Animals, Welfare and the Law

In this objective, practical and authoritative introductory text, the author reveals how the fundamental principles of the human–animal relationship drive the development of animal law.

The book explains the criteria by which the lawful use of animals is determined, and how these criteria impact evolving standards of animal protection and define the responsibilities of people in their interactions with animals. The author identifies twenty-nine key principles which constitute the core knowledge necessary for people involved in debating, assessing and guiding the evolution of society's national and international rulebook of animal welfare law. The book also considers animal welfare and law in the context of a global market through discussion of common issues such as climate change, biosecurity, food safety and food supply.

Based on successful law courses run by the author and his own expertise as an animal law lecturer, prosecutor and specialist legal adviser, the book combines insights from science, ethics and law to provide an essential understanding of what informs society and the law with regards to animals and their welfare.

Ian A. Robertson has the unusual distinction of being both a qualified veterinarian and a barrister (Barrister and Solicitor of the High Court of New Zealand), who has combined his training and experience to become an internationally recognised legal specialist on the subject of animals and the law. Ian undertakes a wide variety of national and international teaching, advising and litigating on the subject of animal welfare and related areas of biosecurity, food safety, fisheries and trade.

Animals, Welfare and the Law

Fundamental principles for critical assessment

Ian A. Robertson

First published 2015
by Routledge
2 Park Square, Milton Park, Abingdon, Oxon OX14 4RN

and by Routledge
711 Third Avenue, New York, NY 10017

Routledge is an imprint of the Taylor & Francis Group, an informa business

© 2015 Ian A. Robertson

The right of Ian A. Robertson to be identified as author of this work
has been asserted by him in accordance with sections 77 and 78 of the
Copyright, Designs and Patents Act 1988.

All rights reserved. No part of this book may be reprinted or reproduced or
utilised in any form or by any electronic, mechanical, or other means, now
known or hereafter invented, including photocopying and recording, or in
any information storage or retrieval system, without permission in writing
from the publishers.

Trademark notice: Product or corporate names may be trademarks or
registered trademarks, and are used only for identification and explanation
without intent to infringe.

British Library Cataloguing-in-Publication Data
A catalogue record for this book is available from the British Library

Library of Congress Cataloging-in-Publication Data
Robertson, Ian A., author.
Animals, welfare and the law / Ian A. Robertson.
pages cm
Includes bibliographical references and index.
1. Animal welfare – Law and legislation. I. Title.
K3620.R63 2015
344.04'9–dc23
2015004469

ISBN: 978-0-415-53562-5 (hbk)
ISBN: 978-0-415-53563-2 (pbk)
ISBN: 978-0-203-11231-1 (ebk)

Typeset in Times New Roman
by Swales & Willis Ltd, Exeter, Devon, UK

Printed and bound in Great Britain by
TJ International Ltd, Padstow, Cornwall

Contents

Preface	vi
Twenty-nine fundamental principles of animal welfare law	ix

1	Introduction	1

PART I
Animal welfare and the need for a critical perspective ... 7

2	What's so important about animal welfare and law?	9
3	The need for critical assessment rather than emotional reaction	32

PART II
The foundational principles of animal welfare law ... 39

4	Religion and reaction: the foundations of animal welfare law	41
5	National law: the public's voice of what is acceptable	76
6	International law is international 'persuasion'	185

PART III
Putting the principles and law into practice ... 231

7	Critically assessing the use of animals in research	233
8	Critically assessing the use of animals in agriculture	249
9	The continuing journey of animal welfare and law	266

Suggested key further reading	277
Index	280

Preface

The idea for this book began with a conversation with another lawyer practising animal law. The original intention was to produce a book that took a world-view of animal law, assessing the development of law regarding animals between different countries and cultures. The concept had merit, but along the way we found that we had overlooked some of the 'fundamentals' which included agreement on definitions and approaches in respect to the subject matter itself. As the project continued, we discovered that we shared different ideas about definitions of 'animal protection', the role of industry, the balance of animals as stakeholders in association with other stakeholders, and approaches to key issues such as practical benefits of animal protection by focusing on people's responsibilities rather than simply the legal classification of animals as property. It had the potential to be a brilliant book that demonstrated contrasting perspectives of two professionals who both practice animal law. However, the foundational differences resulted in us going our separate ways. The experience was valuable none the less, since it demonstrated that although sharing the same label of 'animal law lawyers', the differences of opinion that separate members of the public may also be found in the legal fraternity and those who practice and teach 'animal law'.

The next milestone in the development of this book occurred at a dinner table. Twelve people who had been invited to an animal law function were getting acquainted as the dinner commenced, and one of the women at the table (who I subsequently discovered was a very active animal rights campaigner) asked me what I did for a living. After explaining that I began my professional career as a veterinarian, and had added a law degree and now worked as an animal welfare legal expert, she (initially) appeared impressed. She was less impressed when I told her that one of my roles involved working as a law lecturer teaching the subject of animal law to undergraduate and postgraduate lawyers. Actually, to say that she was 'less impressed' is an understatement. She was bordering on horrified as she leaned forward and said, 'You don't mean to tell me you're teaching lawyers how to undo all the good work we are doing?' Before I could respond, a legal colleague sitting at the same table (who also works as a prosecutor dealing with animal welfare cases) answered for me. He leaned forward to the woman in question, and said: 'Ian teaches animal welfare law in a way that enables his students to subsequently participate sensibly in debates, decision making, and the Courts.'

Preface vii

That prompted further discussion on what it took to ensure that people participating in the development of animal welfare and law were sufficiently informed so that they could contribute in a way that was balanced, authoritative, and realistic.

During that discussion, I had the opportunity to describe the contents of the course I was teaching to both undergraduates and postgraduates. Upon consideration of the contents of the course by the people at the table, one of them remarked, 'You should write a book.' That remark and the encouragement of all those at the table (including the person who had initially expressed so much concern about lawyers being taught the subject of animal law) resulted in renewed commitment to provide a book that addressed the fundamental principles of animal welfare and law.

Other authors have acknowledged that the writing of any book frequently requires the support and understanding of many people. This is just such a book, and this Preface provides me with the opportunity to convey my thanks and appreciation to some of those people.

The first 'thank you' goes to the students representing a variety of disciplines (including biological sciences, law, veterinary medicine and others) whose participation, questions and feedback, over many years of lecturing, particularly in Australia, New Zealand and the UK, are reflected in the contents of the animal law course and this book. In contrast to certain dogmatic views about animals and law in human society, I have consistently found that most students are keen to understand the plethora of contrasting views regarding animals and law, subsequently demonstrating an ability to critique arguments for change and/or retention of the status quo.

Additional thanks goes out to fellow professionals who also represent a wide number of disciplines (including lawyers, enforcement personnel, veterinarians, scientists, ethicists, policy advisors, journalists and others) who have raised questions on a significant range of civil and criminal issues involving animals and law. Your questions and feedback are also reflected in the book.

It's always nice to receive constructive feedback and I am also appreciative for the feedback of the lawyers who are already recognised experts in areas involving matters of animal welfare and the law (e.g., litigants in veterinary professional indemnity insurance, criminal animal welfare prosecutors) and who provided feedback indicating how the material has added depth and meaning to what they do on a daily basis.

Similarly, while the contents of the animal law course are not intended to make lawyers out of veterinarians or scientists, it has been both personally and professionally rewarding to receive feedback on how much the contents of the animal law course, and an understanding of the legal responsibilities attached to these professionals, has also been of value to veterinarians as part of their daily practice. Discussions applying the content of this book to a variety of 'real-life situations' in everything from a well-intended individual bringing in their neighbour's unwell dog (without the neighbour's knowledge or consent), to issues of providing legal guidance to the veterinarian wanting to fulfil their ethical guardianship role in cases where there is suspected family violence and animal abuse, have also helped to shape the contents.

viii *Preface*

Additionally, there are the legislatively appointed inspectors who've commented how an understanding of the fundamental principles addressed in this book have provided clarity in respect of their appointed responsibilities, and a greater understanding regarding the principles and activities they perform on a daily basis. This has addressed a wide range of practical issues, including distinctions between animal 'protection' and 'welfare', how to run a good animal welfare investigation, and navigating the legal complexities attached to their delegated powers and responsibilities. Again, attention to your involvement in matters of enforcement, and subsequent legal assessment of investigations, has been included in addressing the fundamental principles of animal welfare law.

My thanks also go to the team at Earthscan/Routledge who approached me in respect of this book, and have tirelessly supported its development.

In addition to the professional feedback and support that has provided the source of so much information, there are friends and family who have supported me throughout my animal law career, regularly assisted with the development of initiatives such as International Animal Law and education courses, and consistently encouraged me to get on with the writing of the book (including being very understanding as I repeatedly requested that they read and re-read sections of the manuscript). I'm a fan of 'credit where credit is due', so the final product, and the benefits that ensue to readers and animals alike, belong to each member of this 'team' of individuals who have given their care, time and support to me and the purposes which we have worked together towards. The reference to 'friends' includes all those I have worked with throughout both my veterinary and legal career, and includes the animals – as well as the people they own (and yes, I am one of those) – for the fun, trust and magic they had shared with me as their friend, veterinarian and lawyer.

So, to past and present students and colleagues, to friends and family – please accept my deepest and most genuine thanks. I trust that each of you will recognise something of yourself in this book, and feel proud in the part you had to play in its creation. To each reader, I trust that this book serves you well in whatever role you fulfil where your activities impact on animals, humans and the world we all share.

Twenty-nine fundamental principles of animal welfare law

These twenty-nine fundamental principles constitute the main principles that are not only described and demonstrated throughout the book, but also the principles that would save an extraordinary amount of time and conflict if they were understood in relevant animal welfare debates, forums and decision making.

1 PRINCIPLE: Religion was the first 'law' regarding animals, and contemporary animal law continues to reflect religious foundations in its standards and religious, cultural and traditional-use exemptions.
2 PRINCIPLE: 'Animal welfare' is a multifactorial international and domestic public-policy subject, incorporating scientific, ethical and economic issues as well as religious, cultural and trade considerations.
3 PRINCIPLE: 'Animal welfare law' is society's binding rule book governing human–human, and human–animal interactions that involve an animal's welfare.
4 PRINCIPLE: The terms animal 'rights', 'interests', 'protection' and 'welfare' do not have the same meaning in law. Confusion is often caused by incorrect interchanged use of these terms.
5 PRINCIPLE: The subject of 'animal law' has three elements. Animal law (1) involves an animal, (2) takes account of the unique nature of animals as animate objects, and (3) involves the relationship between animals and humans.
6 PRINCIPLE: Issues of animal welfare (and the law's governance of relevant human–human and human–animal interactions) are inseparably connected with practical realities of human economic, environmental, or societal interests.
7 PRINCIPLE: The multifactorial nature of animal welfare means that no singular argument is likely to be the sole determinant in matters involving animal welfare and law; however, as a prerequisite to permissibility, all actions and initiatives involving an animal and its welfare must comply with the applicable law (i.e., is it 'lawful'?).
8 PRINCIPLE: Western concepts of liberty and freedom hold that every practice is permitted unless specifically prohibited by law.
9 PRINCIPLE: The law has a responsibility to balance and prioritise the interests of all stakeholders, where animals and humans are each one, but not the only, stakeholder.

x *Twenty-nine fundamental principles*

10 PRINCIPLE: Speciesism exists and consequently human interests are often prioritised above the interests of animals; however, it is a fanciful misconception to state that the law 'always' prioritises human interests above the interests of animals, because such a statement overlooks the practical reality that humans and animals have many interests in common, and frequently benefit from their co-dependent relationship.

11 PRINCIPLE: The law's demonstrated definition of animal protection/welfare centres on four key words (i.e., pain, distress, unnecessary and unreasonable) and can be summarised as the prevention of an animal's unnecessary and/or unreasonable pain or distress of an animal. This is the sole and continued interest of the animal and its experience that is protected by law.

12 PRINCIPLE: The law functions by first establishing benchmark criteria regarding standards of human (legal) responsibility (and potential liability) regarding the care and treatment of animals (i.e., prevent unnecessary and unreasonable pain and/or distress of animals). The law then qualifies a person's (legal) responsibility in terms of the circumstances of the animal.

13 PRINCIPLE: The degree and nature of legal protection attached to an animal depends significantly on the circumstances in which it is located and demonstrates that the law's substantive consideration is on the purpose/use of the animal and its correlating dependency on the human-caregiver, rather than simply the species of the animal.

14 PRINCIPLE: Although the black letter law[1] concerning human legal responsibilities regarding animals varies from jurisdiction to jurisdiction, leading animal welfare legislation shares similar key features.

15 PRINCIPLE: Contemporary animal welfare law can be viewed as 'specialist property law' because of the property's unique ability to suffer pain and distress.

16 PRINCIPLE: While debates regarding the legal classification of animals as property will continue for the foreseeable future, it is the focus on ensuring people's compliance with their legal responsibilities concerning the treatment of animals – rather than the animal's legal categorisation – that determines the practical well-being of an animal on a day-to-day basis.

17 PRINCIPLE: Empirical evidence (i.e., science) is a key informant of the law, and is commonly used as a basis for providing credibility to national and international standards setting.

18 PRINCIPLE: Government will always be an important stakeholder in any issue of animal protection because it has the responsibility of balancing and prioritising the interests of all stakeholders.

19 PRINCIPLE: Government is similar to other businesses in that it has its key drivers, economic constraints, and differing degrees of expertise, in its decision makers and decision making.

20 PRINCIPLE: There is an identifiable development of incremental change from a sovereign state having no animal legislative protection for animals, to animal protection law (criminalising blatant acts of cruelty), to animal welfare law (incorporating the 'positive duties of care'). The speed of the 'incremental change' in legislation is influenced by key drivers including

---

1 'Black letter law' is a term to describe rules of law that are established by long-standing precedent and therefore generally widely known, accepted and undisputed.

cultural norms, economic expediency and aspirations for trade in the global marketplace.

21 PRINCIPLE: Enforcement is a methodology of facilitating people's compliance with their legal responsibilities and accountabilities. Prosecution is a part of the enforcement process, but the effectiveness of animal protection legislation cannot be assessed solely by reference to the number of prosecutions brought before the courts.

22 PRINCIPLE: Effective enforcement requires informed leadership, clear legislation, penalties that fit the offending, and adequate resources.

23 PRINCIPLE: Status claims of national 'leadership' in animal welfare and animal welfare law are undermined when the alleged national 'leadership' standards are recognised as functioning on legal minimums which derive 'leadership' status by reference to international 'lowest-common-denominator' standards functioning on an inclusionary principle which enables nations with substantially inferior national standards of animal care to participate in international dealings.

24 PRINCIPLE: The multidisciplinary and multifactorial complexities of animal welfare are underpinned by fundamental principles regarding the human–animal relationship and illustrate why animal welfare issues cannot be approached in a black-and-white fashion, as if each issue had a simple singularly correct perspective or solution.

25 PRINCIPLE: Evolution of animal protection legislation is inherently associated with politics, and politics is a manifestation of power. Conceptually, national supremacy and autonomy of each legal jurisdiction to make its own laws may be superseded if the nation state is a member/signatory to a supranational organisation, treaty and/or convention, and consequently has obligations in respect of the values and/or laws of the supranational organisation to which it belongs. Circumstances involving supremacy of power create potential tensions where democratic values and standards regarding animal protection compete with supranational primary trade values.

26 PRINCIPLE: Constructive contribution to current and continuing debates on matters that are relevant to animal law requires the ability to understand and recognise the foundational rules of the human–animal relationship as an essential ingredient to critically assessing issues associated with the human use of animals.

27 PRINCIPLE: Objective, authoritative and practical critical assessment requires informed and balanced consideration of the range of conflicting and competing subjective opinions attached to the subject of animals and their welfare, in order to understand and appropriately prioritise the interests of animals as one of many stakeholders associated with matters of animal welfare.

28 PRINCIPLE: Law will continue to evolve by a process of incremental change in response to human needs, developing science and technology, and the capability of stakeholders to influence other stakeholders regarding acceptable standards of human–human and human–animal interactions in the global commons.

29 PRINCIPLE: The foundational principles of the human–animal relationship are evident in past, present and likely future animal law.

1 Introduction

People and animals: one world and a common future

Almost every aspect of human society relies on animals, and an understanding of how the law sets out people's responsibilities for animals is relevant to anyone who has direct and/or indirect business, professional, or personal interests involving animals.

The lifestyle of almost every individual is touched in some way by animals, and human uses of them, from the food they eat, their clothes, their medicines, to almost every use and interaction involving animals including sports, entertainment, and the companionship many people enjoy with their pets. Humankind's uses and relationships with the enormous range of species occurs across the globe, affecting national and international, economic, environmental and social interests. One way of recognising the enormous impact that animal-related events have on people is to look at some past animal-related events that have 'gone wrong'.

Economic, environmental and social impacts

Mentioning 'mad cow disease', 'foot-and-mouth disease', 'bird flu', or 'swine flu' is usually enough to have people agreeing that issues of animal-related disease control have a significant impact not just on the animals who suffer from the disease, but also on people and economies. Consider 'mad cow disease': Creutzfeldt-Jakob disease (CJD) is a degenerative neurological disorder that is incurable and invariably fatal. When the UK announced, on 20 March 1996, that a new variant of CJD[1] had been identified in ten victims, and it could not be ruled out that there was a link with consumption of beef from cattle with bovine spongiform encephalopathy (BSE), the British beef market collapsed almost overnight. Consumption of beef across the European Union (EU) dropped 11 per cent in 1996, and the BSE crisis cost the EU an estimated US$2.8 billion in subsidies

---

1 Creutzfeldt-Jakob disease (CJD) is a degenerative neurological disorder (brain disease) that is incurable and invariably fatal. See R.G. Will et al. 1996. 'A New Variant of Creutzfeldt-Jakob Disease in the UK', *Lancet*, 347: 921–5.

2   *Introduction*

alone to the beef industry,[2] with the cost to the UK estimated to be in excess of £4 billion.[3] That national loss affected the wider UK public, and wasn't restricted simply to farmers, animal transporters and others whose livelihoods dealt directly with the culled and slaughtered animals.

Disease outbreaks are not the only category of disease-associated risks associated with animals that have enormous potential impacts on people. There are a wide range of ongoing disease categories which warrant constant attention. They include exotic diseases, endemic diseases, re-emergence of controlled diseases, emergence of previously unknown diseases (e.g., novel virus combinations) and human-induced risks which are either inadvertent (e.g., failure in containment systems in laboratories) or deliberate (e.g., bioterrorism). Management of animal-related diseases faces increasing challenges including, for example, increasing globalisation and speed of trade, the development of genetically modified material, the spread of people into new habitats the movement of products, people and animals across national boundaries, climate change, a looming shortage of appropriately trained animal health professionals, and resource constraints that compromise border control and biosecurity efficiencies.[4]

So what does the law have to do with disease control, and the array of other animal-related activities that occur every day, from companionship and entertainment through to agriculture and research? Law has many roles in society, one of which is to manage the risks to the public as it endeavours to balance and prioritise society's varied, competing and often conflicting interests. In this respect, the law may be viewed as the rule book for managing the risks to the wider public by governing the function, procedure and standards of human–human, as well as human–animal, interactions.

Identifying those who have 'direct and/or indirect interests involving animals'

The law applies a broad net of responsibility – and potential liability – regarding the treatment of animals. There is a lengthy list of professions, businesses and organisations whose members have a vested interest in matters and responsibilities related to animals. They range from research laboratory scientists to those working in biosecurity and the fashion industry. Less well-known examples include a number of people whose business, professions and personal activities

---

2 D. Powell. 2001. 'Mad Cow Disease and the Stigmatization of British Beef', in *Risk, Media, and Stigma: Understanding Public Challenges to Modern Science and Technology* (London: Earthscan), pp. 219–28.

3 J. Deane. 1997. 'Chancellor Warned Over Rising Cost of BSE Crisis', *Press Association News*, 27 June 27.

4 Alan W. Bell et al. 2011. 'The Australasian Beef Industries – Challenges and Opportunities in the 21st Century', *Animal Frontiers*, 1(2): 10–19.

involve areas of 'private animal law'.[5] For example, social workers, lawyers, veterinarians and enforcement agencies are among those who are increasingly recognising that animal abuse is a potential indicator of domestic violence. Research demonstrating the link between domestic violence and animal abuse[6] has consequently raised questions about how to assist professionals (e.g., veterinarians) in fulfilling their guardianship role to animals and people under the care of the professional.[7]

The use of animals and animal products in fashion, furniture, food, entertainment, security, medicine, agriculture and a range of other uses, means that the following list is just a small sample of the people and organisations who – whether they like it or not, and whether they are aware of it or not – are likely to have legal responsibilities and/or an impact upon societal standards of acceptable animal welfare:

- lawyers, policy advisers, politicians, enforcement personnel;
- health professionals including veterinarians, doctors, medical paraprofessionals;
- economists, accountants, financial advisers; and
- scientists representing a range of specialties including biology, food quality, ethics, social services, environmentalists, behaviouralists, psychologists.

Those people who have associated legal responsibilities regarding the standards of care concerning those same animals involved. And where there is responsibility, it is not unusual to identify relevant legal liability as well. The list of people and professions who have interests, and therefore legal responsibilities attached to their direct or indirect involvement with animals extends well beyond what most people would consider 'obvious'. However, some things are not that simple. The terms of animal 'rights', 'interests', 'protection' and 'welfare' do not have the same meaning in terms of the law. Confusion is often caused by incorrect interchanged use of the terms.

Understanding the fundamental principles of animal law is also valuable in predicting the future of animal welfare, and distinguishing realistic initiatives from aspirational ones. That same understanding explains why, in order to protect animals *and* the public, it is important to ensure that all people who have dealings concerning animals do so in a way that is not only 'lawful', but also demonstrates a degree of reliable competence.

---

5 'Public animal law' refers to matters that are commonly acknowledged and discussed in terms of their relevance to, and involvement of, animals. In contrast, 'private animal law' refers to issues involving animal law that occur in less public arenas. Issues of family violence and related animal abuse, for example, frequently occurs behind 'closed doors' in the privacy of people's homes, hence the term 'private animal law'.

6 Andrew Linzey (ed.). 2009. *The Link Between Animal Abuse and Human Violence* (Brighton: Sussex Academic Press).

7 I. Robertson. 2009. 'A Legal Duty to Report Suspected Animal Abuse – Are Veterinarians Ready?' in Linzey (ed.), *The Link Between Animal Abuse and Human Violence*, pp. 263–72.

4 *Introduction*

Even outdated legislation has value

Some of the referenced law may be viewed as 'old', or has already been superseded. For example, the Animal Protection Act 1911, which formed the basis of England's animal welfare laws for almost a hundred years, was superseded by the Animal Welfare Act 2006. On the other hand, many nations and states around the world have animal welfare laws that remain a hundred years behind that of existing contemporary animal welfare leaders. Law is an evolving record of the human–animal relationship, and even 'outdated' law from existing leaders has benefits for the purposes of comparison and contrast of a nation's progress, or not, in this subject.

In theory, when people are 'better informed', they make better decisions. This assumption overlooks the fact that information in isolation, or an inability to actually apply the information, may result in knowledgeable individuals, but not necessarily better decision making that benefits the wider populace.

With this in mind, this book's chapters begin by posing questions for the reader to consider prior to reading the chapter contents, and subsequently pose additional questions at the end of the chapter as a way for the reader to see if they can identify the relevant animal–human issues, and apply the chapter content to critically assessing those issues. To further develop this question-learn-apply formula, two specific chapters (7 and 8) of this book are dedicated to two of the more contentious uses of animals. The principles used in assessing these two uses (i.e., use of animals in agriculture, and the use of animals in research) can then be applied by the reader in critically assessing almost any other use of animals.

How much do you already know?

There is frequently a difference between what people know, and what they think they know – even if they have considerable previous experience working in the related field.

As a prerequisite to reading the rest of this book, it is highly recommended that the reader answer the questions below. There are only twenty questions. In addition to providing you with a useful outline of the information that you can expect to cover, this will provide you with an idea of your current familiarity with – and assumptions about – the foundational principles of animal welfare and law.

Additionally, the questions provide a useful self-assessment for the reader of what has been learnt by comparing answers to the questions *before* reading, and their answers *after* reading the book. Each chapter follows this similar pattern, of providing the reader with questions to consider prior to reading the chapter, and then posing further questions at the end of the chapter which enable the reader to apply the chapter contents in critically assessing relevant animal-related issues.

Introduction 5

Who/what dictated how you should view animals?

The starting point of the human–animal relationship

- What were the three key concepts that established past and present cultural/ societal attitudes concerning animals? Explain how these concepts have resulted in differing attitudes concerning human responsibilities regarding animals.
- Name five key figures (and their doctrines) who were instrumental in establishing 'societies' rules' regarding humankind's treatment of animals.
- Name and explain the key moral philosophies that apply to, and explain, the enduring conflicts of opinion about human responsibilities regarding animals.
- Using examples, identify which of these philosophies underpin the law.
- Explain the role of 'law' in animal welfare, and the human–animal relationship.

Can you recognise historical informants in contemporary law?

- By reference to contemporary animal welfare law, demonstrate where the foundational concepts (regarding the human–animal relationship) have been translated and codified in to law (or not)?
- Define and distinguish (with reference to relevant authority) 'the animal' and the 'legal animal'.
- Name and explain the three elements of 'animal law'. To illustrate your answer, apply these three elements to at least five uses of animals in human society.
- What are the four key words used in contemporary animal welfare law that are central to the legal definition of animal welfare? Using these four words, provide the legal definition of 'animal welfare' in one line. Define and distinguish each of the identified four key words.
- Name the six elements/owner-rights that legally define and identify 'property'. Explain how each of those elements applies to animals in contemporary animal welfare law.
- Explain how enforcement of practical animal protection is assisted, or hindered, by the law's categorisation of animals as 'property'.
- Define and distinguish the concepts of animal welfare, animal protection, animal cruelty, animal rights and animal interests.

Who's governing global animal welfare?

- Identify (with a rationale for your answer) the key governors of animal welfare law – nationally, and internationally.
- Identify (with a rationale for your answer) who leads the development of animal welfare – in theory, and in practice.
- Is animal welfare law keeping up with contemporary issues, debates and technologies? Explain your answer with examples.

6 *Introduction*

Are you criticising or critically assessing the uses of animals in human society?

- Explain what it means to 'critically assess'.
- Explain the difference between 'critical assessment' and 'legal assessment'.
- With reference to the foundational principles, explain how the law balances and prioritises the interests and conflicts of key stakeholders attached to the use of animals in research.
- With reference to the foundational principles described in this book, explain how the law balances and prioritises the interests and conflicts of key stakeholders attached to the use of animals in agriculture.
- 'The key professions influencing the development of animal welfare are sufficiently trained in matters of animal welfare': critically discuss this statement.

Part I

Animal welfare and the need for a critical perspective

This first part of the book introduces the concepts of animal welfare and animal law, the importance of using correct terminology, and how law which governs the human–animal relationship is integral to wider economic, social and environmental issues. Given the need for objective, authoritative and realistic perspectives to balance an area that commonly attracts strong emotive, subjective and anthropomorphic views, Part I demonstrates the need for, and benefits of, critically assessing the roles of animals in society and the interdependence between animals and people.

As a result, readers should be able to gain a clearer understanding of the foundational principles which inform society and underpin the law which governs people's responsibilities regarding animals.

2 What's so important about animal welfare and law?[1]

Well, lots, as history, philosophy and the evolution of animal welfare law all indicate. But not least is humanity's consideration for animals, its dependence on animals. And the relationship people have with animals. In fact, the law is a record of that evolving relationship since it reflects society's changing attitudes regarding animals throughout time.

Shifts in scientific knowledge and public knowledge about the lives of animals have resulted in significant changes in attitudes by the public, and therefore the politicians, and consequently the law, regarding what is acceptable (or not) regarding human treatment of animals. Issues of food, fashion, and exploitation have all attracted significant attention. For example, scientists have expressed concerns about the use of animal medicines in the food chain;[2] clothing fabrics have become a target for scrutiny with certain animal-derived fabrics (e.g., fur products) attracting considerable debate;[3] the pleasure principle has begun to clash with notions of what is acceptable human entertainment[4] (e.g., bullfighting) and questions have been raised as to whether continued use of animals in research is justified.[5]

---

1 Addressing the question of 'what is so important about animal welfare' at the start of this book was inspired by an occasion where a senior government decision maker, whose responsibilities included making substantial decisions on matters of animal welfare, asked the author this exact question.

2 S. Schwarz, C. Kehrenberga and T.R. Walsh. 2001. 'Use of Antimicrobial Agents in Veterinary Medicine and Food Animal Production', *International Journal of Antimicrobial Agents*, 17(6): 431–7; Frank M. Aarestrup, Henrik C. Wegener and Peter Collignon. 2008. 'Resistance in Bacteria of the Food Chain: Epidemiology and Control Strategies', *Expert Review of Anti-Infective Therapy*, 6(5) (October): 733–50.

3 Andrew Linzey. 2006. 'An Ethical Critique of the Canadian Seal Hunt and an Examination of the Case for Import Controls on Seal Products', *Journal of Animal Law*, 2: 87–119; Robert Galantucci. 2008–09. 'Compassionate Consumerism within the GATT Regime: Can Belgium's Ban on Seal Product Imports be Justified under Article XX', *Cal. W. Int'l L.J.*, 281: 284–5.

4 Charles E. Friend. 1973–74. 'Animal Cruelty Laws: The Case for Reform', *U. Rich. L. Rev.*, 201.

5 Andrew Rowan. 1997. 'The Benefits and Ethics of Animal Research', *Scientific American*, 276(2); Bernard E. Rollin. 2006. 'The Regulation of Animal Research and the Emergence of Animal Ethics: A Conceptual History', *Theoretical Medicine and Bioethics*, 27(4): 285–304.

10 *What's important about animal welfare law?*

Prompted by globalisation and a heightened awareness of how animal health issues have a bearing on human health issues, the focus on animal welfare – and the law that governs animal welfare – has resulted in considerable demands from the public for greater accountability, transparency and assurances about the well-being of both themselves and animals. Some countries are doing better than others at keeping up with those demands.

The laws of some countries have added weight to the enforcement mechanisms for violations of the cruelty laws; and discussions about what constitutes humane and sustainable treatment of animals have moved further into the courtrooms in terms of numbers of cases and attention to those cases. At the same time, public debates on issues of animal cruelty extend beyond the courtroom and onto broadcasting and printed media and the Internet.

Differences in world-views are typically tied up with a mix of cultural, religious and political perspectives. The current reality, however, demonstrates that humans and animals alike live in a global village where all living systems share a measure of reliance on, and risk from, each other.

Issues of animal welfare and law are not the centre of international concerns. However, this book demonstrates how animal welfare is an important piece of the global jigsaw in a world where the majority of animals continue to rely primarily on the human caregivers for their physical, health and behavioural needs.[6] Matters such as food supply, food safety and environmental degradation all illustrate that the current and future well-being of humans is closely associated with how well people do, or do not, look after the welfare of animals. What else is so important about animal welfare? People have an obligation to comply with the law, and risk substantial penalties if they don't. The terms animal 'rights', 'interests', 'protection' and 'welfare' do not have the same meaning in law. Confusion is often caused by improper interchanged use of the terms.

The ability to understand the terms, and navigate the assumptions as part of being able to assess critically is naturally invaluable in trying to make sense of the substantial amount of written material on the subject of animal law, and making sense of polarised world-views regarding animal protection.

Interestingly, while all people have an established attitude regarding animals (even having *no* attitude is arguably a way of thinking or feeling about animals), few have actually questioned 'why' they think/feel about animals the way they do, or 'what has informed them'. By contrast, it is expected that the reader will have an insight about what informs different people, cultures and societies. That in turn enables the reader to apply that insight to predicting (e.g., people's responses to suggested initiatives), and authoritatively participating in, debates that address current issues, and the future of animal welfare and law.

---

6 Section 4 Animal Welfare Act 1999 (New Zealand); see also Section 9(2) Animal Welfare Act 1999 (England and Wales).

'Balanced, authoritative, and practical'

How, then, can we understand the drivers of national and international governments and organisations amongst the myriad of competing, conflicting and contrasting messages, agendas and motivations of stakeholders involving animals? It is anticipated that the contents of this book will assist readers in distinguishing, for example, leadership based on sound principles from 'just politics'. By identifying basic principles that underpin people's attitudes and the law, it is expected that readers will subsequently be able to rationally assess any use of animals in a 'balanced, authoritative, and practical' manner. The adjectives 'balanced', 'authoritative' and 'practical' are three key words that need to be applied in critically assessing the uses of animals in human society.

'Balanced' refers to the ability to recognise the variety of stakeholders with regard to matters of animal welfare *and* understand their different viewpoints in a way that is objective and unbiased.

'Authoritative' refers to the ability to accurately reference the reasoning and powers associated with contrasting arguments dealing with the subject of animal welfare and law. This naturally includes familiarity with relevant law, but involves more than simply quoting the law to include an understanding of current law in reference to its underlying origins and history of development.

An understanding of relevant principles and law doesn't infer that people are bound to agree with the current status of the law regarding animals; however, an informed understanding of how the law has developed to its current state (rather than just knowing what the law states, and applying one's own interpretations rather than the Courts) is arguably one of the necessary prerequisites for recognising and balancing perspectives, arguments and agendas that are frequently highly emotive.

'Practical' is considered broadly synonymous with 'realistic', 'pragmatic' and 'rational'. Although purists may choose to get embroiled in the distinctions between the formal definition of each word, this book's use of the word 'practical' is reflected most closely in the definition of applying 'sensible and practical' reasoning regarding what can be achieved or expected. Such a definition doesn't infer that all contemplated change is simply aspirational, but it does involve a recommendation to assess uses and ideas for change in a way that takes account of current and future reality.

Constructive contribution to current and continuing debates on matters that are relevant to animal law requires the ability to critically assess issues associated with the human use of animals. Objective, authoritative and practical critical assessment requires balanced and fair consideration of the range of conflicting and competing subjective opinions attached to the subject of animals and their welfare.

Animal law may be viewed as the younger cousin of environmental law

Decades ago, when environmental protection and relevant law was 'new' in comparison to the traditional 'pillars' of law (i.e., contract law, criminal law, tort law,

12 *What's important about animal welfare law?*

criminal law and public law), a person could, with comparatively few exceptions, build what they wanted where they wanted with little regard to the environmental consequences. That situation obviously changed enormously once the concept of environmental protection was accepted, understood and advanced. Nowadays, there is a raft of laws, regulations and environmental impact assessments that apply before implementing any action involving air, land, or water.[7]

Animal law today has substantial similarities to the early days of environmental law. Like early environmental protection, the subject of animal welfare and relevant law is still a relatively new subject, and consequently the subject of animal welfare and associated law is often confused and/or misunderstood, and acceptance ranges from dismissal, prejudice and/or resistance, through to amusement, curiosity and, increasingly common, enthusiastic support.

Despite a minority of lawyers who persist in thinking that legal issues involving animals are dealt with simply by treating them 'just like other property',[8] and consider the idea of a legal specialty known as 'animal law' somewhat novel, there are other professionals who have immediately recognised the importance of animal welfare and law as a subject warranting study as a distinct discipline. One head of a law school described animal law as 'the younger cousin of environmental law', and promptly authorised the course to be offered to undergraduates and postgraduates, making the University of Canterbury the first law school in New Zealand to offer courses on animal law. Auckland, Massey and Otago all followed suit.[9] The adoption of animal law courses in New Zealand academia mirrors the trend in countries around the world where stakeholders are increasingly recognising the need for authoritative education and understanding on the subject of animal welfare. The shift reflects the increased recognition of the importance of animal welfare to a vast range of economic, environmental and sociological human interests.

Shifts in academia, government, non-government organisations, the professions and the Courts all demonstrate that in spite of misunderstandings, curiosity, or even suspicion about what animal law entails, there *is* a legal discipline of animal law. Whatever preconceptions or subjective views individuals may have on the subject, the facts demonstrate that today, animal welfare is a subject that is increasingly recognised as having significant importance to people, profits and the planet.

---

7 Patricia Birnie, Alan Boyle and Catherine Redgwell. 2009. *International Law and the Environment*, 3rd edn (New York: Oxford University Press). As an example of primary legislation, see also the Resource Management Act 1991 (New Zealand), the Environment Act 1986 (New Zealand), and existing equivalent legislation in alternative legal jurisdictions; Paul R. Portney and Robert N. Stavins. 2000. *Public Policies for Environmental Protection*, 2nd edn (Washington, DC: RFF Press).

8 This is the personal experience of the author. It is acknowledged that many legal jurisdictions do continue to treat animals simply as property. However, legal jurisdictions with contemporary animal welfare law demonstrate legislative distinction between 'animate' vs. 'inanimate' property.

9 This became New Zealand's first course on animal law, which was taught at the University of Canterbury. Courses on animal law were subsequently offered at Auckland University, Massey University and Otago University, constituting four out of New Zealand's six main tertiary-education providers.

What's important about animal welfare law? 13

Two hundred years ago, when early animal protection pioneers suggested that there should be a set of legal theories, principles and laws focusing on protecting animals as something more than any other inanimate property, their proposal was greeted with amusement, scorn and outright resistance by many decision makers of the day. Now there is an increasing amount of literature published by legal scholars which evaluates humans' treatment of animals. Governments are implementing and/or updating animal protection legislation, and law enforcement personnel are better informed on matters of both public, and private, animal law. Furthermore, there are hundreds of animal protection organizations – varying in their approach, but none the less focused on ensuring that animals are represented as stakeholders in decisions affecting their well-being.

There are a growing number of lawyers who are well informed about matters pertaining to animals, and the legal responsibilities of people responsible for matters of animal welfare. An increasing number of law schools around the world are adding animal law to their curricula, and more lawyers are spending part, or all, of their practices on animal law issues. Animal law in legal practice addresses as many areas as animals are involved in people's lives, covering individual civil/tort cases (e.g., injuries to and by animals, veterinary malpractice), impact litigation (e.g., assessment of industry/retail practices with respect to large numbers of animals in agriculture and research), animal control/sheltering issues, to matrimonial disputes, and providing for animals in wills and trusts. Issues of criminal animal law feature in government agencies and departments which have a number of roles, including the responsibility to ensure that standards of animal welfare are complied with in order to meet public expectations, and provide assurance regarding standards that form part of international trade agreements and obligations.

Important wider considerations regarding legal standards of animal welfare have wide application to a significant range of social, economic and environmental impacts including, among others, international trade (e.g., disease control, live exports, biosecurity, border control), research (e.g., medicine, genetic modification, xenotransplantation), civil animal law matters (e.g., sale and purchase of performance animals, veterinary malpractice, pet custody battles), smuggling of wildlife, issues associated with food supply and safety (e.g., traceability, animal slaughter and transport) and conservation.

Legal jurisdictions around the world vary considerably in the degree that they have developed legal concepts concerning animal protection. With increasing recognition of the impact of animal welfare of human interests, many countries have some kind of animal protection law. However, early legal development in this area has proceeded largely on an ad hoc basis, without a genuine understanding of how each piece fits into the big global picture. 'Animal law' endeavours to bring those pieces all together in one recognised legal discipline, with recognised legal specialists,[10] providing specialist advice that promotes wider consistency and uniformity in animal welfare standards and law.

---

10 Given that animals are classified as 'property' under the law, well-informed lawyers in this area might be viewed as 'specialist property lawyers'.

14   *What's important about animal welfare law?*

Critically important definitions of 'animal welfare law'

Each discipline has a 'language' of its own, and animal welfare law is no different. There is a strong possibility that despite having just introduced the concept of animal welfare law, little, if any, preliminary consideration has been given to the meaning of the words used in that term.

In forums, meetings and other events discussing concepts of animal law, it is common for participants to make assumptions that there is an agreed definition that attaches to the words and terms which form the core of 'animal welfare law'. Experience demonstrates that this assumption regarding the basics of animal law is ill-founded. Debates and responses provided by 'public consultation',[11] for example, frequently demonstrate various levels of understanding about perceived inconsistencies in animal law. A failure to recognise the range of vastly different personal and organisational definitions, and a subsequent failure to agree what definitions will be applied, underpins many of the problems in communication between discussion participants, with a natural cost and consequence on the subsequent time, effort and outcomes involving animal-related initiatives.

It is therefore vital, in the first instance, to have clarity regarding the definitions and terms that attach to 'animal welfare law'.

First of all, what do we mean by 'law'?

It's helpful to take a moment to consider what the law is, in order to provide clarity about the term 'animal welfare law'.

The term 'law' is used to define a framework of rules and regulations which govern a country, society, or community. Broadly speaking, law fulfils a number of functions which include prescribing prohibited behaviours and penalties, rules of interaction in respect of people's personal arrangements (e.g., property, business), a forum for settling disputes and enforcing obligations, and a system of government which includes rules regarding responsibilities and obligations between the government and its people, and between its citizens.

Different types of legal systems exist around the world.[12] Countries which are currently recognised as global leaders in terms of their animal welfare legislation and supporting systems share common origins in that they were derived from the English system which utilises common law and statute law.

---

11 Public consultation is a term describing a regulatory process which invites the public to express their views on matters which affect them. The process is formal, and traditionally requires the governing body to provide sufficient information to ensure that those persons potentially affected (by a proposed decision), have the opportunity to voice their opinion, pose questions and communicate any relevant concerns. Subsequently, the governing body has the responsibility to fairly consider the views of stakeholders and set out the reasoning for their decision.

12 Civil law, religious law, common law and totalitarian law are examples of alternative legal systems that exist. 'Hybrid law' is an additional term used to refer to a legal system that has a mixture of civil law, common law and religious law.

What's important about animal welfare law? 15

Legislation is a general term used to describe the laws enacted by the governing body (e.g., Parliament). This body of law, also known as 'Statute Law', creates Acts of Parliament (e.g., the Animal Welfare Act 2006) and constitutes the primary source of legal authority for central and local government. Legislation arising from the process of Parliament is the highest form of law. A statute can override the common law, i.e., judicial precedent, and can repeal previous legislation.

Subsidiary/subordinate/delegated legislation is made by virtue of powers contained within the primary piece of legislation. Subsidiary legislation may be referred to in alternative terms including, for example, 'orders', 'regulations' and 'resolutions'.

While a statute traditionally provides the starting-point for legal consideration, 'common law' is a term used to describe the law developed by the Courts in the process of ruling on cases ('case law'). The common law[13] evolved over a number of centuries in England and operates through the doctrine of precedent, and the development of legal principles through cases and judgments. The operation of case law and the doctrine of precedent involve applying legal principles, decided in past cases, to new cases with similar facts. Case law functions through a hierarchical Court system whereby Court decisions generated from a superior Court will be binding on a lower Court. The underlying philosophy of case law is that the system promotes certainty and fairness.

Judges, collectively known as the 'judiciary', have the responsibility of utilising the doctrine of precedent in their rulings, which accounts for why case law is widely referred to as 'Judge made law'.

Law is broadly divided into public law[14] (e.g., administrative law, environmental law, constitutional law, criminal law) and private/civil law[15] (e.g., tort law, land law, property law, family law, contract law).

The law governs human–human and human–animal interactions, and applies legal responsibilities based on minimum standards of mandated human behaviours.

Obviously there is no singular law that applies to all people. There are a number of countries which operate on the basis of Westminster (British) law which are considered global leaders in the field of animal welfare legislation.[16] Some

---

13 As a system of law, common law can be contrasted with other legal systems throughout the world. The civil law system in Europe, for example, requires the precise exposition of its laws in statutory codes.

14 The law of relationships between individuals and the government. 'Public international law' is an expression which refers to rules governing relationships between nations.

15 Law that deals with the relations between individuals (or private legal entities such as an institution or organisation), in contrast to relations between individuals and the government.

16 England, Scotland, New Zealand and certain states in Australia may be included in the list of available examples which are based on the principles of Westminster law. It is noted that the laws in these jurisdictions are particularly familiar to the author, and consequently this book utilises examples from these jurisdictions to illustrate the principles of animal law and leading contemporary animal welfare legislation.

16 *What's important about animal welfare law?*

sovereign states (e.g., Switzerland, Holland, Germany) operate on legal systems that are not based on principles[17] of Westminster law but also have a recognised global leadership in the field of animal welfare law. Additionally, it is of value to the student of animal law to recognise that there are other communities that demonstrate societal attitudes and expectations expressed via 'rules' akin to legislatively prescribed law, concerning the treatment of an 'animal'.

So how do we define 'animal law'?

Despite the fact that individuals and groups may vary in terms of their cultural, religious, and social perspectives regarding how animals should be treated, most people none the less hold strong views about their own (i.e., people's) inherent rights associated with what they consider their property. The law has a long history of balancing potential conflicting views of individuals by setting out societal rules regarding the use, exchange and protection of people's property. Legal concepts controlling property have relevance to animal protection because animals have traditionally been classified by the law as 'property'.

The fact is that wherever people have interactions with other people that involves property – or animals as property – there is likely to be a rule of some kind (aka 'law') governing the rules of that interaction.

Even where legislation regarding animals has not been developed to any great degree, there are still 'rules' that exist regarding animals. For example, if a farmer does not look after their farm animals according to the 'rules' of good animal husbandry, then the results will be self-punishing to the farmer given that the production and/or working value of those animals is likely to be diminished. Extending this point, and stating the obvious to further make the point, if an animal is not properly fed, then it will get sick and may eventually die. These 'natural laws'[18] apply, irrespective of the existence (or not) of 'positivist' man-made law and explains why in many societies which rely heavily on their animals for their livelihood (e.g., as work animals, and/or a source of food), it is not uncommon for the animal's owner to do whatever they can to take care of their animal, irrespective of whether or not there is prevailing legislation. There are clear advantages to having established national animal protection law. National governance through legislation ideal applies an equal (although minimum standard) responsibility on all persons within a particular society. In terms of *global* governance, established national animal welfare legislation governing standards of animal welfare (and associated subjects such as disease control and biosecurity) also provides important marketable 'assurances' for persuading potential trading partners in the global marketplace.

---

17 Animal welfare law refers to primarily criminal law, although the foundational principles are broadly applicable to both criminal and civil matters.

18 Defined as a 'body of law or a specific principle held to be derived from nature and binding upon human society in the absence of or in addition to man-made laws' (*Webster's Dictionary*).

'Animal law' is more than just 'law that involves an animal'

This book defines the subject of animal law as a sub-discipline of law, and having three elements. The first is obvious: it deals with an animal. The second element recognises the unique nature of animals, where the 'unique nature' refers to the fact that despite animals being legally classified as 'property', they are animate property (i.e., animals) rather than inanimate property. This distinction is reflected in the fact that the law recognises that animals suffer 'pain' and 'distress' – in contrast to inanimate objects. The third element is that animal law deals with issues that affect the human–animal relationship.

Consider how the three elements fit with the single largest use of animals – as food for the human consumer: (1) animals are involved; (2) they are defined as animals so there are a substantial number of laws, both nationally and internationally, dictating the standards relating to raising, transporting and slaughtering the animals in a manner where a central consideration is the requirement to minimise the animal's unnecessary pain and/or distress; and (3) it involves the human–animal relationship. This sometimes proves to be problematic to recognise for a number of people, until it is pointed out, for example, that issues of disease control and animal welfare have a direct effect on the safety and quality of the food consumed by people, and thereby the animals' 'relationship'[19] with people.

It should be noted that these three elements reflect an underlying principle: that the law addresses concepts of animal protection (and the animal's 'experience') in the context of 'responsibility' and 'uses' – not simply as species. It is also valuable to note that this framework of human responsibilities regarding animals and their uses, fits neatly to both national legal obligations and international arrangements.

Law applies responsibilities regarding the treatment and uses of animals

Unsurprisingly, the largest portion of animal welfare law involves those that live closest to humankind; these include uses, for example, as companion animals, working animals and animals used in agriculture. This should not be surprising for a number of reasons. Firstly, there is the fact that the number of rules regarding the welfare of the property (i.e., animals) obviously has a direct impact on the value of the property itself. Secondly, the number of rules also reflects the fact that individuals and society in general have largely assumed a moral position that reflects a sense of 'responsibility' to ensure that animals in the care of people

---

19 A broad definition of relationship is applied in this book and incorporates concepts of 'connection', including 'cause and effect'. The third element of animal law which recognises the relationship between humans and animals takes account of environmental, economic and social subjects including disease control, zoonoses, public health and safety, in addition to wide uses of animals for companionship, and as working animals, research subjects, sports, entertainment and a source of food and animal products.

18   *What's important about animal welfare law?*

should be treated humanely. Thirdly, people have self-interests (e.g., food safety) which warrant rules/law to ensure that risks to the general public are minimised.

Essentially, the law reflects a scale of 'responsibility' regarding animals, depending on their uses, and reliance on human care-givers. For example, there are legal obligations regarding companion animals which largely reflect the law's approach that if an animal is significantly dependent on a human being for its food, water, shelter, health and overall well-being, then it is appropriate to apply equally significant legal accountabilities to the caregiver. Similarly, if society wishes to benefit from animals (e.g., in agriculture or research), then people justifiably have a greater duty of care to those animals in comparison to those that exist in the wild.

Although legislation has attracted criticism for allegedly providing less protection to animals that exist in the wild, objective assessment demonstrates that there it is none the less logical to expect that there are comparatively fewer rules regarding the welfare of wild animals, given that they have a greater degree of autonomy than their domesticated counterparts who rely predominantly (and in some cases, completely) on their human caregiver.

It is noteworthy that the starting-point for 'ownership' and therefore responsibility in respect of 'wild animals' is that they belong to the state or the Crown.[20] However, when wild animals are lawfully taken or killed (e.g., when trapped). responsibility for their well-being attaches to the person by whom they have been taken or killed.[21]

While considering the responsibilities associated with 'wild' animals, it is important to remember that the power of law hinges on the words used and the legal definition applied to those words. Consequently, in respect to 'wild' animals, the simple dichotomy between 'tame' and 'wild' does not reflect the reality of animal life in most legal jurisdictions, nor can the distinction be applied without difficulty. There is a question, for example, regarding 'feral' animals, given that there are a number of species (e.g., cats) which would traditionally be considered as 'tame'; none the less, there are established 'feral/wild' populations. Assessments of whether animals are 'domesticated', 'tame', 'feral', or 'wild' will depend on the piece of legislation being considered, and, as is the norm with the majority of legal assessment, careful consideration of all the facts and relevant circumstances.

Defining an 'animal' through the legal lens

The definition of an animal is fundamental to any discussion involving the law about them, but it is a preliminary consideration that is commonly overlooked.

The legal definition of an animal is particularly important when considering legal views of animals for at least two reasons. Firstly, it is important for the reader to be aware that the legal definition of an 'animal' may vary considerably depending

---

20 This is demonstrated, for example, in section 9 of New Zealand's Wild Animal Control Act 1977.

21 Section 36 of New Zealand's Animal Welfare Act 1999 provides an example of where this principle is applied, in that the section applies an obligation on persons who have set traps to inspect them.

on the discipline, context and reference. The second reason is because it is the legal definition of an animal which determines what legislative protections are provided for an animal, or not.

One of the most common oversights of people considering animal welfare law is the application of the mistaken assumption that the definition of an 'animal' in one piece of legislation has the same definition in another piece of legislation.

To avoid the common pitfall of thinking that the law is not consistent in defining an 'animal', it is imperative to recognise and understand that the law is consistent in its methodology but not its definition throughout legislation. Incorrect assumptions, or a failure to understand that there is a 'consistency' in how the law defines an animal, observably results in misunderstandings, and subsequent (and frequently avoidable) irritation and conflict.

The word 'animal' must be interpreted in light of the specific piece of legislation under which it is being considered. Quite simply, there is not one ubiquitous legal definition of an animal that applies across all legislation in any given jurisdiction, or a singular definition that applies in different legal jurisdictions. Furthermore, the word 'animal' may be interpreted broadly or narrowly in a piece of legislation. Some pieces of law, for example, apply a definition that encompasses a wide variety of species, while other legislation is extremely specific in that it will, for example, exclude/include an animal depending on its age. In addition to application of the legal rules of legislative interpretation, this methodology enables legislation to appropriately address the individual circumstances of the species, uses and wider circumstances, thereby subsequently enabling a clearer ability to identify the relevant human responsibility – and potential liability.

Defining animal 'welfare' through the legal lens

When asked to define 'animal welfare', some people, say that it's 'got something to do with an animal not feeling pain'. 'Happy animals' and 'not being cruel', or 'treating animals nicely' are also common responses. Whatever definition is used, they all share a common thread which implies there is a responsibility on humans to ensure that animals don't suffer unnecessarily.

There is no universal definition of animal welfare, in spite of the substantial variety of definitions that have been tabled by almost as many individuals, professions and organisations. Undoubtedly, each definition has been influenced by the personal and professional activities/roles, perspectives and agendas of their proponents.

The World Organisation for Animal Health,[22] for example, has an international role as an intergovernmental policy and standard-setting body. Its definition states: 'Animal welfare is a complex international public policy issue, with important scientific, ethical economic, cultural, religious, and political dimensions with important international trade policy considerations.'

---

22 The OIE is the World Organisation for Animal Health which, in French, is known as the *Office International des Épizooties* (OIE).

20   *What's important about animal welfare law?*

Similarly, a scientific perspective is reflected in the following definition:

> Animal welfare means how an animal is coping with the conditions in which it lives. An animal is in a good state of welfare if (as indicated by scientific evidence) it is healthy, comfortable, well nourished, safe, able to express innate behaviour, and if it is not suffering from unpleasant states such as pain, fear, and distress. Good animal welfare requires disease prevention and veterinary treatment, appropriate shelter, management, nutrition, humane handling and humane slaughter/killing. Animal welfare refers to the state of the animal: the treatment that an animal receives is covered by other terms such as animal care, animal husbandry, and humane treatment.[23]

Whatever definition of 'animal welfare' is used by individuals, organisations, or disciplines, considerable attention to the *legal* definition of animal welfare is necessary because as a prerequisite to *any* implementation of *any* animal welfare initiative, the activity *must*, in the first instance, be 'lawful'.

Reference to the purposes and offences of animal welfare legislation demonstrate that there are four key words which form the legal pillars of animal welfare: 'pain', 'distress', 'unnecessary' and 'unreasonable'. The one-line summary of the law's definition of animal welfare can be explained as the responsibility on the care-giver to ensure that the animal does not experience what the law deems as unnecessary or unreasonable pain, suffering, or distress.

Foundational and fundamental principles of animal welfare law

Law may be viewed not just as the rulebook, but also the history of rules, regarding human–human dealings involving animals, as well as human–animal responsibilities. Underpinning society's rulebook regarding animals is society's list of underlying beliefs and attitudes concerning animals.

Obviously understanding what drives people's attitudes – whether those 'people' are individuals in the general public, or key decision makers whose judgments impact the wider public – goes a significant way to understanding and explaining the current laws regarding animals, *and* how future law is likely to evolve.

Principle

A 'principle' is described as 'a fundamental proposition that serves as the foundation for a system of belief or behaviour or for a chain of reasoning'.

This book identifies principles of animal law that form the pillars for understanding how animal law is constructed and operates. For example, understanding that the law's definition of an animal is consistent in its methodology but not

---

23   OIE. 2010. *Terrestrial Animal Health Code 2010*: web.oie.int/eng/normes/mcode/en_glossaire.htm.

What's important about animal welfare law? 21

its definition throughout legislation avoids the repeatedly demonstrated anguish exhibited by people who lament that the law is not consistent. It has consistency, if you know what you're looking for in terms of the principle.

Similarly, principles addressing the subject of animal law, the role of law, the construction of law, and matters pertaining to concepts of 'state autonomy in a global market place' provide clarity for the reader, and concurrently assist in avoiding/recognising the myths, misinterpretations and agendas of varying stake-holders in the arena of animal law.

Where to draw the line between human and animal interests is a matter of opinion

The law usually draws that line on the basis of species. Speciesism[24] is a term that refers to the assignment of different values to beings and their interests on the basis of their species.

Philosopher Jeremy Bentham is touted by many animal advocates as a key figure in the development of animal protection. Bentham rejected the idea that faculties of reason and discourse were sufficient reason to draw a moral distinction between humans and animals. He is also one of several authors who have pointed to circumstances where animals may be seen as having greater cognitive abilities than various groups of human beings including, for example, human infants,[25] or those who are mentally impaired. However, humans are generally recognised as being the dominant species on the planet primarily because of their cognitive abilities, which distinguish humankind from other species.

Slaves, women, children – and animals? It's a flawed argument

Philosophers, including Peter Singer and Tom Reagan, have argued that speciesism is based on the same type of prejudices as sexism and racism. Some legal academics have pointed to legal changes in respect of slaves, women and children, inferring that if society's attitudes change, then the law which once denied legal rights to humans previously classified as property (i.e., slaves, women and children) can change to dismantle the property status in respect to animals too. Steven Wise is an example of a lawyer who has proposed that having redressed human injustices to women and slaves, the same approach should be taken with animals.[26]

This comparison and analogy is understandably an attractive argument to those who are of the view that the legal status of animals as property is 'a significant hurdle

---

24 R.D. Ryder. 2009. *Animal Revolution: Changing Attitudes toward Speciesism* (Oxford: Berg Publishers).
25 Jeremy Bentham. 1789 (1970 edn). *An Introduction to the Principles of Morals and Legislation*, eds J.H. Burns and H.L.A. Hart (London: Athlone Press), Chapter 17, para 4.
26 S.M. Wise. 2000. *Rattling the Cage: Toward Legal Rights for Animals* (New York: Basic Books).

22 *What's important about animal welfare law?*

for animal advocates'.[27] As appealing as this logic may initially appear, the analogy has attracted considerable criticism. Despite the enthusiasm of animal advocates to unite references to race, gender and age to the campaign for animals having legal personhood too, it has been noted that such an argument is fatally flawed. Indeed, it has been noted that in addition to stating the obvious – in that slaves, women and children are all 'human' – it is the distinction between people and animals that was used as the basis for advocating provision of legal rights to slaves, women and children in the first place.

As appealing as analogy is as a form of persuasion, it is far from being an ultimate argument. United States Federal Court Judge Richard Posner is one of the eminent authors in animal-related legal debates; he categorically states: 'Analogy is a treacherous form of argument . . . legal rights have been designed to serve the needs and interests of human beings, having the usual human capacities, and so make a poor fit with the needs and interests of animals.'[28] While debates regarding the legal classification of animals as property will continue for the foreseeable future, it is the focus on ensuring people's compliance with their legal responsibilities concerning the treatment of animals – rather than the animal's legal categorisation – that determines the practical well-being of an animal on a day-to-day basis.

The law 'draws the line' at species

In terms of which species are protected by the law, humans unsurprisingly err on the side that prioritises humans above other species, including those who are young, or mentally incapacitated, simply by virtue of their membership as humans. This is 'speciesism', as Singer and others have labelled it.[29]

The debates reflect the constant collision between perceived differences versus the similarities between humans and animals. Despite the fact that humans are learning more about animals, and that there are similarities between species in respect of certain characteristics (e.g., the ability to experience pain), there are none the less fundamental differences in how each species experiences the world. Science seeks to understand and bridge the gaps, but the fact remains that, because of physiological and mental differences, it is still impossible for humans to truly understand how other species think and feel.

This has given rise to people frequently anthropomorphizing in areas where the science has not been able to provide sufficient evidence, and where there is a collision between personal but polarised opinions on the differences or the similarities between humans and animals.

---

27 Bruce A. Wagman, Sonia S. Waisman and Pamela D. Frasch. 2000. *Animal Law: Cases and Materials*, 4th edn (Durham, NC: Carolina Academic Press).

28 R. Posner. 2006. 'Animal Rights: Legal, Philosophical, and Pragmatic Perspectives', in Cass R. Sunstein and Martha C. Nussbaum (eds), *Animal Rights: Current Debates and New Directions* (Oxford: Oxford University Press, 2006), p. 57.

29 Angus Taylor. 1999. *Magpies, Monkeys, and Morals: What Philosophers say about Animal Liberation* (Peterborough, Ontario: Broadview Press).

What's important about animal welfare law? 23

Those dealing with animals would have little problem in acknowledging that many animals exhibit behaviours which reflect emotions commonly experienced by people. Animals have been described as 'happy' (e.g., to see their owners), 'sad', or 'fearful' at the prospect of punishment. Physiologically, there is substantial evidence to demonstrate that animals experience 'pain' and 'distress', and that they 'suffer'.

It is the parallels of 'pain', 'suffering' and 'distress' that the law, supported by science, ethics and public expectations, has referenced as central pillars within animal welfare legislation. However, the law continues to draw a clear line between animals and humans on the basis of species. Human nature is that we inherently 'protect our own' in what appears to be laid out in a hierarchal order that moves in order of priority from the individual and/or the family, to the community, the nation, the region, and our species. Posner states: 'If we (humans) were cats, we would protect cats.' Human law is 'speciesist'.

The bottom-line reality is that while the law provides protection for other species by putting responsibilities on humans regarding animals, law – whatever the jurisdiction – clearly distinguishes between humans and non-humans. It's speciesist. Like it or not, it's where the law currently sits. Not everyone likes the species distinctions applied by the law, and people are entitled to their opinion – just as opinion is divided on whether or not animals should be legally classified as property.

Animals are legally classified as property – but no, not like a chair[30]

In general, most people talk about owning property without giving much thought to what the meaning of 'property' really means. In legal terms, the concept of property and 'property rights' relies on the existence of a system of authorised government and law which recognises the concept of property.[31] 'A bundle of rights' (like a bundle of sticks) is one of the most common metaphors used in describing what a property owner may do with their property.[32] This naturally raises questions about the identification of those rights. Six rights have been identified in this

---

30 M.D. Hauser, F. Cushman and M. Kamen (eds). 2005. *People, Property, or Pets?* (West Lafayette, IN: Purdue University Press), p. 3.

31 The dominant view is that this relies on 'legal positivism' which is a school of jurisprudence whose advocates believe that the only legitimate sources of law are those written rules, regulations and principles that have been expressly enacted, adopted, or recognised by an authorised governmental entity or political institution. Legal positivism attempts to define law by firmly affixing its meaning to written decisions made by governmental bodies that are endowed with the legal power to regulate particular areas of society and human conduct. If a principle, rule, regulation, decision, judgment, or other law is recognised by a duly authorised governmental body or official, then it will qualify as law, according to legal positivists: http://legal-dictionary.thefreedictionary.com. An alternative view, known as 'natural law theory', suggests that rights arise naturally as a matter of fundamental justice, independent of government.

32 Eric R. Claeys. 2011. 'Bundle-of-Sticks Notions in Legal and Economic Scholarship', *Econ Journal Watch*, 8(3): 205–14: http://econjwatch.org/articles/bundle-of-sticks-notions-in-legal-and-economic-scholarship.

24 *What's important about animal welfare law?*

metaphorical bundle and include: (1) the right to title (e.g., formal documented identity as the owner of the property); (2) the right to use the property; (3) the right to profit by use of the property; (4) the right to exclude others from using the property; (5) the right to transfer (e.g., sell the property to another owner), and (6) the right to destroy (e.g., in matters involving an animal this means the right to kill or 'euthanase' the animal).

The commonly held view is that an owner can do 'anything he wants' with 'his' property. This is simplistic – and fundamentally incorrect. The legal system was essentially 'designed by humans for humans'[33] and quite simply, property 'rights' under the law are not absolute, but are inherently *limited* according to socially acceptable justifications which balance owner autonomy with clear limits on the scope of that owner autonomy.[34] In so doing, property law provides a process for reconciling the competing goals of individual owners and society in general. Similarly, the rights associated with property ownership of animals has been limited according to what society, enunciated by the law, considers acceptable and 'lawful' in terms of an animal's suffering, pain and/or distress.

Some people believe that the legal classification of animals as property constitutes 'a significant hurdle'[35] to their protection. They say it has been alleged that in order to achieve full rights for animals, it is necessary to elevate the legal status of animals by dismantling their property status and providing them with legal 'personhood'. Balanced critical thinking mandates consideration of alternatives to voices which claim that enhanced legal status for animals is necessary in order to effectively promote the well-being of animals. One of these alternatives strongly maintains that such views are unrealistic and unnecessary. This is because the law has a long history and demonstrated proficiency for protecting property, and therefore *practical* protection may be given to animals by effectively using the property status[36] rather than dismantling it.

In the hands of proficient lawyers, animals can benefit, in practical and realistic terms, from their legal status. Federal Court Judge Richard Posner states 'There is a sad poverty of imagination in an approach to animal protection that can think of it only on the model of the civil rights movement.'[37] According to Posner, 'Animal protection codification' and approaches to the question of animals' welfare that are more conservative methodologically and politically are more effective than what Posner describes as 'rights mongering'.[38, 39]

---

33 Posner, 'Animal Rights: Legal, Philosophical, and Pragmatic Perspectives', pp. 57–8.

34 John G. Sprankling. 2012. *Understanding Property Law* (Newark, NJ: LexisNexis).

35 Wagman et al., *Animal Law: Cases and Materials*, p. 39.

36 C. Lowder. 2012. 'The Case for Animals as the Property of Humans', in Sprankling, *People, Property or Pets?*

37 R. Posner. 2006. 'Debates on Animal Rights', in Sunstein and Nussbaum (eds), *Animal Rights: Current Debates and New Directions.*

38 Ibid., p. 59.

39 The legal concept of animal *welfare* operates on a system that classifies animals as 'property', and focuses on the legal responsibilities of people regarding animals. Accordingly, animal welfare is distinguished from concepts of 'animal *rights*'.

What's important about animal welfare law? 25

Leading contemporary animal welfare legislation acknowledges the unique nature of animals, in that they are animate property distinct from inanimate objects. While the debates continue, the reality is that for the foreseeable future, the property paradigm will continue. Additionally, the welfare paradigms enacted in countries with progressive animal welfare legislation promotes protection of animals by applying legal responsibilities to humans to provide for the needs of animals in their care, and to refrain from treating animals cruelly, on the basis that animals are unique/animate property that experiences pain, suffering and distress.[40]

This means that 'yes, animals are still legally classified as property in contemporary animal welfare legislation' – but 'no, not like a chair'.

Clarifying the terminology: 'rights', 'welfare', 'protection' and 'interests'

The following definitions for the purpose of distinguishing concepts of protection, rights, interests and welfare may be helpful. Readers could use the definitions as a 'template' for identifying and interpreting how other authors have used each term:[41]

* Animal protection – an 'umbrella term' which includes, and has been used synonymously with the terms animal rights, animal interests, and animal welfare. The concept promotes initiatives which broadly seek to secure and enhance the well-being and interests of animals as a distinct stakeholder.
* Animal rights – a predominantly moral view holding that animals should be treated humanely. For the sake of clarity, it is recommended that the reader consider animal (moral) rights, distinct from legal concepts of animal welfare.
* Animal interests – a term attributed to 'traditionalists' who, 'for the sake of consistency of argument have suggested that animals might best be described as having interests'.[42]

---

40 Sovereign states such as England and Wales, Scotland, New Zealand and Australia are examples of countries where legislatures have updated their legislation to incorporate positive duties of care which recognise that certain care is due to animals, different from any owed to inanimate property.

41 The author has had occasion, for example, when, in speaking with another 'animal law lawyer' (in the US), difficulties in communication were evident. It was subsequently identified that the other lawyer was using animal 'protection' and animal 'rights' synonymously, and was working with animal 'legal rights' alongside strong views about animal (moral) rights. In contrast, the author works as a prosecutor in animal 'welfare'. The experience served to illustrate the importance of clarifying the definition of relevant terms, and objectives, from the outset.

42 Simon Brooman and Debbie Legge. 1997. *Law Relating to Animals* (London and Sydney: Cavendish), p 81. Interest in this context refers to an advantage, benefit, or perceived entitlement that belongs to a particular stakeholder.

26 *What's important about animal welfare law?*

- Animal welfare – the lawful use of animals which, as set out in legislation, criminalises blatant acts of cruelty to animals, and applies 'duties of care' to provide for the needs of animals in the care of a person. The legal responsibilities are applied with the intent of minimising the unnecessary or unreasonable pain, suffering, or distress experienced by an animal.

Animal 'rights': a hijacked term that 'misses the point'

While the subject of animal law cannot be limited to discussions about animal rights, the topic of animal rights is an inherent aspect of any book on animal law because it is a term that obviously engenders so much confusion.

Simon Brooman states, 'Unfortunately, the word "rights", has been "hijacked" by some philosophers who have struggled to find a definition of what a moral "right" actually is in relation to humans and whether "rights" exist at all.'[43] The ensuing confusion that seems to exist in relation to the use of the word 'right' has arguably contributed to the creation of alternative terms such as animal 'interests', used by Peter Singer, and the term 'animal protection'.[44] The terms of animal 'rights', 'interests', 'protection' and 'welfare' do not have the same meaning in terms of the law. Confusion is often caused by incorrect interchanged use of the terms.

From a legal perspective, property cannot have rights. Consequently, animals, legally classified as property, cannot be the bearers of legal rights. In situations where individuals choose to explore the concept of rights as it applies to animals, it's generally a prudent prerequisite to distinguish moral rights from legal rights, as these terms do not necessarily share the same values or definitions. Furthermore, any discussion where the parties agree that animals may have legal rights still runs the risk of confusion, until there is agreement on the manner in which the word 'rights' is used. The term 'rights' has been used in a variety of ways, including analogous concepts of human rights,[45] fundamental rights,[46] and correlative concepts that infer rights on the basis that if humans have a duty to treat animals well then the animals have a right to be treated accordingly.[47]

In summary, opinions regarding the question of whether or not animals can have 'rights' can be categorised in at least six different ways:

---

43 Ibid., p. 79.
44 It has been this author's experience that the terminology of animal 'protection' and animal 'interests' are frequently used as umbrella terms, and may encompass considerations of both rights and welfare, the degrees of which may vary significantly dependent upon the jurisdiction and the user.
45 Brooman and Legge, *Law Relating to Animals*, p. 79.
46 Ibid., p. 80.
47 B. Mepham. 2006. 'The Ethical Matrix as a Decision-making Tool, with Specific Reference to Animal Sentience', in J. Turner and J. D'Silva (eds), *Animals, Ethics and Trade: The Challenge of Animal Sentience* (London: Earthscan), pp. 134–45.

What's important about animal welfare law? 27

- Animals cannot have rights because legal property cannot have rights.
- Animals are unable to fulfil 'the social contract'[48] and consequently cannot have rights.
- Animals are morally entitled to rights akin to human fundamental rights.[49]
- Animals are morally entitled to rights akin to human basic rights.[50]
- Humans have a moral obligation to give fair consideration to the 'interests' of animals.
- Animals have 'welfare rights'.[51]

Radford brings a valuable perspective and balance to the argument which demonstrates that both humans and animals benefit from their relationship, and, while

---

48 Philosophers like Immanuel Kant have questioned whether animals can be rights bearers in light of their inability to fulfil the social contract to claim a right and fulfil the corresponding duty to others. The social contract has two parts: first, the ability to claim the right, or enforce the legally recognised expectation against others; second, acceptance of the duty not to infringe the rights of others. A few simple questions amply illustrate the problem. Which animal can make an informed decision to enter into a contract? Or give testimony in a Court of law? Or vote? Or participate in political debate? Animals clearly cannot be parties to such a contract because they have no concept of legal duties, or of fulfilling legal duties owed to others. Consequently, animals cannot enforce their own legal expectations or give an undertaking to respect the rights of others. Accordingly, the term 'animal rights' has received criticism on the grounds that it is a legal farce: Brooman and Legge, *Law Relating to Animals*, p. 80.

In terms of the social contract, it has been said that 'Animals cannot have rights for the same reason they cannot have duties, namely that they are not genuine "moral agents". It is relatively easy to see why animals cannot have duties, and this matter is largely beyond controversy. Animals cannot be "reasoned with" or instructed in their responsibilities; they are inflexible and unadaptable to future contingencies; they are subject to fits of instinctive passion which they are incapable of repressing or controlling, postponing or sublimating. Hence they cannot enter into contractual agreements, or make promises; they cannot be trusted; and they cannot (except within very narrow limits and for purposes of conditioning) be blamed for what would be called "moral failures" in a human being. They are therefore incapable of being moral subjects, of acting rightly or wrongly in the moral sense, of having, discharging, or breaching duties and obligations.' Expressed another way in terms of the human/animal relationship, animals do not have the ability to fulfil the criteria to enter into legal agreements with humans: ibid., p. 82.

In spite of Posner's warning that 'analogy is a treacherous form of argument', a number of animal rights advocates have none the less drawn an analogy with the rights of human counterparts, namely the young or mentally incapacitated who, although incapable of claiming rights on their own, may have proxies or attorneys who are empowered to speak and represent their interests. Posner, 'Debates on Animal Rights', p. 57; J. Feinberg. 1974. 'The rights of animals and unborn generations', in J. Blackstone (ed.), *Philosophy and Environmental Crisis* (Athens: University of Georgia Press).

49 Brooman and Legge, *Law Relating to Animals*, p. 80.
50 Ibid., p. 79.
51 The term 'animal welfare' has been interpreted by a minority, albeit uncomfortably, to suggest that animals have some set of limited rights. It is argued that if humans have a legal duty not to harm animals or be cruel to them, including a positive duty to treat animals according to specified legislative standards, then it follows that animals have a right to be treated accordingly. See Mepham, 'The Ethical Matrix as a Decision-making Tool'.

28 *What's important about animal welfare law?*

unacceptable practices do occur, animal protection legislation has demonstrably improved the quality of life for animals. This forms the basis for pointing out that those arguing about animal rights miss the point that the nature of the legal obligation in the human–animal relationship is less about the property classification or questions about 'rights', but more about duties associated with 'responsibility' to appropriately care for those who rely on the care-giver. According to Radford, property is more than simply a designation of ownership. It actually revolves around a concept of relationship that allows for a sense of responsibility and value.[52]

Joel Feinberg's definition of animal welfare provides significant clarity for those still seeking to distinguish animal welfare from animal rights. He states that animal welfare involves 'duties regarding animals', in contrast to animal rights which are defined as 'duties to animals'.[53] It is these 'responsibilities' attached to the standards of care in the human–animal relationship that are captured in the legal definition of animal welfare and is clearly demonstrated in the name of the relevant legislation which is the Animal Welfare Act, not the Animal Rights Act.

Retaining balance about the welfare paradigm

History demonstrates that animal protection has developed through a process of incremental change. American academic lawyer Gary Francione, for example, describes what he has termed 'legal welfarism' as explicitly supporting 'animal exploitation as morally justifiable'.[54] Mike Radford, an English academic lawyer, in referring to Francione's views, counters by saying that exploitation is an inevitable consequence of social interdependence, 'it is the nature of the exploitation which is important'.[55]

With due respect to Francione, this author, like Radford,[56] unequivocally rejects Francione's opinion. Legislation is not a panacea, and naturally has its limitations in ensuring that animals are provided with the highest standards of animal welfare. None the less, the law has made a considerable difference to the well-being of animals by ensuring that animal welfare practices do not fall below legislated minimum standards.

While not excusing instances where people have abused their position of power, the reality is that the human race is part of the animal kingdom, not separate from it, and that all forms of life exploit their environment in order to survive. To suggest otherwise has been described politely as 'fanciful'.[57]

---

52 M. Radford. 2001. *Animal Welfare Law in Britain* (Oxford: Oxford University Press), p. 10.

53 See Feinberg, 'The rights of animals and unborn generations'. Feinberg's distinction that duties regarding animals (welfare) are not the same as duties to them (traditional rights theory) was exemplified by pointing out that while people might have duties regarding the care of places, monuments and/or buildings, for example, that did not infer that humans had legal duties to those things (e.g., the places, monuments, or buildings).

54 G.L. Francione. 1995. *Animals, Property, and the Law* (Philadelphia, PA: Temple University Press), p. 258.

55 Radford, *Animal Welfare Law in Britain*, p. 10.

56 Ibid., p. 394.

57 Ibid., p. 10.

What's important about animal welfare law? 29

Animals have benefited from animal welfare law

Certain purists may take the view that the notion of animal welfare law is misguided;[58] however, a balanced, practical and objective view quickly demonstrates that the law has made a considerable difference to the well-being of animals by ensuring that standards of animal welfare do not fall below legislated minimum standards.

Public awareness reflected in public policy, and the ability of authorised and empowered authorities to enforce animal welfare standards as set out in contemporary animal welfare legislation, means that many animals are treated considerably better than what would likely have been their traditional lot. With due respect to the perceptions of the isolated few, welfare is the current paradigm and not so much a government conspiracy as a responsibility.

Although debates continue and undoubtedly there will continue to be shifts in what is considered good animal husbandry and practice, the law's involvement is seen across the board in almost every use of animals – but particularly so in the area of greatest use of animals, which is their role as food for the human consumer.

More food is required to feed more and wealthier people

Not all stakeholders are steak eaters – but most still are.

The world's population doubled to 6 billion in the latter part of the twentieth century, and it was developments in agriculture (e.g., 'factory farming') that averted predicted global food shortages and consequent human hardship. Currently estimates suggest that 35 per cent of the world's surface is used for agriculture, and that agriculture uses 70 per cent of globally available water.[59] Consequently, there are concerns about how to reduce the impact of the food production system on the environment,[60] in the face of predictions that, despite growing competition for land, water and energy, the global population and corresponding consumption growth will increase to a figure of 9 billion people by 2050,[61] and a consequent need to produce twice as much food as is currently produced.[62]

There are numerous texts and papers providing estimates based on varying assumptions, that correlate food production with the planet's 'human carrying

---

58 Ibid., p. 394.

59 J.L. Buttriss. 2010. *Nine Billion Mouths to Feed by 2050: The Challenge of Establishing a Sustainable Food Supply* (London: British Nutrition Foundation).

60 H. Charles et al. 2010. 'Food Security: The Challenge of Feeding 9 Billion People', *Science*, 327(5967) (12 February): 812–18.

61 The US Bureau of the Census projection for world population in the year 2050 is 9.10 billion: US Census Bureau. 2000. 'Total midyear population for the world: 1950–2050'. International Data Base: www.census.gov/ipc/www/worldpop.htm. The 2000 United Nations Population Division 'low', 'medium' and 'high' projections for 2050 are 7.87, 9.32 and 10.93 billion respectively: United Nations. 1999. 'Long-range World Population Projections: Based on the 1998 Revision', ESA/P/ WP.153, 27 December; see also Department of Economic and Social Affairs, United Nations, New York: www.sciencedirect.com/science/article/pii/S0306919202000027.

62 Buttriss, *Nine Billion Mouths to Feed by 2050*.

30 *What's important about animal welfare law?*

capacity', and consider how human dietary demands might be met by a combination of cereals and 'animal protein per day'.[63]

The consumption of 'meat' is set to increase

The bottom line of these calculations demonstrate that there is going to be an increased demand for 'animal protein', that as such the single dominant use of animals in the world is likely to continue to be as a source of food for people.[64]

The link between animal and human health, associated with issues pertaining to food supply and food safety, is referenced in programmes and proposals that have become a common term for those involved in the concept of 'One Health'.[65]

A word on vegetarianism . . .

Some people have an ideal world-view that promotes reduction, or even abolition of the consumption of animals by humans. Supporters adopt dietary choices that result in abstinence, to one degree or another, of consumption and/or utilisation of animals or animal products. Dismissing the vegan lifestyle or labelling it as 'wrong' lacks any sense of fairness and objectivity. However, it would be fair to say that, for the time being, the vegan lifestyle is unlikely to be embraced by the larger part of either current, or foreseeable, society. The reality is that the consumption of meat will increase, not decrease.

Total agreement is not expected

Given the divergent opinions regarding animals and the enormous number of stakeholders attached to issues of animals, their welfare and the law governing their uses, then total agreement on what the law provides in terms of animal protection is unlikely, probably unrealistic, and therefore not expected. None the less, the responsibility for making decisions that lawfully, reasonably and responsibly balance and prioritise the interests of stakeholders is the domain of governors in government, industry and a range of non-government organisations.

Putting animal law in context of global governance

Stakeholders attached to the subject of animal law vary geographically, as well demographically. As people's interdependence has expanded from the local community to the international marketplace, the 'rules' that govern local, national

---

63 Bernard Gilland. 2002. 'World Population and Food Supply: Can Food Production Keep Pace with Population Growth in the Next Half-Century?', *Food Policy*, 27(1) (February): 47–63.

64 Bernard Hubert et al. 2010. 'The Future of Food: Scenarios for 2050': www.soils.org/publications/cs/pdfs/50/Supplement_1/S-33.

65 Paul-Pierre Pastoret. 2012. 'Reducing Hazards for Animals from Humans', *Italian Journal of Public Health*, 9(2).

What's important about animal welfare law? 31

and international expectations have also been established, modified and updated. Law provides a record of not just how society's attitudes have developed, but also of how society's attitudes differ enormously throughout cultures, countries and regions of the world.

The global market has inherent risks which national and international governors alike have a responsibility to manage. They also have the responsibility to develop and apply standards of animal welfare in a manner that lawfully, sustainably and fairly balances and prioritises the enormously varied, competing and frequently conflicting interests that exist. Thus, if a nation is free of a particular pest or disease (e.g., bluetongue, or foot-and-mouth disease), then it's obviously in that nation's best interests to ensure that its trade policies and border control procedures minimise the risk of those conditions being introduced. Clearly this is particularly important where such introduction would result in serious economic, environmental and/or societal consequences.

The theory is that where people are better informed, that awareness will subsequently be reflected in their decisions.

Fundamental principles

It is obvious that the field of animal welfare covers an extensive range of subjects with infinite variance in people's opinions between polarised views that vary depending on the species, location, culture nuances and personal opinions regarding both the animals and the people involved. So it stands to reason that this book does not, because it cannot, tell the reader what they should or should not think.

However, despite the obvious disparity in people's attitudes and levels of responsibility concerning animals and their welfare, there are consistent recognisable fundamental principles that underpin the human–animal relationship, and the human–human 'rulebook' dictating the wide number of issues associated with animals.

What this book does do is provide the reader with an authoritative introduction to the legal perspective of people's responsibilities regarding animals, and their welfare. Then, armed with sufficient information regarding fundamental societal and legal principles, and the ability to think critically, the reader (who is expanding their reading and research in to areas of their personal interest) should be in a position to avoid the common confusions and pitfalls that students encounter as they venture into the field of animal welfare law, where animals and humans each represent one, but not the only, stakeholder.

3 The need for critical assessment rather than emotional reaction

Law: it's a rulebook written by society

The role of law has been described as 'the instrument which society uses to strike balances between competing interests'.[1] In a nutshell, law is important because in contrast to ethical or subjective optional perspectives, law binds people, obliging them to behave according to specified standards, and applying penalties for failing to comply accordingly.

The nature of law and the direction of its evolution are in a state of continuous transformation that balances existing conditions, knowledge and justified beliefs with shifting societal expectations, and what constitutes the public good. Law has always had a pivotal role in the epistemological perspective, and thereby, in setting standards of what is acceptable in human society. However, society is inherently made of competing and conflicting ideas about what is acceptable. Additionally, there are individual and community interests that the law has a responsibility to balance and prioritise. It is a considerable oversimplification to state that law achieves this by reference to established and evolving 'rules'. However, the simplification serves the purposes of the book in this instance since it highlights the principle that the rules contained in law define what is 'lawful'.

The rule of law puts everyone on an even playing field

The rule of law operates on the concept that no one is above the law. The logic underpinning the rule of law is that the fundamentals of truth, and therefore law,

---

1 Matthew S.R. Palmer. 2002. 'A Perspective on Balance and the Role of Law', in David Carter and Matthew Palmer (eds), *Roles & Perspectives in the Law: Essays in Honour of Sir Ivor Richardson* (Wellington: Victoria University Press). Palmer states: 'Where the role of law is clearly established, such as in the "black-letter" areas of employment, commerce, and taxation, law is the instrument which society uses to strike balances between competing interests. In "red-letter" socio-political areas of law, such as indigenous rights, human rights and constitutions, where the role of law is less well-established, debate tends to focus on whether law, and the Courts, are the appropriate instrument by which to strike a balance.'

The need for critical assessment   33

operate on principles which can be discovered, but which cannot be created through an act of an individual's will.

Essentially, the rule of law pertains to the relationship between the powers of government and the rights of individuals. The most important application of the rule of law is the principle that government authority is legitimately exercised only in accordance with laws that are properly drafted, communicated, adopted and enforced in a procedurally correct manner. The rule of law functions on an amalgamation of standards and expectations that incorporate concepts of liberty, justice and fairness in that relationship. Consequently, the phrase 'rule of law' has been applied to a variety of concepts which include theories about law and order, separation of powers[2] and the administration of justice, democracy, freedom and equality.

The rule of law encompasses concepts of legality which incorporate fundamental concepts such as the expectation that no punishment shall be imposed without law (*'nulla poena sine lege'*[3]) and that penalties should not be enforced retrospectively. Concepts that may already be familiar include the presumption of innocence,[4] legal equality,[5] double jeopardy[6] and habeas corpus.[7]

Central to the theory of the rule of law is the expectation that the state will not act arbitrarily in dealing with its legal citizens.[8] This expectation holds that everyone, including the government, is equal before the law, and that the law must provide certainty while remaining flexible enough to develop over time.[9] By 'acting arbitrarily', it is meant that the state and its officials should not behave towards legal citizens of the state in a manner which is random, unreasoned, or impulsive and which has no clear justification in law.

The law has an obligation to fulfil its responsibilities in a way that is systematic, reasonable and careful in respect of its dealing with all its legal citizens (cf., just selected groups of legal citizens), setting standards regarding human–human and human–animal responsibilities, and balancing the (frequently emotive) perspectives and arguments attached to those legal responsibilities.

---

2   This refers to the division of power between the three branches of government – the legislature, the executive and the judiciary – with a view to ensuring that no one branch can act unconstitutionally.

3   The principle that there must be no crime or punishment except in accordance with fixed, predetermined law, comes from the Latin expression *'nullum crimen sine lege, nulla poena sine lege'*. A. Mokhtar. 2005. 'Nullum Crimen, Nulla Poena Sine Lege: Aspects and Prospects', *Statute Law Review*, 26(1): 41–55 (Oxford University Press).

4   The legal concept that everyone is 'innocent until proven guilty'.

5   The legal concept holding that all individuals are given the same rights without distinction to their social status, religion, or political beliefs.

6   A legal concept stipulating that a person can only be punished once for the same crime.

7   The right of a person to be advised of the crimes he or she is accused of, and to request that relevant matters be reviewed by the appropriate judicial authority.

8   The origins of this concept date back to Magna Carta of 1215 and the Bill of Rights of 1688.

9   Additional relevant concepts hold that judges should be free to fulfil their responsibilities independently of central government, that the judicial system must be accessible to all citizens, and that natural justice (*'audi alteram partem'*, namely the fundamental right to be given notice and a fair hearing) is equally available to all citizens.

34 *The need for critical assessment*

Being 'objective, authoritative and practical' rather than just 'emotional'

This chapter reflects the ultimate purpose of this book, which is to be familiar with the fundamental principles that underpin human 'rules' about interactions that involve animals, and combine that information with the ability to think critically about the uses of animals in society. That objective clearly has two parts. Firstly, information gathering is essential to understanding any subject, and identification of the fundamental principles of animal welfare and law provides readers with the ability to make sense of the substantial amount of information on the subject, and consequently be discerning over what is valuable and what is not.

Critical thinking is not argument for argument's sake. It should expose misinformation, fallacies and propaganda. It also plays an important role in recognising and building cooperative and constructive solutions in a balanced, authoritative and practical way in any forum, debating any use, involving animal welfare and the law.

There is substantial material available on the subject of critical thinking. Consequently, this chapter seeks to briefly outline some of the key points relating to animal welfare and the law.

The whole subject of animal welfare and law is a highly emotive subject. People vary in respect of their emotional perspective regarding animals. For example, in considering the companionship role of animals to humans, some people view their animals as members of the family similar to any other human being. Others may not see animals as members of the family, but none the less are in agreement that people have a responsibility to treat animals well. At the other end of the scale, there are those who view animals simply as a commodity for human use similar to any other inanimate object. What is needed is constructive contribution to current and continuing debates on matters that are relevant to animal law; this requires the ability to critically assess issues associated with the human use of animals. Objective, authoritative and practical critical assessment requires balanced and fair consideration of the range of conflicting and competing subjective opinions attached to the subject of animals and their welfare.

An informed reader should be able to identify emotive text and put that, too, in the context of its delivery, deliverer and the deliverer's agenda. For example, some animal welfare academics have accused humans of being 'schizophrenic' in respect of their attitudes involving animals.[10] Recognising the fundamental principle that the law applies responsibilities to the human care-giver depending on the circumstances of the animal will help the reader of this book put descriptors such as 'schizophrenic', 'unhappy' and other similarly seductively emotive terms in context of an authoritative understanding of the principles which guide the law.

---

10 Francione, G.L. (2005) 'Animals, Property, and Personhood', in M.D. Hauser (ed.), *People, Property, or Pets?* (West Lafayette, IN: Purdue University Press), p. 79.

The need for critical assessment   35

The reality is that emotion continues to innately attach to most discussions involving animals, and particularly those in which humans empathise, to one degree or another, with the animals concerned.[11] The law has a responsibility to balance the interests of all stakeholders, where animals are one, but not the only stakeholder at the stakeholder table.

The problem with not thinking critically

Despite the fact that everybody thinks, research has indicated that applying rational, open-minded and evidentially informed thinking on a subject is not something that comes naturally to most people. Undisciplined thinking has frequently been the basis for people accepting partial, uninformed, or distorted information and subsequently adopting beliefs (with consequent behaviours) that demonstrably over-generalise, contain fallacies, self-deceptions and bias, right through to blatant prejudice. Informed people are undeniably valuable to the public's well-being. They rationally apply widely held standards of humane treatment of the animals themselves. Effective enforcement requires informed leadership, clear legislation, penalties that fit the offending and adequate resources.

A critical reader will also be able to think beyond simple 'face-value' reports, statements and considerations dealing with issues on animal welfare. For example, one government minister, when referring to traditional agricultural practices, stated that the public should accept that 'where there are livestock, there are dead stock'.[12]

The benefits of thinking critically

There are many definitions of critical thinking, but the key terms and concepts are in this statement: 'critical thinking is the application of a disciplined system of criteria to collect relevant information, followed by application of objective and authoritative reasoning that supports justified conclusions'. Critical thinking is an important element of all professional fields and academic disciplines, but in the context of animal welfare and the law, one of the first lessons is that critical thinking necessitates thinking beyond the interests of one or a limited group

---

11 Conservation efforts in respect of some species have been benefited, for example, by media which anthropomorphically attributes human characteristics to animals. The elephant, dolphin and koala are examples of such species. See Praveen Singh. 2005. 'Narrative in Wildlife Films: How It Shapes Our Understanding of the Natural World and Influences Conservation Choices', Master's Thesis, Montana State University: http://scholarworks.montana.edu/xmlui/bitstream/handle/1/2285/singhp0505.pdf?sequence=1.

12 In 2011, New Zealand Minister of Agriculture David Carter, in response to allegations that over 100,000 lambs predictably die annually during lambing season as a result of exposure to New Zealand's cold winter conditions, responded, 'Where there are livestock, there are dead stock.'

36 *The need for critical assessment*

of stakeholders. Critical thinking can clarify objectives, examine assumptions, identify hidden values and agendas, objectively evaluate supporting evidence, and asses proposals on their merits. Like law, critical thinking requires application of a disciplined process which is based on evidence not opinions, and finally, proof.

There are further close parallels with law. Critical thinking requires the ability to identify issues and succinctly state them, to gather facts by means of a thorough investigation, to assess the information by reference to relevant foundational principles of law, give due consideration to the credibility of the proposed theories, and then apply conclusions and judgements that will guide future decisions and may/will, in turn, be tested. Constructive contribution to current and continuing debates on matters relevant to animal law requires the ability to critically assess issues associated with the human use of animals. Objective, authoritative and practical critical assessment requires balanced and fair consideration of the range of conflicting and competing subjective opinions on the subject of animals and their welfare.

A critical thinking checklist

This brief overview of the benefits of critical thinking, and the traits that identify it, naturally lead to the question of how to think critically.

Readers are encouraged to supplement this brief introduction to critical thinking with further reading. In the meantime, the questions below have proved useful for those studying and assessing animal law, to evaluate the material created/being reviewed:[13]

- Does the work critically assess the subject being addressed? In contrast to critical assessment, is the content biased, myopic, unrealistic, impractical, inadequately researched, and/or overly subjective?[14]
- What are the relevant facts (e.g., statistics, trends, credible forecasts)?[15]
- Given that there is an obligation to be 'lawful', what are the current national/internal law/obligations attached to the current/proposed change?

---

13 These questions are not presented in any definitive order of importance, and it is possible that some, and not all, of the prompts/considerations may be useful in context of the reader's area of interest.

14 The author has used a number of useful 'tools' in assisting students of animal law to think objectively about issues associated with animal law. Among these tools is one referred to as the 'should/could' rule, which encourages students to review their work and review each instance that the word 'should' (implying a subjective world-view) occurs. Then, where appropriate, replace the word 'should' with 'could'. This simple exercise forces consideration of the practicalities as to whether a recommended course of action is warranted, and simultaneously identifies the barriers and alternative 'do-able' and 'affordable' outcomes.

15 This reflects principles of critical thinking associated with requirements for factual evidence that is accurate, credible and verifiable.

The need for critical assessment   37

- Who are the relevant stakeholders?[16] What are their drivers/motivators/interests? What do they each stand to gain/lose (e.g., from retention of the status quo, or proposed change)? What are the stated and inferred/unstated assumptions of the stakeholders? Who is/are the key 'people'/representative of each stakeholder? What is the hierarchy of power between the respective stakeholders? What are the relevant conflicts (e.g., conflicts of interest)?
- What is the problem (if any) with retaining the status quo? Define, specifically, the barriers and proposed outcomes. What is the proposed outcome? What are the alternatives? What are the relevant costs/benefits per stakeholder of the proposed change?[17]
- What is the central argument? What are the key issues?[18] Does the material clearly demonstrate 'why' there is a need for change (i.e., the basis for the central argument)? 'What' is the rationale for identification of the 'key issues'?
- Has all the relevant information been gathered and assessed? What are the key criteria for selecting 'relevant' information? Is the information credible? Is the information verifiable (i.e., not hearsay[19])? What are the demonstrable

---

16 Certain stakeholders will be a constant, while others may vary according to the discipline, or circumstances. For example, lawfulness is a usual prerequisite to decision making and associated risk assessments so commonly featured on matrices or association diagrams listing stakeholders. Alternatively, Mepham's ethical matrix has been applied to various issues which commonly identify stakeholders as 'the organism, users/consumers, producers/providers, and the environment/biota' with interests of 'well-being, autonomy, and justice': B. Mepham. 2006. 'The Ethical Matrix as a Decision-making Tool, With Specific Reference to Animal Sentience', in J. Turner and J. D'Silva (eds), *Animals, Ethics and Trade: The Challenge of Animal Sentience* (London: Earthscan), pp. 134–45.

17 The acronym 'SPIN' ('situation, problem, implication, need') has been used as one tool to assist in assessing the need (or not) for change. Similar 'tools' include SWOT ('strengths, weaknesses, opportunity, threats') analysis, and SMART objectives ('specific, measurable, attainable, realistic, time-bound'). Information on each of these tools, and many more similar assessment tools, is readily accessible via the Internet. FILAC is the author's acronym for 'facts, issue, law, application and conclusion'.

18 It is helpful to state these clearly and precisely, and readers are encouraged to present the issue(s) in one line wherever possible. Constructing the central argument in the form of a closed 'yes/no' question is often advantageous.

19 There is a legal definition of 'hearsay' which illustrates the meaning of the term. Hearsay is identified as a statement that was made by a person other than a witness, and is offered in evidence at the proceeding to prove the truth of its contents (Section 4 of the Evidence Act 2006 (New Zealand)). Hearsay constitutes information that is unverifiable since it was gained or acquired from another person, rather than the speaker's direct knowledge. For example, X, who is not to be called as a witness, tells witness Y he saw person Z repeatedly kicking a dog. Witness Y tries to tell the Court what X told him as evidence that Z repeatedly kicked a dog. Y's statement is hearsay and will be admissible only if it falls within one of the exceptions to the general rule against hearsay, for example, the Court decides that, in the circumstances, the evidence of Y is sufficiently reliable that it can be considered reliable evidence.

38   *The need for critical assessment*

conflicts/agreements in the information? Is the information up-to-date and authoritative? What is the credibility of the documentation/records/research/ published material relied upon?

- Have counter-arguments and alternatives been clearly and authoritatively identified? Have the associated needs, assumptions, implications and practical consequences of each alternative (including the proposal and counter-arguments) been addressed?
- What examples are provided to illustrate/support/demonstrate the points being made? Are the examples on point with the central argument, or do they demonstrate confusion? Have alternative counter-examples been identified, considered and tested?
- Is the argument appropriately and authoritatively structured? Is the argument logical (e.g., are causal associations and alleged claims valid and authoritatively researched/demonstrable)? Have alternative explanations been adequately identified?
- Is the decision appropriately balanced and prioritised in consideration of the 'big picture' [20] and proper risk-management protocols?
- Are the definitions, allegations and interpretations accurate and verifiable?
- Is the conclusion/solution well-reasoned in consideration of relevant law, accepted principles/criteria and achievable standards? What are the identified key criteria for assessing/prioritising solutions? Can the conclusions be corroborated? What (if any) are the potential conflicts of interest? Does the proposed conclusion/hypothesis plausibly explain the evidence, and is it consistent with the known facts?
- What are the implications/consequences of accepting or rejecting the conclusion/judgement?

20 'Big picture' is an idiom referring to consideration of the entire perspective on a situation or issue: www.merriam-webster.com.

Part II

The foundational principles of animal welfare law

This second part of the book includes three chapters which identify the origins of the foundational principles which underpin the human–animal relationship, and how these principles continue to be evident in, and shape, national and international animal law. Chapter 4 shows how religious beliefs created an original framework that established the place of animals in human society, and how humankind's dominant position subsequently evolved through the influence of scientists, philosophers and society. Chapters 5 and 6 then demonstrate how the key principles and standards which define the protection, use and experience of animals permeate both national and international legal systems.

Part II
The foundational principles of animal welfare law

4 Religion and reaction
The foundations of animal welfare law

This chapter looks at the foundational concepts that historically informed people's attitudes, beliefs and relationship regarding animals. In addition to providing the opportunity to consider the basis of their own attitudes regarding animals, readers will also be able to understand opinions other than their own regarding animals. The chapter identifies who or what established the foundational attitudes regarding animals (whatever the legal jurisdiction) which became the first 'rule book' (i.e., law) of humans dealings regarding animals.

It also familiarises readers with animal welfare law terminology – very important in helping to avoid the common confusions that occur when students of animal law undertake wider reading on the subject. Other publications frequently demonstrate that authors have applied significantly different definitions to the same terms with a view to communicating what amounts to contrasting opinions, concepts and underlying agendas. For example, the terms 'animal rights', 'protection', 'welfare' and 'interests' have all been used interchangeably by philosophers, lawyers and scientists, each reflecting their own opinions, field of expertise, and fluency in a discipline other than their own. This chapter provides readers with clarity of terms so that they can identify the law's verifiable definition of animal welfare.

By the end of this chapter, you should be able to:

- authoritatively explain the historical beginnings of people's polarised opinions regarding animals, and explain how those early influencers continue to account for enduring conflicts of opinion about human responsibilities regarding animals;
- using examples, identify which philosophies underpin the law;
- identify the key figures and milestones that shaped the current status of animals under law; and
- explain the role of 'law' in animal welfare, and the human–animal relationship.

Why are people's attitudes regarding animals so different?

Why do people have polarised personal opinions regarding animals? Psychologists have explained that people's attitudes regarding different people, objects, issues,

42 *Foundations of animal welfare law*

or events are the result of a *learned* tendency to evaluate things in a certain way.[1] So what experiences shape a person's conscious and unconscious beliefs about animals, and why do they hold often wildly divergent attitudes and behaviours towards them? What informs *your* personal beliefs, opinions and attitudes regarding animals? Social roles and social norms, for example, can have a strong influence on attitudes.[2] Experience and observation are two additional factors which have been shown to influence views. Or are you simply a product of good advertising that promotes the 'charismatic megavertebrate'?[3]

Consider how you feel about marine mammals like dolphins and whales, for example – should they be protected? The number of established sanctuaries and organisations[4] reflect opinions of a large number of people who believe that these creatures warrant protection.[5] However, what about consideration for situations where one of these creatures is necessarily killed as part of established cultural and religious beliefs? The law certainly provides exemptions[6] on these grounds. Several cultures, for example, consider the successful hunting and killing of an

---

1 D. Hockenbury and S.E. Hockenbury. 2007. *Discovering Psychology* (New York: Worth Publishers).

2 Social roles deals with how people are expected to behave in a particular role or context, while social norms broadly refers to society's rules for what behaviours are considered appropriate.

3 The book *Animals, Equality and Democracy* by Siobhan O'Sullivan (Basingstoke: Palgrave Macmillan Animal Ethics Series, 2011), for example, argues that the key to understanding why we treat some animals better than others is whether they are in public view or not. Some readers agree with the central argument but have expressed concern that it is overly simplistic to argue that animals behind closed doors (e.g., laboratory animals) are less cared about by the public. The suggestion may underpin what has been described as the 'charismatic megavertebrate' argument for determining why certain species of animals are apparently more publicly popular – pandas, elephants, other companion animals that you can see and empathise with – in contrast to pests and rodents that are small, hide in the bush and are more active at night (when humans are traditionally sleeping): D.R. Towns and M. Williams. 1993. 'Single species conservation in New Zealand: towards a redefined conceptual approach, *Journal of the Royal Society of New Zealand*, 23 (June): 61–76.

4 E. Morgera. 2004. 'Whale Sanctuaries: An Evolving Concept within the International Whaling Commission', *Ocean Development & International Law*, 35: 319–38.

5 J.B. Master. 1998. 'International Trade Trumps Domestic Environmental Protection: "Dolphins and Sea Turtles Are Sacrificed on the Altar of Free Trade"', *Temp. Int'l & Comp. Law Journal*, 423; Peter Bridgewater. 2003. 'Whaling or Wailing?', *International Social Science Journal*, 55(178) (December): 555–9.

6 Articles XX and XXI of the General Agreement on Tariffs and Trade 1994, for example, allow Members to justify on a number of non-trade policy grounds measures that would otherwise be inconsistent with their obligations under the WTO Agreement. These grounds include protecting the environment, public health and public morals, and preventing deceptive practices. 'Public morals' can vary in time and space, depending upon a range of factors, including prevailing social, cultural, ethical and religious values: R. Galantucci. 2008. 'Compassionate Consumerism Within the GATT Regime: Can Belgium's Ban on Seal Product Imports be Justified under Article XX', *Cal. W. Int'l L.J.*, 39: 281–313.

Foundations of animal welfare law 43

animal to be a rite of passage from childhood to adulthood.[7] Experience has demonstrated that people, somewhat begrudgingly, will acknowledge that in today's multicultural global society, it is acceptable to accommodate exemptions that result in the killing of selected animals, usually with a proviso that the killings are 'not too many, just a few'. However, people often visibly and audibly demonstrate complete rejection of any suggestion that perhaps it should also be acceptable on cultural and religious grounds to kill a few people so long as the number of people killed was 'not too many, just a few'. The distinction, although clearly stretching the point, has served to illustrate deeply held beliefs that distinguish the value applied to the life of humans and animals. The scenario then dovetails in to considerations of what has informed the beliefs that makes that distinction. Why is it acceptable to kill a whale and not a person? If dolphins and whales are considered simply 'extra-large tuna', why is it more acceptable to kill a tuna than a dolphin or a whale? These, and other questions motivate consideration of what informs people's underlying beliefs not just about the differences in value between human and animal life, but why people value one species of animal above or below another.

This book offers the opportunity to consider the variety of perspectives that exist on the subject of animal law.

In some instances, this will require unlearning some of the misinformation that exists regarding animals and the law, but, as with so many areas of law, it is only possible to comprehend the present legal situation by understanding what informed past developments.[8]

The historical roots of contemporary debates about animals

Historical perspectives of animal law do much more than simply educate about the origins of modern-day arguments. They also provide an opportunity to learn from the past. An examination of historical developments enables readers to trace current thinking back to the early concepts which have shaped people's current beliefs and relationship with animals.

Several commentators have already canvassed the historical and philosophical basis for the fundamental concepts that drive some, but clearly not all, of

---

7 As a rite of passage, the killing of one's first caribou, for example, served as an important indicator in Aboriginal communities as to whether a young man is prepared to assume responsibility as a family provider: David C. Natcher. 2008. 'The Social Economy of Canada's Aboriginal North', College of Agriculture and Bioresources University of Saskatchewan, Paper submitted to Northern Research Forum: www.rha.is/static/files/NRF/.../Anchorage2008/natcher-nrf-submission.pdf. Similarly, under the Marine Mammal Protection Act (MMPA), native hunting is broadly guaranteed, with only a general provision that the take 'not be wasteful': Nancy Lord. 2000. 'Two Worlds, One Whale. The Belugas of Alaska's Cook Inlet are the Victims of a Cultural Divide Between Science and Tradition', *Sierra* (July–August): http://vault.sierraclub.org/sierra/200007/belugawhale.asp.

8 M. Radford. 2001. *Animal Welfare Law in Britain* (Oxford: Oxford University Press), p. 94.

44   *Foundations of animal welfare law*

the doctrines being advanced in animal law. Understanding their contributions in the historical context will frequently enable readers to understand different perspectives, and put contemporary issues involving animals and the law in the context of wider national and international concerns.[9]

Records demonstrate that ancient Greeks, while advocating respect for animals[10, 11] identified key differences between animals and humans that subsequently meant that animals were ranked below humans. Man was different because, for example, man had government, society, the 'gift of speech', and perceptions of good and evil. Aristotle's position, that human and non-human animals exist in different moral realms evidenced by the 'differences' between them, informed Western concepts for nearly two thousand years.[12]

This list of differences included the 'irrationality' of animals. However, it is interesting to note that the Greeks none the less considered animals to be morally culpable for their actions, were put on trial, and if found guilty of crimes against society, the animals might be banished or put to death. A similar belief, which also included putting animals on trial in Courts of Law and assigning them their own legal counsel, was manifested in the Middle Ages and punishments often included excommunication and death. One documented record from 1386, for example, refers to a prisoner who had caused the death of a child by mutilating the face and arms of the child to such an extent that the child had died as a result of the consequent haemorrhage. The local Court decreed that not only should the prisoner be hanged, but that the prisoner's head and legs should be mangled with a knife before the hanging. The prisoner was dressed in a new suit of clothes, attended by armed men on horseback, and the hangman even provided himself with new gloves and a new rope for the occasion. The criminal, in that instance, was a sow that had taken to eating an infant in the street.[13] See Case Study 1.

---

9 For example, René Descartes (1596–1650) alleged that animals did not feel pain due to an 'absence of intellect'. His influential views consequently led to widespread abuse of animals for centuries, as experimenters and commercial agriculturalists used his theories to deny even the most minimal of humane considerations to animals. Pope Pius XII provided Papal support for these views, declaring that 'the cries of animals should not arouse unreasonable compassion'. The legacy of this Catholic view contributed to legal and moral views regarding animals which persist today, and have caused difficulties in framing European legislation concerning animals: Simon Brooman and Debbie Legge (eds). 1997. *Law Relating To Animals* (London: Routledge-Cavendish), pp. 8–10.

10 Mary Ann Violin. 1990. 'Pythagoras – The First Animal Rights Philosopher', *Between the Species*, 6: 122–7, cited in Taylor, Angus. 2009. *Animals and Ethics* (Peterborough, Ontario: Broadview Press), p. 34.

11 Brooman and Legge, *Law Relating To Animals*, p. 32.

12 Ibid., p. 6.

13 H.L. Carson. 1917. 'The Trial of Animals and Insects: A Little Known Chapter of Medieval Jurisprudence', *American Philosophical Society Journal*, 56: 410–15, at 410.

Foundations of animal welfare law   45

> ## Case Study 1: Understanding those comical and macabre historical cases
>
> Criminal trials of animals are recorded as having taken place in Europe as early as the thirteenth century and continued until the eighteenth century. The court transcripts were sometimes comic, and at times macabre, depicting the unusual and disturbing trials of animals in medieval Europe which were held with the solemnity of a human criminal trial, despite the fact that the defendants were not human.
>
> Animals could be charged and required to appear as defendants before church and/or secular courts, with the offences alleged against them ranging from criminal damage to murder. In ecclesiastical courts, animals were routinely provided with lawyers to assist their case. If convicted, it was usual for an animal to be executed, or exiled. However, judgment didn't always go against the animal. For example, in 1750, a female donkey was acquitted of charges of bestiality due to witnesses testifying to the animal's virtue and good behaviour while her human co-accused was sentence to death.
>
> (See Anila Srivastava. 2007. '"Mean, Dangerous, and Uncontrollable Beasts": Mediaeval Animal Trials', *Mosaic: A Journal for the Interdisciplinary Study of Literature*, 40(1): 127.)
>
> A wide variety of species were put on trial and included domesticated animals (e.g., pigs, bulls, horses and cows) and pests (e.g. rats, birds, insects). E.P. Evans explained that according to the medieval mind, the only way to deal with the ravages of miniature noxious and misbehaving creatures was to resort to divine aid, by capturing and bringing some of them to justice via a trial conducted by the human emissaries of God. In 1457, for example, a pig was found with six piglets around the mutilated body of a 5-year-old child. The pig was duly arrested and put on trial, convicted of maiming and killing the child. Eight witnesses actually turned up and testified against the pig. The pig was detained as a prisoner during the course of the trial, and subsequently sentenced to death by hanging. The court was less convinced that the piglets had participated in the crime of mangling the deceased, and acquitted the piglets – although the owner was forced to pay bail before the piglets were returned.
>
> (See E.P. Evans. 1906 (2009 edn). *The Criminal Prosecution and Capital Punishment of Animals* (Lawbook Exchange, Inc.), and Sadakat Kadri. 2006. *The Trial: Four Thousand Years of Courtroom Drama* (New York: Random House).)

In modern times, most criminal justice systems consider that non-human creatures lack moral agency and so cannot be held culpable for their actions.

46 *Foundations of animal welfare law*

A few voices throughout history sought to draw attention to similarities (rather than the differences) between humans and animals, and consequent responsibilities that reflected a concept of stewardship rather than simple domination. For example, one of Aristotle's pupils, Theophrastus (371–c. 287 BCE http://en.wikipedia.org/wiki/Theophrastus),[14] argued against eating meat on the grounds that it robbed animals of life and was therefore unjust. He also drew attention to animals' ability to reason, sense and feel.[15] Eighteenth-century philosopher Julien Offray de La Mettrie also sought to point out the similarities (rather than the differences) between animals and humans. La Mettrie argued that René Descartes' views regarding animals (which alleged that animals could be viewed simply as machines with reflexes) could be applied to humans. La Mettrie's ideas offended the theologians' ideas that men were unique because they were made in the image of God and had a unique relationship with God. La Mettrie had to flee to escape the wrath of the theologians' response, eventually seeking sanctuary in the Court of Frederick the Great of Prussia.[16] Ancient philosophers, including Seneca, Plutarch and Porphyry, also taught that the concept of universal benevolence incorporated a stewardship regarding the care of animals.[17] The Bible, which is commonly referred to as authority for giving mankind 'dominion'[18] over animals, none the less contains references that advocate treating animals in a compassionate and kind manner,[19] and an Italian Catholic friar called Giovanni Francesco di Bernardone (1181–1226) was pronounced a saint in 1228, and became widely known as Saint Francis of Assisi, the patron saint of animals.[20]

However, these voices were largely exceptions to generally help philosophy and law that focused on the differences between animals and humans, and classified them as property, thereby giving licence to their owners to do as they wished with them. These beliefs, when coupled with the belief that animals did not feel pain, resulted in treatment that, in hindsight, modern Western culture would classify as abuse of animals. However, at the time, it was widely accepted that, as endorsed by early theology, human use and abuse of animals was the natural order of things. It is the 'abuse' component of that formula that has changed with time.

Human uses of the seventeenth-century animal

As has been the case throughout history, animals have been widely used in human society. They were not only used for food (e.g., meat, milk, and eggs), but animal

---

14 Tiziano Dorandi. 1999. Chapter 2 'Chronology', in K. Algra et al. (eds), *The Cambridge History of Hellenistic Philosophy* (Cambridge: Cambridge University Press), pp. 52–3.
15 Taylor, *Animals and Ethics*, p. 35.
16 Brooman and Legge, *Law Relating To Animals*, p. 10.
17 Ibid., p. 7.
18 Genesis: 1:26–28.
19 Deuteronomy 25:4, Proverbs 12:10.
20 Augustine Thompson, O.P. 2012. *Francis of Assisi: A New Biography* (Ithaca, NY: Cornell University Press).

Foundations of animal welfare law 47

products were used in everything from clothing to making candles. Animals formed part of wider society. For example, horses were used in agriculture, industry, transport and the military. Animals were also used in entertainment. For those that had the financial means, horse racing and hunting were common sports. For the lower classes, animals were used for baiting[21] and fighting.

Animals are still different to humans ... aren't they?

The attitudes regarding animals were formed in large part by theologians, philosophers and scientists, who, in the beginning, largely focused on the differences between humans and animals. In contrast, today we have recognised that humans and animals also share a significant number of similarities, and despite still 'using' animals, 'abusing' has become the subject of criminal law which sets out considerable penalties for cruelly treating animals and/or not providing for their needs. How we got to that point, however, continued to be highly influenced by religion, philosophy and science. As cultured, advanced and self-aware as modern man likes to think he is, there are deep-rooted attitudes which indicate that humankind still remains the puppet on the end of the foundational strings established long ago by those same three drivers: religion, philosophy and science. Each of those drivers has contributed to deeply held beliefs regarding the differences versus the similarities between animals and humans, which continue to be the consistent root of conflicting opinions.

Religion: the first 'law' licensing humans to use animals

Animals are different, 'because God says so'

Theology was the cornerstone on which cultural and societal attitudes regarding animals were founded, and as such, religious teachings constituted the first 'law' regarding our relationship with animals.

From the earliest of times, humankind has believed that we are not only superior to animals, but also that animals are fundamentally different from humans. Why? Almost universally, the first answer has been 'Because God says so.'

'Dominion' based on 'differences' between humans and animals was widely interpreted in a way that provided people with a licence to use animals, rather than a responsibility of stewardship regarding them.

For example, the Qur'an puts an animal's status below that of human beings, while encouraging Muslims to treat animals with compassion and to refrain from

---

21 Bullbaiting, for example, involves tying a bull to a stake and setting one or more dogs onto it. The objective of the sport was for the dog to take hold of the most sensitive part on the bull, its nose, and tenaciously drag the bull to the ground until it is dead. One of the characteristic traits of the modern bulldog is it having a condition known as 'lock jaw', and is still recognised as having a tenacious bite. The present-day custom of the running of the bulls ('bull running') also had its beginnings in earlier times. In the sport, the bull was chased through the town until it became exhausted, and it was subsequently set upon by the dogs. Variations include throwing the animal off a bridge, or forcing it to jump into a river.

48   *Foundations of animal welfare law*

abusing them.[22] Similarly, in Buddhist thought, animals are seen as beings that are different in their intellectual ability than humans.[23]

Christian teaching informed the traditional Western view of humans' and animals' place in the world, and clearly established the starting point that man was in a position of 'dominion'.[24] The predominant interpretation of Christian 'dominion' was that man had a God-given licence to do as he pleased with animals and could use them to serve his own interests.

Here's how animals are 'different'

Humans' superiority was taught from the earliest of times, by Judeo-Christian religions that gave power to humans and confirmed that animals were essentially for their use.[25] The Bible, which is the cornerstone handbook of Christian faith, is the authority for Western society's attitude to animals. According to Christianity, the basis for man's dominion was enunciated by God who gave mankind 'dominion over the fish of the sea, and over the birds of the air, and over the cattle, and over all the earth, and over every creeping thing that creeps upon the earth'.[26]

St Thomas Aquinas

Religious doctrine continued to inform social attitudes regarding animals, and central figures such as St Thomas Aquinas (1225–74) used the authority of divine revelation to reinforce Christian views that placed mankind at the top of the natural world's hierarchy.[27] The writings of Aquinas stated that 'men, being made in the image of God, are above other animals'. Different interpretation of religious teachings, potentially influenced by the motivations of those advocating their own definitions,[28] resulted in dominion being defined as a licence to use and abuse animals, rather than apply a duty of stewardship. In view of how religion dominated early Western society, it is unsurprising that people considered that they had a God-given right to use animals any way that they pleased.

---

22 'Seest thou not that it is Allah whose praises are celebrated by all beings in the heavens and on earth, and by the birds with extended wings? Each one knows its prayer and psalm, And Allah is aware of what they do': Qur'an 22:18.

23 BBC. 2009. 'Buddhism and Animals': www.bbc.co.uk/religion/religions/buddhism/buddhist-ethics/animals.shtml.

24 St James Bible, Genesis 1:26–28.

25 Brooman and Legge, *Law Relating To Animals*; St Thomas Aquinas (1225–74).

26 St James Bible, Genesis 1:26.

27 Aquinas discussed in T. Regan and P. Singer (eds). 1989. *Animal Rights and Human Obligations*, 2nd edn (Pearson), pp. 109–10.

28 Paul Waldau refers to these as 'religious views, or at the very least opinions dressed up in language derived from religious traditions': Paul Waldau. 2006. 'Seeing the Terrain We Walk: Features of the Contemporary Landscape of Religion and Animals', in Paul Waldau and Kimberley Patton (eds), *A Communion of Subjects: Animals in Religion, Science and Ethics* (New York: Columbia University Press), pp. 41–61.

Foundations of animal welfare law   49

Challenging early theological doctrines

The Christian Church's self-appointed monopoly on being the singular authority on societal values crumbled as it became clear that established, long-held, dogmas were, in short, 'wrong'.

According to the Church, the earth was the centre of the universe. Astronomers, including Copernicus (1473–1543), Kepler (1571–1630), Galileo (1564–1642), Newton (1643–1727) and Laplace (1749–1827), were just some of those who established that contrary to long-held Church doctrines and God-inspired scriptural interpretations, the earth was not flat; and nor was earth the centre of the universe.

Challenges were also made to early theological views regarding mankind's God-given uniqueness on the basis that he was created in the image of God. Scientific opinion postulated that humans themselves might be accurately described as animals, and key figures such as Charles Darwin classified humans as part of the primate order, and suggested that the human species came not from God but had developed by a process of evolutionary change. Scientists repeatedly discovered that animals and man shared significant similarities in their organs, systems and senses.

When it was accepted that the earth was not the centre of the universe, and that there was serious cause to believe that men were more like other primates rather than being uniquely God-like, it is unsurprising that other Church doctrines were also challenged. This included challenges to the Church's monopoly on being the singular access to God and therefore the authority on God's expectations and definitions. Religious 'splinter groups' enabled prevailing orthodox religious attitudes regarding animals to be challenged and, with time, societal and legal standards regarding animals have shifted. 'Dominion' still allows animals to be 'used' by people, but it is no longer an acceptable part of that definition for animals to be abused.[29]

Religion, in culture and society, is not simply a historical driver

Modern exemptions to expectations on the basis of religion

Science and philosophy, by way of additional disciplines such as ethics, policy and politics, continue to inform animal law. So does religion, not just by its influence

---

29 Paul Waldau writes, 'In neither 1900 nor 1950 would religious believers in North America, Europe, and other parts of the industrialized, "developed" world have been well described as "concerned" about the earth's nonhuman animals. Some believers were compassionate, no doubt, but institutions and religious rhetoric were, on the whole, insensitive to nonhuman animals' interests. Indeed, the vast majority of religious believers were not only unconcerned but also ignorant and blind insofar as nonhuman animals were concerned': Waldau. 2003. 'Religion and Animals: A Changing Scene', in D.J. Salem and A.N. Rowan (eds), *The State of the Animals II* (Washington, DC: Humane Society of America), p. 87: http://animalstudiesrepository.org/cgi/viewcontent.cgi?article=1004&context=sota_2003.

50   *Foundations of animal welfare law*

on societal norms, but also its contribution to legal exemptions based on religion, culture and/or tradition. Some consider that such exemptions should not constitute a valid reason to excuse actions that are harmful to animals. Despite these subjective opinions, the fact is that the law does just that. Bullfighting, described by some as 'legalised cruelty' for human entertainment, is one clear example. But entertainment activities are not the only area where religious and cultural values conflict with modern concepts of treating animals 'humanely'.

Where old religion conflicts with modern science: religious slaughter

The continuing exemptions

Religion was the first 'law' regarding animals, and contemporary animal law continues to reflect religious foundations in its standards and religious, cultural and traditional-use exemptions. There is substantial legislation providing exemptions to legislative norms on the basis of religious freedom, or culture. However, some practices that seem controversial today had their beginnings many centuries ago. For example, significant controversy has developed where old practices conflict with knowledge, science and requirements to ensure that animals are humanely slaughtered. Slaughter without stunning is a practice that is efficient at bleeding out an animal. Meat declared fit for the consumption by Muslims is labelled 'halal' and dictates what is lawful for Muslims to eat. Halal food laws are based on interpretation of the Qur'an, the Muslim scripture.

The prescribed method of slaughter requires a knife cut that severs the front of the throat, the carotid artery, wind pipe and jugular veins but leaves the spinal cord intact. The animal is positioned in order to have its blood completely drained and is left to exsanguinate.

This ritual method of slaughter as practiced by followers of both Islam and Judaism has been described as inhumane by some animal welfare organisations. For example, in 2003, the Farm Animal Welfare Council (FAWC), an independent advisory group, concluded that the way halal and kosher meat is produced causes severe suffering to animals. On the other hand, halal and kosher butchers deny that their method of killing animals is cruel and claim that a quick loss of blood pressure causes the brain to be instantaneously starved of blood, leading to loss of consciousness and allegedly there is no time to start feeling any pain.

After widespread media coverage on the controversy, initiatives to inform the public via labelling were instigated. In 2008, the UK food and farming minister stated that halal and kosher meat should be labelled when it is put on sale, so that members of the public could decide whether or not they want to buy halal-slaughtered meat.

The legal requirement in some countries – that animal slaughter must be humane, and not cause the animal unreasonable or unnecessary pain, suffering, or distress – has led to the central issue of whether or not halal slaughter complies with this legal requirement. Questions have also been specifically raised about

Foundations of animal welfare law 51

whether or not pre-slaughter reversible stunning is a way of ensuring that the interests of all parties are satisfied.[30]

Legal opinions assessing the 'lawfulness' of the practice take into account the existing law,[31] supporting legal documents,[32] and scientific research into humane commercial slaughter methods.

In New Zealand, animal welfare legislation provides for standards to be set, that apply to all persons responsible for the welfare of animals being killed in commercial operations. Section 12 of the Animal Welfare Act 1993 states: 'a person commits an offence who, being the owner of, or a person in charge of, an animal, kills the animal in such a manner that the animal suffers unreasonable or unnecessary pain or distress'.

The issue demonstrates that religion is not a thing of the past, but continues to colour the lens of each person's ideal world-view with 'traditional', 'cultural' and 'religious' values. See also Case Study 2 below.

Case Study 2: Halal slaughter: Tension between religious roots and contemporary animal welfare

Religion has been a keystone of the human–animal relationship not just in terms of people's responsibilities for animals in their care, but also for the processing of animals for human food. In many traditionally Western countries, animal welfare and food safety law reaches into every stage of the farm-to-fork process which naturally includes supervision of slaughter practices.

(continued)

---

30 Insensibility of the animal during the entire slaughter process is a requirement of New Zealand law. During halal slaughter, the animal dies due to anoxia following the severance of major blood vessels supplying the brain. New Zealand is of the view that animals killed by this method of slaughter may experience pain or distress for several seconds or minutes prior to death, unless they have been rendered insensible to pain at the time of slaughter. For this reason, under New Zealand law, all stock and farmed game must be rendered insensible to pain by an approved method prior to commercial slaughter. Pre-slaughter mechanical or electrical stunning, or slaughter by an alternative method which renders the animal instantaneously insensible to pain – each represent ways in which this legal requirement may be met. New Zealand law also requires animals to be slaughtered as soon as possible after stunning, to minimise the time between stunning and the death of the animal, so that the risk of the animal regaining sensibility is minimised.

31 In New Zealand, for example, animal welfare legislation provides for standards to be set, that apply to all persons responsible for the welfare of animals being killed in commercial operations. Section 12 of the Animal Welfare Act 1993 states: 'a person commits an offence who, being the owner of, or a person in charge of, an animal, – (c) Kills the animal in such a manner that the animal suffers unreasonable or unnecessary pain or distress.'

32 For example, New Zealand refers to the Animal Welfare (Commercial Slaughter) Code of Welfare 2010: www.biosecurity.govt.New Zealand/animal-welfare/codes/commercial-slaughter.

52 *Foundations of animal welfare law*

(continued)

In jurisdictions with established animal welfare law, slaughter practices generically, in the first instance, must comply with established animal welfare standards which reflect the overall purpose of animal welfare legislation to minimise unnecessary pain or distress to the animal. This requirement is considerate of context of wider criteria including, for example, available technologies, as well as relevant economic criteria and consumer expectations.

As a starting point, religious slaughter practices are usually required to comply with the established animal welfare and food safety law. There is a natural tension that develops when traditional slaughter practices are seen as inconsistent with contemporary animal welfare standards and/or legal requirements. Where those tensions have come into direct conflict, litigation has sometimes been either contemplated, or initiated. One of the key areas where the tension between traditional religious requirements and contemporary animal welfare legislative requirements has occurred is in relation to the pre-stunning of animals prior to their slaughter and subsequent consumption as human food.

In terms of the slaughter process, pre-stunning has been implemented in order to alleviate avoidable pain or distress in the time interval between the neck incision and the animal's loss of consciousness. The practice of pre-stunning an animal has arisen as a point of contention. According to Jewish law and to Muslim law, 'slaughter is carried out with a single cut to the throat'. Some religious groups accept reversible pre-stunning prior to the cut. However, certain more orthodox groups take the view that a stunned animal is to be considered injured and unhealthy, and therefore, from their religious perspective, the meat derived from the animal is not fit for human consumption. Those more orthodox groups have subsequently contested the need for pre-stunning, arguing that making pre-stunning mandatory is in conflict with religious freedoms.

The legal situation in respect of pre-stunning differs from country to country and court cases have demonstrated the complicated issues and tensions of humane animal slaughter versus civil liberties. For example, in the United States, the Humane Slaughter Act (7 U.S.C. section 1901) exempts ritual slaughter, and this exemption has been upheld as constitutional. In France, ritual slaughter is permitted, with some restrictions. In *Jewish Liturgical Association Cha'are Shalom Ve Tsedek v. France, 27 June 2000 (App. No. 27417/95)*, the Grand Chamber of Rights interpreted Article 9 of the European Convention on Human Rights in a manner that provided for ritual slaughter falling under Article 9's guarantee of the right to manifest religious observance.

In contrast, in February 2014, Denmark's minister for food, agriculture and fisheries signed a regulation which banned ritual slaughter of animals without prior stunning. The Muslim and Jewish communities in Denmark strongly opposed the decree, arguing that it constituted an infringement upon religious freedom. In May 2010, the New Zealand government, in the

> interest of animal welfare, required that all animals slaughtered for commercial purposes be stunned before being killed. Members of New Zealand's small Jewish community went to the High Court alleging that the ban infringed on their constitutional rights. The government withdrew its position prior to the matter being heard in court. New Zealand currently requires halal meat be stunned before slaughter, while kosher meat – which is killed only for a small domestic market – does not have the same restriction.

Philosophy and morals: how should animals be treated?

The realisation that the Church didn't have a monopoly on communication with God was logically one of the societal shifts that prompted the 'independent thought' that marked the Renaissance. Independent thought has evolved into the various recognised disciplines, of which ethics and philosophy are two[33] natural starting points for consideration of the wider issues associated with animal welfare and the law.

Law is demonstrably shaped by, and gives exemptions to, societal standards in consideration of the combined trilogy of religion, tradition and culture, and must similarly take account of ethical and philosophical considerations of human responsibilities concerning animals.

Ethics and philosophy, translated into 'policy', provide background and explanation for many of the legal doctrines, rules, 'policies' and material, that contribute to further discussion about what it means to critically assess and apply knowledge about the history of animal welfare to contemporary issues. Undoubtedly the interplay between the two areas of philosophy/ethics and the law is compelling for many reasons, one of which is the clash of personal world-views about what people 'should' and 'should not' do.

Policy: today's philosopher and ethicist

Defining philosophy

Philosophy has been defined as 'a study of problems', including those connected with questions about 'existence, knowledge, morality, reason and human purpose'.[34] Philosophy comes from the Greek for 'love of wisdom', so by root definition could imply that concepts of knowledge and understanding (i.e., 'wisdom') are highly valued. Philosophy demonstrates an approach to asking questions (with sub-disciplines of epistemology, metaphysics, ethics, and logic) that challenges, if necessary, established concepts.

---

33 While acknowledging that every discipline is likely to require familiarity with a specific terms and methods, the reader might consider psychology and policy (e.g., analysts, advisers) as additional examples of disciplines that involve substantial independent thought and 'thinking about thinking'.

34 J. Teichmann, and K.C. Evans. 1999. *Philosophy: A Beginner's Guide* (Oxford: Wiley-Blackwell), p. 1.

54   *Foundations of animal welfare law*

Defining ethics

Again, purists may be uncomfortable with any suggestion that the scope of ethics might be condensed into a simple definition; none the less, ethics has been described as 'a set of principles of *right* conduct' and 'a theory or a system of *moral* values'.[35] Even to the layperson, the words 'right' and 'moral' immediately denote a strongly subjective element to ethics, given that moral judgements of what is right or wrong, or corresponding terms of good or bad vary enormously between individuals, cultures and societies.

Despite individual variation on what is ethical or not, individual 'values' (of what is important and right) and community notions of 'morality' (denoting what society broadly accepts as appropriate/acceptable rules of conduct) can be recorded in a set of ethical principles that outline what is considered important and right, and appropriate for the time and circumstances. Ethics can be viewed as a set or system of moral values, which frequently deal with the expectations that form the relationship between an individual and a larger group. For example, each profession (e.g., lawyers, veterinarians, doctors and others) has a set of ethical standards to which members are expected to adhere while acting in their professional capacity.

In terms of animal welfare and law, policy advisers may be viewed as special advisers to the government,[36] who bring together elements of philosophy and ethics. Governments and other organisations with domestic policy interests employ advisers to help them shape and advocate policies, and consequently policy advisers have a significant potential influence on ministers' policy decisions, addressing a range of domestic and/or foreign issues. Policy advisers are frequently an unseen level of government and governance, fulfilling a range of important functions which include guiding ministers and other government leaders by questioning established but potentially outdated standards.

Philosophy in animal welfare and law

Philosophical questions about animals

In the eighteenth century, moral philosophy, accompanied by natural and political science, raised questions regarding people's responsibilities regarding animals. The change in thinking was initially restricted predominantly to the well-educated, but eventually in the UK, a small number of influential people argued that Parliament needed to intervene in order to prevent excessive cruelty to animals. Man's relationship with animals, and particularly treatment of animals, was recognised by

---

35 www.thefreedictionary.com/ethics.

36 It is noted that policy advisers assist in providing policies and overall direction to a number of organisations including, for example, companies or private/public-sector organisations. However, for the purposes of examining animal welfare and law, a focus is given to the role of policy advisers in government.

Foundations of animal welfare law 55

a number of philosophers as having a negative influence on human character. A number of key philosophers were instrumental in developing animal welfare law, despite the fact that their focus was on protecting animals primarily because it shaped human beings' relationship with each another.

Identifying key philosophers who shaped today's animal law

A number of key philosophers and accompanying moral theories have shaped the development of animal law.[37] This book refers to a select few that are consistently referred to in discussions regarding animal welfare and the law.

René Descartes (1596–1650)

French philosopher René Descartes was also an acclaimed mathematician and writer, whose theories regarding animals had profound negative consequences for animals.

Descartes proposed a mechanistic theory of the universe, attempting to demonstrate that all things in the world could be mapped out without allusion to subjective experience.[38] Descartes extended this theory to animals. Central to Descartes' views was his opinion that the human mind was separate to the rest of the physical universe, and that it linked human beings to the mind of God. In contrast, the non-humans were automata and did not possess souls, minds, or the ability to reason. As such, while non-humans could see, hear, and touch; they could not suffer or feel pain.[39, 40] Descartes' views arguably led to animals being denied even the most minimal of humane considerations in commercial agriculture, or vivisection, as described by Nicolas Fontaine:[41]

> They administered beating to dogs with perfect indifference, and made fun of those who pitied the creatures as if they had felt pain. They said that the animals were clocks; that the cries they emitted when struck, were only the noise of a little spring which had been touched, but that the whole body was without feelings. They nailed poor animals up on boards by their four paws to vivisect them and see the circulation of the blood which was a great subject of conversation.[42]

---

37 Scott Wilson. 'Animals and Ethics', *Internet Encyclopedia of Philosophy*: www.iep.utm.edu/anim-eth/.

38 René Descartes. 1641. *Meditations on First Philosophy*, cited in John Cottingham, 'Descartes, René', in Ted Honderich (ed.), *The Oxford Companion to Philosophy* (Oxford: Oxford University Press, 1995), pp. 188–92.

39 René Descartes. 1637. 'Discourse V', in J. Veitch (trans.), *René Descartes: A Discourse on Method*, Everyman edn (London: Dent, 1912), Part V, pp. 43–6.

40 Mary Midgley. 1999. 'Descartes' Prisoners', *New Statesman*, 24 May.

41 N. Fontaine. 1738. *Memoires pour server a l'histoire de Port-Royal*, quoted in L.C. Rosenfield, *Beast-Machine to Man-Machine* (New York: Octagon Books, 1968).

42 Descartes, 'Discourse V', in Veitch (trans.), *René Descartes*.

56   Foundations of animal welfare law

Descartes' views received papal support from Pope Pius XII, who said that the cries of the animals should not arouse 'unreasonable compassion'.[43]

John Locke (1632–1704)

British philosopher John Locke argued in 1693 that animals have feelings and that unnecessary cruelty toward them was morally wrong. However, the focus was again on the affects that cruelty would have on people, rather than any depth of consideration to the animal. Locke indicated that in his opinion, 'tormenting and killing of beasts' by people, particularly children, would 'harden [people's] minds even towards men'.[44]

Immanuel Kant (1724–1804)

German philosopher Immanuel Kant argued that humans have duties only toward other humans and not to non-humans, but repeated the views expressed by Locke that cruelty to animals was morally wrong solely on the grounds that it was bad for humans. He stated 'Animals are there merely as a means to an end. That end is man.'[45] However, he noted that 'cruelty to animals is contrary to man's duty to himself, because it deadens in him the feeling of sympathy for their sufferings, and thus a natural tendency that is very useful to morality in relation to other humans is weakened',[46] and that 'he who is cruel to animals becomes hard also in his dealing with men'.[47] Kant continued earlier thinking that recognised a link between violence to animals and the characteristics of people who inflict that suffering to them.

Kant went further by pointing out various professions that would be desensitised to violence as a consequence of their work: 'Our duties towards animals, then, are indirect duties towards mankind.'[48] While Kant's presumptions about butchers, doctors and vivisectionists might be out of step with current thinking, his ideas do reflect the findings of contemporary research.[49] They conclude that acts that inflict suffering to one individual (irrespective of the species) may desensitise the perpetrator of the violence to the suffering of other living beings.

---

43 Brooman and Legge, *Law Relating to Animals*, p. 10.
44 John Locke. 1693. 'Some Thoughts Concerning Education', in *The Works of John Locke in Ten Volumes*, 10th edn, Vol. 9 (London, 1801), pp. 112–15.
45 Immanuel Kant. 1775–80 (1963 edn). *Lecture on Ethics*, L. Infield (trans.) (New York: Harper Torchbooks), p. 239.
46 Immanuel Kant. 1797. 'The Metaphysical Principles of the Doctrine of Virtue', paras 16 and 17, cited in Regan and Singer, *Animal Rights and Human Obligations*.
47 Kant, *Lectures on Ethics*, p. 240.
48 Ibid., pp. 240–41.
49 Historically, there has been significant amount of research done on the potential relevance of animal abuse to violent crimes against people and property. This in turn has prompted interest from stakeholders including local government, law enforcement, social workers, legislators and the public.

Foundations of animal welfare law 57

Jeremy Bentham (1748–1832)

In contrast to the attitudes that developed in France and further afield as a result of the views and influence of René Descartes, English law developed in an alternative direction.

English philosopher Jeremy Bentham described animals as 'sensitive beings' who, like humans, 'may be the objects of benevolence',[50] and suggested that if ethical behaviour was to direct men's actions towards producing 'the greatest possible quantity of happiness', then it was logical that both humans and animals were represented in consideration of 'those whose interests is in view'.[51]

He wrote, 'The question is not, can they reason? Nor, can they talk? But, can they suffer?' This quotation remains as one of the most widely cited quotations by those addressing any one of a number of subjects that consider the relationship between humans and animals, and human responsibilities regarding animals.[52]

Bentham continues to be one of the most quoted figures pertaining to the development of animal law. His view – that people have a responsibility to ensure animals do not experience unnecessary and/or unreasonable suffering – continues to be the foundational principle of virtually every society that embody laws regarding animal protection.

After Bentham, the issue of cruelty to animals was no longer seen from a solely anthropocentric point of view, but also from a theriocentric one which considered the protection of animals for their own sake.[53]

John Rawls (1921–2002)

American philosopher John Rawls is a recognised figure in moral and political philosophy. His contractualist theories of morality construe morality to be the set of rules that rational individuals would choose under certain specified conditions to govern their behaviour in society. In his book, *A Theory of Justice*, he argued against including animals within what he described as the principles of justice. Rawls believed that humans, by way of their justice system, are not required to give strict justice to creatures lacking the capacity for a sense of justice.

---

50 Jeremy Bentham. 1789 (1970 edn). *An Introduction to the Principles of Morals and Legislation*, eds J.H. Burns and H.L.A. Hart (London: Athlone Press), Chapter 5, para 10: www.academia. edu/328046/Jeremy_Benthams_Quantitative_Analysis_of_Happiness_and_Its_Asymmetries.

51 Ibid., Chapter 17, para 1 and para 2.

52 Jeremy Bentham's statement 'the question is not, Can they reason' nor, Can they talk? But, Can they suffer?' raised further questions about the status of animals and became of great importance to the modern anti-vivisectionist cause: A.H. Maehler and U. Trohler. 1987. 'Animal Experimentation from Antiquity to the End of the Eighteenth Century: Attitudes and Arguments', in N. Rupke (ed.), *Vivisection in Historical Perspective* (London: Routledge).

53 Ibid.

58   *Foundations of animal welfare law*

Peter Singer (b. 1046)

Australian philosopher Peter Singer specialises in applied ethics. His book, *Animal Liberation* (1975), is widely considered as a seminal text in animal rights/liberation theory. Relevant to the use of animal law terminology, Singer doesn't argue for animals to have the same rights as humans, but instead argues that their 'interests' (e.g., in avoiding suffering) be fairly considered.[54] Singer is regarded as a utilitarian,[55] who assesses the appropriateness of a decision and/or act by its consequences and as a benchmark where the needs of the many outweigh the needs of the few. This correlates with Bentham's view, for example, which holds that 'the greatest happiness of the greatest number is the foundation of morals and legislation'.[56]

Singer's principle of equality does not limit itself to a particular species and, while not advocating equal or identical treatment of any group, Singer's theories do advocate at least a starting point that gives equal consideration to each group's interests. Speciesism is naturally a barrier to purist application of Singer's theories.

The moral status of animals is a hotly debated topic, and one which is understandably influenced by the subjective opinions of those who debate the issue. Individual opinions have relevance because the collective of individual opinions becomes 'public opinion'. Public opinion, in turn, affects assessments made by legislators and policy makers who take account of public opinion, and accompanying existing philosophical frameworks.

In broad terms, there are two leading contemporary theories which address the moral position of animals.[57] The first is the theory of 'inherent value', which holds that 'the needs of the one are equivalent to the needs of the many'. In contrast, the second theory of 'utilitarianism' broadly advocates that 'the needs of the many outweigh the needs of the one'.[58]

Inherent value

Historically, the animal rights theory is associated with the eighteenth-century German philosopher, Immanuel Kant. In Kant's view, human beings have an intrinsic worth or dignity, and should therefore be treated 'always as an end and never as a means only'.[59] In other words, because humans had individual worth,

---

54 Peter Singer. 1995. *Animal Liberation*, 1995 edn (London: Pimlico), pp. 4–5.

55 There are recognised forms of utilitarianism such as act utilitarianism, preference utilitarianism and rule utilitarianism. The reader may choose to pursue individual studies addressing each of these subcategories of utilitarianism.

56 Jeremy Bentham. 1843. *The Commonplace Book*, in J. Bowring (ed.), *The Works of Jeremy Bentham* (1843), Vol. 10, p. 142.

57 Other philosophers have sought to avoid using a single moral theory in addressing the issues associated with the human–animal relationship, and there are those who have noted the difficulties of a hypothetical amoral approach. None the less, inherent value and utilitarian moral theories continue to be the dominant theories used: Brooman and Legge, *Law Relating To Animals*, pp. 95–6.

58 Ibid., p. 76.

59 I. Kant. 1785. *Fundamental Principles of the Metaphysics of Morals*, Thomas Abbott (trans.) (Englewood Cliffs, NJ: Prentice Hall, 1949).

Foundations of animal welfare law 59

then the human individual and their experience should be given priority. Other rights theorists, including American philosopher Tom Regan, argued that the principle should be extended to animals.[60]

Reflecting the consistent underlying principle of animal law, Regan draws attention to the similarities and differences between humans and animals, and focuses on the similarities in his arguments:

> Animals, it is true, lack many of the abilities humans possess. They can't read, do higher mathematics, build a bookcase, or make baba ghanoush. However neither can many human beings, and yet, society and the law broadly stipulates that such people should not be considered as having a diminished inherent value, or less of a right to be treated with respect, than do others. It is the similarities between those human beings who most clearly, most non-controversially have such value, and not our differences that matter most.

The 'inherent value' rights-based theory put forward by Regan promotes the concept that animals possess innate worth because similarly to humans, animals, according to Regan, deserve consideration and on the basis that they are 'experiencers of life' with inherent value of their own.[61]

Inherent value of animals in contemporary animal welfare law

The inherent value concept gives weight to concepts that hold that the interests of the individual animal warrant due consideration.

On a practical legal aspect, there are arguments that allege the property status of animals undermines the inherent value concept, while the second element of animal law[62] accommodates considerations of the inherent value/experience of an animal and its ability to experience pain and distress.

Arguments that consider that the inherent value concept is undermined by legislation that seeks to protect and prioritise just human interests tend to overlook the fact that humans *and* animals alike face competing and conflicting interests as stakeholders whose interests are to be represented, balanced and prioritised in a decision-based system that is predominantly utilitarian.

---

60 German philosopher Albert Schweitzer is another philosopher who held similar views. He is attributed with coining the phrase 'reverence for life' in consideration of his pursuit of the 'ethic of universality' and his critique of previous attempts to define the concept of morality: A. Schweitzer. 1923. *Civilisation and Ethics* (London: A & C Black Ltd), p. 254.

61 Regan, T. 1989. 'The Case for Animal Rights', in Regan and Singer, *Animal Rights and Human Obligations*.

62 The three elements of animal law are that it (1) deals with an animal, (2) acknowledges the unique nature of animals as animate property that is capable of experiencing pain and distress, and (3) involves the relationship between humans and animals. The expectation that animals should not suffer unnecessary and/or unreasonable pain or distress therefore constitutes the 'interest' of animals that is protected by animal welfare law.

60 *Foundations of animal welfare law*

Utilitarianism

Utilitarianism is reflected in the view that 'the rights of the many outweigh the rights of the one'. It has been alleged that humans prioritise human interests in most circumstances above the interests of animals. However, such statements are accurate in a limited degree given that wider consideration demonstrates that the welfare of humans and animals alike is inseparable. Radford provides clarity and accuracy to notions of exploitation by referring to the true breadth of the human–animal relationship in stating:

> other species have long since been integral to our society, and exploitation is an inevitable consequence of interdependence. It is the nature of the exploitation which is important . . . the interaction of animals with men need not be prejudiced inevitably in our favour; and they, too, may benefit, and often do.

So speciesism exists. Consequently human interests are often prioritised above the interests of animals – but in law, not always. The practical reality is that humans and animals have many interests in common, and frequently benefit from their co-dependent relationship.

Contemporary animal welfare legislation does give consideration to the interests of animals in respect of obligations to minimise their experience of unnecessary and unreasonable pain, distress and suffering. Decisions take into account what is 'appropriate to the species, environment and circumstances of the animal'.[63] The law functions by firstly establishing benchmark criteria regarding standards of human responsibility regarding the care and treatment of animals (i.e., prevent unnecessary and unreasonable pain and/or distress of animals), then qualifies that responsibility in terms of the circumstances of the animal, particularly its use and associated dependency on its human care-giver.

Opinions vary on how much consideration and importance should be given to animals' interests – just as they do over other aspects of society. In a democratic system where the expressed voice can have a significant bearing on societal rules, the law largely reflects society's collective voice. 'The greater public good' – which forms the basis for a utilitarian approach – continues to be a pivotal consideration of governance.

Bentham promoted two particular criteria in respect of making moral decisions: firstly, to ensure that each stakeholder's interests carried the same significance; and secondly, that any act should only be undertaken after giving due consideration to all competing interests and recognising the best possible equilibrium between the satisfaction and frustration of the interests of those affected by the proposed/decided action.[64]

---

63 Section 4 of Animal Welfare Act 1999 (New Zealand).
64 Brooman and Legge, *Law Relating to Animals*, p. 91.

Foundations of animal welfare law 61

Animal interests in utilitarian law

Bentham's views have raised questions among those involved in matters of animal protection. Bentham's first criterion was that each stakeholder's interests should carry the same significance. Some believe that animals' interests are all too often either not considered at all, or not sufficiently enough. This has resulted in allegations that animals and their interests are 'voiceless'.

As always, the law is one of the key governors that must appropriately balance and prioritise the competing interests, and the question of whether or not animals are represented in the eyes of the law is clear – at least in jurisdictions where animal protection legislation has been enacted. In these jurisdictions, animals are lawfully stakeholders, and the interest of animals that the law recognises is their protection from suffering unreasonable and/or unnecessary pain and/or distress. On a utilitarian basis, animals' specific legally recognised interest is considered in questions of law.

Utilitarianism ultimately depends on a cost–benefit analysis. The crucial challenge for this theory is what are the appropriate factors to consider and what criteria are to be used to measure them. The answer in respect of animal and human interests alike, depends on the issue, the law, and all the circumstances.

Again, opinions will vary but there is a useful method which will assist readers to assess them. This tool will enable the reader to determine which stakeholders are represented in an argument, and then gauge if the interests of *all* stakeholders are accurately and fairly considered. Material that overly represents one stakeholder, whether that be government, non-government, producer, retailer, consumer, the animal, or other stakeholders (e.g., the environment in considerations of 'bio-prejudice'[65]), may reflect the same bias and oversight of interrelationships reflected in myopic arguments which infer that all human exploitation of animals results in negative consequences for the animals.[66]

Animal welfare legislation makes animal interests a mandatory consideration.

In the context of animal law, both utilitarian and inherent value theories agree on the basic tenet that animals and humans possess common qualities which warrant protection. Differences occur about where to draw the line in considering the circumstances where those individual protections should be forfeited. Inherent value advocates that each individual has an in-built quality which should not be surrendered, except in the most extreme circumstances. In contrast, utilitarianism demands equal consideration, but the benchmark for overriding an individual's personal right occurs when the needs or desires of the many outweigh the needs or desires of the few/individual. Public opinion has shifted from excluding animals

---

65 The term is used here to describe a bias – either for or against – a stakeholder based on its classification as a living organism. In context of animal law, bioprejudice has been used synonymously with 'speciesism', but as the 'bio' (biology) prefix of the word demonstrates, bioprejudice refers to all natural systems and not just animal species. Therefore bioprejudice may, for example, take the environment into account as a relevant stakeholder.

66 Radford, *Animal Welfare Law in Britain*, p. 10.

62 *Foundations of animal welfare law*

in that consideration, to a point where contemporary animal welfare law sets out that the suffering of animals is a mandatory consideration in all decisions involving legal standards pertaining to their welfare.[67]

Enter science: 'And will you be wanting facts with that?'

When it comes to animal law, readers may find that the word 'science' is defined in many different ways. Opinions about what constitutes science, or scientific methodology, vary substantially. People's perceptions about what constitutes science can vary enormously, depending upon their familiarity with particular sub-disciplines (e.g., biology, physics, ecology), and variation in how authoritative the discipline itself can be. For some people, it is a contributing argument, while for others, it is the ultimate amoral voice of authority that either endorses or discredits a particular concept.

Science is one of the key disciplines that continues to inform the development of the human–animal relationship, and the consequent standards applied by the law in respect of people's legal obligations concerning animals. The legal definition of 'animal welfare' demonstrates this by stating that legal standards of animal welfare (i.e., the obligation to minimise unnecessary and/or unreasonable pain or distress of animals) represent a benchmark pointing to what constitutes 'good practice and scientific knowledge'.[68]

No examination of the development of the law as it relates to animals would be complete without considering the impact of one key figure: Charles Darwin (1809–82). Darwin was not the first scientist to consider the theory of natural selection[69] and the similarities between humans and other primates. However, he remains the scientist whose theories radically changed and established the role of science in debates and laws pertaining to concepts of animal protection.

Darwin brought the discipline of science to a predominantly theological and philosophical debate. Historically, mankind had focused on the differences between humans and animals, but Darwin's crucial contribution was that his findings attached scientific credibility to arguments that sought to shift the focus from the differences between humans and animals to the similarities. Darwin's findings scientifically demonstrated that animals shared some remarkable similarities with humans not just in form, but also in respect of characteristics including pain, suffering and sentient qualities:[70] 'Darwin provided strong arguments which

---

67 See the legal definition of animal welfare as described in Chapter 1.

68 Section 10 of the Animal Welfare Act 1999 (New Zealand), for example, creates an offence for failing to ensure that the physical, health and behavioural needs of animals are 'met in a manner that is in accordance with both good practice and scientific knowledge'.

69 Linnaeus, Erasmus, Darwin and Lamarck are other scientists who had suggested a similar idea in the eighteenth century. Charles Darwin himself was prompted to make his own theories public earlier than he had anticipated, after he discovered that another scientist, Alfred Russell Wallace, had independently come to the same conclusion and was due to publish.

70 C. Darwin. 1871 (1981 edn). *The Descent of Man* (Surrey: Princeton University Press), pp. 34–5.

Foundations of animal welfare law   63

put humans alongside animals in terms of many characteristics and advocated a moral approach to our decision making regarding animals based on scientific evidence.'[71] He added scientific reasoning to philosophical debates and intuitions that noted the similarities between humans and animals not just in terms of physical characteristics but also in terms of mental abilities including memory, attention, curiosity, imitation and reason.[72]

Moreover, Darwin's theory of evolution provided empirical evidence that animals and humans shared common origins,[73] thereby undermining the traditional orthodoxy advocating that humans were different because men were made in the image of God, and that animals existed solely for the benefit and exploitation of mankind. These theological theories were incompatible with the science of Darwin's theories which demonstrated that humans, rather than being uniquely different to 'animals', were in fact similar to animals on the basis that humans had essentially evolved from animals. Darwin unequivocally stated that 'man bears in his bodily structure clear traces of his descent from some lower form',[74] and referred to facts which all pointed 'to the conclusion that man is the co-descendant with other animals of a common progenitor'.[75] 'Man in his arrogance thinks himself a great work worthy of the imposition of deity', stated Darwin in 1838, 'more humble and I think truer to consider him created from animals.'[76]

Darwin's theories interpreted to support each of the polarised opinions

Despite this clarity, there is an apparent dichotomy in how Darwin's theories have been interpreted.

The first interpretation is based on Darwin's theory of 'survival of the fittest', and the 'differences' between humans and animals. It supports the idea that man is the 'fittest' and therefore at the top of the evolutionary pyramid. As the ultimate 'predator', this theoretically gives humans a natural licence to use and exploit other species as they wish.

The alternative interpretation places more weight on Darwin's theory of evolution, which focuses on the similarities between humans and animals, and findings that 'animals differ from humans in degree but not in kind'. Advocates of this interpretation promote the idea that the consideration of 'like should be treated alike' supersedes attention to the differences that allegedly support questionable human uses of animals.

---

71 Brooman and Legge, *Law Relating to Animals*, p. 16.
72 Darwin, *The Descent of Man*, pp. 34–5.
73 James Rachels. 1990. *Created From Animals: The Moral Implications of Darwinism* (Oxford University Press: www.jamesrachels.org/CFA.htm), cited in Brooman and Legge, *Law Relating to Animals*, p. 16.
74 Darwin, *The Descent of Man*, p. 65.
75 Ibid., p. 607.
76 Rachels, *Created from Animals*, cited in Brooman and Legge, *Law Relating to Animals*, p. 16.

64   Foundations of animal welfare law

Darwin's theory of evolution gave scientific credibility that contributed to the shift in humans' attitudes regarding animals. J. Howard Moore stated 'whatever the inhabitants of this world were before the publication of *The Origin of the Species*, they never could be anything since but a family'.[77]

Is old anthropomorphism the new empathy?

The similarities between animals and humans have long constituted one of the primary reasons why science continues to use animals for selected purposes (e.g., research and experimentation). That same similarity has been interpreted by animal interest groups as providing sufficient cause to cease those same uses on the moral grounds that they experience life in a way similar to humans.

However, characteristics which were once considered the exclusive domain of humans have now been formally identified in animals. For example, historically, when qualities of language, emotions and sentience were used as descriptors in association with animals, the labels attracted criticism on the basis that they were simply exercises in anthropomorphism. However, research science has identified that animals do indeed possess each of these qualities.

The law ... and science

Law distinguishes humans from all other species and acknowledges that no singular argument is likely to be solely determinant in matters involving animal welfare and law. However as a prerequisite to permissibility, all actions and initiatives involving an animal and its welfare must comply with the applicable law.

Science continues to be one of the strongest contributing voices for providing justification of development and decisions in respect of animals, law and related policy. Contemporary animal welfare legislation specifically states that legal standards of animal welfare will be informed by what constitutes good practice and sound 'scientific knowledge'.[78]

Science is also charged with the responsibility of applying a disciplined scientific process and empirical evidence to balance enormously varied individual moral judgements which are frequently presented on the basis of 'common sense'. Radford points out that the feelings of 'right minded men can be highly subjective, and reliance on common-sense at the expense of reason provides too great an opportunity for the prejudiced, the bigoted, and the ill-informed to hold sway'.[79] In short, science adds 'reason' to shifting conceptions about what constitutes 'common sense', according to the 'right minded' people.

---

77 J. Howard Moore. 1906. The Universal Kinship (Chicago, IL: Charles H. Kerr & Co.): www. angusrobertson.com.au/books/the-universal-kinship-moore-j-howard-1862/p/978131 3784580?gclid=CJeinJm08sQCFVBvvAodvm0Ajg.

78 Section 10 of the Animal Welfare Act 1999 (New Zealand).

79 Radford, *Animal Welfare Law in Britain*, p. 118.

Foundations of animal welfare law   65

While science informs the law, there are clear distinctions between their respective roles. Science identifies, and may rank, the elements that are important to an animal's welfare. However, translating the science into law that determines levels of protection is not a simple or straightforward exercise. Consequently, while science is very persuasive to legal determinations, it is not the only factor that is taken into consideration. It is the law's role to consider the animal's interests in a wider context that takes into account ethical, economic, environmental and societal issues. This is illustrated, for example, in the English High Court case of *RSPCA v DEFRA*[80] The legal issue here concerned the legality of using 'ventilation shut down'[81] to euthanase a large number of potentially infected birds, given the risks to the public associated with an outbreak of avian influenza (bird flu). The RSPCA maintained that there were more humane alternative methods available to kill the birds. The Court's decision included consideration of national law and international animal welfare obligations,[82] the advice of independent agencies' expert evidence (agencies that had the responsibility 'to inform, through its *scientific* panels, the European Commission and others on matters requiring *scientific* risk assessment'[83]), and issues of proportionality and the input of 'scientific bodies'.[84]

Ultimately, the Court rejected the RSPCA's argument and found that the then secretary of state had acted *intra vires*. Furthermore, the Court gave consideration to concepts of what was necessary and/or reasonable given the circumstances, in respect of the animals by referring specifically to balancing of the wider issues with the obligation to spare animals 'any *avoidable* excitement, pain or suffering in the cause of disease control'.[85]

This case is particularly valuable in demonstrating that although scientific opinion is a key contributor to the development of animal welfare law, science cannot in and of itself be the sole consideration that the law takes into account.

Does the law expect too much of science?[86]

Science can provide robust empirical evidence that fosters informed decision making. However, not all would agree that science actually delivers on this aspirational responsibility, or that it is appropriate to expect science to do so.

How credible is law's source of reliable evidence?

---

80 *RSPCA v DEFRA* [2008] EWHC 2321: www.ala.org.uk/sites/default/files/2008EWHC2321.pdf.
81 This is a method of killing birds by cutting off the ventilation in buildings in which birds are housed, so as to kill them by hypothermia or organ failure: Para 4 of the *RSPCA v DEFRA* judgment.
82 Including reference to European Union requirements, and EU Directives paras 9–23 of the *RSPCA v DEFRA* judgment.
83 Ibid., para 27, emphasis added.
84 Ibid., para 29.
85 Ibid., para 71, emphasis added.
86 Peter Sandøe, Stine B. Christiansen and Björn Forkman. 2006. 'Animal Welfare: What is the Role of Science?', in J. Turner and J. D'Silva (eds), *Animals, Ethics and Trade* (London: Earthscan), p. 47.

66 *Foundations of animal welfare law*

The reality is that science, and scientists, don't always speak with one voice. Nor is it realistic to assume that science is always objective, or able to consistently provide a definitive answer to relevant animal welfare questions. With this in mind, it is often necessary for legislators to develop law on the basis of incomplete or even conflicting evidence.[87]

Authors such as Peter Sandøe[88] have commented on the role of science, pointing out its limitations. Sandøe says that while 'science cannot stand alone when it comes to understanding animal welfare',[89] this does not mean that science can be ignored. According to Sandøe, 'common sense and science depend on each other to reach sound conclusions about animal welfare'.[90]

Implementing 'the precautionary principle'

Historical development in respect of animal welfare issues in jurisdictions with contemporary animal welfare law demonstrate that the cut-off point between acceptable and unacceptable has shifted, by a process of incremental change, in the direction that gives stronger emphasis to animal welfare.

This shift is recorded in laws that identify the baseline standards of human responsibility regarding animals. Scientists have commonly been asked to assist the law in 'drawing the line' by identifying specific cut-off points of what is acceptable, and what is not, by way of 'good practice and scientific knowledge'.[91] For example, science and scientists have contributed strongly to panels and published works dealing with a variety of issues, including the keeping of laying hens and the castration of piglets. Still, there continues to be a considerable degree of confusion about where to 'draw the line'. The discipline has been used as a tool of persuasion by animal interest groups and politicians alike. This has raised questions that perhaps too much is expected of science.[92] One result is that the 2009 Treaty of Lisbon suggested that implementation of a precautionary principle in favour of animals should be the appropriate starting point.

Contemporary animal welfare law puts significant emphasis on preventing an animal from feeling unnecessary pain and suffering. The argument of 'if in doubt, then don't' essentially captures the concept broadly known as the 'precautionary principle'.

However, when science is incapable of proving that an animal experiences pain or suffering, then there have been circumstances where decision makers have

---

87 In New Zealand, for example, it was the scientific community that largely influenced the debate on the definition of 'animal' and its impact on research, testing and teaching. During the development of the Animal Welfare Act 1999, some research being conducted was on the foetus rather than the dam and medical researchers were anxious that such research came within the jurisdiction of animal ethics committees: Personal email to author from N. Wells, 14 February 2007.

88 Sandøe et al., 'Animal Welfare', p. 42.

89 Ibid., p. 48.

90 Ibid.

91 Section 4 of the Animal Welfare Act 1999 (New Zealand).

92 Sandøe et al., 'Animal Welfare', p. 50.

Foundations of animal welfare law 67

abandoned the common sense referred to by Sandøe.[93] They placed too much reliance on science demonstrated by their reliance on it, as the sole authority to provide the cut-off points.[94]

The different approaches of New Zealand and the UK to the issue of protection from pain and suffering as applied to lobsters provides a useful example. New Zealand decided that certain invertebrates (crabs, lobsters and crayfish[95]) should come within the scope of the Animal Welfare Act, as they are capable of suffering even though they have a comparatively simpler nervous system than human beings. In contrast, and contrary to specific recommendations to consider New Zealand's position, the UK initially chose not to include invertebrates in the list of animals provided with legislative protections, on the grounds of 'insufficient scientific evidence' that these creatures felt pain. To the detriment of the lobster, and other animals where common sense does not prevail in the absence of science, legislators have applied an approach that considers animals being unable to suffer or feel pain till such time as credible science advances sufficiently to prove otherwise, rather than applying the precautionary approach.

Navigating the conflicts between morals, science and law

What is it about animals that needs protecting?

There are people who view and treat animals simply as property to be used for human interests. Others recognise an interdependence between human welfare and animal welfare, and some go so far as to say that animals have an inherent value which should be protected. In short, 'what needs to be protected' varies. Animal welfare law says that what needs to be protected in respect of the animals is safeguarding them from unnecessary or unreasonable pain or distress.

The law is amoral

There is a difference between immoral and amoral. An immoral act has been defined as an act or belief that conflicts with generally or traditionally held moral principles. By contrast, an amoral act is defined as something that is neither moral nor immoral. Both science and the law, for example, are considered to be examples of disciplines which are amoral, in that they lie outside the sphere to which moral judgements apply in that their judgements focus on truth rather than moral assessments.

Distinguishing moral 'rights' from legal rights/obligations

In examining the terminology used to describe the human–animal relationship, the law has been affected by differing views of morality and public opinion. However, it

93 Ibid., p. 48.
94 Ibid., p. 47.
95 Section 2 of the Animal Welfare Act 1999 (New Zealand).

68 *Foundations of animal welfare law*

is appropriate to reaffirm that while morality and law are mutually influential, there is a difference between what some call natural law, or moral rights; and positivist law which focuses on legal rights as set out by the governing legislative body.

It might be helpful for the reader to consider a *moral* right as a personal view of what 'should' be done or not done. In contrast, a *legal* right may be viewed as the ability to call on the legal authority of a particular jurisdiction to enforce an expectation (e.g., protection, or concept of justice) that is provided for under the established legal system. That is, the law of the land establishes societal structure by way of rules that dictate and enforce what 'must', or must not, be done.

Personal moral concepts of what a person 'should' or 'should not' do are distinct from what a person 'must' or 'must not' do according to obligations set out under the law. This raises the question: 'what is law?' There are two broad and contrasting responses to this question. The first is positivist law, and the second is natural law.

Positivist law

Legal positivism attempts to define law by referencing its meaning and authority to written decisions made by authorised bodies (e.g., government) that are endowed with the legal power to regulate society and human conduct. If a principle, rule, regulation, decision, judgment, or other law is recognised by a duly authorised body or official representative, then, according to legal positivists, it will meet the requirements of being recognised as 'law'.

The essence of law from a positivist perspective is that the only binding rules are those enacted by the authorised governing body. This means that if a rule concerning a person's behaviour is advocated by anyone or anything other than a duly authorised body (or the officially recognised official representative of the authorised body), then the alleged rule will not qualify as law. In the minds of legal positivists, until a rule is legitimised by the authorised body – irrespective of how many people may or may not support the concept within society – the rule is simply not acceptable law. Legal positivism is often contrasted with natural law.

Natural law

Natural law[96] has been defined as a body of law or a specific principle held to be derived from nature and binding upon human society in the absence of, or

---

96 Although arguably related, this term is not to be confused with the term 'natural justice', which originally encompassed two very distinct doctrinal requirements (i.e., the right to a hearing; and the right to be heard by a relevant state authority). In the administrative law sphere, the term 'natural justice' has expanded well beyond those requirements today and there are now many administrative law scholars, and some judges, who now attempt to subsume those doctrinal considerations, along with many others, under a general formula of 'fairness'. In criminal and civil law generally, the term 'natural justice' also has a general usage as denoting the way in which a Court, tribunal, or even the legal system itself, ought generally to comport itself. In that sense, the term is prescriptive, as well as descriptive.

Foundations of animal welfare law   69

in addition to, positive law. According to proponents of natural law, all written laws must be informed by, or consistent with broadly held principles of morality, religion and justice. If all fail to comply with this criterion, then it is deemed as unfair and inappropriate to be called 'law'.

Readers will recognise an inherent problem with the requirement for a law to conform to subjective views of 'morality, religion, and justice'. Reference to a higher natural law has been made, for example, in denouncing societal practices (e.g., homosexuality, or the treatment of animals in research and agricultural practices). Legal positivists generally acknowledge the existence and influence of alternative drivers of human opinion, but commonly contend that such views are personal and aspirational, pointing out that in the absence of a political system applying penalties for expression of anti-social personal opinions, individuals who express them suffer no adverse consequences for doing so. Society, via the law, applies state penalties such as fines and/or imprisonment to those who contravene legislatively established obligations and responsibilities.

Law is not a panacea – but it is an essential component of animal welfare law

As a prerequisite to implementation of any action or proposal, it must first be 'lawful'. Consequently, although law in and of itself is not a panacea, it constitutes an essential element that must be included in any human–human dealings involving animals, and human–animal interactions. This stems from the reality that in legal jurisdictions which have contemporary animal welfare legislation, there are legal obligations applying to people whose acts or omissions affect the welfare of animals. The question of how far that regulation should expand is a continuing debate.

The need for continued state involvement

Government has the primary responsibility for managing each stakeholder's interests in a democratic society. It has long been held that where there is a conflict between the animal's well-being and human interests, that animal's well-being is commonly relegated to second place. In 1796, Lawrence stated 'experience plainly demonstrates the inefficacy of mere morality to prevent aggression', and suggested that 'a law made for the protection of beasts' was consequently necessary.[97] Lawrence was not alone in recommending that it was appropriate for central government to provide protection for animals against ill-treatment. Often this treatment arose because of a belief that animals were simply 'property'. A relatively small number of people were engaged in the debates about the treatment of animals, but they included influential figures whose activities contributed to a growing voice suggesting that central government had a responsibility to reflect shifting public attitudes towards animal welfare.

---

97 John Lawrence. 1796 (1802 edn). A philosophical and practical treatise on horses and on the moral duties of man towards the brute creation (London: Symonds) (www.biodiversitylibrary. org/bibliography/26577), cited in Radford, *Animal Welfare Law in Britain*, p. 82.

70 *Foundations of animal welfare law*

There is an important distinction for the reader to recognise that the law does not dictate that the animal's interests or that its well-being must always be prioritised above other interests. What the law does dictate is that in dealings which involve animals, humans have a legal responsibility to ensure that those interactions do not fall below legally prescribed standards.

Perhaps the simplest argument for continued involvement of the state in matters of animal welfare can be made simply by imagining what would happen if society was unfettered by the state in its dealings regarding animals. In terms of human–animal interactions and the animal's welfare, this can quickly and easily be assessed by comparing the treatment of animals in legal jurisdictions where contemporary animal welfare is established with those where it is not.

In addition to anticipated deterioration of standards of treatment for the animal, ungoverned animal welfare has serious implications for each member of the public as well. Remembering that the third element of animal law deals with the inseparable 'relationship' between animals and humans enables the reader to recognise that there would be serious concerns about a raft of assurances that any member of the public might take for granted. A constant supply of safe food is perhaps the most obvious example, as is the expectation that border control and biosecurity associated with international trade policies would continue to control diseases that impact wider society, the environment and the economy. In short, the risks to each person's livelihood and lifestyle would be significantly increased.

Despite the fact that there is an intimate connection between matters of animal welfare and human welfare, there is naturally a continued tension when issues or attitudes see a competition between animal and human interests. Views with the inability or unwillingness to factor in the inseparable connection between human and animal welfare are often identifiable by persons' or organisations' criticism of, or resistance to, government interference on positions based on 'animals *or* humans' rather than 'animals *and* humans'. There is obviously a need to ensure that minimum standards and uniform rules exist. Initiatives such as voluntary schemes, and arguments suggesting reliance on public opinion and market forces, may contribute to initiatives seeking greater efficiency and effectiveness, but they do not negate the need for government intervention in safeguarding animal welfare. It is noteworthy that as a general rule, even organisations that express dissatisfaction with the decisions of government, do not suggest that there is no role for government whatsoever. The practical reality is that the democratic system puts responsibility for governing the competing and conflicting interests of society on central government.

Is government 'getting it right'?

The belief that government and the law will always be necessary is not meant to imply that recourse to the law will always be the most effective means of ensuring animal and human protection and welfare. Law can be technical and confusing, which accounts for the fact that, similar to other disciplines, there are specialists in

Foundations of animal welfare law   71

each sub-discipline including, for example, 'specialist property lawyers'[98] in dealing with issues of animal law. Additionally, seeking recourse via the Courts can be expensive and time-consuming, with no guarantee or certainty of the eventual outcome. It reflects the commonly held sentiment that the law is frequently a very poor first port of call – but it is a very effective, although often expensive, last resort.

Government, via its legislative, judicial, and executive branches,[99] is administratively the final decision maker in respect of what constitutes lawful standards of animal welfare. Given the differing drivers of people's opinions, it is not unusual that government decisions attract criticism, and one of the more common criticisms is that 'the government should do something'. But governments, like any business, are subject to resource constraints and do not enjoy the luxury of 'bottomless pockets', and government expenditure must be supported by the tax-paying public. Governments' decisions may be fallible because of their reliance on humans with varying skills, motivations and understanding.

These realities support the observation made decades ago that 'legislation alone will not provide the animals with an adequate charter'.[100] This reality has been recognised by animal welfare groups who, in addition to utilising the law to advance their objectives, also use education, campaigning and research to influence the behaviour of consumers. Their aim is to bring pressure on producers and retailers, and ultimately government, to change accepted norms regarding standards of animal treatment. For example, PETA is an example of one animal welfare group that has had substantial influence in respect of the practice of mulesing[101] in Australia. The 'Boycott Australian Wool' campaign began in January 2004 when PETA began to organise against the practice of mulesing on merino sheep by pressuring overseas apparel retailers to cease selling products containing Australian wool. On 8 November 2004, the Australian sheep and wool industry taskforce made a public commitment to retailers to phase out the practice.[102] Compassion

---

98   The reference to specialist 'property' lawyers refers to the fact that animals are classified under the law as 'property'. Animal welfare law distinguishes animals as a sub-category of property in as much as animals are 'animate' property which feel pain, suffering, and distress.

99   Many of the contemporary legislative leaders of animal welfare have developed from the British parliamentary system known as the Westminster system of government, and consequently Parliament (the Legislature) is the highest law-making body. However, the Westminster system and Federal/State systems (e.g., Australia) share common features that separate the powers and responsibilities of the Executive (which conducts the government, deciding on policy and administering legislation), Judiciary (i.e., Judges who have the responsibility to apply the law to cases that come before the Court), and the Legislature.

100 Ruth Harrison. 1964. *Animal Machines* (London: Vincent Stuart), cited in Radford, *Animal Welfare Law in Britain*, p. 178.

101 Mulesing is an animal health practice used by many merino wool growers to prevent fly strike. The practice involves the surgical removal of skin folds from around the breech of young merino sheep.

102 R.K. Bowmar and H.R. Gow. 2009. 'Alternative Strategic Responses to the Animal Welfare Advocacy: The Case of PETA, Merino Wool and the Practice of Mulesing', Department of Agriculture, Food and Resource Economics, Michigan State University, 1 February, 17th International Farm Management Congress, Bloomington/Normal, Illinois, US.

72 *Foundations of animal welfare law*

in World Farming (CIWF) and the 'good egg awards'[103] provide another example of initiatives implemented by a non-government organisation in respect of animal welfare. Retailers including the Body Shop (which markets its products as being 'free from animal testing'), Marks & Spencer, Coles supermarkets, Burger King, and McDonald's, are just a few of the retailers who have implemented changes demonstrating that good animal welfare is good business.

The politics and politicians of animal welfare

The development of any social justice movement has always required its champions, and animal law is no different in that respect.

On 3 April 1800, Scottish Member of Parliament Sir William Putney introduced a Bill to the House of Commons to prohibit bullbaiting. Putney drew attention to the social vices associated with the sport, and allegations that the sport was associated with 'many disorderly and mischievous proceedings',[104] while other Members of Parliament (MPs) in support of the bill made reference to the cruel nature of the sport, saying that 'to tie the poor animal to a stake and set upon him a number of ferocious dogs, was cruel, disgraceful and beastly'.[105] On that occasion, the Bill was defeated 43 votes to 41.

In 1809, Thomas Erskine presented a Bill to the House of Lords to prevent malicious and wanton cruelty to animals. Instead of looking at arguments revolving around issues of public disorder, Erskine focused on securing protection of animals against ill-treatment and suggested that man's biblical 'dominion' be reinterpreted in a way that viewed animals as being the subject of a moral duty. Instead of focusing on the differences between humans and animals (language, reason, or the possession of the soul), Erskine referenced the similarity between humans and animals in providing a basis for constitution of a moral duty regarding them.[106] Despite Erskine's strategy, the Bill was again lost.

Richard Martin was an Irish politician of the early 1820s, who is now recognised as one of the early champions of animal protection law. However, when he first suggested to the British Parliament that law should be enacted to stop blatant cruelty of animals, he, like his forebears, was jeered, ridiculed and laughed at, and his suggestion was met with outright hostility.

These early campaigners would have undoubtedly been very gratified to learn that their efforts prompted such enormous changes that now serve animals and people alike.

---

103 H. Buller. 2010. 'The Marketing and Communication of Animal Welfare: A Review of Existing Tools, Strategies and Practice', *European Animal Welfare Platform*: www.animalwelfareplatform.eu/documents/MarketingReportBuller.pdf.

104 R. Thorne, ed. 1986. *The History of Parliament: The House of Commons 1790–1820*, Volume 33, columns 202 and 209 (2 and 18 April 1800) (London: Boydell and Brewer): www.historyofparliamentonline.org/volume/1790-1820/survey/appendix-ii.

105 Ibid., Volume 35, column 213 (18 April 1800).

106 UK Government. 2006. *Parliamentary Debates*, Volume 14: www.publications.parliament.uk/pa/cm/chron.htm.

Foundations of animal welfare law   73

In 1964, Ruth Harrison's book, *Animal Machines*, resurrected the issue of animal treatment. Her work focused on the impact on animals following the development of factory farming after the Second World War, in response to the public's demand for lots of meat at cheap prices. Public awareness was raised further after the Bramble Report (1965),[107] commissioned by the UK government which resulted in the first piece of legislation that specifically addressed the welfare of farmed animals. The Report proposed the concept of the Five Freedoms as the basis of good animal welfare; specifically:

- freedom from thirst, hunger and malnutrition;
- freedom from discomfort;
- freedom from pain, injury and disease;
- freedom to express normal behaviour; and
- and freedom from fear and distress.

Shortly after, Peter Singer's book, *Animal Liberation* (1975),[108] drew attention to the role of animals in human society, and human moral responsibilities regarding them.

Human and animal interests are now balanced and prioritised in a democratic system[109] by a majority rule theorem which applies utilitarian-based methodology. The methodology applies a cost/benefit assessment of what constitutes the greatest good (i.e., 'public good') for the majority. Governing then, involves finding a balance between competing interests and identifying the means to achieve commonly held goals, despite disagreement about the means to get there. There are many examples in the state where the individual's freedom and property are considered sacrosanct, and yet these same freedoms may be abridged in the name of 'greater good'. Incarceration for a wide range of antisocial behaviour, constitutes an obvious example. Animal law itself provides an example of how the traditional rights associated with owning property (i.e., the animal) may be abridged (i.e., the animal may be seized and/or destroyed by authorised representatives of the state) in the event that the owner/person in charge of the animal fails to comply with the state's standards of animal care.

Opinion that seeks to separate any part of animal welfare from politics fails to recognise that as a matter of law, it is the responsibility of decision makers to take into account all relevant considerations including matters of scientific knowledge, ethical perspectives and international obligations. Failure to do so may be legally challengeable on grounds that the decision maker has failed to properly exercise

---

107 'Report of the Technical Committee to Enquire into the Welfare of Animals Kept under Intensive Husbandry Systems', referred to in Radford, *Animal Welfare Law in Britain*, p. 169.
108 Peter Singer. 1975. *Animal Liberation* (London: Pimlico).
109 Democracy is defined a government by the people (i.e. rule of the majority), where ultimately the supreme power is vested in the people and exercised by them directly or indirectly through a system of representation (e.g., through the election process): www.merriam-webster.com/dictionary/democracy.

74 *Foundations of animal welfare law*

their authority and discretion, or that they have simply delegated their decision-making responsibilities to advisers.

Although it risks stating the obvious, it is none the less equally obvious that there are people who readily overlook that legislation is the product of the political process. Legislation is a reflection not just of scientific and ethical perspectives, but also a product of existing government priorities, international obligations, individual politicians, legislative resources, and a host of competing and conflicting interests of experts, science, the media, public opinion, and existing law. As a consequence, concludes Radford, 'the law is rarely, if ever, neutral or entirely objective, and never finally settled', and 'is always an expression of power'.[110]

That power must increasingly be applied to matters of animal welfare for at least two reasons. The first is based on the fact that there is increasing research demonstrating that the welfare of animals is inseparably connected to the welfare of humans. Technology enables this knowledge and awareness to be communicated to an international audience in minutes. Greater awareness by people about their dependency on animals, accompanied by concerns by members of the public for the well-being of the animals themselves, is significant to decision makers for several reasons, not the least of which is the fact that public awareness translates into votes. Secondly, globalisation of trade means that the human and animal welfare is accompanied by global-sized risks. Consequently, risk management assessments are part and parcel of balancing, and prioritise stakeholder interests.

Public opinion has been successfully used in areas related to both public[111] and private[112] animal law. Despite allegations from some critics that the well-being of animals is predominantly driven by irrational sentimentality regarding cruelty to animals, the fact is that public consensus largely admonishes against cruelty, whether that cruelty is inflicted upon people or animals. Since Jeremy Bentham first turned people's attention to animals' ability to feel pain, it is arguable that it is only our understanding of pain, as informed by science and shifting societal opinion, that has shaped our thinking about what constitutes 'cruelty', ever since.

Helping readers to think critically is a key objective of this book. So, here are some questions to consider and answer:

---

110 Radford, *Animal Welfare Law in Britain*, p. 167.
111 Examples include issues such as disease control, agricultural methods, and international trade.
112 For example, there is a significant body of research demonstrating that there is a link between domestic violence and animal abuse. People involved in seeking solutions point out that 'violence is violence, and victims are victims, no matter what the species'. As a repeated demonstration of the inseparable link between human welfare and animal welfare, and in responding to those with limited understanding of the true nature of violence, it has also been pointed out that implementation of solutions for one (i.e., humans or animals) consistently translates into benefits for the other. The link between domestic violence and animal abuse constitutes an example of 'private' animal law because it is one of the areas of animal law that commonly occurs behind the closed doors, and in the privacy of, people's homes.

Foundations of animal welfare law   75

- Who are the stakeholders involved in halal slaughter? By reference to the material in this chapter, discuss the roots of conflicting opinions on the subject of halal slaughter. In your discussion, it would be valuable to consider the alternative opinions including, for example, not just the trade markets that prefer meat from animals slaughtered according to halal requirements, but also those people who choose to consume meat derived from animals who have been slaughtered according to standards and procedures that are significantly different to halal methodologies.
- Spain is a country that has supported the concept of giving rights to the Great Apes, while concurrently legalising bullfighting. Assess this apparent contradiction of animal protection with reference to underpinning drivers of human responsibilities concerning animals, and the politics of animal law.

5 National law

The public's voice of what is acceptable

This chapter demonstrates how foundational opinions and attitudes have (or have not) been translated and codified into contemporary animal welfare law at the national level. This is done by referencing the principles of animal welfare legislation of selected jurisdictions which are reputedly global leaders in matters of animal welfare.

By the end of this chapter, readers should be able to:

- by reference to contemporary animal welfare law, demonstrate where the foundational concepts (regarding the human–animal relationship) have been translated and codified into law (or not);
- explain the consistency, and variation, within legislations reference to the 'legal animal';
- name and explain the three elements of 'animal law';
- state the legal definition of 'animal welfare' in one sentence that encompasses all key terms consistently used in contemporary animal welfare law;
- name the six rights of ownership that legally define 'property', and explain how those elements apply to animals in contemporary animal welfare law;
- discuss how enforcement (of practical animal protection) is assisted, or hindered, by the law's categorisation of animals as 'property';
- distinguish the concepts of animal welfare, animal protection, animal cruelty, animal rights and animal interests;
- list and explain the key features of contemporary animal welfare legislation;
- recognise and describe how the law seeks to balance and prioritise competing and conflicting stakeholder interests where animals and humans each represent one (but not the only) stakeholder; and what informs the law in prioritising stakeholder interests in issues of animal welfare and related matters.

Historical viewpoints regarding animals still dictate to current society and law

This chapter demonstrates how contemporary animal welfare law is the culmination of the religion, philosophy and science that set the foundational attitudes and rules governing human–animal relationships. Those rules are evident in each

National animal welfare law   77

nation's law, and there are common threads (e.g., attitudes that see humans as superior, and animals as property) throughout global society irrespective of how developed (or not) a nation may be in respect of its animal welfare law.

Religious and 'cultural values' carry on being reflected in the principle that animals continue to be viewed as inferior to humans, and available for human use. In particular, religious and cultural values continue to constitute exemptions to what would otherwise be largely regarded as inhumane treatment of animals. Bullfighting in Spain, and the Japanese round-up and mass slaughter of dolphins provide two examples that many people are aware of.

Philosophers, now often referred to as 'ethicists' or 'policy advisers', continue to contribute significantly to society's decision makers. Science continues to be particularly influential for decision makers today given that it theoretically provides an independent, researched credibility. Decision makers understandably rely heavily on science and scientists to balance widely differing personal, subjective and frequently emotional opinions of the public.

In considering how the law addresses animals and the legal issues regarding them, it is important to have a sound understanding of what legislation is relevant, and the principles such legislation contains. Man's superiority is a consistent theme, and animals continue to be legally classified as 'property'. This is balanced, at least in part, by the law's recognition of animals as unique, given that animals are animate property. Additionally, moral values advocating that animals should not be treated cruelly have been incorporated into law; the law's concept of cruelty has evolved as it has been increasingly informed by science about the lives and experience of animals – in particular their ability to suffer pain and distress 'similar to people'.

There is an enormous amount of legislation pertaining to human–human and human–animal interactions involving animals; however, there is one particular piece of legislation that is effectively the jewel in the crown of animal protection law, which is aptly named 'the Animal Welfare Act'. Jurisdictions, having updated and leading animal protection law, are notable for the existence of such legislation in their national laws. It is a key piece of legislation for national residents who have direct and indirect contact with animals. Furthermore, the legislation and standards that are associated with it provide, at least in theory, a reassurance regarding standards of animal treatment and related issues, for international companies, wider industry, and other countries trading in the global marketplace. New Zealand, for example, relies more heavily on its primary agricultural products to provide quality of life for its citizens, than any other developed country in the world. More than 50 per cent of its exports come from primary industries. With so much at stake, it is unsurprising that New Zealand continues to aggressively protect and promote its reputation for high standards of animal welfare, given that such a reputation is critical to selling its 'quality' animal products to international trading partners.

Even a cursory comparison of animal protection legislation amongst different countries quickly demonstrates that there is a vast difference between each legal jurisdiction in respect of the existence, and standards, of animal protection law.

78 *National animal welfare law*

However, some jurisdictions are clearly much further ahead in their thinking about, and enactment of, animal protection law.

The single interest of animals protected by law can be described in four key words

In practical terms, this means that as a starting point, owners of animals retain the rights associated with property ownership in respect of animals, including the right to title, use, profit, exclusion, sale and destruction[1] of an animal. However, the owner's property rights are abridged in so far as, although the owner or legally authorised person in charge has the right in respect of *what* he does (i.e., destroy the animal), the law dictates the standards pertaining to *how* that right is implemented.

A key principle for those seeking to understand legal animal welfare concepts is that the law reflects a scale of human 'responsibility' regarding animals and correlating legal protections of animals and human liabilities, depending on the use of the animal and its reliance on its human care-giver(s).

Specifically, the human care-giver, or persons having dealings with animals, must ensure that the animal does not suffer unnecessary or unreasonable pain or distress as a result of either an act, or omission, on their part. In prescribing legal responsibilities in respect of these identified legal interests of animals, leading contemporary animal protection law constrains the previously unfettered property rights of the owner under common law.

The four key words that underpin all animal protection law and the two limbs identifying criminal offending, are 'pain', 'distress', 'unnecessary' and 'unreasonable'. The first limb of legislative responsibility simply asks whether or not an animal has experienced pain (i.e., a negative sensation/experience in response to a noxious stimuli) or distress (e.g., stress that is of such a degree that results in physiologic compromise to the individual). If the animal does not experience either pain or distress, then there is simply no offence under animal welfare law. If, however, the animal has experienced pain or distress, then the second limb of the legislative test queries whether or not the suffering (pain or distress) was either necessary (i.e., which goes to the nature of the act or omission, e.g., were there alternatives that good practice and/or scientific knowledge demonstrate were available and/or preferable?) or reasonable (i.e., which considers the degree of suffering, e.g., were there available options, based on good practice or scientific knowledge, that would have alleviated the pain and/or distress experienced by the animal?).

These four words underpin what continues to be referred by various synonyms (e.g., humane, anti-cruelty) and forms the underlying theme of animal protection from its inception to current – and future – animal welfare and protection standards.

---

1 Synonyms in the field of animal welfare include 'euthanase' and 'kill'.

Question: who's got leading animal protection/welfare law?

There was a time when the British Empire was so large that there was always at least one part of its territory in daylight. The size of the Empire during the nineteenth and early twentieth centuries, and the fact that wherever the Empire ruled it imposed its laws, goes some way to explaining why Westminster law still continues to have such a strong influence on issues of animal protection globally. Despite differences in animal welfare standards that clearly occur between countries, there are also a number of important similarities which can be traced back to the countries' legislative roots with Westminster law.

Recognising the common thread of Westminster law that occurs in some jurisdictions, but not others, assists in understanding why some jurisdictions appear further ahead in their animal law than others. It also assists in understanding the seemingly ad hoc development of animal law in different jurisdictions. One of the legacies of British rule was that its colonies throughout the world adopted Westminster law, as it was at the time as the basis for the legal system. Consequently, and despite their common beginnings, each legal jurisdiction subsequently developed in different ways to address local issues, culture, politics and prevailing attitudes regarding the uses of animals.

Beyond welfare and toward dignity of animals?

The principles of Westminster-based animal protection law are widely referenced as the current benchmark of global leadership in terms of welfare law. However, there are jurisdictions that have already extended animal protection law beyond standard welfare concepts. For example, the Swiss Animal Protection Act of 16 December 2005 protects not just the welfare but also the dignity of animals.[2] But as attractive as this development may be to certain people, the initiative is not without its problems. Law functions better when there is clarity, but the term 'dignity' raises questions in a number of areas, including definitions, boundaries and enforcement. What is meant by 'dignity' in the context of human responsibilities for animals? What constitutes – and what is the difference between – a violation of dignity and failure to respect dignity?[3] How does the law deal with inconsistencies involving a 'failure to respect', 'violation' and 'protection' of dignity and 'taking account of dignity' in the Swiss Federal Constitution?[4]

Despite these challenges, the Swiss initiative potentially redefines a public standard of the relationship between people and animals, and reflects an agenda to

---

2 Art. 1 TSchG: www.admin.ch/ch/d/sr/455/a1.html.
3 'The Dignity of Animals and the Evaluation of Interests in the Swiss Animal Protection Act' – a position paper issued by the Ethics Committee for Animal Experimentation of the Swiss Academies of Arts and Sciences: www.samw.ch/dms/en/Ethics/Ethics . . . /e_dignity_of_animals_2010.pdf.
4 Federal Constitution of the Swiss Confederation of 18 April 1999 (SR 101): www.admin.ch/ch/e/rs/101/index.html (English-language version).

80   *National animal welfare law*

move people's attitudes further away from viewing animals as mere commodities toward increased recognition of them as individual beings. Switzerland, Germany, the Netherlands and South Korea are nations whose laws have incorporated reference to the inherent value of animals. Inclusion of dignity and specific notation to the innate value of animals as experiencers of life may be incorporated by wider legal jurisdictions in the future, but for many nations the implementation of welfare law mirroring Westminster welfare standards remains the predominant leadership contemporary norm.

The Victorian empire established many of today's legislative leaders

Given that Westminster law derived from early English law, a familiarity particularly with the development of animal protection law in England's Victorian era is essential to any study of animal protection law.

This is because Westminster law of the nineteenth and early twentieth centuries has had such a profound global impact on principles of animal law. Consequently, because 'the Westminsters' are globally recognised for their leadership in animal protection law, this book primarily references the principles of animal welfare legislation from jurisdictions that have Westminster law.

The champions of Westminster's early animal protection legislation

The early 1800s demonstrated significant changes in animal protection, and although the 20-year time span must have seemed lengthy to its early pioneers, hindsight demonstrates the enormous impact of their early accomplishments.

In 1800, Sir William Putney introduced the first bill to put down bullbaiting. The proposal was opposed by William Windham on the grounds that it was 'anti-working class', and the Bill failed by a narrow margin of just two votes (43 to 41). Just two years later, in 1802, a second Bill to abolish bullbaiting was introduced by William Wilberforce. Windham again opposed the motion on the basis that bulls derive satisfaction from baiting, and it was unconstitutional to deny the working class their pleasures, particularly when the upper-class reformers had their own 'rich sports', such as hunting and racing. The Bill was lost by 64 votes to 51.

In 1809, former Lord Chancellor, Lord Erskine introduced a Bill to protect 'domesticated' animals which included, for example, cattle and horses. On this occasion, Windham opposed the Bill on the grounds that it might prejudice the rights of property, that men should be trusted to regulate their own behaviour and that the legislation would be too difficult to enforce. Lord Erskine's Bill was also lost.

Erskine subsequently assisted another Member of Parliament, Richard Martin, in producing a Bill to Parliament in 1821 'to prevent the ill-treatment of horses and other animals' by third parties. The 'Ill-Treatment of Horses Bill' introduced by Richard Martin, MP was greeted with derision and laughter. The Bill was lost.

National animal welfare law 81

Martin persevered and the following year (1822), he introduced the 'Ill-treatment of Horses and Cattle Bill'. The Bill received Royal assent on 22 June 1822 and became the first notable legislative success of the animal protection movement in the world. The Act, commonly referred to as 'Martin's Act', made it an offence to 'beat, abuse, or ill-treat any horse, mare, gelding, mule, ass, ox, cow, heifer, steer, sheep or other cattle'. Despite the legislative success, enforcement was problematic, and Martin himself took to the streets with the intent of bringing offenders to Court.

Between 1823 and 1826, Martin continued to advocate for extensions to the 1822 Act, and introduced additional Bills, seeking to prohibit various baiting and fighting sports, and extend legislative protections to dogs, cats, monkeys, and horses awaiting slaughter.[5] In 1835, Joseph Pease, MP secured most of the reforms which Martin had attempted to introduce during the 1820s.[6]

The 1840s: state involvement in societal issues

In contrast to the resistance experienced by Erskine, Martin and other early MPs advocating the need for state involvement to protect against cruelty to animals, by the 1840s, the state's involvement in matters of animal protection was widely accepted by the public and politicians alike.

By the late 1840s, prosecutions for animal welfare offences had increased. Enforcement addressed not just offences that were committed in public places, but the state also assumed power to enter the previously sacrosanct location of private property[7] in order to enforce legal standards of animal protection. For example, despite the existence of legislation prohibiting cruelty of animals, there was considerable evidence that horses in knackers' yards were still being callously treated, either by being left without food and water for considerable periods of time in anticipation that they were simply going to be slaughtered, or, in other instances, were not given sustenance of any kind and consequently they died of dehydration and starvation. The shift of government attitudes resulted in the enactment of legislation governing the activities of knackers' yards was ratified in just two months.[8] The speed of the legislative enactment was extraordinary even by modern standards.[9] The enactment established that contravention of the regulatory regime could result not only in a fine or imprisonment, but potentially the

---

5 Michael Radford. 2001. *Animal Welfare Law in Britain* (Oxford: Oxford University Press), p. 39.

6 Ibid., p. 45.

7 It is noteworthy that even today in an allegedly advanced Western society, there are still minorities that cling to notions that privacy should supersede accountability for criminal actions. For example, research has demonstrated a link between domestic violence and animal abuse, and offenders still commonly allege that the state has no right to interfere with what happens behind the 'closed doors of a person's home'.

8 Cruelty to Animals Act, 1835 7 & 8 Vict., c87; An Act to Amend the Law for Regulating Places Kept for Slaughtering Horses.

9 Radford, *Animal Welfare Law in Britain*, p. 63.

82   *National animal welfare law*

applied penalty could deny the offender of their means of livelihood by denying them the necessary licence to operate as a knacker.

The 1849 Cruelty to Animals Act strengthened animal protection law by widening the ambit of liability to include both the perpetrator of criminal offending, as well as those who caused or procured acts that were considered cruel under legislation. As a consequence, it was possible to prosecute the master and servant for criminal animal law offending. In essence, this was the beginning of 'vicarious liability'[10] under animal welfare law.

In contrast to the social attitudes and resistance of early Westminster law which viewed animal protection concepts as somewhat eccentric, by the early 1900s, the idea that animals should be protected was increasingly accepted, and actually promoted as a benefit that would 'elevate the human race'.[11] Consideration given to issues of animal cruelty by early legislatures was therefore a mixture of concern for the animal, and significant consideration regarding the effects that cruelty to animals might have on the human character. One early Court decision stated: 'Cruelty is degrading to man; and a society for the suppression of cruelty to the lower animals . . . has for its object, not merely the protection of the animals themselves, but the advancement of morals and education among men.'[12] As public attitudes acknowledged a responsibility regarding animal care, and as legislation reflected the shifting public attitude, then animal protection moved from being seen as something eccentric, to being something that was positive.

The animal was consequently included in legal assessments of animal cruelty. The important shift in terms of animal protection law was that the law turned its assessment of matters involving animal cruelty from a focus on devaluation of people's property, to considering the impact of alleged offending on the experience of the animal, which included the physical and mental components of an animal's pain and/or distress. This meant that legal liability could rise from committing an act or omission that constituted animal cruelty in the eyes of the law.

A principle piece of legislation was enacted in 1911. The Protection of Animals Act 1911 gave legislative protection to 'any animal', although it excluded wild animals, food animals and animals used in research. To a large degree, the 1911 Act marked the true beginning of 'contemporary' animal protection law, not only because of its legislative attitude to concepts of animal cruelty, pain and distress; but also because it influenced global development of animal protection by virtue of its promulgation as law throughout the world as part of the British Empire. Although remonstrating against acts of cruelty, the 1911 Protection of Animals Act was not at that time considered to be a significant milestone in the development of animal protection law. Instead, it was viewed as an amalgamation of existing laws. It reflected Victorian and Edwardian views and was constrained by

---

10 This term refers to the tort legal doctrine that imposes responsibility upon one person for the failure of another, with whom the person has a special relationship, i.e., employer and employee: http://legal-dictionary.thefreedictionary.com.

11 *Re Wedgewood* [1915] 1 Ch 113, 122, CA (*Swinden Eady LJ*).

12 Chitty J in *Re Foveaux* [1895] 2 Ch 501, 507.

National animal welfare law 83

a conscious decision not to introduce 'any amendment which was not necessary'.[13] Under the Protection of Animals Act 1911, cruelty was defined by reference to a number of specific acts which were considered 'cruel'. For example, it was an offence to 'cruelly beat, kick, ill-treat, override, overdrive, overload, torture, infuriate, or terrify any animal; or cause, procure, or, being the owner, permit any animal to be so used'.[14]

Early legislation functioned on criminalising blatant acts of cruelty

Early concepts of 'anti-cruelty' focused on what people should not do to animals. The purpose of early legislation focused on prohibiting humans from inflicting blatant acts of cruelty on animals by dictating what people could *not* do.[15] This 'negative duty' is in contrast to contemporary legal concepts of animal welfare law which, while retaining the anti-cruelty concepts defining what any person must *not* do to an animal (legally referred to as 'ill-treatment'), also dictates what owners and persons in charge of animals *must do* in meeting the needs of animals in their care, supervision, or under their control. This obligation to be proactive in providing for animals' needs explains why legal concepts of welfare are described as 'positive duties of care', which the law applies to people who own, or who are in charge of, animals.[16]

In spite of the fact that early animal protection legislation clearly had its difficulties and that like any other law, animal protection has evolved by a series of incremental steps; it pays to remember that protection of the animal *for the animal's sake* constituted an enormous achievement by its early animal protection advocates.

Defining the animals that were the subject of (early) legal protections

Early legislation, despite its good intentions, had its limitations. One of the assumptions that is still widely applied by people involved in the subject of 'animal law' is that the word 'animal' applies to all animals. Determining the appropriate legislative definition of an animal has been problematic from the earliest times where the law sought to provide protections for animals.

Early legislative protections were afforded only to domesticated and captive animals, and did not extend to their 'wild' counterparts. A domestic animal was defined as a 'horse, ass, mule, bull, sheep, pig, goat, dog, cat, or fowl, or any other

---

13 House of Commons debates, 30 June 1911, column 745 referred to in Radford, *Animal Welfare Law in Britain*, p. 196.
14 Protection of Animals Act 1911 s1(1)(a).
15 Early Courts applied a broad definition of cruelty which considered people's acts *and* omissions that resulted in an animal's suffering.
16 Section 4 Animal Welfare Act 1999 New Zealand.

84   *National animal welfare law*

animal of whatsoever kind or species, and whether a quadruped or not which is tame or which has been or is being sufficiently tamed to serve some purpose for the use of man'.[17] It is a lengthy, cumbersome definition that, as a consequence, forced the Courts to consider concepts of 'tameness' and degrees of 'control' of animals. Making the distinction, however, proved problematic.

The problems associated with considerations of 'tameness' can be illustrated by considering the many states of cats. Some cats are obviously more docile than others. 'Domesticated' often refers to an animal that is reliant on its human care-giver for its needs (e.g., food, water, shelter, health care). But what about the 'feral' cat? Or the 'stray' cat? Are these terms simply variations of the domesticated animal, or something more akin to a 'wild' animal? Depending upon the legal jurisdiction, this may raise questions about whether the animal in question benefits, or not, from legal protections provided under animal welfare legislation.[18]

Similarly, degrees of 'control' can vary markedly depending on the circumstances in which an animal is found. Is a beached whale, stranded on the foreshore, 'controlled'? Is the whale an animal under the Act? Would the whale be deserving of protection under the law from someone who attacked the live animal with a knife? A Court case in 1912 determined that the whale, which was indeed attacked by a person with a knife while the animal was still alive, was not protected by the Act because the Court at the time considered that captivity or confinement meant 'something more than temporary inability to get away from a particular spot'.[19]

Recognising the 'development continuum' of animal protection legislation

It's worth noting that the development of animal protection law in England exemplifies the criminal law 'development continuum' of animal protection legislation that continues to be demonstrated in different jurisdictions around the world.

Animal protection law in Westminster bases legal systems developed in various stages from a state of 'no law', through to law that prohibited blatant acts of cruelty (e.g., England's Animal Protection Act 1911), and almost a hundred years later, enacted the Animal Welfare Act 2006 which retained offences for intentionally cruel treatment of animals, and added legal obligations on owners and persons in charge of animals to proactively provide for animals in their care. The future challenge may be recognising where animal protection law progresses beyond welfare to the innate (inherent) dignity of animals rather than focusing on minimising pain and distress. From early religious law which dictated that men

---

17 Section 15 Protection of Animals Act 1911: www.legislation.gov.uk/ukpga/Geo5/1-2/27.

18 New Zealand has produced secondary legislation which distinguishes between feral, wild and domesticated cats – Animal Welfare (Companion Cats) Code of Welfare 2007: www.biosecurity. govt.nz/animal-welfare/codes/companion-cats.

19 *Steele v Rogers* (1912) 76 JP 150, 151 (Pickford J).

National animal welfare law   85

had unfettered rights to use animals as they pleased, Westminster law transformed the prevailing law from a situation where there was little if any protection of animals for their own sake, to a point where a wide range of species benefited from at least some degree of protection provided by the law.

Awareness of this continuum provides readers with a useful reference point to compare and contrast the law from various jurisdictions/regions. In terms of animal welfare legislation, for example, it is a relatively straightforward exercise to ascertain whether a nation demonstrates 'almost nothing' in respect of animal protection law, or a slightly more advanced state focusing primarily on 'anti-cruelty', or animal law that reflects the principles of leading animal 'welfare' by a combined focus on anti-cruelty and the 'positive duties of care', which are the legislative enactment of principles set out in the Five Freedoms, stated as:

- freedom from thirst, hunger and malnutrition;
- freedom from discomfort;
- freedom from pain, injury and disease;
- freedom to express normal behaviour; and
- freedom from fear and distress.

Incremental change is founded on much more than just sentimentality

As demonstrated in the previous chapter, theology, philosophy and science provided the basic concepts regarding people's relationship with animals. The early views of these influences that focus on the differences between people and animals, the superiority of mankind, and the God-given licence to use animals as people pleased, provided the context for further developments in the area of legislative protections for animals. It would be wrong to assume that legislative protections of animals resulted simply from people's change of attitude regarding animals reflecting a greater sympathy toward them.

To put the animal protection movement in context, it is helpful as a starting point to recognise that the protection of animals was part of a greater shift that occurred during the nineteenth century, which considered the well-being of various apparently inferior groups, including slaves, children and the poor. It remains surprising to learn that protection for animals, benchmarked by the establishment of the RSPCA in 1824, actually preceded legal protections of children by approximately sixty years.[20]

---

20 Radford, *Animal Welfare Law in Britain*, p. 48. It is worth taking a moment to consider why people might be surprised at this disjunct in legislative protections. When examined, the surprise is often rooted in the timeless assumptions pertaining to a hierarchy of interests where human interests, which include children as members of the human race, are prioritised on the basis of human superiority.

86 *National animal welfare law*

Recognising common features of incremental change

Principles of law that address issues of animal cruelty and welfare are relatively commonplace today, so it is sadly too easy to overlook the enormity of the animal protection achievements of historical individuals such as Lord Erskine,[21] William Wilberforce,[22] Richard Martin,[23] and others who began what might aptly be described as the modern-day animal protection movement. Their influence on changing legal and social attitudes regarding animals in England spread throughout the British Empire and consequently continues to have significant relevance to public attitudes concerning animals throughout the world. Insights as to their contributions in driving the development of animal protection legislation provides insights as to what might prove useful (or not) in furthering constructive incremental changes regarding concepts of animal law today.

The evolution of animal protection legislation demonstrates a number of features that are common to the complexities of incremental change. These features of incremental change are clearly evident in the field of animal law and include:

- Use of an established, responsive, legislative system that enables the public's voice to be represented by members of government.
- The establishment and resourcing of organised enforcement systems to effectively implement legislated responsibilities.
- The involvement of educated and influential individuals possessing qualities of passion, patience and persistence, combined with the requirement for education and support of the public.
- Although it may be debated whether law leads public perceptions, or whether public perceptions drive the law, the law is generally described as being predominantly reactive (rather than proactive) in respect of societal issues. This reality highlights that the education of the public (e.g., regarding the similarities between humans and animals) is another feature that contributes to incremental change.

---

21 Lord Thomas Erskine (1750–1823) was a member of the House of Lords, and Lord Chancellor in England. He introduced a Bill to the House of Lords for the prevention of malicious and wanton cruelty to animals. The House of Lords accepted the Bill, but it received considerable opposition in the House of Commons and it was defeated. Lord Erskine refused to be discouraged and reintroduced the Bill in the next session of the House of Lords. The Bill was eventually accepted and enacted into Statute.

22 William Wilberforce (1759–1833) was a British politician who is largely known for leading the parliamentary campaign against the British slave trade, which resulted in the Slave Trade Act 1807. He also championed the campaign to ban bullbaiting (1802) and establish the Society for the Prevention of Cruelty to Animals.

23 Richard Martin (1754–1834) was an Irish politician who is famous for his work against the cruelty to animals, particularly ill-treatment of horses, and sports that involved baiting and fighting. He championed what is recognised as the first notable legislative success of the animal welfare lobby in the world, and is now referred to as 'Martin's Act'.

National animal welfare law 87

- The public's voice, championed by the higher ranks of society and reflected in votes, logically constitutes a major driver for any politician and, thereby, a government. For example, the early political champion of animal reforms, Richard Martin, was well aware of the importance of drawing attention to public support, and made a point of referring to the 'millions of well thinking people' around the country that he was allegedly in correspondence with, and who shared his opinions regarding matters of animal protection.[24]

Richard Martin's (1754–1834) involvement in matters of animal protection illustrates another important principle to those involved in the incremental change of animal protection law – that 'an individual, working alone, could only achieve so much', and that in order to achieve greater effectiveness it is necessary to have an organisation that is specifically authorised to deal with matters of animal protection. The establishment of the Society for the Prevention of Cruelty to Animals (SPCA) continues to stand as an example of such an organisation. Despite precarious beginnings when initially established, the SPCA had a profound influence in the legal protection of animals, and is recognised internationally as a major voice in issues involving animals and their welfare.

Animal law is 'specialist property law'

What are the elements of legal 'property'?

'Animals are property': this brief, but succinct, statement underlies our interaction with animals, our use of them, and importantly, the legal obligations on humans regarding them.

Understanding the legal classification of animals as property is fundamental to understanding the development and application of the law concerning animals. 'Animals are property' is at the core of most significant doctrines, cases and daily reality for both animals and the humans that have direct or indirect contact with them.

The law gives six 'rights' to the property owner

It is likely that the reader will, like most people, have read references to 'property' in the preceding material, without necessarily considering how 'property' is legally defined. Take a moment to consider these questions: What actually identifies 'property'? What is it that distinguishes something as property belonging to one person, and not another?

The elements of legal property have been described as a 'bundle of rights' that are in the possession of the owner. There are six 'rights' of property ownership, each of which have application to animals and issues of animal protection:

---

24 Radford, *Animal Law in Britain*, p. 74.

88   *National animal welfare law*

- the right of title or 'ownership';
- the right to use the property;
- the power to exclude others from using the property;
- the right to profit from use of the property;
- the right to sell/transfer title of the property; and
- the right to destroy (e.g., in reference to an animal, this is described as the right to euthanase) the property.

In a system of law that is particularly interested in protecting property interests, the legal elements of property as they apply to animals can be viewed from two perspectives: firstly, how those property rights serve the human interests vested in animals and, secondly, how human responsibilities in respect of property might serve the animals' interests.

Animals have consistently been viewed as property

Given that religion was people's 'first law' that dictated man's position of dominion, it is unsurprising that animals have been treated as property throughout history.

God-given rights continued to inform and underpin comparatively recent views on what constituted legal property. William Blackstone, an eighteenth-century jurist, is commonly recognised and referred to as the authority for setting the foundational legal concepts of property in Westminster law. Blackstone asserted that 'whatever airy metaphysical notions may have been started by fanciful writers', it was, in Blackstone's opinion, none the less a situation that 'dominion given to men by God' had the effect that although initially everyone took from 'the public stock', this 'communion of goods' was superseded as men gathered 'animals as were of a more tame antiquated nature' and established a 'permanent property in their flocks and herds . . . *as absolute a property as in any inanimate beings*'.[25]

Animals were recognised as property and moreover, as *inanimate* property. The law has a long history of protecting the property interests of the owner, and the inherent rights of property owners to do with their property as they pleased. Between 1671 and 1831, there were more than fifty statutes addressing legal issues involving game, deer, cattle and fish; and unlawful activities of poaching, hunting, wounding, maiming, killing and destroying animals which were deemed to be the property of their owners.

None of the law's focus at the time was on preventing suffering to the animal. Instead, the law's focus was on concerns such as maintaining public order, and protecting owners from damage to their property by a third party without either the express or implied consent of the property's/animal's owner. These legal

---

25 *Commentaries on the Laws of England*, Book II, 1765–1769, p. 3; see also William Blackstone. 1765 (1979 edn). *Commentaries on the Laws of England* (Chicago, IL: University of Chicago Press), emphasis added.

objectives were reflected in the existing systems of law and available remedies at the time. For example, if a domestic animal was injured or killed, then the owner might sue in trespass for compensation under *civil* law; but *criminal* proceedings by the state were only instigated if it could be proved that the 'barbarous treatment of a beast' reflected malicious intent of the perpetrator towards the *owner* of the animal.[26] It is notable that human interests received the primary focus of available legal protection, while the interests of the animal were comparatively non-existent.

Activities associated with animals, such as the driving and slaughtering of cattle, and beating of horses, were commonplace in Victorian society and consequently weren't viewed as threats to public order. Additionally, as the focus of the law was on protecting the value of the property, there was little involvement by the law if the devaluation of the property was attributable directly to the owner of the property itself, or with his consent.

The legal categorisation of animals as property has been a constant feature of debate regarding animal protections. However, it might be more accurate to note that the real issue of debate concerns the well-being of animals which, according to some, is dependent on animal's legal classification as property. Despite the fact that some early debates drew attention to the animal's ability to experience pain and thereby sought to distinguish animal property from other inanimate objects,[27] the rights of the property owner were none the less considered sacrosanct.

Animal protection law fettered the previously unfettered property rights of the animal owner

Legitimacy: 'Everything is permitted except what is expressly forbidden'

In addition to understanding that property owners had a prima facie right to do as they pleased with their property, it is also important to understand the boundaries that were attached to this principle.

The property-owner's rights to do as he pleased with his own property was intimately associated with the continuing prevailing legal principle that people were allowed to do as they pleased with their own property *unless* there was a law expressly forbidding a certain activity in relation to the property. Put succinctly, every act or omission was permissible unless it was expressly forbidden by law.

In most Western legal jurisdictions, and particularly those that follow the principles of Westminster law, the independence of individuals exists less because of the provision of positive legal rights, and more because of this principle which establishes the existence and primacy of liberties and freedoms *unless* those freedoms

---

26 E.B. Nicholson. 1879. The Rights of an Animal (London: Kegan Paul), cited in Radford, *Animal Welfare Law in Britain*, p. 9.

27 Jeremy Bentham. 1789 (1970 edn). *An Introduction to the Principles of Morals and Legislation*, eds J.H. Burns and H.L.A. Hart (London: Athlone Press).

90 *National animal welfare law*

are *specifically* abridged by law. This has been described in the Courts as being a state where 'everything is permitted except what is expressly forbidden'.[28]

This principle is plainly evident today. Largely utilitarian law making takes into consideration matters of public good (e.g., safety) when applying boundaries to an otherwise unfettered freedom of the individual. This principle is also clearly demonstrated in the development of animal law, where the animal owner was historically free to treat animals as he wished. Subsequently, that freedom was curtailed as the state enacted laws in respect of animal protection.

As continues to happen today, state initiatives curtailing individual freedoms were met with considerable resistance. It is one thing to encourage the public to voluntarily accept a moral responsibility to treat animals well; quite another to persuade government to go through the procedural hurdles accompanying the establishment of law, which ultimately results in criminalising behaviours that once were 'legitimate' as of right to law-abiding citizens. The power of the law in setting societal norms (which are enforced by criminal law and the application of penalties) is illustrated in this context. By legitimising a practice, the law can be said to be morally endorsing its continuation. In contrast, by criminalising selected practices, the law theoretically reflects standards which are morally unacceptable to the majority of society.

Law has developed by a series of checks and balances, largely in response to the public majority and prevailing public opinion. Today, people question any edict from the government that seeks to restrict their freedoms. In that respect, people have not changed, so it should be unsurprising that there was resistance by Victorian citizens to the state seeking to fetter their rights, and criminalise their previously legitimate handling of animals.

State vs people: fettering the rights of the property owner with 'negative' duties

The legislative approach of fettering people's rights explains why the nature of animal cruelty protection was traditionally negative in character, proscribing what people could *not* do to an animal. The features of anti-cruelty law (and successive welfare law) are still based on common-law principles which continue to recognise ownership entitlements and liberties associated with animals as property.

Early arguments against state interference

There is a tension between state control of people, and the inherent right of people to control themselves independently of state involvement. In the early eighteenth century, state governors were in the process of dealing with a number of societal issues, which included giving protection to children, and addressing the plight of the poor, in addition to initiatives dealing with the protection of animals. Criticisms

---

28 *Malone v Commissioner for the Metropolitan Police* (no. 2) [1979] Chancery Division 344.

National animal welfare law 91

levelled at animal protection advocates Lawrence, Erskine, Martin and Pease illustrated the depth of societal conventions in Victorian times, when people expected to be able to do as they pleased with their property, free from any interference of the state, both in public and in the privacy of their own home.

It helps to remember that the legal 'bundle of rights' that attached to property was then broadly applied to women and children, as well as animals. In short, the Victorian way of life, authorised by its Judaeo-Christian roots and supported by the law, prioritised the white Christian male property owner.

The man's place as the head of the household was recognised and validated by the law which gave him legal power and authority. For example, prior to 1870 in England, a wife had no legal standing, and was described as little more than a necessary chattel of the husband. As such, the husband was legally entitled to chastise his wife for 'misbehaviour'. Despite common perceptions that the phrase 'the rule of thumb' had something to do with carpentry, the measurement reference is more widely believed to have had its beginnings in the seventeenth century with a British judge who allegedly ruled that an Englishman could legally beat his disobedient wife using a stick *provided that* the stick was no thicker than the width of the husband's thumb.

The authority of the Victorian patriarch is further demonstrated in that historically the father was empowered by society and law to discipline his children as he chose. It was said that, other than 'murder or very serious physical assault' then, in civil matters, the Courts 'considered that the views of the father prevailed over all others'.[29] In short, the law gave dominion, accompanied by significant power to the white Christian male and extended further rights and authority to those who also owned property and land.[30]

However, the balance between the state's power and the historical power held by the patriarch shifted. In Western cultures, many of the powers invested in the patriarch were subsumed to the state. This shift was viewed by many people as a derogation of the previously sacrosanct authority of the patriarch, and his God-given right to do as he chose with his own property.

Resistance was largely based on arguments alleging that interference with property constituted an invasion of privacy and personal freedom which undermined man's natural (i.e., God-given) rights regarding the use of his personal property. However, there was a moral view held by an influential minority that animals should not be treated 'cruelly'. This was expressed in the alternative as an expectation that people should treat animals 'humanely'.

The term 'humane' highlights another principle that is fundamental to understanding animal welfare law. Essentially, contemporary animal welfare law can be viewed as 'specialist property law' because of the property's unique ability to suffer pain and distress.

---

29 Radford, *Animal Welfare Law in Britain*, p. 49.

30 Compare and contrast the protections provided to women, children and animals in Victorian times with the protections provided to minority groups in cultures and legal jurisdictions where unfettered patriarchal authority is still evident today.

92 *National animal welfare law*

What is meant by 'humane' treatment?

Despite allegations that humans 'put humans first', there is a broad principle of animal protection that accepts human use of animals, provided the use is humane. In 1995, the Banner Committee, for example, considered that the law, while incorporating principles that revolved around the principle of 'harm', extended consideration beyond simply physical mistreatment. The Banner Committee held that:[31]

a   Harms of a certain degree and kind ought under no circumstances to be inflicted on an animal.[32]
b   Any harm to an animal, even if not absolutely impermissible, none the less requires justification and must be outweighed by the good which is realistically sought in so treating it.
c   Any harm which is justified by the second principle ought, however, to be minimised as far as is reasonably possible.

Additionally, the Farm Animal Welfare Council[33] was commissioned by the UK government to provide a report addressing the implications of cloning for the welfare of farmed animals. The report adopted the Banner Committee's principles, suggesting that a procedure may be considered intrinsically objectionable within (a) above if:

1   It inflicts very severe or lasting pain on the animals concerned.
2   It involves an unacceptable violation of the integrity of a living being.
3   It is associated with the mixing of kinds of animals to an extent which is unacceptable.
4   It generates living beings whose sentience has been reduced to the extent that they may be considered to be mere instruments or artefacts.

Contemporary concepts of animal welfare naturally incorporate consideration to a wide number of national and global issues, but in respect of the legislatively protected animal, the public and politicians have largely agreed that decisions and outcomes involving animals must be both 'humane' as well as 'sustainable'.[34] Obviously from an animal welfare perspective, the focus is on the meaning and application of 'humane'.

31   DEFRA. n.d. 'Archive: Animal Welfare: Government Response to FAWC's Report on the Implications of Cloning for the Welfare of Farmed Livestock': http://webarchive.nationalarchives. gov.uk/20130402151656/http://archive.defra.gov.uk/foodfarm/farmanimal/welfare/govresponse/ cloning-resp.htm.
32   In other words, there are situations in which cost–benefit analysis or utilitarian calculations should not be regarded as the sole test of acceptability. Decisions should also take account of the appropriateness of the proposed action, and its consequences.
33   Website for the Farm Animal Welfare Committee: www.gov.uk/government/groups/farm-animal-welfare-committee-fawc.
34   D. Ibrahim. 2006. 'The Anti-Cruelty Statute: A Study in Animal Welfare', *Journal of Animal Law and Ethics*, 1: 175–89.

National animal welfare law 93

Considering what constitutes humane treatment of animals emphasises the three elements that define animal law. Firstly, it involves an animal. Secondly, animal law takes account of the unique nature of animals as animate objects, and thirdly, animal law involves the relationship between animals and humans.

In terms of the law, 'cruelty' and 'humane' are more specifically set out in the offences which describe, in one line, the purpose of all animal protection law: prevention of 'unnecessary and/or unreasonable pain and/or distress'.

This one-line benchmark of preventing an animal from suffering pain and/ or distress creates two tests in terms of legal assessment of culpability. Firstly, did the animal, in fact, suffer pain and/or distress? If not, then there is clearly no offence. However, if it is proven that the animal did in fact suffer, and then the second consideration is whether or not the suffering was necessary.

Test 1: did the animal suffer 'pain and/or distress'?

Although definitions may vary between individuals and disciplines including the law, there is widespread agreement that almost all species, including mammals, birds and fish, suffer as a result of experiencing pain and distress.

'Suffering'

Like the words 'cruelty' and 'humane', the word 'suffering' is another term frequently used in a generic and synonymous manner. Suffering is a state of being, which goes beyond simply being an experience that is 'unpleasant' or 'undesired'.[35]

The causes of pain and/or distress vary widely, and include, for example, physical injury, noxious stimuli and/or the absence of important positive stimuli. Clinical signs may vary according to the condition, and include, for example, thirst, hunger, breathlessness, nausea, pain, fear, anxiety, boredom and other negative experiences. Suffering may manifest physically, and/or as mental and/ or emotional pain, including unpleasant feelings, sensations or perceptions, 'cognitively processed and interpreted by the animal according to its species-specific and individual nature, and past experience'.

Whatever the combination of causes, symptoms, behavioural changes and clinical signs, the result for the individual is significantly 'unpleasant' or 'undesired' experience that varies in intensity (e.g., from significant to excruciating) and duration (e.g., short-term 'acute' pain and/or distress, to long-term 'chronic' pain and/or distress).

---

35 Suffering means an unpleasant, undesired state of being which is the outcome of the impact on an animal of a variety of noxious stimuli and/or the absence of important positive stimuli. It is the opposite of good welfare and may be associated with elevated levels of thirst, hunger, breathlessness, nausea, pain, fear, anxiety, boredom and other negative experiences. It can manifest as physical, mental and/or emotional pain, including unpleasant feelings, sensations or perceptions, cognitively processed and interpreted by the animal according to it species-specific and individual nature, and past experience.

94 *National animal welfare law*

Importantly, pain and/or distress are less about the 'opposite of good welfare' and more about the result, or consequence, of poor welfare.

For the purposes of law, 'suffering' is an umbrella term that encompasses conditions of pain and distress. The terms 'pain' and 'distress', in conjunction with the words 'unreasonable' and 'unnecessary' are key words which form the starting point of legal assessments considering whether or not an offence under the animal protection law has been committed.

The law distinguishes between suffering pain and suffering distress

It's important to remember that legislation is not in the habit of using multiple words to describe the same thing. This means that where different words are used, legislative interpretation infers that government intended to convey a distinction between the words, or terms, used. With this in mind, legal interpretation of pain is therefore different from the legal interpretation of distress.

As a consequence, the presence of both terms in primary animal protection/welfare legislation means it is important for the reader and those professionally involved in the field of animal law to also be clear about the distinctions between each term. For example, the fact that there is a difference between 'pain' and 'distress' is critical for a prosecutor in applying the distinctions to the relevant fact pattern and circumstances of the case, in order to prove the elements of any alleged offending. An animal may, for example, experience pain but not necessarily distress or vice versa. Alternatively, despite appearances (e.g., a cow with a low body-condition score, commonly referred to as a 'skinny cow'), the evidence may not establish that the cow actually experienced pain and/or distress.

There are problems for experts tasked with assisting the Court by distinguishing between pain and distress if, for example, they rely on simple generic definitions. A common generic definition of distress, for example, is 'suffering from anxiety, sorrow, or pain'. Utilising such a definition would simply create a circular argument that distress is pain and pain is a distress. Clearly, a deeper understanding of distress is necessary, particularly when circumstances further warrant distinguishing 'distress' from concepts of 'stress'.

The Courts commonly turn to experts to assist them in these deliberations, so it is important that any expert witness to alleged animal welfare offending should also have a clear understanding of the distinctions between the terms in order to fulfil their duty to the Court. Despite the fact that many individuals, publications and professionals make frequent reference to the line 'pain and distress', it is often apparent that many of society's animal welfare experts (e.g., veterinarians) are unfamiliar with the legal definitions that attach to their professional duties. Furthermore, many have demonstrably failed to turn their minds to the difference between the key legal meaning of pain and distress. For example, while a considerable number of veterinarians are naturally conversant with matters pertaining to an animal's physical health, questioning frequently reveals that they lack understanding of the legal concepts of welfare, despite the fact that the legal definition of animal welfare applies to almost everything a veterinarian does. Some veterinarians have been called into a criminal investigation of animal welfare offending. In these circumstances, the enforcement officer in charge – and subsequently the Court – is likely to rely upon the veterinarian making clear distinctions between pain and distress, as well as explaining the causes, nature and degree of the pain/distress observed.

Pain – human and animal parallels

Pain is a natural, and frequently beneficial, experience of humans and animals alike. Pain prompts even the most basic of living organisms to withdraw from noxious stimuli, or teach individuals the lessons that will be essential for survival in the future. Leading behaviourists have recognised that it is the balance of pleasure and pain (e.g., underlying systems of reward and punishment) that represent a normal, and frequently essential, aspect of life for any living creature.

Eighteenth-century publications demonstrate the early introduction of qualifiers regarding pain. Primatt, for example, wrote 'pain is pain, whether it be inflicted on man or beast'.[36] Most people understandably associate 'pain' as something that they would prefer to avoid altogether. The recognition where pain is beneficial provides a useful starting point: For the realistic objective is not to avoid all pain, but to minimise unnecessary pain. With the law, like the realities identified in the life sciences benchmarks, it is not the complete absence of pain, but the minimisation of 'unnecessary' or 'unreasonable' pain that is the essential consideration in respect of responsibly looking after the individual's interests (whether that 'individual' be human or animal), and balancing the interests of the individual with the best interests of society as a whole.

Many people agree on the legal definition, but are uncomfortable about clarifying the difference between the terms 'pain' and 'distress' – that includes even the experts. Veterinary professionals, for example, widely promote themselves as the 'animal health and welfare experts'. Animal welfare legislation supports this view, given the veterinarian is the only professional specifically referred to in animal welfare legislation. The law officially expects veterinarians to demonstrate the knowledge and integrity for making potentially key assessments regarding an animal's pain or distress, including whether or not it is possible to treat an animal or necessary to euthanase it. On this basis, it isn't uncommon for attending veterinarians to be called upon as expert witnesses in legal proceedings considering whether or not criminal animal welfare offending has occurred. Yet many involved in enforcement are surprised to note that a number of veterinarians demonstrate difficulty in clearly or authoritatively distinguishing concepts of pain and distress, or for that matter clearly and credibly classifying a basis of categorising acts and/or omissions as either 'unnecessary' and/or 'unreasonable'.

---

36 Humphrey Primatt. 1776. *A Dissertation on the Duty of Mercy and Sin of Cruelty to Brute Animals* (London): Google Books: Online Library of Free eBooks.

96 *National animal welfare law*

Defining pain

While it is acknowledged that assessments of pain in humans are not without their challenges, the fact remains that one of the simplest ways to determine whether a human being is experiencing pain or not, is simply to ask them. By contrast, assessing the presence, location and degree of pain in animals is much more difficult.

In general terms, pain may be broadly described as an 'unpleasant' sensory stimulus which results in the recipient withdrawing from the painful stimulus. However, there's more to considerations of pain than simply withdrawal from a noxious stimulus – even unicellular organisms will withdraw from a noxious stimulus. Assessments regarding the nature and degree of pain must extend beyond simplistic questions of whether, or not, an animal can experience pain.

For an animal to be classified as experiencing 'pain', additional elements need to be considered. Evidence of a nervous system and sensory receptors, physiological shifts in response to noxious stimuli, and external reactions (i.e., clinical signs, behavioural responses) are some of the scientific references for determining whether or not a species/animal experienced pain. Ancillary tests (e.g., blood tests, biopsies, post-mortems) in conjunction with assessment of records (e.g., production records) are additional tools that assist in determining whether or not an animal experienced pain/distress, and if so, the nature and degree of the pain/distress experienced. To serve the law, all of these materials (commonly referred to in law as either evidence and/or exhibits) may be produced in Court.

It is common for definitions of pain to be restricted to disease states or physical conditions that cause tissue damage.[37] These definitions obviously focus on the physical appearance of the animal involved. But pain is not limited simply to physical injuries. Individuals can experience 'emotional' pain too.[38]

Not everyone agrees that animals experience 'emotions', despite the fact that many people who have had interactions with animals would have no problem ascribing emotions to animals (e.g., fear, anxiety, happiness and contentedness). Others believe that attributing human emotions to animals is simply being overly anthropomorphic. As a result, some definitions used to describe pain in animals avoid reference to emotional states and, for example, define pain as 'an aversive sensory experience caused by actual or potential injury that elicits protective motor and vegetative reactions, results in learned avoidance and may modify species-specific behaviour, including social behaviour'.[39]

---

37 International Association for the Study of Pain: Pain Definitions (cited 10 September 2011). 'Pain is an unpleasant sensory and emotional experience associated with actual or potential tissue damage, or described in terms of such damage', derived from J.J. Bonica. 1979. 'The Need of Taxonomy', *Pain*, 6(3): 247–8: www.iasp_pain.org/AM/Template.cfm?Section=Pain_Defi . . . isplay.cfm&ContentID=1728.

38 B. Lynn. 1984. 'Cutaneous Nociceptors', in W. Winlow and A.V. Holden (eds), *The Neurobiology of Pain: Symposium of the Northern Neurobiology Group, held at Leeds on 18 April 1983* (Manchester: Manchester University Press), p. 106.

39 M. Zimmerman. 1986. 'Physiological Mechanisms of Pain and its Treatment', *Klinische Anaesthesiol Intensivether*, 32: 1–19.

National animal welfare law   97

Despite the demonstrated reluctance by certain people to describe an animal's pain by reference to people's pain, the fact remains that by legislating against the infliction of unnecessary and/or unreasonable pain in animals, the law demonstrates that it accepts that animals are prima facie capable of feeling pain.

The similarities between animals and humans underpin their continued use in activities such as research. Pain, and the prevention/minimisation of it, is well researched in humans because people are understandably highly motivated to avoid pain. Analogies to human experience are commonly referred to in the Courts to help understand the animal's experience. Accepting that they experience pain in similar ways to human beings, also leads to recognition that there are different types of pain.

Immediate injury, for example, may result in observable signs of an animal being in pain. Some species appear to make attempts to mask these clinical signs, theoretically on the grounds that external signs exhibiting pain potentially attract the attention of would-be predators; however, immediate injury usually results in observable signs that an animal is in pain. Physical manifestations (e.g., limping), vocal sounds (whimpering or crying or groaning), or simply a change and demeanour (the animal is described as 'quiet') have all been terms used by owners, and observed by veterinary clinicians. Additional signs and physiological references may be used to identify the presence and degree of pain including, for example, changes in heart rate, respiratory rate, temperature, production rates, and results to standard laboratory tests.

Acute pain is widely described as pain that is either of a short duration and/ or varying intensity. The animal's ability to cope with the injury and the ensuing pain will naturally vary depending on the nature of the injury itself. For example, a relatively minor wood splinter in the paw is likely to result in less pain than a broken leg. The response of different species, and different individuals within the same species, may vary enormously.

Chronic pain is usually regarded as a condition which persists over a prolonged period of time. Chronic pain has been described as much more insidious and generally has greater significance in terms of welfare assessments. It is not simply a longer version of acute pain, it actually represents conditions which potentially have a much more extensive and detrimental effect on the animal's physiology, behaviour and consequent physical and mental states. It is relevant that the presence, or absence, of symptoms cannot be relied upon to determine whether or not an animal is experiencing pain, or whether or not there are significant welfare problems. For example, on-farm assessments of potential welfare problems commonly requires whole-of-farm reviews that examine farm infrastructure, stockmanship skills and capabilities, feed supply, and the physical environment, in addition to matters pertaining to the animals' health and body condition. This approach imputes responsibility on the assessor, and the legally responsible human care-giver, to fulfil their legislative welfare responsibilities by more than simply looking for obvious signs of pain.

98 *National animal welfare law*

Distinguishing stress from distress

Stress involves a state where the animal is coping, albeit with biological or physiological shifts/responses in order to enable it to cope. All animals, including humans, experience a degree of stress. Stress may elicit a variety of biological and physiological responses, many of which are recognised as being beneficial to the individual (e.g., fight-or-flight responses), and well within the individual's capacity to cope. The appearance of a dog in the backyard may cause distress, for example, to the family cat, but provided the cat is able to escape or safely ensconced inside the house behind the window, then the cat is unlikely to experience significant physiological detriment. Similarly, the family dog with a larger-than-life appetite may experience a certain amount of stress at not being fed quite as much as he would prefer, but he is unlikely to suffer any significant physiological consequences from being fed only as much as he needs.

Stress is significantly different from distress. Circumstances may occur where the stress is sufficiently high that the individual's system is unable to cope. 'Distress' is a term used to describe a state where the cumulative effects of biological or physiological costs/stresses, either singularly or cumulatively, results in the individual being unable to cope and detrimental effects on an individual.

Distress is an exacerbated state of stress, whereby the individual's physiological mechanism becomes unable to respond or function normally. Various definitions and descriptors have been used to describe distress, each reflecting the discipline and/or purpose of their provider. For example, the Australian Code of Practice for the Care and Use of Animals described distress as 'Acute or chronic response of an animal caused by stimuli that produce biological stress which produces observable, abnormal physiological or behavioural responses'.

Moberg distinguishes 'stress' and 'distress' in biological terms, by stating 'Stress is the biological response elicited when an animal perceives a threat to its homeostasis.'[40] The nature of this response varies between individuals and is influenced by previous experience, genetics, age, physiological status, environment and season. The result is an alteration of the animal's normal biological functioning as it attempts to adapt or to cope with the stressor. Consequently, alterations may be seen in behavioural responses (e.g., movement of the animal away from threatened response, postural changes), the autonomic nervous system response (e.g., changes in heart rate, blood pressure, gastrointestinal activity); neuro-endocrine and/or production responses (e.g., failed reproduction, altered metabolism); and/or competency of immune responses which may, for example, result in increased incidence of disease.

Evidence that an animal has experienced pain and/or distress is not in and of itself sufficient to establish that an offence has been committed. The second part of the test requires that it must be proved that any pain and/or distress experienced by the animal was either unnecessary or unreasonable.

---

40 G.P. Moberg. 2000. 'Biological Response to Stress: Implications for Animal Welfare' in G.P. Moberg and J.A. Mench (eds), *The Biology of Animal Stress* (Wallingford: CAB International), pp. 1–21.

Test 2: was the animal's suffering 'unnecessary' or 'unreasonable'?

Defining 'unnecessary' and/or 'unreasonable'

The concept of what constitutes 'unnecessary or unreasonable' in respect of an animal's pain or distress is central to considerations of legal determinations regarding animal cruelty. It underpins the offences related to the roles of animals and human society (e.g., transportation, slaughter, agribusiness and research), and debates reflecting frequently polarised opinions about animals.

Despite varying opinions on what is necessary or not, the incorporation of an offence based on causing (by an act or an omission) 'unnecessary or unreasonable pain and/or distress' to an animal has undoubtedly been enormously beneficial in the development of animal protection.

Mirroring the consistent objective to minimise an animal's pain or distress, it may be said that the law's test of 'necessity' is met if there is a sufficiently beneficial (largely utilitarian) reason for the pain and/or distress of an animal. This same principle applies not just to animals but also to people, where the freedoms provided to an individual and the law, are also balanced by responsibilities to wider society.

The consistent thread through animal protection is a consideration to preventing an animal from experiencing 'unnecessary or unreasonable' pain and/or distress. However, determinations of what is considered 'necessary' vary considerably, according to the circumstances of the animal concerned which, in turn, have a bearing on the responsibilities of the human care-giver.

For example, the same animal may experience different levels of protection depending upon the circumstances in which it is kept. This can be illustrated by imagining a single hen which is the subject of legal protections if it is kept as a family pet, but may have no protections whatsoever if it is kept in a commercial operation. Similarly, an individual rabbit may be the subject of protections under the law if it is kept as a pet, but the same animal may be subjected to tests in the name of research that would otherwise be an offence. The same rabbit may be killed as a pest if it is in the wild and constituting a threat to other interests, such as agribusiness.

Circumstances such as these have given rise to the claim that the law is schizophrenic in respect of animals. It would be more balanced, and objective, to recognise that this diversity of treatment and protection simply reflects the reality that the law protecting animals has been developed on an ad hoc basis that has traditionally reflected the purposes, and therefore the circumstances, to which animals have been put, rather than their species. The law functions by firstly establishing benchmark criteria regarding standards of human responsibility regarding the care and treatment of animals (i.e., prevent unnecessary and unreasonable pain and/or distress of animals), then qualifies that responsibility in terms of the circumstances of the animal, particularly its use and associated dependency on its human care-giver.

100 *National animal welfare law*

It is noteworthy that the obligations on the human care-giver also vary according to the species, environment and circumstances (e.g., purposes) in which the animal is kept. Using the same example of a rabbit, the pet rabbit is protected under legislation from blatant acts of cruelty. Its owner has a duty to provide for the animal's needs. In contrast, if the same rabbit was used for research purposes, then the obligations on the laboratory owner are comparatively much more stringent. Similarly, eradication schemes in agribusiness are the subject of a vast array of decision-making criteria and regulations. In short, the degree and nature of legal protection attached to an animal depends significantly on the circumstances in which it is located, and demonstrates that the law's substantive consideration on the purpose/use of the animal and its correlating dependency on the human care-giver, rather than simply its species.

The issue usually centres on what is 'necessary'

Unsurprisingly, different stakeholders will have differing perceptions about what is necessary. Leading animal welfare legislation provides a prescriptive list of considerations for the Court in determining whether or not pain and/or distress experienced by an animal was necessary (Animal Welfare Act 2006). These include consideration of:

- whether the pain and/or distress could reasonably have been avoided or reduced;
- whether the conduct which caused pain and/or distress complied with any relevant law, relevant licence, or code of practice;
- whether the conduct that caused pain and/or distress was authorised for a legitimate purpose (e.g., benefiting the animal, protecting a person, property, or another animal);
- whether the pain and/or distress experienced by the animal was proportionate to the purpose of the conduct; and
- whether the conduct was, in consideration of all the circumstances, that of a reasonably competent and humane person.[41]

The list, while comprehensive, is not an exhaustive inventory of considerations to which the Court may have regard. Furthermore, the list of considerations applies what has been viewed by some as a third-person test. In addition to determining whether or not the animals suffered, and subsequently whether or not the pain and/or distress was necessary (in the sense that the pain and/or distress was inevitable), then the law considers whether a reasonably competent and humane person (sometimes referred to as the 'reasonable man') would have tolerated the animal's pain and/or distress?[42]

---

41 Section 4 Animal Welfare Act 2006 (England and Wales).
42 Radford, *Animal Welfare Law in Britain*, p. 252: this three-tiered test was recognised prior to the advent of the Animal Welfare Act 2006 (England and Wales), and the concept is illustrated in section 4(3)(e) of the Animal Welfare Act 2006 (England and Wales).

National animal welfare law   101

It's worth noting that the offence of causing an animal to suffer unnecessary or unreasonable pain and/or distress can be the result of an act, or an omission (to act) by a person. Furthermore, it is not a fundamental requirement that the person knew that the act, or failure to act, would result in unnecessary or unreasonable pain and/or distress of the animal. Liability can attach if the Court determined that the person knew, 'or ought reasonably to have known' that the animal would suffer as a result of the person's act or omission. If the relevant legislation creates a strict liability offence[43] in respect of animal welfare offending, and the prosecution shows that the person was prima facie guilty, then the defendant subsequently has the onus of proof[44] to show the Court that they complied with existing legislative defences.

How subjective is '(un)necessary' through the legal lens?

Opinions vary on whether the Courts and the legislators have got it 'right', irrespective of the criteria that have been almost prescriptively set out. The term 'unnecessary' has attracted criticism by a number of people on the basis that the term is inherently changeable and consequently allows a very subjective viewpoint. Criticism has suggested that the lack of definition leaves Courts without clear direction. It alleges that Courts are overly reliant on scientific interpretations to guide their decisions. Critics claim that legislative and judicial claims of objectivity and independence are, as a result, unreliable.

The counter-argument to these criticisms is that such arguments miss the point of having the term 'necessary' as a deciding legal criteria attached to determinations of animal welfare offending. The criticisms demonstrate a common 'straw man' argumentative approach, which concentrates and undermines one element, whilst ignoring the wider picture. The fact is that the Courts are not solely reliant on science, any more than they are forced to rely on just one witness, or one expert, or one version of events. In determining what currently constitutes 'good practice and sound science'[45] the Courts take account of multiple factors which include relevant facts, evidence and the wider circumstances. Judges have considerable personal experience and skills in distinguishing relevant admissible evidence from views that are less credible, reliable, or truthful. Judicial findings include both objective and subjective commentary. Adjudicators in the Court have some latitude. However, this should not be construed as meaning that adjudicators are unfettered in their decisions. The reality is that adjudicators, despite potentially varying personal opinions, also have an obligation to follow guidelines in respect of their judgments and sentencing decisions. Similarly,

---

43 See, for example, section 13(1) of the New Zealand Animal Welfare Act 1999, which states that 'it is not necessary for the prosecution to prove that the defendant intended to commit an offence'.

44 'Onus of proof' is a legal expression that identifies which person/party to a proceedings has the responsibility for providing proof to address the legal issues in question.

45 See, for example, section 10 of the New Zealand Animal Welfare Act 1999.

102 *National animal welfare law*

lawyers presenting their case to Court, are equally bound to comply with legal principles and professional guidelines. The prosecution, for example, in cases of alleged criminal animal welfare offending, have an obligation to evidentially prove 'beyond reasonable doubt' that firstly, the animals did indeed suffer (or experience pain or distress), and secondly, that the pain and/or distress was either unnecessary or unreasonable.

The notion of what is or is not unnecessary varies according more than simply law and science. Other factors include cultural differences, public awareness and political integrity.

Different stakeholders have different drivers, opinions and agendas which inform their concept of what is 'necessary'

While food production remains the primary use of animals, in a comparatively small number of legal jurisdictions, standard practices for animals raised in industrial 'factory farming' conditions are also being questioned. The size of commercial hen cages, sow stalls in pig production systems, and veal crates, are examples of agricultural practices which have been the subject of legal challenge and change. In assessing what is necessary, and distinguishing that from what is unnecessary or unreasonable and by inference, what is unlawful, the judiciary, by reference to the relevant law, applies a decision-making process that demonstrates a legal rigour.

Assessment of the almost prescriptive list of considerations that exist in jurisdictions with leading animal welfare law demonstrates that there is a considered logic in respect of assessment in judging whether the pain and/or distress experienced by an animal was 'necessary', or not. Recognising the logic is valuable in responding to frequently subjective opinions that may disagree with, for example, sentencing outcomes, or other matters involving legal protection of animals. Proponents will often disagree on how a particular stakeholder interest should be prioritised. Certainly, many non-government organisations that are active in the area of animal protection, advocate improved standards that benefit the animal. In comparison, industry has often been described as prioritising profit, which underpins their activities such as marketing and animal husbandry on the basis that higher standards of animal welfare generally translate into better production per animal, and a marketable point of difference to a cheering and safety conscious public. By contrast, the government has the responsibility for establishing and enforcing standards of animal welfare which apply a broadly utilitarian approach to ensure a functioning society. As a consequence, while promoting standards of the best practice, compliance and enforcement activities benchmark 'minimum (legal) standards'. These three elements illustrate how different stakeholders involved in matters of animal welfare have different drivers, and aspirations.

One common thread running through all this is that the government will always be an important stakeholder in any issue of animal protection. It has the responsibility of balancing and prioritising the interests of all other stakeholders.

National animal welfare law   103

Critics remonstrate that this state of affairs demonstrates inconsistency and a lack of clarity in the law. But the law's underlying logic becomes clear when each situation is considered in terms of the degree of dependency (of the particular animal) on the human care-giver for its needs. Obviously, the reliance of a dog which is kept as a household pet, is significantly different to those of a similar animal living in the wild (e.g., a wolf). Similarly, the circumstances/purposes of a pig or chicken kept as an individual animal on a lifestyle block may be significantly different than another pig or chicken raised in a commercial environment.

Balancing considerations of 'currently lawful' with the views of what is 'morally right'

Western principles of liberty and freedom mean that people can largely do what they choose unless restricted by law. For example, in terms of criminal law and animal protections, it is not necessary for individuals or companies to be able to point to express legal authority for treating or using animals in a particular way, so long as the practice is not deemed unlawful.

If not prohibited by law, a practice will generally be considered lawful, and hence, by implication, 'legitimate'.[46] This inference is potentially problematic in that it provides a seductive basis for subjective arguments suggesting that 'if it's not legally wrong, then it must be morally right – or at least, acceptable'. This is a flawed reasoning. It overlooks concepts of what is morally acceptable in the shifting tides of public opinion.

Sometimes the law shifts perceptions of what is acceptable to the majority of the voting public, and sometimes it's vice versa. What is morally acceptable to the majority of the public changes, illustrated by changes in perception of issues such as slavery, prostitution, homosexuality, abortion, alcohol and smoking. Concepts about what is acceptable or not in respect of animal treatment are included in that list.

It is important to note that in a democratic society, the law allegedly reflects the majority view, rather than all views regarding what is right or wrong. Consequently, rather than inferring that because a practice is lawful it is therefore morally right, it would be more accurate to state that a lawful practice implies that the practice is morally acceptable 'to the majority' 'at the time'.

Understanding these principles explains why the law, in taking account of the interests of all stakeholders, might be seen as immoral to certain people who, at the time, do not represent the prevailing majority view.

Consider the practice of using traps and snares to capture and kill animals. Public opinion varies on many aspects regarding the use of such devices, including their design, the species they should be used on, and the obligations attached to their use. The regulatory process of assessing and eventually prohibiting a particular trapping device on the basis that it is cruel is potentially a protracted process. At first glance, it might appear that because of the difficulty in monitoring the range of devices and humane use of the traps by their operators, a total

---

46 Radford, *Animal Welfare Law in Britain*, p. 113.

104   *National animal welfare law*

ban on traps might be more effective in ensuring protection for animals. The total ban would make interpretation regarding the use of traps much easier, and prevent the development of new traps that were potentially cruel – but animals are not the only stakeholder to the decision, and banning traps would disadvantage an entire industry that has had public sanction for years. Consequently, the more protracted regulatory process remains necessary to balance the interests of all stakeholders.

Similar principles apply to various practices in the agricultural industry. A number of widely used practices (e.g., veal crates, sow stalls, hen cages) have attracted criticism and, with time, have been banned or modified in a number of jurisdictions. For those advocating the ban of various practices, the time period to implement the prohibitionary law may appear inordinately long, but again, there are wider considerations to be taken into account. This includes, for example, the farmer, who may have made a considerable financial investment in equipment which was, initially, lawful on the basis that it was not at the time of installation unlawful.

Legislative exemptions exist in certain circumstances, where conduct that would normally be viewed as a legal offence, is not illegal, provided that the treatment complies with prescribed and authorised standards. The use of animals in research, for example, is an obvious example. Similarly, a number of animal husbandry practices that occur in agribusiness (e.g., debeaking of birds, tail docking in pigs) would be deemed unlawful and cruel if those same practices were applied to pet animals.

Despite the fact that the use of a certain device or practice may attract criticism or dispute, the people using the practice or device are, under the law, able to go about their business relatively unhindered. This position is consistent with Western concepts of liberty and freedom, which hold that every practice is permitted unless specifically prohibited by law.

Provided that the animal does not suffer unreasonable or unnecessary pain or distress, then this principle broadly applies in respect of animal uses including agriculture, sports, entertainment and the wider variety of roles that animals have in human society; clearly, this has very practical implications for aspects of animal protection.

Death is not necessarily a singularly determinative indication of unnecessary or unreasonable pain and/or distress

Relevant to the discussion of unnecessary or unreasonable pain and/or distress is the fact that it is not unlawful to kill an animal,[47] provided that it is done in a lawful manner. The method of killing is a key consideration for the law, and is consistent with the law's approach that, whether the killing of an animal is lawful or not, revolves significantly (although not exclusively) around the obligation to ensure that animals do not suffer unnecessary or unreasonable pain or distress.

---

47 Naturally, this excludes species which may be protected by legislation, e.g., endangered species. Bats, whales, dolphins, and certain species of reptiles, fish, amphibians and insects, for example, may be considered protected species.

National animal welfare law 105

The death of an animal is not prima facie evidence that the animal has suffered. It may be an indicator that unlawful treatment of an animal has resulted in an animal's death as a consequence, but determinations of unlawfulness, and whether or not the animal suffered, relies on the relevant law, and the relevance, admissibility and weight of the evidence.

The Court will have to consider all the circumstances in determining whether or not an offence has been committed, and may require consideration to the species of animal involved, the methodology used, and individual circumstances of the people involved. For example, after an attack by the neighbour's dog on his child, the father of the child entered his neighbour's property and cut the throat of the dog. Although this act was likely to result in charges being laid for offences (e.g., trespass), the act in itself did not constitute an animal welfare offence when the evidence identified that the individual who killed the dog was a professional slaughterman at the local abattoir, and the evidence, including testimony from expert witnesses, could not demonstrate 'beyond reasonable doubt' that the animal suffered. Death in itself is not considered to be a welfare issue, but the manner in which the animal died will be relevant.

The law focuses on human 'responsibility' in order to deliver welfare for animals

Should animals continue to be legally classified as property? The question of how law defines property is a central issue to past and present animal protection debates, given that although legislation has implemented enormous changes regarding how animals can be treated, animals are still traditionally categorised as 'property'.

In response to a question that asks 'how *should* animals be treated', it is valuable for the reader to observe that, in the first instance, the word 'should' inherently invites subjective opinions which vary enormously between people according to strongly divergent religious, cultural and/or philosophical/moral roots.

By this stage, the reader will recognise the drivers that shape people's subjective opinions and that polarised personal opinions are often flagged by the use of the words 'should' and 'shouldn't'. Consequently, the responses to the question of whether or not the legal categorisation of animals as property 'should/shouldn't' be changed, are often driven by both varying opinions and interests.

'Animals are property' is touted by those promoting their own views of necessary changes as 'the highest hurdle for animal advocates to clear'.[48] In contrast, others advocate that animals gain sufficient and *practical* protection in their daily lives by maintaining their property status,[49] on the basis that one of the universal strengths

---

48 B.A. Wagman, S.S. Waisman and P.D. Frasch. 2009. *Animal Law: Cases and Materials*, 4th edn (Durham, NC: Carolina Academic Press), p. 73.

49 H. Landemore. 2005. 'Why should One Reject the Motion Intending to Remove Animals from the Status of Property?', in M.D. Hauser, F. Cushman, and M. Kamen (eds), *People, Property, or Pets? (New Directions in the Human-Animal Bond)* (West Lafayette, IN: Purdue University Press), p. 65.

106 *National animal welfare law*

of the law is in its focus on what can and cannot be done with property. In terms of international law and its potential benefits for animal protections, the legal concepts of property also provide commonality between different legal jurisdictions.

The legal status as 'property' does have potential drawbacks for the animals.[50] For example, the owner's right to destroy the animal may result in it being put to sleep irrespective of considerations to the animal's health or alternative options such as the possibility of re-homing. Commercial uses of animals have also attracted significant attention and concerns have been expressed that animals may be too readily viewed as just another commodity, and that their welfare is compromised as a consequence of competitive pressures and business imperatives.[51]

How effective is animal welfare law?

This question raises at least two issues for consideration: The first issue is whether or not leading animal welfare legislation deals with each of the drawbacks just referred to. Does animal welfare legislation apply legal protections to animals in commercial operations? Leading animal welfare legislation provides a broad definition of an animal. So, provided that animals in commercial operations fall under the legal definition of an animal and do not fall outside of the legal protections due to some other legislative exemption, then the law's recognition of animals as animate property results in legal responsibilities being broadly applied to people and organisations who have animals in their care. Contemporary animal welfare law creates a very broad net of legal responsibility that attaches not just to the immediate care-giver ('person in charge') and owner (of the animals). In addition, legislatively defined vicarious liability extends legal responsibilities to managers, directors, employers and other people who may not have a hands-on interaction with the animal, but whose acts, omissions and decisions none the less affect an animal's welfare.[52]

One of the obvious practical advantages of extending this liability to wider decision makers is that it reduces the risk of animal's welfare being compromised to unacceptably low standards for the purposes of profit or other business interests. Undoubtedly, commercial operations utilising animals have the objective of being profitable like any business, but the broad net of legal responsibility and liability, means that consideration of the animal's welfare (i.e., protection from unnecessary and unreasonable pain or distress) is prioritised alongside other business objectives.

The second issue is that it is a matter of opinion whether or not the drawbacks referred to by advocates for dismantling the legal property status of animals, would actually be overcome by changing their legal status.

---

50 Radford, *Animal Welfare Law in Britain*, p. 103.

51 Ibid.

52 See, for example, sections 164 and 165 of the New Zealand Animal Welfare Act 1999. Similarly, section 3 of the Animal Welfare Act 2006 (England and Wales) applies a broad interpretation to the definition of those who have 'responsibility for animals'.

National animal welfare law 107

The American lawyer Gary Francione has consistently argued that animals can never be fully protected while they continue to be viewed as property under the law. Francione states that 'the property status of animals means that their interests will virtually always be ignored whenever it will benefit humans and despite the many laws that supposedly protect animals'.[53] Francione argues strongly in favour of giving animals a 'right not to be treated as . . . property'. In contrast, English lawyer Mike Radford brings balance and real-world pragmatism to the debate by pointing out that the reality is that 'rights are seldom absolute' and 'where the application of one right is incompatible with that of another, something has to give'. Radford goes on to state that 'Leaving aside the difficult question of which animals will be accorded what rights, . . . it is by no means clear that the concept of rights is the panacea to animals as [Francione] has suggested.'[54] An alternative approach to the legal property status of animals has been suggested by American legal academic, David Favre, who has suggested a form of equitable self-ownership for animals that uses legal concepts of guardianship.[55]

Although these novel approaches to animal protection may be persuasive to the American judicial system, it is questionable whether approaches posed by the likes of US academics like Favre and Francione would ever be adopted in legal jurisdictions that operate under the principles of Westminster law. This is because, in contrast to the relationship between the Courts and the state and federal legislators in the United States, jurisdictions following the principles of Westminster law place the Courts in a subordinate position to central government, thereby prohibiting radical changes, such as a change in the legal status of particular species.

The current reality is that for the time being, animals remain legally classified as property. The enactment of animal welfare legislation which limits traditional notions of owners' rights in relation to their property, is arguably evidence of legislative recognition of a difference between animate vs inanimate objects. The difference is due, of course, to the unique nature of the 'property' itself. Consequently, some traditionalist lawyers have found it easier to comprehend the breadth of animal law as a discipline when it's explained as being 'specialist property law'.

Legal categorisation of animals as property is a distraction to the real issue of practical animal protection

The debates about the legal property status of animals is potentially a 'distraction' to the *real* issues of *practical* animal protection. Where standards of animal 'welfare' have been implemented, then in practical terms, the animals' well-being is not limited by its legal status as property, but by initiatives including public education, collaboration (e.g., between industry and government) and adequate

---

53 Francione, 'Animals, Property and Personhood', p. 77.
54 Radford, *Animal Welfare Law in Britain*, p. 103.
55 David Favre, 'Equitable Self-Ownership for Animals', *Duke Law Journal*, 50(2000): 473–502: http://scholarship.law.duke.edu/dlj/vol50/iss2/2.

108 *National animal welfare law*

resources for effective compliance and enforcement. In short, it's about creating a legal framework that requires citizens and nations to be responsible in respect of animal treatment.

Guardianship debates

The Guardianship Campaign began as a well-intended initiative to shift historical attitudes regarding animals as property. The implementation of guardian in lieu of owner has already been enacted in selected US jurisdictions, and is consistent with wider agendas seeking to implement legal personhood, standing and/or alternatives to property-based legal categorisation.

Its proponents view the shift as primarily symbolic and having an educative function, raising awareness about animal care and elevating the status of animals in human society. Opponents recognise the power of changing a word in law. Dictionary definitions may differ from legal definitions, not just in terms of meaning but also in respect of obligations, duties and penalties.

The legal term 'guardian' defines a person lawfully invested with the power, and charged with a legal duty, of caring for another individual by managing their person, property and legal interests. It is a fiduciary relationship. It obligates the guardian to consistently act in the best interests of their ward, and possibly be removed from office on grounds of failure to perform their duties in a suitable manner, or demonstrating a lack of capacity or having a conflict of interests with their ward's interests. There are several types of legal guardian which vary according to the manner of the appointment and the subject of the guardianship. In law, the fiduciary 'guardian' is distinctively different in terms of duties, rights, responsibilities and accountabilities than an 'owner' – despite well-intended and commonly interchanged use of both words in a non-legal context.

Well-intended initiatives implementing a legal-guardian status risk unintended legal consequences. These include derogation of owners' accountability, liability and ultimately responsibility for an animal's care. Understandably, these issues become particularly pertinent in circumstances where multiple parties and lines of accountability are involved and subsequently blurred. For example, governance of stray dog/cat programmes – as well as industry, agriculture and almost every profession, business and individual, with current activities involving animals – would be affected if the guardian was implemented in place of ownership. Even the seemingly obvious and simplest use of animals for companionship raises questions about the authority/responsibility of people to attend to the health care and costs of animals in their care. Other issues arise in a public safety-conscious society; neutering, confinement, muzzling, or euthanasing/slaughtering, adopting, transporting, and consuming are just some of the issues that a ward – or legal counsel acting for the ward – might question on the basis of whether or not the practice is really in the ward's best interests.

To minimise foreseeable societal disruptions that accompany the shift to guardianship requires distinctions in species, uses and responsibilities that require revised systems of compliance and enforcement, which in turn demands considerable

National animal welfare law 109

attention to the age-old question in animal law about where to draw the line? For example, which animals would have guardians and which would have owners?

Creative use of animals' property status

Consequently, creative lawyering that *uses* the property status of animals (rather than anguishes about it) continues to be the preferred current paradigm to further avoid the inherent conflict and confusion associated with novel but potentially problematic concepts of animal rights or self-guardianship. To the extent that the creative use of the property status leads to positive change, it is ultimately helpful to animals and humans alike.

An additional consideration notes that methodical approaches that advocate incremental steps based on sound law are likely to be more palatable to key decision makers such as the Courts and legislatures, and more consistent with wider drivers such as the realities of international trading. US Federal Judge Posner, for example, states 'There is a sad poverty of imagination in an approach to animal protection that can think of it only on the model of the civil rights movement.'[56] He states that it is a 'mistaken' view 'to think that the best way to prevent (animal) cruelty is to treat chimpanzees like human beings'.[57] Posner counsels that questions pertaining to animal welfare would be better served by an approach that is 'more conservative, methodologically as well as politically, but possibly more efficacious, than rights mongering'.[58]

This concept advocating 'responsibilities' regarding animals is reflected in Joel Feinberg's distinction between animal rights and animal welfare, identifying that animal welfare is about legal duties 'regarding' animals, distinguished from concepts of animal rights which advocate that people should have legal obligations 'to' animals. This succinctly captures the substantive difference between concepts of animal welfare versus animal rights.

A key principle in understanding animal welfare and the law is that the law reflects a scale of human 'responsibility' regarding animals and correlating legal protections of animals and human liabilities, depending on the use of the animal and its reliance on its human care-giver(s). Those considerations reflect that the 'real' issue is about governing people's 'responsibilities' regarding animals, which in turn provides a useful reference for consideration of law's development that focuses on the responsibility to protect animals from unnecessary and/or unreasonable pain and distress.

Recalling the three elements distinguishing animal law as a legal discipline,[59] element number two of 'animal law' reflects this principle in that the law recognises

---

56 C.R. Sunstein and M.C. Nussbaum (eds). 2006. *Animal Rights: Current Debates and New Directions* (Oxford: Oxford University Press), p. 58.
57 Ibid., p. 59.
58 Ibid.
59 Law that deals with an animal, recognises the unique nature of an animal as animate property, and the inseparable relationship between animal and human interests.

110 *National animal welfare law*

animals as unique property because animals are capable of experiencing pain and distress. The very definition of an animal supports this interpretation by the fact that legal protections begin when an animal, based on science, is first able to experience pain (i.e., 'any mammalian foetus, or any avian or reptilian pre-hatched young, that is in the last half of its period of gestation or development'[60]) and finishes when the animal is dead (and, the implication is, unable to experience pain). Between these two points in an animal's life and death, animal protection/welfare legislation obliges people to minimise an animal's pain and distress to lawfully prescribed standards. Failure to do so constitutes a legal offence.

Understanding 'offences' in terms of human responsibility

To understand the liabilities which attach to criminal offences, it is very helpful to think of the offences as breaches of legislatively established human 'responsibilities'.

By definition a legal offence is an act/omission (i.e., doing something which is forbidden, or omitting to do something that is required), which breaches a standard or code established by the law. The law broadly defines the 'who, what, when, where, how' of acts or omissions that are consistent with the law's stated objective/purpose (i.e., the 'why') of protecting animals from unnecessary and/or unreasonable pain and/or distress.

While those involved with animals all share a responsibility to protect the animals in their care from unnecessary and unreasonable pain or distress, the standards attaching to what is considered reasonable or necessary may vary. For example, a person who may have primary liability applies to a person who is directly responsible for an animal (e.g., the person who has responsibility for day-to-day care of an animal). In contrast, legal concepts of 'vicarious' liability often applied to those who may not have physical day-to-day contact with animals, but whose decisions none the less affect the day-to-day care of the animals involved. Employers, principals and corporate officials are examples of people/roles where vicarious legal responsibilities/liabilities may apply.

Elements of offending

Each offence has its constituent parts, known as the 'elements' of an offence. These are commonly categorised as either physical elements ('*actus reus*', literally translated as the 'guilty act') or mental elements ('*mens rea*', which refers to the 'guilty mind').

Actus reus

Actus reus is a term that refers to the prohibited conduct, and generally takes into account the external elements of alleged offending, including the circumstances and

---

60 Section 2 New Zealand Animal Welfare Act 1999.

consequences that together made the act an offence/crime. It is usually accepted that for an action to constitute an offence, the defendant's act must be voluntary. Consequently, determinations of liability take into account an individual's abilities, in addition to the circumstances. Autism, and compulsion, and reflex actions (e.g., being stung by a bee while driving) are examples of where the defendant's act might be viewed as the defendant having limited, or no, control over their actions.

An 'act' logically involves *doing* something, such as beating dairy cows with an iron bar. An 'omission' refers to the failure to fulfil a specific legal obligation, such as the care-giver or person who has the responsibility to care for them failing to provide proper and sufficient food to the animals.

Strict liability offending

Offences that are termed 'strict liability' apply to circumstances where there has been a guilty act (*actus reus*) and an identified consequence, but the defendant didn't know about, or intend for the consequence. Strict liability holds that the crime has been committed despite the fact that there was a lack of a guilty mind (*mens rea*). 'Absolute liability' is a term referring to circumstances where an offence requires no *mens rea* and the *actus reus* need not be voluntary. In practical terms, this means that it doesn't matter whether the defendant meant to commit an offence or not.

This is consistent with one of the primary purposes of animal welfare legislation – to ensure that people who own or who are in charge of animals properly fulfil their legal duty to look after the welfare of the animals in their care. This includes a responsibility to take all reasonable steps to ensure that the animal's physical, health and behavioural needs are met according to good practice and scientific knowledge, and wherever practical, ensure that animals in their care receive treatment to alleviate any unreasonable or unnecessary pain or distress.

Many of today's animal welfare offences are identified as strict liability offences.[61] Once the facts of the matter are proven, then in strict liability offending, the burden of proof then shifts to the defendant to prove that the offending was either not their fault, or committed in circumstances where there was/is an available legislative defence.

In the absence of the defendant proving that they met the criteria of a legislatively provided defence, then strict liability holds that the perpetrator is guilty of an offence whether they acted (or failed to act) intentionally or inadvertently. The circumstances of the offending may be considered by the Court as part of the subsequent sentencing and applied penalties.

---

61 A strict liability offence attaches legal liability to a person for acts or omissions regardless of the alleged offenders' *mens rea* (Latin for 'guilty mind'). Parking tickets are an example of strict liability offending where the commission of the act itself means that an offence has been committed. Defences may be put to the Court but it is up to the defendant to provide sufficient evidence to prove that there were reasonable grounds for the offending, rather than the onus of proof being on the prosecution to prove that no excuse existed.

112 *National animal welfare law*

Mens rea *offending*

In addition to the general strict liability offences, animal welfare legislation also recognises more serious offences relating to ill-treatment of an animal. *Mens rea* offences involve knowledge and intent on the defendant's part. The law recognises varying states of mind (e.g., blameless inadvertence, negligence, recklessness, intention/wilful) that either alone, or together, are commonly considered sufficient to prove a defendant's guilt.

Although early Courts were empowered to apply penalties in the event it was proven that an individual's treatment of an animal was 'cruel', they none the less demonstrated a reluctance to convict if the prosecution failed to show that the defendant's *mens rea* was also 'wanton'[62] (i.e., a term incorporating considerations of maliciousness, unjustified, without motive or provocation).

With time, early legislation waived the requirement for the prosecution to prove wantonness. However, in addition to general strict liability offences, contemporary animal welfare law also includes offences that are considered more serious than the general duty of care offences, on the grounds that they refer to general, reckless, or wilful ill-treatment of animals.

Concepts of recklessness and ill-treatment require the prosecution to address the knowledge element of offending, proving what the defendant either knew, or should have known. On this basis, reckless and/or wilful ill-treatment offences are sometimes referred to as *mens rea* offences.

Proving *mens rea* involves proving that the facts of the offence demonstrate intention or recklessness, that the conduct of the person was intentional or reckless, that the person was aware of or reckless in the circumstances, and that they foresaw the consequences to the animal of their intentional and/or reckless actions. Additionally, the prosecution must prove that it was the defendant who committed the acts that constituted the offence, and that the defendant intended to commit those acts. As part and parcel of the charges for ill-treatment offences, the prosecution also needs to choose evidence proving that the animal has suffered.

In contrast to strict liability offending where, once the facts of the matter are proven by the prosecution, the defendant has the responsibility to prove that they were either not the person legally responsible for the animal welfare offending, or there is a legislative defence that they can rely upon, the *mens rea* offences require that the burden of proof remains for the prosecution to prove the *mens rea* components of the defendant's acts and/or omissions. This task is further complicated for the prosecution because, although the defendant has the opportunity to raise evidence countering the prosecution's view, the defendant is not obliged to do so. Moreover, the prosecution must provide sufficient evidence to prove each element of the alleged offences in order to persuade the Court/jury that the defendant committed the offence 'beyond reasonable doubt'.

---

62 12 & 13 Vict., c92; An Act for the More Effectual Prevention of Cruelty to Animals.

Proving criminal offending 'beyond reasonable doubt'

'Beyond reasonable doubt' is a standard of evidence required to validate a criminal conviction

It means that the prosecution must prove the offending to the extent that a reasonable person would believe that the defendant is guilty of the offences they are charged with. In terms of criminal animal welfare offending, that means that the prosecution has the responsibility for proving 'beyond reasonable doubt' that a person's acts or omissions have resulted in an animal's pain and/or distress.

This standard does not involve proof to 'absolute' certainty, or proof beyond 'all' doubt, but it does require that, based on relevant law, evidence and reason, the Court and/or jury are sure that the defendant is guilty of the offence they are charged with. 'Beyond reasonable doubt' is deemed to be a substantially higher standard of proof than the probability (which refers to a lesser standard known in law as the 'balance of probabilities').

The term 'beyond reasonable doubt' refers to a threshold or burden of proof that applies in criminal cases which requires the prosecutor to prove each charge against the defendant or accused to a standard whereby the Judge or jury are sure of the guilt of the accused or defendant. Being 'sure' does not require mathematical certainty, or assessment in 'percentage likely' terms. However, being sure does require that the Judge or jury hold no reasonable doubts about the guilt of the offender.

By comparison, a 'reasonable doubt' refers to an honest and reasonable uncertainty remaining in the minds of a Judge or jury about the guilt of an offender after they have given careful and impartial consideration to all of the evidence. At the end of the legal proceedings, if the Judge or jury have a reasonable doubt about the guilt of the defendant, then the prosecution must be dismissed.

Historically, the Courts were reluctant to define the term 'beyond reasonable doubt', hoping that it was self-evident. However, an explanation of the meaning of the term is routinely provided these days in order to clarify the degree of certainty that the term implies, and distinguish it from comparatively lesser legal benchmarks such as 'the balance of probabilities', which applies in civil matters.

Proving what a defendant knew and/or intended has its unique challenges from a prosecutor's perspective but, like all other elements of each offence, relies on evidence to prove 'beyond reasonable doubt' to the Court/jury that the defendant committed the offence.

It's not what you think, it's not what you know, it's what you can prove

Each of the elements of an offence constituting the *actus reus* and, where indicated, the *mens rea*, must be proved by the prosecution by way of producing evidence. Occasionally, enforcement personnel and/or others involved in legal proceedings either overlook or forget that 'proof' is much more than simple

114　*National animal welfare law*

belief, or personal certainty (i.e., regarding a person's culpability for offending). For example, despite the personal views of an investigator that a defendant will admit/confess to committing an offence without opposition, the reality is that people charged with criminal offending are highly likely to seek out the services of a lawyer whose duty will be to assess the evidence with the purpose of protecting their client's interests which, despite the personal views of the investigator/officer in charge, is likely to constitute significant 'opposition'. Moreover, prosecutors and the Courts will, as a matter of 'principled prosecution', recognise that unfounded personal beliefs are insufficient to fulfil the duty and burden of proof that attaches to the prosecution. To prove its case, principled prosecution must provide 'evidence'.

In general terms, evidence is considered to be anything which establishes a fact or provides a reason for believing something. In legal terms, it is anything offered to prove or disprove the facts (which pertain to each element of an offence) of a matter. Furthermore, each piece of evidence will be considered by the Court for its relevance, admissibility and weight.

All the offences revolve around people's responsibilities to protect the single legislatively recognised interest of animals

By reference to the offences, the singular benchmark for law in terms of animal protection since the 1800s may be described in one phrase: 'the prevention of unnecessary and unreasonable pain and distress of animals'.

Reference to the offences contained within contemporary animal welfare legislation demonstrates that the continued focus of the law is the 'prevention of unnecessary and unreasonable pain and distress of animals'. Almost without exception, the activities which are referred to in law, and to which offences are attached, reference this singular consideration and benchmark. That single legislatively recognised interest of animals as protected by contemporary animal welfare law is reflected in the entire legal journey of the human–animal relationship and animal protection to this point in time. As such, contemporary animal 'welfare' law retains offences from earlier legislation regarding people's 'negative' acts/omissions (i.e., ill-treatment of animals) *and* adds offences to owners and/or persons in charge of animals for failing to provide for their physical, health and behavioural needs ('positive duties of care').

Remembering that 'cruelty' is predominantly a legal concept, and that 'welfare' is a strongly scientific concept, it follows that improvements in animal welfare are the results of incremental changes in disciplines other than just law, including, for example, science and ethics. Consequently, and like other areas of law, animal welfare law is predominantly a reactive, rather than proactive, legal discipline which has been described as 'racing to keep up' with changes in modern-day technology, science and ideas about what constitutes 'good practice'.

Primary legislation demonstrates the existence of 'qualifiers'. For example, concepts of pain and distress are qualified by considerations of what is 'unreasonable' and 'unnecessary'. Similarly, the positive duties of care, setting out obligations on the owner and/or person in charge of an animal to provide for their needs, is qualified by considerations regarding the animals' 'species, environment and circumstances'. Because it is impractical to incorporate details regarding the care of each species, and accommodate shifts in what constitutes 'good practice and scientific knowledge', those details are set out in secondary legislation (known as 'Codes of Welfare', 'Codes of Practice').

There are obvious administrative challenges associated with updating, educating and enforcing compliance with standards/requirements of law, and it is important for governments and governors to be clear that in terms of the law, people's actions regarding animals only become unlawful when those actions or omissions fail to meet the most basic benchmark of minimum standards. In practical terms, this means that although legal standards are advised by other disciplines such as ethics and science, the law cannot compel people to treat animals in a way that would comply with standards of 'best practice'.

It is important to recognise that minimising the pain and/or distress of animals does not in itself mandate that people provide best standards of animal care.

The law's minimal standards are not the same as standards of 'best practice'

The minimisation of pain and/or distress focuses on a continued assessment of preventing the negative by implementation of 'negative duties' (i.e., criminalising blatant acts of cruelty/ill-treatment) and implementation of the 'positive duties of care' (i.e., providing animals with the legislatively identified needs). Criminal law therefore has a focus on minimum standards, in that it only becomes involved when conduct towards animal falls below a minimum standard. Legislation, enforced by criminal law mechanisms, makes no requirement of stakeholders to improve upon a benchmark defined primarily on this lowest common nominator ('minimum standards'). Consequently there is a distinction between the law's 'minimum standards' and recommended, albeit unenforceable, standards of 'best practice'.

Distinguishing best, standard and minimum practice

The legal benchmark for legal offences is not based on standards of 'best practice', or arguably even on standards of 'usual practice', because the offences take effect when a person has breached what the law considers as 'minimum standards' of practice.

Incremental change, guided by scientific progress and public expectations mark the evolution of animal protection. Its laws referencing 'minimum standards' present a problem for those who fail to recognise the distinction between best standards and minimum standards, and/or who are not clear in their communications. For those who profess leadership in matters of animal welfare law on the basis that their national standards reflect those of the international community, here's a problem: that statement clearly overlooks the fact that the standards of the international community are based on 'minimum standards'. It is argued that minimum standards

116　*National animal welfare law*

are necessary in order to include as many parties as possible to agreements, and to facilitate wider interests of trade – balanced, wherever necessary, with public interest/safety.

By contrast, a model that incorporates notions of 'best practice' regarding people's responsibilities concerning animal's welfare goes well beyond minimal standards of practice. In traditional terms, 'best practice' refers to a method or technique that is superior to alternative methodologies, and frequently infers that the methodology/technique delivers superior results.

In practical terms of animal welfare law, 'best practice' often infers that the methodology/technique further minimises the potential risk of an animal experiencing unnecessary or unreasonable pain or distress. For example, secondary legislation specifically distinguishes between minimum standards and best practice in respect of matters of stockmanship, feed and water, the physical environment, and other husbandry practices. The minimum standard in respect of providing food to dairy cattle, for example, states that 'when the body condition of an animal falls below 3 (on a scale of 1–10), urgent remedial action must be taken to improve conditions'.[63] This is in contrast to the 'recommended best practice' which makes reference to 'target live weights', what the body-condition score of animals 'should be' at calving, and making reference to the actual procedure used in assessing body-condition score by going so far as to suggest that animals 'should be assessed at the same time each day'.[64] In essence, minimum standards set out benchmarks which the responsible person in charge of animals 'should not' fall below. This is in contrast to standards of best practice which set out benchmarks which the person responsible for animals 'should' aspire to.

For many advocates of enhanced animal protection, these traditional benchmarks of 'best practice' do not go far enough, because they continue to focus primarily on animal husbandry practices, rather than acknowledging, and practically incorporating laws, that recognise the intrinsic value of an animal and its experience (e.g., its sentience).

Differences of opinion regarding responsibilities concerning animals are often bound up with differing religious and cultural perspectives, and are influenced by wider economic and political drivers. Consequently, a shift to best practice rather than to a system that references simply 'minimum standards' would necessitate much more than simply a reconsideration of animal husbandry practices, and arguably require a considerable – and quite possibly a generational – shift in people's sense of responsibility. Again opinions vary. Examples include interventionist technologies utilising production animals, such as multiple ovarian embryo transfer, xenotransplantation, and utilisation of hormones such as bovine somatrophin (BST) to stimulate milk production.

As a result, the law continues to focus on the most basic interest of animals (i.e., the prevention of their unnecessary and/or unreasonable pain or distress). Even

---

63　Animal Welfare (Dairy Cattle) Code of Welfare 2010 (New Zealand), p. 9.
64　Ibid.

in instances where the law has acknowledged the sentience of animals and heard scientific evidence of 'happy' animals, it continues to benchmark the key criteria of 'pain' and/or 'suffering'.

The offences reference minimum standards of what is 'necessary'

The offences are all benchmarked according to minimum standards regarding what is acceptable, or not, in consideration of what constitutes 'unnecessary and/ or unreasonable pain or distress of an animal'.

In essence, this reference point has never changed since the inception of animal protection law. What has changed is the level at which those standards reflect society's concerns and expectations regarding the welfare of animals. What was once acceptable in the past is now no longer so. Examples abound – commonly known ones in the commercial sector involve farrowing crates, veal crates, and cage sizes for laying hens. Additional examples which have attracted varying degrees of media attention include piston firing on legs of horses, tail docking of dogs and skinning animals before they lose consciousness at slaughter.

The law attaches liability to the persons considered responsible for an animal's well-being according to various criteria that take account of the species of the animal, its environment, its role and other relevant circumstances. The offences will hinge on whether or not the animals experienced pain or distress, and whether the pain or distress experienced was necessary/reasonable, or not. The offences themselves are wide-ranging and had their origins in early nineteenth-century animal protection legislation. Important developments and extensions to the early offences have extended what is considered 'unnecessary or unreasonable' in the eyes of the law to include a wider range of activities, and added a prospective element so that offences include not just unlawful acts/omissions that have been inflicted upon an animal, but also acts/omissions that are 'likely to' result in an animal's unnecessary and/or unreasonable pain and/or distress.

This understanding provides context for the long list of criminal offences which, for example, addresses issues associated with activities including:

- administration of drugs and poisons;
- fighting and baiting;
- killing an animal inhumanely and/or unlawfully keeping it alive;
- piercing and branding;
- research, testing and teaching; and
- (non) treatment of ill or injured animals.

The law applies a broad net of liability

Potential liability for offending attaches to people who have direct and/or indirect responsibility for ensuring compliance with standards of animal welfare. Having recognised that offences are created for failing to ensure that an animal is protected

118   *National animal welfare law*

from unnecessary and/or unreasonable pain and distress, the next obvious question is 'who does this legal obligation apply to'?

In instances where it is shown that there have been breaches of relevant animal welfare law, then investigators and prosecutors consider issues of liability (i.e., who is legally responsible, and the subject of potential criminal charges).

This process involves identifying all persons that have had dealings, in one way or another, directly and/or indirectly, with the animals that have been the victims of animal welfare offences. The list of people includes owners, persons in charge of animals (whether or not their involvement/interaction with the animal was temporary or permanent, or of a long or short duration), those who may not have had direct contact with animals but whose responsibilities none the less affected the animals welfare (e.g., employers, directors, agents, managers on the basis of the legal principle of vicarious liability). So, to fairly ensure the application of justice and demonstrate responsible consideration to the 'totality of offending', transportation of an animal where it was subsequently shown that the animal was unfit for transport may result in charges being laid against the farmer (as either the owner or the person in charge of the animal), the truck driver, and the trucking company (on the basis of vicarious liability).

Similarly, if it is then shown that animals have been underfed (i.e., the owner or person in charge has failed to provide animals in his care with proper and sufficient food and water), then charges may be laid against the farmer (and/or associated personnel) as the owner and/or person in charge, and relevant agents, managers, employers, or company directors. Logically, this is entirely appropriate, given that the decisions of people in the management chain can have a direct bearing on the well-being of animals. Decisions that are made at boardroom tables, for example, to prioritise profits in a manner that results in an animal's unnecessary suffering are potentially just as liable under the law as the person who has direct hands-on dealings with the affected animals.

The broad net of liability is further exemplified by considering the potential liability of relevant professionals who are usually assumed to have the best interests of the animals in mind. For example, enforcement personnel may inappropriately overlook the responsibility/culpability of professionals such as veterinarians, farm advisers and contractors.

Animal health professionals, like other professionals throughout the workplace, experience potential conflicts of interest. The veterinarian, for example, has potential conflicts between the animal's welfare, the potentially compelling wishes/instructions of the animal's owner, and the veterinarian's own business/ profit/reputational interests. But veterinarians, by virtue of their professional responsibilities and their own professional code of conduct (e.g., to provide professional services to animals 'in the direct *care*'), fit fairly and squarely within the legal definition of a person in charge (i.e., a person who has an animal within their '*care*, and supervision, or control'). This reality also demonstrates one of the steps in legal assessment where 'all' persons associated with animal welfare offending are identified. Consideration of the relevant law, facts and circumstances then identifies the legal responsibilities, and who have fulfilled their responsibilities – or not. Criminal charges may then be considered. Legislation traditionally provides specific protections from liability for those exercising legitimately authorised powers of appointment, and those persons cannot be held personally liable for anything done or not done while properly exercising their powers/responsibilities as set out in the legislation. However, those protections/immunities may be lost if it is shown that the person has acted outside the scope of their powers ('ultra vires'). Similarly, even though legislation may contain recognition that what constitutes 'necessary' and 'reasonable' in respect of the 'circumstances' of working animals (e.g., police, military), those considerations/exceptions apply only in instances where the animal is performing working duties (e.g., in the course of protecting human health/safety and/or enforcing the law/specific role). Otherwise, the usual responsibilities to avoid ill-treatment and ensure the animal with its needs, still apply.

The law functions by first establishing benchmark criteria relating to standards of human responsibility regarding the care and treatment of animals (i.e., prevent unnecessary and unreasonable pain and/or distress of animals), then qualifies that responsibility in terms of the circumstances of the animal, particularly its use and associated dependency on its human care-giver.

Where there is an offence, law traditionally provides a defence

The law recognises that in certain circumstances, there may be valid reasons why individuals have not fulfilled their legal responsibilities/obligations. In terms of the law, these are known as 'defences'.

A keystone of law is that a person is 'Innocent until proven guilty'. The prosecution has, in the first instance, the responsibility for providing the Court with evidence that supports its allegation that the defendant has committed an offence.

The onus of proof

The prosecution has the responsibility to prove that the defendant committed the actual acts that made up the offence in both strict liability and *mens rea* offending.

Strict liability

Once the prosecution has shown that there is sufficient evidence to establish that there is a case, then in respect of strict liability offences, the onus then shifts to the defendant to prove that they were not at fault.

Defences broadly available to the defendant under contemporary animal welfare law require the defendant to prove that they took all reasonable steps to try and meet their legal obligations under the relevant section (despite the fact that those obligations have not actually been met); that the breach occurred in an emergency or in circumstances of stress and was necessary for the preservation, protection or maintenance of human life; or that at the time of the alleged offending, there was a

120 *National animal welfare law*

relevant legally recognised standard of practice the acts (or omissions) in question were either complied with or exceeded.

A point to note about the prescribed defences: the defence demands that the defendant took 'all' reasonable steps – not just 'some' reasonable steps.

Additionally, determination of what constitutes 'reasonable steps' will take account of facts and circumstances associated with the people and the animals involved, and what is considered (e.g., in the wider industry) to be 'usual practice'. For example, farmers with large dairy herds or flocks of sheep know that pasture growth declines in winter, and that it is their responsibility to either reduce the number of stock on the property ('stocking rate'), or provide feed supplementation if there is insufficient pasture growth on the farm. This is to ensure the animals are provided with proper (i.e., food type and quality) and sufficient (i.e., food quantity) food. If a farmer fails to plan ahead to ensure that there is sufficient food for the animals in his care, and animals subsequently starve to death and investigators identify that many more are in the process of starving requiring euthanasia on humane grounds, then prosecution of the farmer may ensue.

'Usual practice' refers to more than just what is done, and encompasses consideration regarding 'how' a practice is implemented. For example, if the farmer inappropriately applies animal husbandry practices in a manner which is subsequently shown to have resulted in animals suffering unnecessary or unreasonable pain or distress, then the farmer and potentially the associated professional (e.g., the attending veterinarian) may face prosecution. Induction of dairy cows provides a useful illustration. In cases where dairy cows have suffered following the inappropriate pre-injection assessment (e.g., though they have insufficient body condition to receive the induction injection, the veterinarian none the less administers to the cows the drug that is in his sole control – the drug cannot be sold to the farmer to administer) and post-injection care is also shown to have fallen below expected standards, then the farmer may seek to rely on a 'reasonable excuse' of relying on the veterinary professional's decision to inject/induce the animals. In principle, prosecutions give due consideration to the liability on all parties to an alleged criminal animal welfare offending; the reality is that both the farmer and the administering veterinarian may face prosecution.

And there is a list of 'reasonable excuses' that defendants commonly seek to rely on. For example, reference to the weather (e.g., unforeseen heavy snowfall in winter) is a common excuse proffered (by defendants in the agricultural sector who are facing prosecution). The Courts/prosecution balance that consideration with the knowledge that winter is predictably cold and that snowfall in certain areas is not uncommon. 'Personal circumstances' (e.g., financial, marital, emotional) have also been submitted by defendants for the Courts' consideration as a 'reasonable excuse'. While these matters are more likely to have relevance to this sentencing rather than determinations of liability, the presence or absence of evidence demonstrating a defence is important to the prosecution as well as the offence. Evidence of an unavailable defence goes directly to the prosecution's legal assessment in respect of whether or not a prosecution is warranted.

Mens rea

Mens rea offences differ from strict liability offences because the onus of proof is different. In *mens rea* offences, the onus remains on the prosecution to prove not just that the act (or omission) occurred, but they must also prove the defendant's state of mind, and that they acted deliberately. The defendant may choose to produce evidence advocating that the prosecution is incorrect, *but they are not obliged to*. The responsibility for proving the defendant's state of mind rests, prima facie, with the prosecution. This requires a prosecution to provide facts and evidence to prove that the defendant (and not somebody else) committed the acts that constituted the offence, and that the defendant meant to do them.

The defence, in *mens rea* offences, may simply rely on demonstrating that the prosecution has failed to adduce sufficient evidence to prove every element of each alleged offence 'beyond reasonable doubt'.

Common-law defences

In addition to giving consideration to any specific defences contained within relevant animal welfare legislation, legal assessment by prosecutors also consider potential common-law defences that may be raised by defence counsel. In that event, the prosecution has the onus of negating those defences to the legal standard of 'beyond reasonable doubt'.

Examples of common-law defences include self-defence or defence of another, compulsion, necessity, impossibility, alibi and provocation. In order to rely on a common-law defence, the defence counsel must, in the first instance, provide a credible narrative linking the evidence of the case being considered, with the available defence. The prosecution then has the responsibility to negate the defence.

The defence only bears an evidential burden in respect of these defences. In other words, before the prosecution has to negate a common-law defence, there must be a credible narrative in the evidence on which to base a defence. For example, if an individual is caught committing an illegal act (e.g., stabbing a dog to death), but the evidence credibly demonstrates that there is either a statutory or common-law defence (e.g., the person was acting to protect a human life), then the onus is on the prosecution to prove beyond reasonable doubt that no such threat existed. The example is based on an actual case and first impressions can be misleading, given that the person had stabbed a dog more than 32 times with a kitchen knife. However, the same perceptions might change when the full facts of the matter revealed that the killing occurred in circumstances when an uncontrolled dog attacked a female jogger and was in the process of severely mauling her. The (potential) offender (unrelated to either the jogger or the dog) witnessed the incident from the kitchen and grabbed a kitchen knife on his way out to try and assist. He was not prosecuted – he could rely on a legislative defence based on protecting the jogger.

122   *National animal welfare law*

'Exemptions'

There are certain practices that would be considered criminal offending, but for the existence of exceptions on the grounds that they are widely considered as acceptable and 'usual practice'.[65] In jurisdictions with contemporary animal welfare legislation, 'qualifiers' exist for traditional legal standards of animal welfare. These 'qualifiers' are often overlooked by those pointing to required standards and claiming that the law is permitting an unlawful practice. For example, qualifiers exist in respect of legal obligations to meet an animal's physical, health and behavioural needs. The qualifier to that obligation is that assessment must be made in consideration of the 'species, environment and circumstances'. This has relevance to arguments posed by people alleging that cages housing layer hens which are too small to enable the animals to exhibit 'normal behaviour', concluding that the cages are therefore unlawful. The obvious reality is that the use of these cages is permissible in a number of legal jurisdictions, largely on the basis that the law takes account of 'the circumstances' (i.e., the agricultural practice and purposes of food production and the economy). Factually, there are a number of jurisdictions where public opinion regarding the unacceptability of these cages has resulted in industry and legal shifts. In New Zealand, for example, the traditional battery-hen cage is being replaced by larger 'enriched' cages and the law has given industry ten years to phase out the older cage before it will be officially deemed unlawful practice.

In addition to selected exemptions in respect of agricultural practices, certain research projects also qualify as prescribed exemptions to legal obligations dictating the minimum standards of animal welfare. Some experiments are non-invasive and simply assess the animal's choices (e.g., in food). However, others cause the animal a degree of suffering. If this practice occurred outside the laboratory, then the people involved would face potential prosecution. However, under strict controls regarding the person, place and project, and consideration to research principles such as the 3Rs (i.e., research principles advocating Reduction, Refinement and Replacement of animals in the laboratory setting), then the legislative benchmark outside the laboratory in terms of what is 'reasonable' or 'necessary' shares in comparison to what is permissible, under those strict controls which happen inside the laboratory.

Additionally, there are exemptions on the grounds of religious, cultural, or heritage reasons. Spain continues to legalise bullfighting which has been described

---

65 The Treaty of Amsterdam, for example, states: 'Desiring to ensure improved protection and respect for the welfare of animals as sentient beings, have agreed upon the following provision, which shall be annexed to the Treaty establishing the European Community, in formulating and implementing the Community's agricultural, transport, internal market and research policies, the Community and the Member States shall pay full regard to the welfare requirements of animals, while respecting the legislative or administrative provisions and customs of the Member States relating in particular to religious rites, cultural traditions and regional heritage.': Treaty of Amsterdam amending the Treaty on European Union, the Treaties establishing the European Communities and certain related acts – Protocol annexed to the Treaty of the European Community: 'Protocol on protection and welfare of animals', 1997 OJ C 340.

as legislatively endorsed cruelty. Despite increasing opposition from the public and decreasing attendance, bullfighting continues as a regulated sport promoted within tourism and legally exempted on cultural grounds, despite the fact that in any other circumstances the treatment of the bull, which includes lancing, mutilation and death, would be considered a criminal offence.

A wide number of practices utilising animals in sports, entertainment, medicine, religious rights, cultural norms and 'heritage' have attracted criticism. They demonstrate conflicts within the theoretical and applied law, as well as particularly divergent public opinion. Examples include fox hunting in Britain, dolphin slaughter ceremonies in Japan, and orthodox halal slaughter methods (which don't accept the use of pre-stunning techniques).

It's not about species – it's about the animal's purpose/use

Those who understand the principles of animal welfare law will recognise that the degree and nature of legal protection attached to an animal depends significantly on the circumstances in which it occurs. That same understanding enables recognition that the law's substantive consideration is on the purpose/use of the animal and its correlating dependency on the human care-giver, rather than simply its species. This reality is amply illustrated when considering the law as it applies to working animals.

Although personal opinions may vary on the 'necessity' of putting animals at risk for the purposes of warfare and/or enforcement (e.g., police dogs), the law recognises and accepts that certain working animals will be at greater-than-normal risk that is part and parcel of their role.

The legal definition of 'service animals' (aka 'working' animals) may vary from jurisdiction to jurisdiction. However, it's usual for animals in the military and enforcement (e.g., dogs and horses) to be considered working animals. These may also include guide dogs for the blind. Consideration is being given to the different types of risks that might apply to other 'working' animals, such as the farm dog, in comparison to its more 'pet-orientated' counterparts.

Despite the law's recognition that the 'circumstances' of a working animal may put it at unique risk, the designation of 'service/working' animal is not a licence for human care-givers to ignore traditional legal obligations. 'Exemptions' (e.g., police dogs on front-line duties) usually apply only to times when the animal is functioning in their specific working role. For example, in respect of animals used in the defence force and the police, legislation[66] has applied at least two provisos to this distinction and subsequent use of animals in the military and enforcement. First of all, the animals involved can only be used in ways that are broadly considered a 'substitution' for humans. In other words, the uses must be consistent with something a person could, at least in theory, do. Secondly, the use of animals in the military and/or enforcement can only be for specific purposes of protecting human health or safety, or enforcing the law, and cannot be used in wider research that is not necessary for these purposes.

---

66 Section 179 of the Animal Welfare Act 1999 (New Zealand).

124 *National animal welfare law*

Outside of these two legislative provisions, the treatment of the animals involved comes under the standard legal criteria set out in the relevant Animal Welfare Act (or equivalent).

Placing penalties in the context of compliance and enforcement

Are animals 'victims' of crime?

Remembering that criminal law is generally accepted as involving matters between the state and the offending individual, it logically follows that of the person found guilty of offences against the state (which represents society) has obligations to pay what is commonly referred to as their 'debts to society'. This raises questions about compensation to the victims.

Historically, the victims of crimes did not have defined statutory rights and there were no formal mechanisms for information concerning the impact of the offending upon the victim to be conveyed to the sentencing Judge. However, in recent times, legislation has been enacted to address these issues, and the Court will commonly order a victim impact statement (or equivalent) to be prepared and provided to the presiding Judge. The victim impact statement provides details of the charge about any physical injuries, property loss and any other affects (e.g., psychological harm) suffered by the victim. It is easy to see how this has application if the 'victim of crime' is a person. However, there is a question of whether or not animals fall within that legal definition of a 'victim', in order for the prosecution to justifiably argue successfully that suffering of an animal has occurred and that the Court can justifiably view animals as 'victims of the offending' in determining the appropriate sentence.

Animals are generally not strictly defined as 'victims' under law because firstly, the term is largely restricted in law to humans, and secondly, because property – albeit 'unique' property that can experience pain and distress – cannot have 'rights', and therefore cannot be a victim.

It is important not to lose sight of the fact that animal protection legislation benefits both animals and humans. Issues of animal welfare (and the law's governance of relevant human–human and human–animal interactions) are inseparably connected with practical realities of human economic, environmental, or societal interests.

Additionally, a broad definition of a 'victim' acknowledges the practical reality that the animals are like other 'victims' often completely reliant upon – and at the mercy of – their human 'care-giver'. Consequently, it is not unusual for prosecutors to suggest that the Court might justifiably view the animals affected as victims. The discretion to accept the prosecutor's submissions, or not, lies with the Court/presiding Judge.

The Court's judgments risk subjective criticism, which often comes from individuals who are not fully aware of the legal nuances of the relevant law, or the relevant facts and admissible evidence pertaining to a matter. Judges usually have no problem in applying law that recognises people have responsibilities for animals who are entirely reliant, and therefore vulnerable to, the skills and aptitudes of their human care-giver.

For example, the Court in New Zealand has stated: 'just as we have legislation to protect children and other vulnerable members of our community, this [animal welfare] legislation is to protect animals who perhaps have an even greater vulnerability to human neglect whether that be through incompetence or deliberate action'.[67]

The three broad categories of penalty objectives are . . .

If a prosecution is pursued and a defendant convicted and penalised, then there are three ways that penalties may be applied in ways that serve to protect the animals associated with criminal animal welfare offending. Importantly, considered sentencing addresses not just the welfare of current animals owned or managed by the offender, but other animals who the offender may come in contact with.

Better penalties demonstrate a practical and holistic/total consideration for the well-being of the animals that either have, or may, suffer at the hands of the offender. With this in mind, there are three broad objectives attached to the penalties:

Firstly . . .

First of all, it is desirable to ensure that the animal is removed from the circumstances in which the offending occurred, and ideally, is not returned to the same situation. In terms of animal welfare penalties, this is called 'forfeiture' (or deprivation), and involves the transfer of legal title of the animal from the offender to another party (e.g., an animal interest group like the SPCA). Alternatively, subject to the circumstances and defined criteria (e.g., confirmation by a veterinary expert that the animal is unlikely to recover and warrants being euthanased on humane grounds), the animal may be euthanased.

Secondly . . .

Secondly, it is important to ensure that after being found guilty of animal welfare offences, the offender doesn't simply leave the Court and go out and buy/ obtain another animal who potentially becomes the next victim. In the range of

---

67 Judge Neave, in *MAF v MacGregor* 06/12/07, Judge Neave, DC Christchurch CRI-2007-009-13715 [paragraph 8].

126 *National animal welfare law*

animal welfare penalties, this is commonly referred to as 'disqualification'. It is not unusual for the Court to apply conditions to disqualification. These conditions will depend on the circumstances, but have included prohibiting the person from having anything to do with the particular species, owning animals, participating in the keeping of animals, or dealing with animals in any way where they are responsible for control of an animal's welfare.

The legal definitions of words used in the disqualification, and the conditions attached to any disqualification and/or confiscation, matter considerably. Early Court rulings asserting that disqualification and/or custody involved the physical control of an animal solely by the offender meant that it was possible for the physical control to be shared between two more people.[68] For example, if the disqualification addressed primarily issues of ownership/title by the offender, then potentially another person (e.g., a family member living in the same household as the offender) may actually have legal title, but the animal, in practical terms, if living in the same household with the offender, was still potentially vulnerable to the offender's behaviours.

In many jurisdictions, the problems posed by allowing 'shared control' have since been addressed; however, prosecutors and Courts who are alive to the potential of technical exemptions, often recommend/apply a broad conditions to any disqualification, thereby preventing even potential employers (e.g., farm managers) from engaging farm workers who are disqualified from owning or 'exercising any authority' over animals.[69]

Thirdly . . .

Thirdly, in denouncing the offending, contemporary animal welfare legislation empowers the Court to apply a range of additional penalties. Once, imprisonment for animal welfare offending was largely unheard of. And the imposition of monetary fines alone were widely seen as sufficient punishment in view of stated opinion that 'it's only an animal' and that the offender had 'already lost money by damaging his own stock'. In contrast, it is more common (in jurisdictions holding and applying their leading animal welfare law) for offenders to receive a prison sentence. For example, a farmer who beat his dairy cows with an iron bar and metal milking cups to the point that many exhibited clinical signs of fractured/broken legs and were subsequently euthanased on humane grounds, was sentenced to over two years in prison.[70] More details of this case are included in Case Study 3. Depending on the offences and circumstances, additional penalties may be available to the Court and be applied.

---

68 *RSPCA v Miller*, cited in Radford, *Animal Welfare Law in Britain*, p. 236.
69 Section 169 of the Animal Welfare Act 1999 (New Zealand).
70 *MPI v Lourens Barend Erasmus*, Priestly J., [2013] New Zealand High Court, New Zealand CRI-2012-463-69.

Case Study 3: Yes, you can go to prison for animal welfare offending

Despite a growing number of people who demonstrate support for the concept of responsible animal care, it's still not uncommon to hear some individuals express surprise that not only are there significant financial penalties for animal welfare offending, but that people 'actually go to prison' for mistreating animals.

The Courts demonstrate flexibility in addressing individual circumstances such as disqualifying persons from owning or being in charge of certain species of animals, rather than all animals (e.g., certain breeds of sheep require specific facilities and handling in order to attend to usual sheep husbandry practices of shearing and crutching as opposed to goats) or ordering the involvement of selected advisers and consultants to provide reports not just to the respective government department, but also to the Court.

For example, when a farmer's criminal history and overall lax animal husbandry practices revealed a pattern of neglect that had escalated to warrant being charged for aggravated cruelty of farm stock, it was submitted by the prosecution that external intervention was necessary in order to stop and prevent a reoccurrence of the same or similar conduct. The Court took all matters into account including the conduct of the accused, the impact on the animals, and community expectations. The Court stated 'as humans, we have the power to dominate almost every other living being on the planet . . . we eat them, we live with them. Every person who owns other living beings must ensure they are not harmed'. The Court went on to say that 'the suffering that these animals endured must have been horrific . . . You [the accused] have a duty to either get rid of the animals or look after them.' The Court was of the view that both specific and general deterrence were paramount considerations in sentencing the accused. The farmer was convicted and ordered to pay an aggregate fine of $5,000 plus Court costs, including directives which included instruction to return to provide reports and return to the Court for judicial monitoring. He was also instructed to attend and engage in relevant animal husbandry courses. With respect to the prosecution's submission that the accused should be disqualified from owning animals, the Court adjourned the decision for a period of six months (after the second judicial monitoring), in order to reassess the animal husbandry skills of the accused. Despite the fact that farming was central to the livelihood of the accused, the Court warned the accused that if any indiscretions were reported, then the Court would have no hesitation in accepting the application of the prosecution to impose a disqualification on the accused. The Court also warned the accused that any breach of the Court order would almost certainly see him receive a term of imprisonment.

(continued)

128   *National animal welfare law*

> *(continued)*
>
> *(Department for the Environment and Primary Industries v Brendan Fitzgerald*, Hamilton Magistrates' Court (Australia), McGarvie J, 21 May 2014)
>
> Penalties for animal welfare offending must follow the principles set out in relevant sentencing law (legislation and precedential cases), and sentences for animal welfare offending routinely involve a mix of financial penalty, disqualification from owning animals and imprisonment. While imprisonment used to be highly unusual, those who have experience in animal welfare enforcement largely agree that the occurrence of imprisonment for serious animal welfare offending has increased significantly in the last decade. Despite the fact that farming may be essential to the producer's livelihood, farmers may none the less be sentenced to imprisonment, as was the case involving Laurens Barend Erasmus, who had broken cows' tails, and hit cows on the hind legs with a steel pipe and stainless-steel milking cups. One hundred and fifteen of the 135 dairy cow herd exhibited one or more breaks in their tail. Twenty-five of the cows were euthanased due to the severity of the pain and distress associated with their injuries, which included broken and fractured legs, swollen joints, weeping lesions and infections subsequent to being hit with either the steel pipe and/or stainless-steel milking cups. On the basis of sentencing criteria which take into account considerations of the nature, duration and degree of the offending, the defendant was ultimately imprisoned for a period of two years and one month.
>
> *(Ministry for Primary Industries v Laurens Barend Erasmus*, High Court (Rotorua, New Zealand) 13 February 2013)

Sentencing

Matters of animal cruelty in animal welfare have generally attracted wide public criticism, and advances in technology and greater public access to information means that decision makers are under greater scrutiny than before, to be transparent in the accountability for their decisions relating to animal welfare issues. Despite the fact that judgments may understandably be influenced by the personal views of the Judge, the fact remains that (Westminster) law obligates Judges to abide by identified legal principles and procedure. Failure of the Judge to abide by these rules may result in the judgment being appealed. Consequently, while solicitors strive to present 'Judge-proof' arguments to the Court, it is widely recognised that Judges in turn are careful to ensure that they abide by the rules of law in order to ensure that their rulings are wherever possible, 'appeal proof'.

Penalties do more than punish the offender. They also provide practical protections for the animals, including the relieving of:

National animal welfare law   129

- an animal that was harmed, from suffering (e.g., through forfeiture or, potentially, euthanasia, where the animal is relieved from unreasonable/continuing pain or distress);
- animals that might have otherwise come into the possession of the defendant (i.e., disqualification that prevents the convicted defendant from possessing other animals); and
- animals of people other than the defendant who are reminded via the Courts of their legal responsibilities (i.e., 'deterrence' of potential offending).

It is commonly accepted that people who are found guilty of criminal conduct will incur some form of punishment. The law takes a primarily utilitarian approach and therefore punishment of criminal behaviour is justified on the basis of that which has benefits for the individual offender, and for wider society.

The fundamental justifications for punishments meted out by the law include concepts of deterrence (reducing the number and/or reoccurrence of crimes), retribution (to punish the offender for their offences) and rehabilitation (initiatives to assist an offender in returning to society). Imposing sentences is one of the key responsibilities undertaken by judges who themselves are obliged to abide by rules that govern principles and purposes of sentencing. They reflect a number of considerations, some of which may be in conflict. For example, those considerations require taking into account the gravity of the offending, the interests of the victim, and consideration to the maximum penalty prescribed for the offence and consistency of sentences for similar offending. Sentencing law addresses the purposes of sentencing, but doesn't require that one particular purpose be given greater weight than others. It is the Judge's responsibility to ensure that sentencing law is appropriately applied to the relevant facts and evidence of each individual case. It is a multi-layered task, often easier stated than applied.

It's not uncommon for people to read about a media-reported penalty and subsequently provide an extensive personal opinion on the shortcomings and ineffectiveness of the applied penalty – despite the fact that they have no idea about the relevant law, the full facts (beyond what's frequently a very abridged version of reported events), or the wider circumstances attached to the offending. This behaviour isn't restricted to individuals – politicians, organisations and a host of others are notably very quick to point to what they perceive as failings in respect of inadequate penalties – in absence of the full facts. The first point is that, as with any other topic, credibility is protected if the person or organisation is in possession of the full facts before providing a quasi-authoritative opinion.

There's something else that's worth keeping in mind the next time a media piece is being read about criminal charges in respect of animal welfare offending, and the penalties meted out by the Court. While penalties naturally carry a deterrent effect, the real practical sting of the penalty is often the non-official penalty that attaches to being on the receiving end of criminal charges. The time, worry and money attached to defending criminal charges can be enormous. Sometimes it takes years for a matter to come to Court. Defence lawyers and the collection of relevant

130 *National animal welfare law*

evidence also consume considerable amounts of time and money. Oft-times, there is a stigma attached to people who have been publicly identified as guilty of criminal offences involving an animal. And even if the accused person is found not guilty, it's common for the accused to spend years telling friends, family and even strangers, about what happened, their version of events, and provide personal opinion on how they suffered an injustice. In short, the penalty handed out by the Court may be substantial; however, it is often the case that the bigger picture demonstrates a much bigger penalty.

For the student of animal law, it's also interesting to compare and contrast the lessons-to-be-learnt from different legal jurisdictions and enforcement bodies. For example, some jurisdictions demonstrate an apparent mindset on prosecution, operating on a thinly veiled assumption that styles from other areas of enforcement (e.g., fisheries' measure and count basis, or touch street-policing) are equally applicable to the field of animal welfare enforcement. Failure to understand and accommodate the highly subjective nature and nuances of animal welfare enforcement not only incurs avoidable costs for regulatory bodies, but also damages invaluable stakeholder relationships.

Differences in prosecution initiatives are also evident. For example, an appeal by Kathryn Hamilton-Johnson heard in the English Supreme Court against the penalty meted out by the (lower) Magistrates' Court resulted in Hamilton-Johnson's penalty being substantially increased from £260 to £28,000 in consideration of the respondent's (RSPCA's) costs.[71] Reviewing of the case and final judgment would naturally be expected to make for sobering reading for future defence counsel and appellant considering appealing a Magistrates' Court finding in the future. More details of this are given in Case Study 4. Similarly, in Australia, the prosecution in Victoria[72] noted that the accused lacked the basic and necessary animal husbandry knowledge and practices required to ensure and promote the humane welfare of his animals, and was therefore no longer proficient to be a person in charge of farm animals. The prosecution went further and submitted that the welfare of the accused's animals should be the paramount consideration, above any other consideration prejudicial to the accused (for example, any loss of income or livelihood). As part of the specific and general deterrence measures implemented, the accused was sentenced to a Community Corrections Order (CCO) with special conditions, including directions to:

- attend and successfully complete an animal husbandry course;
- attend regular judicial monitoring hearing[73] and provide the Courts with reports that would be referenced at the judicial monitoring hearings; and
- adhere to limitations on the number of animals he could own or have in his care.

---

71 *Kathryne Hamilton-Johnson v RSPCA Supreme Court*, England, 4 March 2000, Case No: CO/3185/99.

72 *Department of Environment and Primary Industries v Fitzgerald*, 21 May 2014, Hamilton Magistrates' Court, Victoria, Australia (unreported).

73 It is noteworthy that this initiative involves the Courts, and not simply the enforcement/ regulatory body.

Initiatives such as these warrant consideration on the grounds that they continue to provide a general and specific deterrence message, but also apply practical penalties which focus on addressing the root of the problem, rather than simply applying a somewhat traditional fine, seizure and/or disqualification option.

Case Study 4: Caution on appeal: the penalty that went from £260 to £28,500 (UK)

The Court demonstrates a hierarchy of escalating authority and decision making, whereby, subject to established legal criteria, a Court decision may be appealed. There is a common belief that the decision and penalty of the lower Court establishes a 'ceiling' that will not, and cannot, be set aside by the higher Court. This is not necessarily the case, as demonstrated by the UK case against Kathryne Hamilton-Johnson that likely gives defence lawyers in the UK reason to pause and carefully consider the basis and risks for lodging an appeal.

Magistrates had convicted Kathryne Hamilton-Johnson of 19 separate offences for causing unnecessary suffering to various animals. She was conditionally discharged for a period of two years and disqualified from keeping domestic animals for five years. She was also ordered to pay £260 to the RSPCA. She subsequently lodged an appeal against her sentence. Her appeal was unsuccessful and the Court determined that it was authorised and appropriate to also revisit the amount of payment ordered. Kathryne Hamilton-Johnson was subsequently ordered to pay £28,500 in consideration of the costs of caring for the animals pending the prosecution, and the RSPCA's legal costs of prosecution.

(*Kathryne Hamilton-Johnson v RSPCA*; Royal Courts of Justice, London (England), Lord Justice Schiemann, 4 March 2000, Citation Case No: CO/3185/99)

Enforcement is much more than just counting prosecutions

Historically, the first animal protection legislation was the result of efforts by a few individuals arguing that it was necessary for Parliament to intervene to prevent excesses of cruelty to animals. Initially, suggestions about legal intervention were robustly opposed on the basis that they would constitute an unacceptable intrusion by the state on people's personal lives. None the less, once it was accepted that it was appropriate for the state to intervene in matters of animal protection, a variety of related interests were addressed by the state, including activities involving animals including research (i.e., vivisection), transportation (e.g., live exports), slaughter, disease control and wildlife protection. The powers of the state are balanced by human rights law, but underpinning concepts of state powers and human rights is

132 *National animal welfare law*

the Court's commitment to the rule of law.[74] The rule of law sets out that, as a matter of applied principle, the starting point is that all citizens are considered equal under the law. The application of the rule of law in a structured society balances each citizen's right to liberty and freedoms with the obligation to refrain from disrupting the lawful activities of others. Consequently, the rule of law precludes against those who hold strongly to one set of views from unlawfully intruding on the activities of other people who do not hold the same views, and creating a situation which 'cannot be tolerated and must unhesitatingly be rejected by the Courts'.[75]

In animal protection law, this means that while people have a right to campaign to change the law, they do not have the right to trespass, threaten, intimidate, or use other unlawful means to interfere with the lawful activities of others who have different views concerning animals.[76] There are numerous examples of activities involving animals where people's opinions drastically differ. Examples include commercial farming operations (e.g., intensive farming methods versus 'free range'), religious slaughter and human consumption of animals (e.g., varying lifestyle choices of vegetarianism and veganism). In all situations where there are conflicting perceptions and practices, the central question for the law is not, at least in theory, whether or not the practice (either an act or an omission) is right or wrong, good or bad, since such determinations are inherently highly subjective. Instead, the central question for the law is whether or not the practice is 'lawful'. This understanding further clarifies that the 'rule of law' stipulates that all citizens are to be considered equal under the existing applicable system of law. Obviously, in order to apply the existing system of law, there must be a system of enforcement.

Law is largely impotent unless accompanied by proper enforcement

Effective enforcement is of fundamental importance, because any measures to improve animal welfare can only be effective if they are properly implemented and enforced. Animal protection legislation secures a measure of animal protection in theory. An adequate means of enforcing that legislation is necessary to ensure that the theory of animal protection is actually put into practice.

Enforcement is a system of creating good law, informing and educating the public regarding their legal duties, instructing and directing those members of the public where necessary, and prosecution of those people whose actions or omissions (in respect of the treatment of animals) have been particularly egregious and/or where the behaviours and/or attitudes of the people involved require the prosecution with a view to ensuring lawfully compliant future behaviours.

---

74 The Rule of Law, in its most basic form, is the principle that no one is above the law, and that all men are equal before the law regardless of appointment or official status. For legal reference, see *R v Metropolitan Police Commissioner*, ex p Blackburn [1968] 2 QB 118, 138 CA (Lord Denning).

75 *R v Caird* [1970] 54 Cr App R 499, 506, CA (Sachs LJ).

76 Section 68 of the Criminal Justice and Public Order Act 1994 (England).

So enforcement is much more than simply hauling offenders off to court because prosecution is the end-stage of an entire enforcement process. Indeed, prosecution could be seen as a failure of all other enforcement activities in addressing non-compliant behaviours. An understanding of this principle of enforcement demonstrates that any person suggesting that effective enforcement can be adequately assessed by counting the number of prosecutions, is simply trumpeting their own misunderstanding, not only about the law but also the enforcement process.

Enforcement has a number of functions besides simply prosecuting. It informs people about the law, educates them as to their legal responsibilities towards animals and thereby assists in the maintenance and improvement of relevant animal welfare standards. Whether by education or deterrence, it can prevent animal abuse. Enforcement enables animals to be removed from the cause of abuse. Additionally it identifies problems and weaknesses in the legislation, which can then provide insights for potential reforms.

The development of legislation from animal protection legislation, with its nineteenth-century language and focus on anti-cruelty, to animal welfare legislation that incorporates positive duties of care, shows the continuing need for legislation that is clear, understandable and updated. But even the best legislation is of little practical effect unless its objectives are adequately understood and implemented by the leadership who have the responsibility for ensuring that its enforcement is properly resourced. Effective enforcement requires informed leadership, clear legislation, penalties that fit the offending, and adequate resources.

Enforcement should be adequately resourced so that officers can fulfil their statutory obligations. Resource considerations include ensuring that enforcement officers continue professional development as part of maintaining their knowledge in respect of relevant legislation, their duties and powers under those pieces of legislation, and their abilities to function efficiently in their animal welfare enforcement role.

Enforcement is a process that facilitates compliance by a process which includes drafting good legislation, shaping public attitudes through education, providing adequate resources to enable effective and efficient monitoring of compliance, principled decision making, and the ability to appropriately penalise those who commit animal welfare offences.

It is a common misconception that 'enforcement' is the same as prosecution, and that the effectiveness of enforcement can be assessed simply by measuring the number of prosecutions. Prosecution, while being an important part of the enforcement process, represents a measure of last resort in the enforcement process. Indeed, rather than representing the effectiveness of prosecution, prosecution may more accurately be interpreted as a failure of all other steps in the enforcement process. Used *properly*, prosecution reinforces to the public that the laws must be complied with. To understand what 'properly' means, it is necessary to understand the concepts of what is commonly known as 'the enforcement triangle' which works on principles of the VADE (Voluntary Assisted Directed Enforced) model of assisted compliance.

The VADE model

The VADE model of compliance (sometimes referred to as 'the enforcement triangle' – see Figure 5.1) refines the broad objectives and principle of enforcement that, in order to maximise effectiveness and efficiency of compliance, wherever possible, persuasion is better than compulsion. With a view to ensuring compliance with established law, the model categorises compliance with the law in accordance with people's knowledge, attitudes and behaviours. Attitudes, for example, may range from 'unfamiliar but willing to comply' (dealt with by conducting a preliminary inspection and subsequently providing education to those to make up the voluntary component of the model), to those that require assistance and/or direction to comply (i.e., requiring a warning or infringement), through to the comparative minority of individuals (often no more than 3 per cent) whose behaviours, often reflecting an attitude demonstrating a blatant disregard for the law, warrants stronger legal intervention (i.e., via the prosecution component of the spectrum of enforcement).

The VADE system is a model of tiered enforcement for achieving effective and efficient compliance. The value of the VADE model's approach of

Figure 5.1 The VADE Model of Compliance

National animal welfare law 135

adopting a series of escalating interventions matching the level of enforcement with the knowledge and attitude of each individual cannot be underestimated. The VADE model acknowledges that, in addition to matching the contrasting psychographics and behaviours between each of the four different groups with graduated enforcement, each group also warrants tailored communication as part of the education process if outcomes are to be genuinely more efficient and effective. For example, those who are unaware of legal requirements but willing to comply may simply need to be advised (e.g., via media) regarding the purpose and benefits of legal initiatives, and it would be potentially inappropriate – even offensive – to approach these people on the same basis as the minority of people who demonstrate a blatant disregard for the law and wider public interests.

Keeping enforcement figures in context

Enforcement numbers are relative. Interpretation in isolation of context and perspective is highly likely to result in misinterpretation. Quoted numbers presented in isolation of wider considerations may seem dramatic, and even persuasive, if time isn't taken to critically assess the information given. Great care needs to be taken in interpreting quotations or numbers out of their context to avoid coming to the wrong conclusions.

For example, quoting the number of successful prosecutions as if an increasing number of prosecutions is a mark of success, is, to the informed individual, blatantly inadequate; potentially, it's a nonsense when prosecution itself is a measure of last resort. It demonstrates a failure of all other steps in the VADE model.

Equally, quoting that 'millions of animals are killed for human consumption every year' understandably sounds very dramatic, but when put in context of the fact that there is a global population of 7 billion people, and the reality that the singular primary use of animals is as food for human consumption, then the figures – when assessed on a 'per person' basis – can then be considered in a way that is much more balanced and potentially more understandable to the individual.[77]

Similarly, while numbers regarding the number of prosecutions are useful to provide a first impression of the volume of animal welfare cases that go before the Courts in respect of animal welfare matters and the associated sentencing outcomes, the figures provide little information on the practical perspectives of animal welfare, such as the prevalence of cruelty, and wider enforcement activities.

Significantly more information is required to understand the wider enforcement activities including, for example, the number of reported incidents of alleged animal welfare offending, the number of resolved incidents, the number

---

77 K. Sharman. 2013. 'Farm Animals and Welfare Law: An Unhappy Union', in P. Sankoff, S. White and C. Black (eds), *Animal Law in Australasia*, 2nd edn (Annandale, Australia: The Federation Press).

136   *National animal welfare law*

of infringements, the number of recidivist offenders, the decision-making policy behind pursuing prosecutions, and the number of matters that are resolved prior to instigation of legal proceedings. Less than 3 per cent of reported allegations of animal welfare offending are eventually prosecuted. The view that this fact shows insufficient fervour in prosecuting animal welfare offending may be off-set by the reality that by far the greater majority of people (e.g., including those involved in agriculture, research, veterinary medicine and other businesses/professions associated with uses of animals) quietly, and lawfully get on with their usual business. Only after raw data has been properly analysed is it likely to provide a reliable informed view of the effectiveness of legislation and enforcement activities. Like any other area of expertise, enforcement entails much more than simply knowing 'something' about animal welfare, or being able to quote the relevant legislation. In addition to having a theoretical knowledge of relevant law, efficient enforcement of animal welfare protections also requires enforcement personnel being alive to the nuances of animal welfare. These include a sound understanding of animal husbandry systems and related matters (e.g., health care, transportation, feed supply and quality, seasonal variances/planning), and a genuine appreciation of the fact that the majority of animal owners are not intentional lawbreakers. Overly enthusiastic enforcement approaches that demonstrate an 'appetite for prosecution' are not only inferior in terms of efficiency and effectiveness, they may also be unlawful (e.g., under human rights provisions) and attract criticism and/or challenge from the Courts, fellow enforcement personnel and the public.

Inadequate enforcement

Inadequate enforcement not only undermines the purpose of legislation, but also damages public confidence in the law's ability to perform.

Who is responsible for enforcement? Implementing enforcement of animal protection legislation belongs to a wide number of agencies who often have a very varied mandate. They range from specialist bodies which focus on one particular activity involving animals (e.g., inspectorates regarding the use of animals in research), to organisations which have a wide ambit of activity, such as the police, where matters of animal welfare form a very small part of their regular activities.

Broadly speaking, however, there are two organisations that are widely recognised as driving, by way of enforcing, standards of animal protection. 'The government' is one, and the other widely known organisation is 'the SPCA' or its equivalent.

State enforcers

Criminal law deals with legal matters concerning the state versus the individual. The state ensures that members of the public comply with prescribed standards of law regarding the treatment of animals.

National animal welfare law 137

As part of the enforcement process, the state provides its appointed representatives with substantial powers.[78] Many of these powers abridge previously held notions that private citizens were entitled to complete privacy on their own land, and could do with their property (in this case, the animal) as they pleased.

Early animal protection legislation criminalising blatant acts of cruelty to animals focused on negative actions of people involving animals. One obvious drawback in terms of providing practical protections to the animal, however, was the fact that the offence had to be committed before the law could theoretically get involved. Contemporary animal welfare legislation, while continuing to incorporate many of the anti-cruelty offences of the former (animal protection) legislation, addressed this problem of its legislative predecessor in a number of ways that included the adoption of a preventative legislative approach, and empowering enforcement, by way of legislatively delegated state powers to appointed inspectors, to act not just when an animal had suffered, or was in pain and/or distress, but to intervene in circumstances where the animal was 'likely' to suffer.

The priority of appointed animal welfare inspectors is, at all times, the alleviation of any unreasonable or unnecessary pain or distress suffered by the animal. With this in mind, the state provides appointed animal welfare inspectors with substantial powers to prevent and/or mitigate the pain and/or distress of the animal and to assemble evidence in accordance with the relevant animal welfare law, where, in the opinion of the appointed inspector, the facts and circumstances provide reasonable cause to believe that breaches of the relevant Animal Welfare Act have occurred.

Those state powers include, for example:

- power to enter onto any land, premises or place at any reasonable time for the purposes of inspecting an animal if the inspectors have 'reasonable grounds to believe' that an animal may be suffering – or likely to suffer – unreasonable and/or unnecessary pain or distress;
- power to search and seize property, including the power to euthanase animals or remove them; and
- lawful assumption of escalating powers of control over the animals and their environment (e.g., the farm), from issuing notices to the respective owner/person in charge of an animal requiring them to take specific actions (to mitigate existing or likely animal pain and/or distress) through to assuming total control and decision making.

Accountability for the use of state powers

Appointed inspectors have the power to override the rights of ordinary citizens in carrying out their statutory functions. Consequently, and in recognition of the substantive, and potentially intrusive, nature of these powers, individuals who are

---

78 Sections 18–23, 53–5 of the Animal Welfare Act 2006 (England and Wales); sections 127–40 of the Animal Welfare Act 1999 (New Zealand).

138 *National animal welfare law*

appointed representatives of the state have significant obligations and account-abilities in respect of how they utilise state powers. Appointed inspectors, for example, must:

- Provide proof of identity, and evidence of their appointment as an appointed inspector prior to exercising any power of entry of inspection.
- Clearly communicate the authority that they are acting under and advise why they believe they have a reasonable belief for utilising their delegated statutory powers. For example, animal welfare officers have a responsibility to discuss proposed action plans with the owner or person in charge wherever possible, and take the owner's concerns into account. These practical measures are generally considered to be part and parcel of exercising statutory powers in a way that is fair and reasonable.
- Maintain adequate records in respect of all uses of their statutory powers. For example, if an inspector enters land, premises, and/or vehicle utilising statutory powers and the owner or person in charge is not present at the time, then the inspector is still under an obligation to leave a notice of entry in a prominent place that provides prescribed details, for example, the date and time of entry, the purpose of the entry, the condition of the animals inspected, identification of any animals seized/removed, and the inspector's name and contact details.

Essentially, it is the government that has the obligation to administer and resource laws that have been enacted. Despite the theory of government commitment, or Memorandums of Understanding (MOUs) which create an informal arrangement between government and non-government organisations, there are many instances where the reality is that in a number of jurisdictions, if it weren't for selected animal protection groups (e.g., the Society for the Protection of Animals – SPCA), which are frequently the nation's largest single prosecution body of animal welfare offending (e.g., Royal Society for the Protection of Animals (RSPCA), England), then enforcement by government might largely be described as inadequate or, at the very least, abdicating responsibilities for cost-effective solutions window-dressed as 'collaboration'. Or the government might consider animal welfare as simply one of a raft of governance responsibilities which requires appropriate – but not singular – focus in terms of limited resources.

The SPCA: the government's unpaid enforcers?

For the public, the relevant national SPCA continues to be one of the foremost figures with the responsibility and presence when it comes to the enforcement of animal protection legislation. The SPCA (and its companion organisations, such as its American equivalent the ASPCA, or the RSPCA) has international and national activities and undertakes activities which involve training of its inspectors, under-cover operations, investigation of complaints regarding the treatment of animals, and education. It remains one of the largest prosecuting bodies of animal welfare issues. When we remember that the SPCA is a charity, these activities are all the more impressive.

Nineteenth-century animal welfare activists like Richard Martin were limited in how much they could do. It was recognised that greater effectiveness would be achieved if a formal organisation was established to protect animals. Thus, on 16 June 1824, it was agreed at a meeting attended by 21 people (including Richard Martin and William Wilberforce, both of whom were early proponents of animal welfare legislation) to establish an organisation to be known as the Society for the Prevention of Cruelty to Animals.

The society was successful in securing convictions for animal cruelty; however, in its early days, it failed to secure sufficient income to meet its needs and as a consequence one of its early founders and the appointed secretary (Arthur Broome) was imprisoned because of the society's debts, and the initial committee reportedly considered dissolving the society. The inevitable outcome was narrowly avoided by the receipt of a timely legacy and the efforts of its new secretary. However, continued financial restrictions and efforts to save money resulted in the suspension of the Inspectorate, and a reduction in the number of prosecutions. Despite these early challenges, the SPCA survived.

One of the key events in the early development of the SPCA was the fact that the society received Royal endorsement. Queen Victoria, in 1837, was a patron of the society and in a time where the values of the sovereign had an enormous impact on the aristocracy and the growing middle classes, her endorsement gave the cause of animal protection social standing and legitimacy.

Unpaid enforcement

The SPCA (and its equivalents across various nations) operates predominantly with little or no government-provided public funding and with limited special legal powers. Despite those limitations, the SPCA makes an enormous contribution to the enforcement of animal welfare legislation.

Criticism has been levied at the state on the grounds that were it not for the SPCA, enforcement of animal protection would be inadequate. In turn, this recognition has attracted considerable additional criticism of respective governments, on the basis that government is abdicating its responsibilities.

Such criticism lends weight to arguments calling for greater transparency and accountability of statutory enforcement agencies. This would give the public an insight as to how the government is really functioning in terms of its ability to provide practical animal protection in the workplace. A specialist organisation which operates privately in the enforcement of animal protection matters has clear advantages. In addition to the obvious expertise, the SPCA theoretically does not compete with other public prosecution departments vying for a piece of the government's annual budget. By comparison, while the English RSPCA relies entirely on its supporting public, the New Zealand SPCA receives government funding.

None the less, provided there is sufficient autonomy, the focus of the SPCA on matters of animal protection potentially means that the animals, and matters of

140 *National animal welfare law*

animal welfare, benefit comparably much more than if they were solely reliant on the government funding.

Both the government and the SPCA are recognised as key bodies prosecuting matters of animal welfare offending. There is a distinction, however, in the focus and potential conflicts of interest. Issues of animal welfare (and the law's governance of relevant human–human and human–animal interactions) are inseparably connected with practical realities of human economic, environmental, or societal interests.

In contrast, the SPCA is widely accepted as having greater focus on the well-being of the animal and potentially fewer conflicts of interest.

Again, 'It's not what you think, it's not what you know, it's what you can prove'

Animal welfare legislation has important implications in safeguarding animal and human victims alike, but the duties, powers and protections – the whole process of enforcement – is largely dependent on efficient and effective identification and reporting of suspected animal welfare offending. Those with the statutory authority and responsibility for ensuring compliance with animal welfare legislation, will normally, in the course of usual practice, investigate a matter following receipt of information that indicates there may be animal welfare offending.

The investigator will then consider whether the requirements of the relevant Animal Welfare Act are being met, based on identification of the relevant facts and application of the law. This assessment requires enforcement personnel to apply the facts and collected information ('evidence') to the component parts ('elements') of offences set out in the applicable animal welfare law. In order to establish an offence, there must be sufficient evidence to prove every element of the alleged offence to a standard that complies with the Court's requirements. Obligations in respect of evidence highlight that the duty of the animal welfare investigator is twofold, namely to mitigate the existing and/or likely pain and distress of an animal, *and* obtain evidence.

The gathering of evidence by investigators is conducted with a view to its subsequent presentation as relevant and admissible in Court, and must be mindful of the fact that in criminal cases, it is the prosecution that carries the burden and standard of proof to prove each element of all charges.

Evidence essentially consists of words and things

Evidence remains the cornerstone of enforcement 'proving' their case

Words of witnesses given by a sworn affidavit, or stated in Court, are an example of words as evidence. 'Witnesses of fact' give evidence of facts of which they have personal knowledge from experiencing those facts with one of their five senses – they must have seen, heard, touched, smelled or tasted something. In the

National animal welfare law 141

majority of cases, this means that witnesses give evidence about what they saw, and what they did.

'Witnesses of fact' are distinguished from 'expert witnesses' because while the witness of fact is limited to providing facts to the Court, the expert witnesses' role is to assist the Court by giving their opinion as to the meaning, explanation for, and accurate context of the facts that have been provided.

Their evidence is admissible if it is deemed to assist the Court in understanding other evidence or ascertaining any fact that is of consequence to the determination of the proceeding. The expert may, for example, base some or all of their evidence on information in textbooks (and other technical or scientific publications) and knowledge learned from others.

To be able to give evidence in Court of inferences taken from any particular set of facts, an expert witness must first 'qualify himself or herself'. Consequently, an expert is defined in law as a person who has specialised knowledge or skill based on training, study, or experience. Expert evidence is defined as 'the evidence of an expert based on specialised knowledge or skill of that expert and includes evidence given in the form of an opinion'.[79]

The credentials of 'expert witnesses' may be challenged in Court by opposing counsel. Both prosecution and defence counsel have the opportunity to cross-examine an expert witness as to their field of expertise in an attempt to discredit the evidence given by the expert witness, and to highlight perceived weaknesses in the expert's areas of knowledge. Evidence can be wide-ranging, including books, documents, photos and videos.

Exclusionary rules of evidence

In generic terms, evidence is defined as anything which establishes a fact or provides a reason for believing something. In legal terms, it is anything offered to prove or disprove a matter under enquiry. However, for the purposes of Court procedure, the nature of evidence is unfortunately not as simple as those definitions suggest.

The law has developed many rules governing the way in which the relevance, admissibility and weight of evidence (i.e., probative versus prejudicial value) is determined in legal proceedings. For example, evidence may be deemed inadmissible to legal proceedings on the grounds that it is deemed to be hearsay,[80] unacceptable opinion,[81] and/or lacks veracity.[82] Additional rules of evidence include considerations to matters of propensity, and whether or not the evidence is considered 'overly prejudicial'.

---

79 Section 4 of the Evidence Act (New Zealand).
80 The most common exclusionary rule of evidence is the hearsay rule. Hearsay is regarded as a statement that was made by a person other than a witness, and is offered in evidence at the proceeding to prove the truth of its contents.
81 An opinion is any inference drawn from observed or known facts.
82 Traditionally, there were two categories of character evidence: evidence of credibility and evidence of propensity.

142　*National animal welfare law*

The relevance and admissibility of evidence is a constant consideration for the investigator during the course of the investigation, because those same rules of evidential relevance and admissibility will be the basis of any subsequent legal assessment determining whether or not there is sufficient evidence to support a prosecution.

The steps of an investigation

Given the responsibilities to mitigate animal pain and/or distress and collect evidence of alleged offending in a manner which complies with established legal procedures and protocols, investigators have an established number of standardised steps to ensure that each stage of the investigation is completed thoroughly and lawfully.

The investigators' assessment would be expected to include not just the animals, but also their environment, the circumstances, and the people who are responsible for/associated with the well-being of the animals concerned. The investigation would include assessment of a wide range of factors including, for example, the physical condition and behaviour of the animals, and any specific conditions in respect of the animals in question. In respect of the environment, the inspector is likely to review the immediate physical space of the animals as well as the local environment, the (un)availability of adequate food, water, shelter. Additionally, the investigator is likely to want to identify and talk to people who are responsible for, and associated with, the animals in question to determine the acts and/or omissions that may have given rise to any subsequently alleged animal welfare offending.

Basically, the investigator will have the responsibility for determining, by way of assessment and evidence collection, if animals are suffering in a manner that constitutes potential offending under the relevant Animal Welfare Act. With this in mind, the investigator may seek assistance or advice from an appropriate expert (e.g., a farm consultant and/or a veterinarian) and collect other relevant information/evidence that would go to supporting or refuting any particular charges under the relevant law.

Following, or even in conjunction with, the inspection, the inspector will determine what enforcement action is necessary to prevent or mitigate an animal's pain and/or distress. While continuing to ensure that all actions are appropriately authorised, implemented and properly recorded, enforcement action options may include, for example, provision of instructions regarding an animal's care, and escalating levels of search[83] and seizure.[84] The inspector must ensure that people

---

83　Opinion varies as to what defines a search. However, a search is accepted as being invasive, and a person's reasonable expectation of privacy is broadly accepted as the touchstone for legal considerations when assessing whether or not state representative actions may be defined as a search.

84　While there is no settled definition of what constitutes a seizure, a person's reasonable expectation of privacy is broadly recognised as the touchstone of legal considerations regarding whether or not state actions may be defined as a seizure. For example, the non-consensual taking by state officials of an item in which a citizen has a reasonable expectation of privacy may constitute a seizure.

associated with the alleged offending are properly informed, and that the exercise of the inspector's powers are conducted in a way which the law determines as fair and reasonable. If an inspector acts outside their specific statutory powers, then the law, via the Court, may rule that the inspector's actions were unlawful. As a result, the evidence collected by the animal welfare inspector may be ruled inadmissible. In addition to jeopardising any subsequent prosecution, unlawful actions by an inspector also risk compensation being paid by the relevant government department for losses associated with the inspector's actions. Following assessment, and depending on the circumstances, it is reasonable to expect that the inspector will follow up in order to ensure that any instructions have been properly complied with. If the owner or person in charge fails to comply, then further legal options may ensue.

In any case, where the requirements of the relevant animal welfare legislation are not being met, then the inspector has a duty to advise the person/people legally responsible for the animals concerned regarding their legal obligations and communicating where, and to what extent, they have failed to meet their legal obligations.

In less serious cases, intervention by animal welfare investigators may be limited to providing information and education in order to help people improve their care and management of animals. But this is not always possible or appropriate. If the people involved are uncooperative or obstructive, or if the circumstances demonstrate an extreme case of neglect, then the investigation may be upscaled with a view to mitigating the pain and/or distress of the animals involved, and collecting evidence with a view to potential prosecution.

'Principled prosecution' means not all potentially prosecut *able* offending is prosecut *ed*

Prosecution guidelines

Prosecutors have been described as 'ministers of justice'[85] in that they do not either win or lose,[86] given that their responsibilities of focus on fulfilling their role fairly and objectively to see that justice is done. As part of the prosecutor's overriding duty to the Court, they must never mislead or deceive the Court, nor in any way allow it knowingly to be misled or deceived. This is illustrated, for example, by the fact that despite the adversarial system which is a feature of Westminster law, prosecutors have an obligation (not an option) to disclose all material in their possession or knowledge which is, or could be, of interest and/or assistance to an accused. None the less, in impartially representing the interests of the community, the role of the prosecutor is to prosecute, not defend, those who have allegedly breached the rules of societal conduct as set out in the law.

---

85 *R v Puddick* (1865) 4 F & F 497, 489; 176 ER 662, 663.
86 *R v Bain* 10 CR (4th) 257, 264.

144   *National animal welfare law*

Evidential sufficiency and public interest

Two key tests are a prerequisite to initiating, or continuing, a prosecution. The first determines whether or not there is sufficient relevant, credible and admissible (to the Court) evidence to provide a reasonable prospect of conviction, i.e., to satisfy a Judge or jury beyond reasonable doubt that the individual being prosecuted has committed the criminal offence for which they are charged. The second assessment determines whether or not prosecution is required in the interests of the public. It is not a rule that all prosecutable offences must necessarily be prosecuted. Discretion whether or not to prosecute will naturally turn on all the relevant law, facts and circumstances of each individual case. Additionally, considerations to the number of victims, and injuries sustained by them, are also likely to be taken into account as part of the decision-making process. Questions of anticipated Court penalties, and practical realities pertaining to correction of the underlying offending/mischief, will also be considered.

There is no mechanical formula given that there are a wide number of relevant facts, circumstances and law to be considered. Decisions to prosecute or not will be affected by a number of factors including, for example, (a) the seriousness of the alleged offence, and (b) determination of whether or not there is a 'reasonable prospect of success' of prosecution.

Generally, the more serious the charge and the stronger the evidence to support it, the less likely it will be that it can properly be resolved by means other than by prosecution. The decision to prosecute or not will naturally be affected by the nature and degree of the alleged offending itself. On occasion, the state of the animal in question may be considered sufficient to demonstrate wilful ill-treatment or deliberate cruelty. Alternatively, there may be instances where the scale of neglect may be such that although prosecution in respect of any one animal may not be appropriate, the total number of animals affected may consequently warrant prosecution.

Traditionally, there is an extensive list of considerations attached to the decision of whether or not to prosecute. Addressing the societal wrong, changing behaviours of the offender and would-be-offender ('deterrence') and upholding the rules of law and justice, are broad principles that underpin those considerations, which are theoretically applied throughout the separate stages in the enforcement process.

Prosecution and 'the attitude test'

The circumstances, history and behaviour of the legally responsible persons are widely recognised to be a relevant consideration to questions as to whether prosecution is warranted, or not.

A Court of Appeal decision has stated, for example,

> The nature and scope of any consultation will depend on the circumstances including the exigencies of the situation and the animal welfare

considerations. The conduct of the owner may also have a bearing on the issue. If the owner adopts an uncooperative or even belligerent attitude, the extent and nature of the obligation to consult may be viewed in a different light. An owner's conduct may make consultation impossible to achieve or at least limit the steps required by the officials to meet the obligation.[87]

The statement demonstrates that there are situations where a person's attitude or conduct makes reasonable communication difficult or impossible. In such circumstances, the inspector's responsibility to consult with the person in charge may be limited or even dispensed with, in favour of the overriding responsibility to mitigate an animal's immediate pain and/or distress.

Maintaining the integrity of the decision-making process

Prosecutors must meet obligations relating to relevant prosecution standards of transparency, reasonableness and lawfulness. For example, consider a theoretical case where there is sufficient evidence to prove that animal welfare offending has occurred as a consequence of the combined acts and/or omissions of a farm manager *and* the attending veterinarian. If the evidence demonstrated that the offending by the farmer and the veterinarian occurred in the same circumstances, relied upon the same evidence, and dealt with the same animals, then criticism might justifiably ensue if it was only the farmer that was charged and the veterinarian's potential culpability was either ignored or simply referred to the relevant professional body on grounds of maintaining cordial professional relationships. Principled decision making in respect of alleged offending in this instance would clearly require an accountability as to why a prosecution was not pursued against the farm manager *and* the veterinarian, given the expectation that criminal liability (under the rule of law) should be applied to veterinarians, or any other professional, as equally as it does to any other member of the public.

'Unprincipled prosecution' may also occur in the event of individuals (e.g., prosecutors and/or enforcement personnel) denigrating their responsibilities to pursue a prosecution to serve what has been described as their own 'appetite for prosecution'. Such behaviour arguably fuels criticism that the conduct of some state representatives is akin to that of 'bullies with a badge', and potentially brings the organisation represented by the decision-maker into disrepute. Legislation has an obligation to be clear, equitable and practical. The 'equitable' portion of that equation demands that responsibility, and legal liability, be applied to all whose conduct has an impact on the welfare or treatment of animals. Courts rely on state management and enforcement personnel to consistently take a principled approach to ensuring that prosecutors bring all appropriate cases of animal welfare offending before the Courts to ensure that disregard of the law (which protects the interests of animals and humans alike) is appropriately censured.

---

87 *R v Summers* CA356/04, 8/12/04 at paragraph 29 (New Zealand case law).

146 *National animal welfare law*

Don't overlook the pressure of prosecution

The significant number of steps and considerations attached to the decision whether to prosecute, or not, are appropriate because whether or not the defendant is found guilty, and whether or not public opinion considers that the applied penalty is sufficient, the fact remains that the process of being prosecuted is likely to constitute a considerable stress for alleged defendants.

Prosecutions inherently involve substantial amounts of time, endeavour and money. The potential impact on the defendant's life, both during the course of the prosecution, and subsequent to it, is considerable.

The decision to prosecute is a serious consideration. The pressure, impacts and potential stigma that may subsequently be attached to the defendant, have, on occasion, been recognised by certain prosecutors as 'an inherent penalty to the prosecution process that may go beyond any fine, forfeiture, or even imprisonment that the Courts may impose'.

In summary, decisions to prosecute are not to be made lightly, which is why there are relevant prosecution guidelines – and accompanying checks and balances to ensure that those applying to power of the state do so in a manner which is lawful, procedurally correct and reasonable. It follows that, in the hands of competent and responsible decision makers, the decision to prosecute should be driven by the evidence and an assessment of the public interests, rather than prevailing media attention, political agendas, or inappropriate subjective perspectives of enforcement personnel.

What's driving the standards of animal law?

The critical importance of enforcement of animal welfare standards naturally raises questions about who sets the standards of animal protection. In theory, in a democratic system of government, state governors set standards of animal protection law after a process which involves various experts and advisers, and consultation with the public, including representatives from industry, non-government organisations, and other interested bodies, such as individual members of the public.

Early development of animal law itself, particularly between 1822 and 1911, was visionary in terms of changing widely held public opinion and usual practice in respect of animal treatment. By a process of incremental change, public awareness and opinion has shifted to a point where there is a widely held public expectation that treatment of animals will not only be sustainable, but that it will also be humane.

Opinions vary as to what leads/determines law regarding animals. It is appealing to say that public opinion influences elected representatives, the key legislative decision makers. However, this raises questions about who influences public opinion. Individual opinion is highly influenced by communications/marketing/promotions by high-profile and highly vocal interest groups and industry, as well as the media's reliance on well-informed (or not) journalists, and other individuals/groups, each with their own drivers and agendas. For example, it might be argued that industry, through marketing to the wider public and lobbying activities to the politicians, ultimately decides relevant standards of animal welfare. Industry is widely described as being driven by profit. In addition to recognising that higher standards of animal welfare are profitable, industry has also recognised the value of marketing good animal welfare, and assurances of food safety/traceability/quality to their paying public.

Additionally, there are a number of non-government organisations who have recognised the power of the public voice in matters of animal welfare, witnessed, for example, in the shift in tactics from historical public demonstrations outside industrial premises to passive-aggressive courtship of industry, retailers and governing bodies. This has also been underpinned by an education of, and relationship with, the paying/voting consumer.

The government

Some would say the government has the 'ultimate say' given that it allegedly sets the relevant benchmarks, and potential 'penalties' for non-compliance with established legal criteria. That said, industry has considerably more flexibility in establishing its trading criteria than government. It must give consideration to national and international trade rules (e.g., those established by the World Trade Organization), but none the less has substantially more freedom in terms of its trading agreements. They include the ability to adapt its agreements to what is deemed economically/politically necessary, and the ability to move its primary operation to another legal jurisdiction with different/less restrictive legal criteria.

There have been occasions when the law has led public opinion by shifting what's lawful, which in turn shifts perceptions about what is socially acceptable, for example, decriminalisation of homosexuality and prostitution in some countries. Arguably, that 'influence' on the law 'goes both ways' and is subject to the practical reality that politicians/legislators are widely driven by, and dependent upon votes from the public, and money representative of 'The Golden Rule' (described as 'He who owns the gold makes the rules').

The reality is that the government, in seeking to be effective and to implement cost-cutting efficiencies, has put considerable effort into 'collaborating' with wider stakeholders (e.g., industry) to facilitate improved compliance with standards of animal welfare. This obviously has significant advantages in respect of outcomes that benefit participating stakeholders. Government, for example, avoids incurring the cost of engaging more investigators by enlisting the wider eyes and ears of stakeholders in monitoring and detecting compliance with standards of animal welfare, and engaging methods of persuasion with the help of industry. Industry benefits from the relationship as well, because it is equally in the interests for national and potentially international markets, to trade on the back of trading-partner perceptions of a well-enforced system, ensuring high standards of animal welfare.

However, as with most arrangements, the collaboration is limited. Industry bodies have obligations to their wider members (e.g., farmers), so, while it is

148 *National animal welfare law*

democratically advantageous to censure the unlawful activities of a minority/one member, membership perceptions that industry bodies and/or representatives have assumed a 'policing' role risks outcomes which are counter-productive to the participating industry itself. So, industry's collaborative support to government in practical terms is limited to matters involving 'compliance'. It has demonstrated a resistance to extending this collaboration to activities traditionally seen as government responsibilities of 'enforcement'.

What constitutes 'ideal' standards of animal welfare differs between stakeholders

Self-interest largely drives the 'ideal' standards of animal welfare. Broadly speaking, non-government organisations advocate for what they perceive as the highest standards of animal welfare, sometimes even exceeding existing concepts of 'best practice'. While taking into account the interests of people, the primary focus of some non-government organisations is heavily focused on the animal. Some non-government organisations arguably go so far as to advocate the animal as 'the' prioritised stakeholder, rather than just 'a' stakeholder, whose interests are to be considered amongst others.

In contrast, industry is driven by profit given that they are answerable to their respective shareholders. Even so, such an attitude does not equate with the fact that industry is a highly motivated stakeholder, given its vested interest in matters of animal welfare. The government has responsibilities to the wider public in terms of public goods, public safety, dominant societal values, food supply and safety, and economic considerations. For example, 'leadership' in the field of animal welfare is frequently driven not by some altruistic moral standing of the government, but because high standards of animal welfare and demonstrated compliance are integral to the nation's economy and society's lifestyle. New Zealand represents a clear example of this situation, and one of the country's previous agricultural ministers is quoted as succinctly stating that New Zealand, and each New Zealander's lifestyle, depends more on the sale of its primary agricultural products than any other nation in the world.

In order to democratically accommodate and appease as many stakeholders as possible to facilitate inclusion and participation, national and international governments set standards which are either the 'lowest common denominator' (e.g., consider national jurisdictions, even those with comparatively 'leading' standards of animal welfare by global comparison), or simply exclude standards of animal welfare in favour of alternative benchmarks and criteria (e.g., the WTO which focuses on creating global trading quality and therefore functions primarily on economic criteria). Issues of animal welfare (and the law's governance of relevant human–human and human–animal interactions) are inseparably connected with practical realities of human economic, environmental, or societal interests.

Significant progress has been made in the field of animal welfare, but there are wider segments of industry and nation states that still have yet to recognise that good animal welfare equates to substantial benefits for animals and people alike.

For example, Indonesia refused to bring in pre-slaughter stunning on the grounds that it contravened established religious requirements. According to a number of animal welfare experts, the real reason for the reluctance was that Indonesian decision makers were simply averse to change – even though practices elsewhere in the farm-to-fork process demonstrated that better standards of animal welfare would actually be practically easier to use and more profitable. Only after higher standards were compelled and implemented did Indonesia identify for themselves that better standards of animal welfare were indeed highly profitable. Despite expectations that stakeholders would enthusiastically embrace change, particularly where they are highly motivated due to high investment, large segments of society, industry and government struggle to keep up with change and, in certain cases, demonstrate a high suspicion of 'new' initiatives.

That's where the animal advocates play an important role in promoting change. While advocating minority views that have been described as 'fringy', the questions posed by such minorities question the status quo and promote change. Radford articulates the relationship between minority groups, public opinion, and legal development:

> it is ... fatal for the law to be too far in advance of public opinion. Such an analysis will offend the moral absolutists, but they delude themselves if they think it is either possible or desirable to use the law as an instrument to impose the views of a minority on to an unsympathetic majority. The onus is on those who are opposed to the status quo to persuade others of the merits of their case. Liberal democracy is dependent upon law that is essentially consensual. Conversely, however, if minorities are not to be subject to [the] 'tyranny of the majority', popular support cannot in itself justify legislation.[88]

Undoubtedly, the debates will continue as to 'who really drives standards of animal welfare', it is highly questionable whether the public is really the determinative stakeholder. The apparent principle is that a prerequisite to change is the requirement for sufficient objective proof of resultant potential/real benefit. Even in the face of that proof, however, some stakeholders will be faster to make the change than others but eventually – in many cases – early adopters of change create contemporary norms. Such is the case with animal welfare changes advocating improved protections and practices involving animals: the changes continue to filter through to people via the media, social networks and other communication systems thereby shifting consumer expectations and choices. In turn, there is political pressure on those who have the power to instigate wider changes which include updating and amending society's legislative rulebook.

The hallmarks of leading animal protection law

Legislation that incorporates the leading principles of animal welfare is but one of the performance criteria that identifies a global leader of animal welfare.

88 Radford, *Animal Welfare Law in Britain*, p. 116.

150   *National animal welfare law*

Commitment of resources to adequate training, administration and enforcement is another relevant point of difference between genuine leadership and simply lip-service to concepts of animal welfare. Effective enforcement requires informed leadership, clear legislation, penalties that fit the offending and adequate resources.

It follows that the implementation of animal welfare law by the judiciary in Court decisions is another performance indicator of whether or not a sovereign state genuinely exhibits global leadership. Animal welfare is a concept that is much more than simply penalising cruel acts of humans towards animals. Unlawful animal welfare has potentially national and international impact that affect humans and animals alike.

In the absence of a global model of best practice, the countries with leading animal welfare law provide a valuable reference for the rest of the global market. So below is an abridged list of what to assess in order to identify global leaders in animal welfare legislation.

1. Is there primary legislation?

The first KPI (Key Performance Indicator) of a nation's commitment to issues of animal protection welfare is the existence of primary legislation whose purposes include the provision of legislative protections of animals from suffering unnecessary and/or unreasonable pain and/or distress. The term 'primary legislation' refers to Statutes, otherwise known as Acts of Parliament. 'Secondary legislation' refers to statutory instruments often called Codes, Orders, Regulations, or Rules which contain further detail regarding rules contained in primary legislation, which are often enforced through 'delegated' powers and/or authority.

There are thousands of pieces of legislation that have relevance to animals. However, the flagship for a nation's animal welfare commitment is frequently reflected in its primary priority of animal protection (i.e., a piece of legislation aptly named the 'Animal Welfare Act', or its equivalent). This is a first stop for any assessment of a nation's commitment to animal welfare. While certainly not the only criteria to be considered, it's important because it establishes the standards from which almost everything else in respect of animal welfare flows – or not.

The four stages of development of primary animal protection legislation

- Stage 1: No legislation whatsoever that protects animals. This may be because the nation is effectively lawless, or animal protection simply doesn't feature on its existing list of laws. In effect, its development reflects pre-seventeenth-century Western law, and as such, these nations could be considered as already four hundred years behind.
- It's important not to confuse laws that involve animals with actual animal protection law. Religion, for example, has traditionally made reference to animals in some manner. This book assesses animal welfare law in context of the traditional operation of (Westminster) legal principles. Claims of respect

National animal welfare law 151

and care for animals based on quotes from religious text are distinguished from state-implemented law (i.e., legislation) which sets standards of care which, if breached, attract penalties (e.g., a fine, imprisonment, or both) for non-compliance.

- Stage 2: Anti-cruelty legislation: This reflects the eighteenth-century Westminster law, where the legislature recognised that in order to protect interests of humans and animals, it was appropriate to implement law that criminalised blatant acts of cruelty. It's at least a start, but comparatively, it too is behind leading nations by 100–200 years.
- Although the US operates under a system of law that demonstrates significant differences to Westminster-based legal systems, various states within the United States none the less provide a wide variety of animal protection law. Assessing the place of each US State on a 200-year anti-cruelty legislative spectrum is difficult, with some states acting progressively and others not.
- Stage 3: Welfare legislation: Animal welfare legislation reflects a legislative development where people have responsibilities beyond simply 'not' doing something (i.e., an act or omission that would cause an animal pain or distress); but also responsibilities to 'actually do' something (i.e., an act) in a proactive means, to ensure animals do not experience unnecessary or unreasonable pain or distress. The legal obligation to take affirmative action is consistent, therefore, with the terminology that refers to these obligations as 'positive duties of care'.
- Stage 4: The existence of enacted 'welfare' legislation that prohibits blatant acts of cruelty and compels positive measures to provide for the needs of animals: Of course, to ensure that paper-stated purposes of legislation are actually implemented, the paper-to-paddock purposes of animal protection law must be backed up with adequately resourced enforcement. The existence of legislation that incorporates anti-cruelty and welfare concepts is not enough to deliver effective animal welfare. Effective legislation must be clear in its drafting as part and parcel of ensuring it is enforceable, and then sufficiently resourced to ensure that the practical value of the legislation is worth more than just the paper it's written on.
- Stage 5?: It is possible that a Stage 5 development in animal welfare legislation will develop alongside emerging technologies and scientific knowledge. For example, forward-thinking neuro-scientists are identifying pleasure centres (distinct from currently identified pain receptors) in animal's brains.

Mirroring existing legal principles that incorporate positive duties of care as well as avoidance of breaches of 'negative' duties (i.e., rules stipulating what people must *not* do, in contrast to positive duties stipulating what people *must* do), then perhaps it may be possible that future assessment of whether or not people have fulfilled their responsibilities regarding animal care will measure the animal's pleasure in addition to considering measurements of pain. This would certainly be consistent with proponents of the concept that a happy animal is one that experiences pleasure rather than simply avoids pain.

152 *National animal welfare law*

2. The animal stakeholder: is the animal's interest clearly stated in the legislation?

The inclusion of the animal's interest is clearly included in the stated purpose(s) of (existing) primary legislation.

Welfare law expanded the benchmark of 'unnecessary or unreasonable pain or distress' from simple prohibition of cruel acts, to actually requiring people to provide for the animal's needs ('positive duties of care'). Animal welfare law continues to give consideration to the attitude or conduct of the offender, but that attention unequivocally assesses the fulfilment (or not) of legal responsibilities in terms of the effect on the animal's experience and needs.[89]

Consequently, a point of comparison between jurisdictions that have primary animal protection legislation is its inclusion and clearly stated purpose to protect animals from suffering unnecessary or unreasonable pain or distress.

Should sentience be a feature of contemporary animal welfare legislation? Some people believe so, and commonly point to European Union legal instruments which referred to 'animal sentience' as their authority.

The European Union's benchmark of sentience

The Treaty of Lisbon (and its subsequent amendments) saw animals being formally acknowledged in an international instrument as sentient. The inclusion of the word 'sentience' has been viewed by many animal advocates as a significant achievement, given that it provides a formal point of reference for all future legislative development on issues involving animals. While its potential impact is considerable, its actual application is, as always, balanced by other interests. The duty on members to 'pay full regard to the welfare requirements of animals' includes responsibility to consider the animal's welfare as 'a' consideration, rather than 'the' central consideration that overrides competing interests. Furthermore, excitement over the inclusion of sentience in EU legislation is tempered when the EU's legal definition of 'sentience' is identified and compared to the purposes and concepts contained within contemporary animal welfare legislation. The interpretation primarily acknowledges that animals are distinguishable from inanimate objects and therefore have an identifiable interest in being protected from experiencing/feeling pain or distress that is unnecessary or unreasonable.

A definition of 'sentience' which sets out that animals can feel pain and distress means that the concept of sentience is already reflected in the standards of leading contemporary animal welfare legislation.

Furthermore, there are questions about whether or not the inclusion of sentience would make any real difference in practical terms for the animals. The

---

89 Section 9 of the Animal Welfare Act 1999 (New Zealand): 'Purpose – The purpose of this Part is to ensure that owners of animals and persons in charge of animals attend properly to the welfare of those animals.'

central issue remains people's responsibility regarding animals and, in turn, the experience of the animal that takes into consideration wider pragmatic realities.

Underpinning the debates is the reality that in law, words have power and that the law is not in the habit of including additional words unnecessarily. Consequently, if legislators were of a mind to simply appease animal advocates and add the word 'sentience' to amend primary legislation that already referenced animal pain and distress, then it is highly likely that legal minds of animal advocacy groups would subsequently argue that the Parliament's addition of the word 'sentience' meant more than simply another way of benchmarking standards of just pain and distress in terms of legal liability. It is foreseeable that animal advocates would seek to implement interpretations consistent with the 'dignity' of an animal, as set out in Switzerland's constitution, or apply other interpretations elevating concepts of an animal's innate value above legal categorisation of animals as animate property.

While debates are likely to be ongoing, it remains that in jurisdictions with leading animal welfare law, the judgments relating to animal welfare offending demonstrate that significant weight is given to the animal's experience. The law recognises animals as a stakeholder whose interests are acknowledged and duly considered.

3. Secondary legislation: is clarity by species provided in credible supporting and secondary legislation?

Primary legislation cannot practically address every individual nuance of caring for each species of animals in their varying roles. To be effective, primary legislation requires the clarity provided by well-drafted secondary legislation.

Regulation through licensing, certification and registration

Primary legislation abridged the traditional freedom of property (animal) owners to do as they pleased with their property. Systems of licensing and certification provide further clarity and controls regarding people's legal responsibilities concerning animals. A licensing system, for example, permits particular activities only if the licensee complies with specific conditions and standards. Failure to comply potentially result in the revocation of the authorisation.

There are a wide number of commercial and professional activities involving animals which attract some form of licensing, certification, or registration. Animal shelters, zoos, riding establishments, animal boarding facilities and slaughterhouses are some of these establishments. The variation reflects the variety of activities and conditions in which animals are used. For example, it shouldn't be a surprise that the specific requirements regulating the confinement and care of large, exotic and potentially dangerous zoo animals is substantially different to the regulations that apply to keeping domesticated cats and dogs in boarding establishments.

154 *National animal welfare law*

The list of regulated activities is substantial, as is the variation between them. But, there is a common thread. For the most part, it illustrates that the consideration toward public interest (e.g., public safety) is accompanied by an obligation to ensure that animals are cared for according to legislatively prescribed standards. Each of the regulatory regimes is always dependent on the legislative provisions which underpin them. Clarity is needed for their practical implementation.

Secondary legislation simplifies primary legislation

It would be cumbersome to put the details of what it takes to look after every species of animal in often vastly differing environments and circumstances into primary legislation. Consequently, an increasing number of jurisdictions, which are updating their animal welfare legislation, use secondary legislation to outline standards of care.

The standards naturally vary according to the species, environment and circumstances of the animal. Terminology within the codes identifies that some standards are considered 'minimum standards' in contrast to 'best practice'; however, the expectations all recognise the dependence of the animal on its human care-giver.

The 'codes' enable modifications to be made to standards of animal care as science develops, and as societal expectations shift. Despite the fact that the process of developing various codes has attracted criticism on the grounds of lengthy delays, it none the less remains a fact that modifying a code is substantially quicker and simpler than revising primary legislation.

The codes are referred to as 'a shield, but not a sword'

For the purposes of legal assessment, the codes have been described as 'a shield, but not a sword'. Prosecutors have historically been limited in their ability to use the codes as a 'sword', because breaching a code of welfare is not, in and of itself, an offence. That said, evidence of breaching the code may be used to support charges alleging criminal offences under animal welfare legislation. For example, evidence that a farmer has not met the required standard of care to provide adequate food to animals in his care as set out in the relevant code, is not an offence. However, the details in the code that refer to the amount of food required by an animal of a certain species may be referred to by a prosecutor arguing that a farmer has failed to provide 'proper and sufficient food', which is a legal obligation set out in primary legislation.

The codes may be used as a shield against prosecution, however, because demonstration by a defendant that they have met, or exceeded, the minimum standards set out in a relevant code of welfare constitutes a legislatively recognised defence. The concept of codes as 'a shield, not a sword' is shifting however. With a view to more effective and efficient enforcement of animal welfare standards, regulation of the codes is in the process of being implemented in selected legal jurisdictions.

National animal welfare law 155

The legal strength/weakness of 'good practice and scientific knowledge'

With the intent of increasing the efficiency of prosecution resources, suggestions have been made about regulating the failure to provide for an animal's needs. Undoubtedly, it's a valuable initiative, but there are inherent problems where those regulations rely on reference to codes that, reflecting the scientific nature of animal welfare, contain the uncertainties of science.

Primary legislation creates an offence for failing to provide animals in a way that meets with 'good practice' and 'scientific knowledge'. The inherent weakness is illustrated simply by challenging the drafter's use of the subjective word 'good'. What is 'good' practice, and who decides it?

Many prosecutions involve animal welfare offending that is so extreme that reference to the codes is almost a technicality. But in the event that legislators seek to translate the codes into regulations associated with penalties, then questions of clarity and credibility are foreseeable.

Furthermore, the codes' reference to minimum standards based on 'good practice and scientific knowledge' may fail to provide sufficient clarity about where to draw the line between best practice, minimum standards, and unlawful (and therefore penalisable).

As a case in point, consider the problem of lameness in dairy cows. It is not an offence to be a person in charge of a cow that is lame. It is an offence to fail to provide sufficient medical care for an animal. But where is the line drawn to clearly determine that the standard of care is so low that it constitutes an offence? 'They should have called a vet' is a common statement given with the benefit of hindsight and subjective opinion. The reality is that the degree of lameness and the impact on the animal can vary enormously, depending on the circumstances, the animal, and the actual cause of the lameness. Additionally, many farmers are very competent in treating lame animals. Even if veterinarians are involved (e.g., one acting on behalf of the state in an animal welfare investigation, and the other being the usual attending veterinarian for the potential defendant), then in the absence of statements by the relevant professional body stating that either veterinarian's opinion and/or methodology is below usual professional standards, then the difference of opinion is simply that. As a consequence, the state veterinarian's views must be accompanied by other compelling evidence before it can reliably be considered that offending has occurred.

Legal determinations rely on the relevant law, and consideration of all the relevant facts, evidence and circumstances. With this in mind, the usefulness of codes relies heavily on their consistency with relevant legal authority and research.

The codes do provide a suitably flexible benchmark

Undoubtedly the codes will evolve with new scientific evidence, but over-reliance on conflicting science is one potential weakness attached to any prosecution relying heavily on the codes to 'prove' or 'benchmark' alleged offending. However, 'scientific knowledge' is constantly changing and it is evident that, like other professions,

156 *National animal welfare law*

there are substantial differences of opinion about what constitutes 'good practice' amongst the scientific community.

Like many issues, finding the balance relies on people to fulfil wider obligations such as transparency and accountability. Flexibility to update the codes with new scientific information and societal requirements of what constitutes good practice is obviously advantageous drafting that assists in preventing primary legislation becoming quickly outdated by failing to keep up with developing science. Unfortunately, the barriers to implementing this flexibility are all too often identified as being attributable to either outdated processes, or problematic people – or simply a lack of understanding between the drafters and the technicians.

Over-reliance on standards that are constantly shifting is problematic enough, but the problems are clearly exacerbated when the content of codes are based on a non-transparent process, or patently relies on authority that is demonstrably inferior and/or unreliable.

Such circumstances demonstrate that it is not just the presence of secondary legislation that constitutes a jurisdictional comparison, but also the quality, authority, and therefore the credibility of secondary legislation that warrants assessment.

4. Is the precautionary principle applied to the definition of the legal animal?

Not all animals are 'legal animals', or protected under animal protection law

It is a common, and incorrect, assumption to think that all animals are protected by the animal welfare law. Determining the breadth of the legal definition of the legal 'animal' therefore constitutes another point of important comparison. Legislation introduced the practice that is still evident in contemporary animal welfare law, that is, of defining which species were included in the statute's use of the word 'animal'.

The definition of 'animal' does not include a human being, but generally includes any 'live member of the animal kingdom'. As a first consideration, the law generally applies protections to animals that are capable of feeling pain. Understanding that the law broadly applies responsibilities in a way that correlates with the animal's vulnerabilities, then it makes sense that the protections vary between circumstances of the animal, such as whether or not the animal is domesticated or wild. In certain circumstances, the law may exclude certain animals entirely according to their use. For example, in the US, animals used in agriculture are commonly excluded from legal protections that the same species of animal – even the same animal – may have if it was used another way (e.g., as a pet). The law excludes a majority of animals, however, including, for example, numerous species of shellfish and insects, as well as most fishing activities.[90]

---

90 It is notable that fish welfare is a developing area of concern as science recognises that fish experience pain and distress. Notably, however, there are strong opinions in both industry and government which continue to provide exemptions which thereby protect significant economic interests of influential stakeholders.

The ability to feel pain, determined by 'scientific evidence', is one of the key criteria identifying animals which will be protected by animal welfare legislation. This reliance on 'scientific evidence' to determine what species do, or do not, benefit from legislative anti-cruelty protections has continued to be a source of irritation for those who take the view that there is too much reliance on science, and that the precautionary principle in favour of the animal should be applied. It has been argued that the relying on science to demonstrate that animals experience pain before providing them with legislative protections, puts the onus of proof in the wrong place, because it can be 'too easily used to justify correlating practices which are clearly undesirable even though this cannot be scientifically proved'.[91]

With this in mind, it is useful to compare not just what animals are protected, and how this protection is consistently applied (or not) amongst animals in the range of animals' roles throughout society (e.g., whether in research, agriculture, companion animals, or other areas), but also to consider which and what reasons the legislators rely on for withholding legal protections from animals that are not given the benefit of the precautionary doubt.

How broad is the definition of an 'animal'

It is incorrect to assume that the legislative definition of an 'animal' provides legislative protections to all creatures other than human beings. Tens of thousands of species fall outside the legislative definition of an animal, and consequently are not subjects of the law's protection.

The law has traditionally given protections to those animals for which people have inherent responsibility, due to the fact that the animals concerned are largely dependent upon their human care-givers. However, there has been a shift that attaches value to wider matters involving, for example, issues of climate change, environmental protection, and conservation of animals. Non-domesticated animals ('wild animals') have been the subject of various laws, but traditionally have been viewed as falling 'outside' the ambit of traditional animal welfare legislation. This has attracted considerable criticism, but indicators are that leading jurisdictions recognise circumstances where the law's protections encompass 'wild animals'. For example, a New Zealand judgment shifted the national (and arguably international) benchmark in convicting an offender for brutally clubbing a number of seals to death. Despite the fact that the defendant sought to argue that seals fell outside the Animal Welfare Act (under which he was charged), the Court concluded that the purposes, wording and structure of the Animal Welfare Act authorised the Court to give consideration not just to the species, but also to the nature of the offending. Consequently, the offender was found guilty of animal welfare offending. The judgment is significant: its practical impact brings previously excluded 'wild animals' within

---

91 Radford, *Animal Welfare Law in Britain*, p. 192.

158 *National animal welfare law*

the protections of animal welfare legislation and broadens the ambit of the law's legal definition of an 'animal'.

Liability: how wide, and how clear, is the net?

A point of comparison between jurisdictions with animal welfare law is consideration of the breadth – and the clarity – of liability that attaches to animal welfare offending.

'Responsibility' is a key underlying concept of all law, including animal law, so another point of comparison is assessing whom the law holds liable when it has been shown that animals have suffered unnecessarily and/or unreasonably as a result of a person's act or omission. Legal liability is determined by the facts, the relevant law and consideration of all the circumstances.

Contemporary animal welfare legislation applies a broad net of responsibility, and potential liability, to persons who, by their acts or omissions, either directly or indirectly, have resulted in unlawful treatment of animals.

Owners and persons in charge

Owners and persons in charge[92] of animals are among those to whom the law attaches legal obligations[93] in respect of duties to ensure that animals are not ill-treated, and to provide the physical, health and behavioural needs of animals in their care.

Strict liability standards not only prevent someone from avoiding liability by claiming ignorance, they also reaffirm the legal expectation that it is ultimately the human care-giver's responsibility to ensure that the animal's treatment complies with legal standards.

However, contemporary animal welfare legislation provides a broad net of liability that extends beyond simply the owner or immediate person in charge of animals.

---

92 The Animal Welfare Act 1999 (New Zealand) defines a person in charge as: 'in relation to an animal, includes a person who has the animal in that person's possession or custody, or under that person's care, control, or supervision'. Under the Act, a 'person' is interpreted far wider than simply a singular human individual. The Act specifies that a person 'includes a corporation sole, and also a body of persons, whether corporate or unincorporate'. These statutory definitions provide the Court with the ability to assign legal responsibility broadly where it is shown that an animal has experienced unnecessary and/or unreasonable pain, suffering, and/or distress in contravention of legislative standards.

93 Strict liability is a legal term that means that a person can be guilty of an offence whether or not they were aware that they were breaking the law. A person's state of mind (referred to in law as the *mens rea* (Latin for 'guilty mind') is not something that has to be proven by the prosecution for offences that are classified as 'strict liability' offences. The prosecution generally need only prove that the person (or persons) committed the act (known in law as the *actus reus*, Latin for 'guilty act'), although consideration of whether the person's offending was committed 'intentionally', 'recklessly', or 'wilfully' may be relevant to other elements of alleged offending.

National animal welfare law 159

Derivative liability

Derivative liability, in practical terms, means that criminal responsibility for either ill-treating an animal or failing to provide an animal with its needs, is extended from the principal actor to other persons, who may also face criminal charges on the basis of their association with the perpetrator and/or their involvement with the animals.

Derivative liability and the legislatively automatic attachment of potential liability to those in the management decision-making chain are highly appropriate. Historically, animal welfare offences have commonly been attributable to either an individual or small group of persons. However, the law has recognised that ownership and decision making that impacts an animal's welfare may extend well beyond the immediate care giver. Corporate ownership of animals, for example, involves a chain of responsibility for animal welfare that extends from employees, through to executive officers and directors. Policies and decisions that prioritise financial concerns that result in compromised feed budgets in animal care and consequent animal welfare offending justifiably warrant attention and potential prosecution.

Derivative liability, therefore, can attach to employers, directors, or officers of body corporates. If an employee, for example, is guilty of an offence under the relevant animal protection legislation, then as an inspector automatically adopts a legal position that the employer too is prima facie liable as well, unless, for example, the employer can satisfy the Court that they establish they had no knowledge of the offending.[94]

Consequently, an employer cannot escape liability by turning a blind eye to animal welfare offending. Indeed, the effect of applying liability to employers for their employees' acts or omissions places a considerable legal responsibility on employers to actively supervise the way in which their employees treat the animals in their care. Employers have a clear duty to prevent offences occurring in the first place, and to mitigate the effects of any harmful actions that may have already occurred. In the case of corporate bodies, this obligation extends right through the chain of command. The burden of proof shifts slightly with respect to directors and other managers, where the onus is on the prosecution to prove that the offending took place with their 'authority, permission, or consent'; or that the directors and/or managers 'should have known that the offence was to be, or was being committed' and that they 'failed to take all reasonable steps to prevent it'.[95] The criteria are particularly important and it is worth drawing attention to the fact that liability attaches not just for what company officers *knew*, but extends to what the Court considers the company directors *should have* known. Similarly, the potential defence points out that it is not enough for the officers to have taken 'some' reasonable steps, but that they have an obligation to take 'all' reasonable steps. Criminal investigators therefore consider the circumstances of each case, and evidence demonstrating that the principal knew, suspected, or even should have known, that there was non-compliance with expected standards of animal care.

---

94 Section 164 of the Animal Welfare Act 1999 (New Zealand).
95 Section 165, ibid.

160 *National animal welfare law*

The law in respect frequently demonstrates that directors, both executive and non-executive, may be held legally liable not just for shutting their eyes to obvious offending ('wilful blindness'), but also for failing to make inquiries about the offending behaviour in a situation where such inquiries should have been made.[96]

Aiding, abetting, counselling

Potential liability is extended further by legislation which attaches liability to any person who '[c]ounsels, procures, aids, or abets any other person to do an act or refrain from doing an act as a result of which an animal suffers unreasonable or unnecessary pain or distress'.[97]

Prosecution

In jurisdictions having leading animal welfare law, criminal liability is relatively clear and comprehensive; liability, at least in theory, is very broad. Consequently, consideration of the breadth – and the clarity – of liability that attaches to animal welfare offending is a key point of comparison between jurisdictions in respect of their animal law.

5. Penalties that fit the crime: do the available penalties reflect the nature and degree of offending?

Appropriate legislative penalties that fit the offending are an important part of assessments concerning sentencing and subsequent disparities between legal jurisdictions. A range of penalties are traditionally available in leading animal welfare law which, upon consideration, addresses the overall objectives of ensuring that the perpetrator is unable to continue causing pain and/or distress to the animal victim (forfeiture); is penalised for their crimes (applied penalty which may be a fine, community service, or imprisonment), and is prevented from simply obtaining another animal (disqualification).

The presence of existing sentencing structures does not, however, guarantee that the penalty will fit the crime. New Zealand legislation provides a good example of how amendments to primary legislation were necessary to enable penalties to more appropriately fit the crime. Initially, cruelty offences were divided simply into ill-treatment and wilful ill-treatment. The more serious offence of wilful ill-treatment put the onus of proof on the prosecution to prove a knowledge/*mens rea* element of alleged offending. Knowledge elements of offences are inherently problematic to prove on an evidential basis in much of criminal law, and particularly so in matters involving alleged animal welfare offending where animals may be located in isolated areas at times (e.g. difficult

---

96 *Sadler & Niederer v New Zealand Food Safety Authority High Court Auckland*, CRI 2005-404-285/286, 6 October 2005.

97 Section 29(h) of the Animal Welfare Act 1999 (New Zealand) 'Counsels, procures, aids, or abets any other person to do an act or refrain from doing an act as a result of which an animal suffers unreasonable or unnecessary pain or distress'.

terrain, seasonal variances) and consequently difficult for the person in charge to regularly check.

In cases where there was insufficient evidence to prove the knowledge and intentional infliction of harm by the perpetrator, then the prosecution would frequently have no option but to lay charges for a comparatively lesser offence, with an accompanying lesser penalty. However, the introduction of an offence of 'reckless' ill-treatment created an intermediary offence between ill-treatment and wilful ill-treatment, and enabled the ability to lay charges that enhanced the ability to apply penalties that more appropriately fit the crime.

Criticism of Court sentences is a common occurrence. Sometimes the criticism simply reflects the author's own subjective view, or (mis)understanding of the full facts and/or legal process. None the less, poorly thought-out legislation that fetters the abilities of enforcement to consider, and apply, charges and penalties that are congruent with the offending, provides genuine grounds for denunciation of sentencing.

Leading penalty regimes not only punish the offender, they also provide practical protections for the animal, which include the ability to remove affected animals from the influence of the offender, and ban the offender from having care, supervision, or control of other animals ('disqualification').

The provision of appropriate penalties that fit the offending, in addition to consistency of offending, consequently constitute a valuable point of comparison between jurisdictions.

In 1822, Richard Martin stated 'If legislation to protect animals is to be effective, it must be adequately enforced.'[98] As Richard Martin discovered at the commencement of the animal protection movement in the early 1800s, the existence of legislation is an important step, but it is not enough alone to change societal behaviour – it never is.

In governance and animal welfare law, the term 'resourcing' refers to money, manpower, machinery, technology and other tools provided for enforcement with a view to demonstrating that the paperwork of animal welfare legislation is not simple rhetoric.

Concerns regarding under-resourcing of animal welfare have prompted calls for 'more funding', and even a dedicated animal welfare ministry. Ideally, the government would obviously have sufficient funds to resource all valuable and worthy initiatives, including all aspects of animal welfare enforcement. However, such lofty aspirations must be balanced by the reality that governments, like any other business, do not have bottomless pockets, and must therefore budget and prioritise in consideration of public needs.

Government departments have historically and understandably attracted criticism when inefficiencies have been identified, so it is a fallacy to assume that 'more money' necessarily translates to greater efficiency. Any assessment of the resources – in conjunction with assessment of the efficiency and effectiveness of available resources – assists in distinguishing genuine political commitment as opposed lip-service.

---

98 Richard Martin, 1822, cited in Radford, *Animal Law in Britain*, pp. 345–95.

162 *National animal welfare law*

6. The nation's blueprint: is there an established animal welfare strategy?

With the vast number of stakeholders attached to matters of animal welfare, each with frequently competing and conflicting interests and agendas, it comes as no surprise that in the absence of an animal welfare blueprint of animal welfare development and collaboration, animal welfare law, policy and implementation is created and implemented on a comparatively ad hoc and splintered basis.

Australia's animal welfare strategy demonstrates an exemplary model of a focused national animal welfare initiative which was formulated to 'guide the development of new, nationally consistent policies' and 'enhance existing animal welfare arrangements in all Australian States and Territories'.[99] The strategy covers the humane treatment of *all* animals in Australia, including livestock/production animals, animals used for work, sport, recreation or display, animals used in research and for teaching purposes, as well as companion, wild and aquatic animals. Importantly, the strategy was developed in consultation with multiple stakeholders including state and territory governments, animal industry organisations, animal welfare groups and the general public. Its goals, objectives and activities reference a range of key considerations as part of putting animal welfare in context of science, national and international benchmarks, and social and economic considerations. The strategy states that it is 'for the entire Australian community including animal owners, the veterinary profession, livestock producers, processors, transporters, animal welfare bodies, researchers, consumers and government agencies'.

However, despite this strategy, Australia continues to demonstrate conflicts and inconsistencies between federal and state/territory animal welfare law/standards. Government has also attracted criticism for its inefficiencies, alongside demonstrably political agendas and subterfuge. None the less, the fact that the usual political window dressing is accompanied by at least some practical initiative which consciously engages stakeholders in developing benchmarks and potentially a voice of consensus (albeit not complete agreement) is definitely a valuable point of jurisdictional comparison.

7. Does the system deliver?

It's one thing for a nation to claim it is committed to standards of animal welfare, and quite another to deliver it. Given the dependence of human well-being on matters of animal welfare, it is important to distinguish where decision makers sit, between genuine leadership and window dressing and political puffery.

Logically, no system can be 100 per cent effective all of the time, but the test of all the preparations (i.e., the establishment of primary and secondary legislation that fairly and clearly identifies and balances the protected interests of all relevant stakeholders, including animals as one of stakeholders) is whether or not the system actually delivers.

99 Australian Animal Welfare Strategy: www.daff.gov.au/animal-plant-health/welfare/aaws.

National animal welfare law   163

Systems to determine and apply appropriate standards of animal welfare, and assigning responsibilities or implementation of established standards, is a complex matter. In addition to determining the current need to balance the interests of all stakeholders, decision makers also have the responsibility to ensure that they are on track to meet stakeholders' future requirements as well. In practical terms, the government is often unlikely to have sufficient resources to be effective for development of, and compliance with, animal welfare standards. Consequently, it relies on high trust relationships with stakeholders in order to share knowledge, foster innovative practice and encourage compliance.

However, real-life situations have a way of revealing whether paper-based assurances and political puffery have genuine substance, or not. For example, consider the implications of a situation where the government officially declares a state of drought in certain regions of the country. The declaration signals the government's recognition that 'normal' conditions do not apply.

Simplistic views of farm agriculture by those with a limited understanding of farming and agriculture in general, traditionally show that if there is insufficient food to feed the animals, then either more food should be purchased, or animals should be culled from the farm. But that view ignores what is really a potentially complicated and inter-dependent system of both farming and wider agribusiness. There are wider factors associated with feed shortages that may result following a drought. Farming involves constant forward planning in converting food to product, so requires attention to multiple factors in the farm-to-fork process. They include attention to seasonal changes, stock numbers and farm maintenance, as well as accurate monitoring of available pasture and food supplements that must take account of topography, the animal's health requirements and physiology, and seasonal fluctuations. In times of unforeseen and extreme climatic conditions, the demand for supplementary food is likely to increase, and be reflected in an increased price.

The increased price may mean that the farmer who does not have enough food stores set aside for stock simply cannot afford to buy sufficient amounts of supplementary feed. Responses saying that the farmer should simply cull the animals overlook the fact that culling the animals (e.g., dairy cows) is potentially an equally difficult option because the animals are frequently 'assets' which are relevant to the financial security of the farming operation (e.g., bank loans). A drought potentially has long-term impacts. Restricted amounts of feed are likely to have a direct impact on successful fertility rates, and consequently significantly impact not just the current year's financial position, but also the operation of the farm for subsequent years as well.

These nuances of animal welfare therefore require that those involved in enforcement of animal welfare standards must do more than simply memorise relevant law and events on the farm calendar. Proper use of the state's powers and responsibilities delegated to appointed officers means that the officers need to have demonstrated knowledge and genuine understanding of the subject of animal welfare. A system of law that delivers compliance with high standards of animal welfare that provides a balanced (e.g., penalties with incentives) system has the potential to provide enormous

164 *National animal welfare law*

benefits to animals and humans (from producers right through to consumers) alike. Of course alternatively, there are equally enormous risks and costs in the event that decision makers 'get it wrong'.

So what does 'a system that delivers' actually look like?

Is there an ideal system of animal welfare protection and governance? And what, if any, is the end point at which it can be said that the interests of animals are fairly represented in the face of continuing cries that animals are 'voiceless'?

A system that delivers must be constantly updated to meet contemporary and foreseeable needs of stakeholders; in relation to animal protection law, that is currently described as 'sustainable and humane'. Assessment of the key features of contemporary animal welfare law illustrates that efficient and effective systems of animal protection law target and deliver this objective of sustainable and humane treatment of animals. It is one, but not the only, responsibility of governors. In order to push the boundaries of current norms, perhaps the visionary question might consider what the legal concept of animal welfare will look like in fifty, a hundred, or even two hundred years from now?

The difficulties and perhaps even the impossibility of predicting exactly what the future of animal protection systems will look like is illustrated by considering how accurate – or not – early eighteenth-century pioneers of animal protection might have been in predicting today's animal protection systems. What is clear is that despite the significant evolution of animal protection over the last two hundred years, the fundamental principles of the human–animal relationship that underpin the law as society's rulebook, appear to be a constant. Despite gradual evolution of animal protection law, essentially the only thing that has changed is the public's understanding and consequent perception of animals. That understanding and perception has been informed by science and communication technology.

Looking forward then, it is likely that standards of acceptable treatment will shift, as public ethics continues to learn more about the pain/pleasure life experience of animals, accompanied by a greater recognition that issues of animal treatment have a direct impact on the personal health, well-being and the life experience of people.

In turn, it is predictable that future governors will continue to rely heavily on science and contemporary ethics to balance competing and conflicting economic, environmental and sociological drivers in order to remain politically and publicly credible in the area of animal welfare. It may be, for example, that the limitations of the Five Freedoms will be superseded, and that the existing focus of current law and standards on preventing unnecessary pain and/or distress will shift to reflect advances in neuroscience which identify both pain and pleasure centres in animals. It is equally foreseeable that improved systems of identification and measurement of the animals' experience may also translate into improved technology-facilitated systems of enforcement.

Pro-dignity initiatives and laws that increasingly recognise the innate value of animals is a possibility. Supporters of incorporating terms such as 'dignity' and 'sentience' into law claim that the initiative is predominantly symbolic and will have an educative function that raises awareness about animals, their well-being, and even their status in human society. Opponents recognise the power of words in law, and the risks that albeit well-intended proposals can result in complications and unintended consequences. These involve, for example, derogation of animals' legal categorisation as property, frivolous litigation and further unforeseen consequences to animal-associated professions, business and practical protections for the animals themselves. Moves in this direction have extended beyond simple discussion given that countries including Switzerland, the Netherlands, South Korea and Germany have laws which incorporate reference to the inherent value of animals.

Civil practice of animal law

Distinguishing 'civil' from 'criminal' animal law

It is common for people to refer to 'the law' as if it operated from one single reference book of rules. While ideally there should indeed be a consistency across all jurisdictional law, it is helpful to understand that in respect of its functions, the law is divided into subsets: criminal law and civil law.

Civil law and criminal law are two broad and separate entities of law with separate sets of laws and punishments. Civil law addresses legal issues between two (or more) individuals (in contrast to criminal law which broadly addresses legal issues between the state and an individual), and involves matters of redress, where one of the key objectives is to put/restore the person who has sustained loss (or 'harm', 'injury', 'damages') in the same position as they would have been ('compensation') in the event that they had not suffered as a result of the actions/ omissions (e.g., 'negligence') of the offender. While this book deals primarily with legislation (and thereby, criminal law) on the basis that this represents a nation's benchmark in respect of legal protections and obligations regarding animals, it is none the less appropriate that in addressing the foundational principles of animal welfare, attention includes an introduction to matters of civil law.

Criminal law

The term 'criminal law' generally refers to the body of substantive criminal laws. That body identifies 'crimes', otherwise known as 'offences', to which various penalties are attached. 'Criminal procedure' describes the process through which the criminal laws are enforced. Specifically addressing the subject of animal welfare law, criminal law prohibits any person from being cruel to an animal (e.g., that people should not ill-treat animals, either recklessly or wilfully) and establishes that human care-givers are obliged to provide for the needs of animals in their care. The manner in which government enforces this substantive law – through the process of investigation, gathering of evidence, and prosecution – is generally considered a procedural matter.

166 *National animal welfare law*

'Primary law', 'legislation', or 'Statute', are the terms used to describe law that is established by the government, and form the body of rules known as 'criminal law'. Breaches of criminal law, which are frequently referred to as either 'crimes' or 'offences', may result in prosecution that generically involves legal proceedings between the state/government and a person,[100] in order to determine if there has been a breach of state-established rules which have been put in place to protect public interests and safety. The fact that the law has historically applied a utilitarian starting point that prioritises people's interests, demonstrates the enormity of the work done by early animal protection advocates in convincing the legislature to protect the animal's interest (in being protected from unnecessary and/or unreasonable pain and/or distress) to an extent that fettered the traditional 'property rights' of the animal's human owner.

The fact that governments and criminal law traditionally centre on the wellbeing of *people* also illustrates the enormous significance of legislation that ultimately legislated to protect animals, and the animal's interest (of being protected from unnecessary pain and/or distress), in and of their own right.

Because criminal law is designed to protect the public, a breach of criminal law is considered an offence against the public, for which the government/state as the public's legal representative takes responsibility for governing and enforcing. This is done with the objective of protecting citizens by ensuring that all individuals comply with the relevant rules.

Criminal law therefore deals with matters that involve legal issues between the state and the individual.[101] Offending is attached to a range of penalties which can include: a monetary fine, forfeiture (e.g., of the animal(s)), disqualification (e.g., from owning/controlling animals for a period of time), and imprisonment. The state is consistently one of the 'parties' to legal proceedings in its role where it is essentially acting as the representative of the public. If the alleged offender is judged guilty of committing a criminal offence, then penalties may be applied. Criminal penalties punish the offender, and are intended, among a number of criteria that the Court must consider in order to deter others from committing similar offences, thereby protecting the public and the state, and maintaining law and order.

Criminal liability has been described as 'the strongest formal confirmation that society can inflict'.[102] Treating animals cruelly, and failing to provide for their needs, has long been established in legal jurisdictions following Westminster principles, as a criminal offence. For those who are prosecuted by the state, the process and experience can be lengthy, expensive and arduous.

---

100 In terms of the law, a 'person' is not restricted to just a natural person, but may also refer to other bodies such as companies, organisations and other established entities.

101 'Individual' may be a person, company, or other legal entity. Such actions are distinguished by comparison with tort law which addresses legal issues and conflicts between individuals.

102 Andrew Ashworth. 1999. *Principles of Criminal Law* (Oxford: Oxford University Press, 2006), cited in Radford, *Animal Welfare Law in Britain*, p. 1.

Civil law

In contrast to criminal law which deals with legal issues involving the state/government and a private individual, civil law essentially deals with legal disputes between two (or more) individuals.[103] According to William Geldart:

> The difference between civil law and criminal law turns on the difference between two different objects which law seeks to pursue – redress or punishment. The object of civil law is the redress of wrongs by compelling compensation or restitution: the wrongdoer is not punished; he only suffers so much harm as is necessary to make good the wrong he has done. The person who has suffered gets a definite benefit from the law, or at least he avoids a loss. On the other hand, in the case of crimes, the main object of the law is to punish the wrongdoer; to give him and others a strong inducement not to commit same or similar crimes, to reform him if possible and perhaps to satisfy the public sense that wrongdoing ought to meet with retribution.[104]

Rather than dealing with matters that might be described as breaching society's rules established to protect and serve wider public interests, civil law has significant dealings with issues of compensation for damages suffered by one particular party. Redress ('compensation') is sought via the law by one party against the other on the grounds that the person has suffered a loss ('damages') as a result of the unlawful actions (or omissions to act) by the other person.

Civil matters in 'animal law' therefore include, for example, issues of damage done to an animal which is legally classified by the law as that individual's property (e.g., veterinary negligence), or damage done by an animal to another person's property (e.g., where uncontrolled animals such as wandering stock or aggressive dogs cause damage). Similarly, civil 'animal' law deals with issues of ownership and/or transfer of property between two or more individuals (e.g., matrimonial disputes, and addressing legal issues of title and responsibilities of animal care in people's wills and trusts).

In each circumstance where an animal has been injured, or where title of the animal is being transferred, the criminal law provides important relevant starting points, one of which being the mandatory consideration as to whether or not the animal involved suffered – or is likely to suffer – 'unnecessary and/or unreasonable pain and/or distress'.

---

103 It is noted that the government/state may be a party to civil proceedings. This may occur, for instance, in circumstances where the state has incurred costs while investigating criminal offending. If the criminal Court does not order the defendant to pay costs, then the government may subsequently seek compensation of costs via the civil Court.

104 D.C.M. Yardley (ed.). 1984. *Introduction to English Law*, 9th edn (Oxford: Oxford University Press), p. 146.

168 *National animal welfare law*

CIVIL COMPENSATION (AKA 'DAMAGES')

For the purposes of assessing and understanding matters of civil law involving animals, there are three key points:

- The starting point is to remember that animals are legally classified as property.
- This is directly relevant from the law which establishes a system of rules and 'responsibilities' regarding property, for example, in respect of control of their own property, and accountability for damage caused and or sustained to property.
- Therefore, in terms of civil matters involving animals, damage can be the result of acts/omissions done *to* animals, and *by* animals.

APPLYING THE PRINCIPLES OF CRIMINAL LAW TO CIVIL MATTERS

It is important to recognise that relevant criminal and civil issues involve much more than simply standards of animal care (e.g., providing animals with sufficient food, water, and suitable environmental/living conditions), but extend to a vast array of systems and products associated with keeping, controlling and using animals. For example, there are established criteria relating to standards in respect of transport vehicles (from airlines moving animals from one country to another, to trucks transporting animals from the farm to the abattoir), confinement systems (e.g., cages for laying hens, farrowing crates for pigs), training devices (e.g., electronic collars for dogs and cats), and hunting (e.g., criteria distinguishing lawful from unlawful traps and snares).

Mirroring the history of animal law, there are people in the animal law field who argue for improved animal welfare protections on the basis of a moral obligation to animals. There is another strategy which links improved standards of welfare for the animals to interests of people. Purists may criticise the approach of combining animal and human interests by realities demonstrating that human and animal welfare are intimately linked. It is the 'delivered outcomes' that provide practical benefits in respect of the welfare of the animals in question, more than simply paper victories.

Decision makers, including the Courts, function on established law as the established (i.e., 'precedent') legal interests of the parties involved. For example, the established legal interest of animals is that people have a responsibility to minimise unnecessary and/or unreasonable pain, distress, or suffering of animals. There is an obvious credibility and strength in arguments that structure legal proposals by reference to established precedent. Such an approach does not require the Courts to entertain subjective and sometimes fanciful concepts that exist beyond the realms of established legal procedure. As a consequence, well-structured arguments that demonstrate a sound understanding of animal welfare legal principles is likely to be much more persuasive to the Court, and in turn, of benefit to the interests of those being legally represented.

With that in mind, civil arguments are frequently more authoritative, credible and acceptable if they will reference established legal principles that are set out before the Courts in criminal animal welfare law. Additional weight can be given to civil arguments by referencing additional considerations that have informed

National animal welfare law   169

criminal law. Those considerations include, for example, property principles, public safety and credible 'science' in determining what is 'necessary' and/or 'reasonable' in terms of the animals as property which can experience pain, distress, or suffering.

The law imposes a duty on all persons to avoid causing harm to others, or to their property. Animals are 'unique property', which may demonstrate that uniqueness in ways that are significantly different from traditional chattels, and be potentially problematic for their owners. In broad terms, civil wrongs involving animals largely fall into one of two groups – either damage done *by* animals or damage done *to* animals.

Damages by *animals*

There is a difference between inanimate and animate property. Species differences are illustrated by imagining that the 'animate property' told to 'sit, stay' is a cat. Cat owners would generally agree that dog owners have significantly better chances of their pet obeying a command to 'sit and stay', than cat owners. Despite these obvious differences, as a general rule, tortious liability applies to animals in much the same way as it does to other chattels/property, in that the person in charge of an animal has a responsibility to be in control of their property/animals at all times, with a view to ensuring that their property/animal does not cause harm to other people or their property.

A range of civil offences reflects a person not fulfilling their legal responsibility to control their animals. For example, an owner of a dog may be penalised if his dog strays, in recognition of the fact that an uncontrolled animal poses potential risks to the wider public/community. If the dog strays onto a road, then the owner may be considered legally *negligent*,[105] in the event that a Court considers that any injury/damage which occurred was a direct result of the owner failing to exercise reasonable care in controlling their dog.

The law has evolved special rules regarding liabilities in respect of harm/damage/injury which occurs in circumstances where animals stray (e.g., are not properly contained and/or contained with either fencing or leads), or pose a recognised danger to the public (e.g., dangerous dogs). Historically, the law was particularly indulgent

---

105 Negligence is a tort which depends on the existence of a breaking of the duty of care owed by one person to another. There are five elements in determining liability for negligence. These are: 1. The plaintiff was owed a duty of care demonstrating an obligation upon the defendant to take proper care to avoid causing injury to the plaintiff. 2. The duty of care was breached by the defendant. 3. The breach of duty by the defendant is directly connected to the injury/harm suffered by the plaintiff. 4. The plaintiff suffered injury/harm/damage as a result of the breach of the duty of care by the defendant. 5. The damage suffered by the plaintiff is sufficiently proximate to the tort being addressed.

'Proximate' imputes that the defendant's culpable conduct be the actual cause of the plaintiff's injury. Damages are less likely to be recovered if the relationship between the defendant's conduct and the plaintiff's injury does not, in the opinion of the Court guided by established tests (e.g., foreseeability) justify imposing tort/legal responsibility on the defendant (see *Donoghue v Stevenson* [1932] AC 562).

170 *National animal welfare law*

to the owners of stock (e.g., cattle and sheep) which strayed on to the highway. In a number of jurisdictions, this has subsequently changed in recognition of the fact that keepers have a responsibility (subject to various legal defences) for the movements and containment of animals, and that the law absolving persons in charge from any liability was out of date with modern society and legal developments.[106]

The same principle of legal responsibility for controlling an animal continues to be demonstrated in a number of other common situations involving animals. For example, an occupier of the premises may be liable (*'occupiers liability'*) if injury is caused by the occupier's animal (e.g., dog) to a person lawfully entering the premises.[107] Additionally, an owner/person in charge of an animal may incur liability in *nuisance*,[108] if his animal/property interferes with a neighbour's right to enjoy their own property, free from excessive noise (e.g., barking) and/or smell, or other unreasonable disturbances. Given the widespread and diverse role of dogs in human society, the law has developed a range of special rules concerning people's responsibilities for controlling dogs, and attaching liabilities for a range of disturbances including attacking, worrying, and/or chasing other animals or people's.

In broad terms, owners and/or persons in charge of animals have a legal responsibility to control each animal in their care, and are liable for property damage caused by the animal. The law demonstrates an acknowledgement that this broad rule should be read in consideration of the species, environment and wider circumstances regarding the animal and its individual circumstances. Down the chain of 'less responsibility means less liability', reduced liability is associated with feral and/or definitively non-domesticated animals in a wild state.

Harm done *by* animals is substantively different to legal issues involving harm done *to* animals.

Damages to *animals*

Damages to animals address circumstances where an animal has usually either been injured or died, but can be awarded to owners on behalf of suffering of the animal.

CALCULATING DAMAGES: 'HOW MUCH IS THE LAW VALUING
THAT DOGGY IN THE WINDOW'?

The starting point is 'fair market value'. Widening concern about harm to animals has raised increasing questions about the law which determines the appropriate

---

106 A 1975 report concerning 'The law relating to liability for animals' demonstrates how the law has changed, and the continuing underlying principles (e.g., control) which none the less continue – Torts and General Law Reform Committee. 1975. 'Law Relating to Liability for Animals': http://132.181.2.68/Data/Library4/law_reports/tortsgenr_300155.pdf.

107 Section 5(3) Animals Act 1971 (England).

108 From the legal perspective, the term 'nuisance' is traditionally used to describe an activity, and/or associated harm, as a result of a particular activity that unreasonably interferes either with the rights of individuals or with the legal rights of the general public: see *Jones v Powell* (1629).

level of damages in cases involving an animal. The legal classification of animals as property has resulted in an animal's value being determined primarily on economic terms. Consequently, if a cow was harmed or killed, then damages were the market value. If the cost of veterinary care and recovery exceeded the market value, then the animal was often euthanased – not on humane grounds, but on economic grounds. Simply put, in many instances where an animal is injured, it makes little economic sense to invest in the treatment and care of an animal if the money to replace the animal is less than the money to repair it. From the law's perspective, this economic reference point is known as the animal's 'fair market value'.

The 'fair market value' may subsequently be adjusted by consideration to a list of individual factors which may increase/decrease the starting-point value. In addition to considerations of the age of the animal, the breed and species (e.g., purebred or 'mixed breed'), and reference to the cost of simply replacing that animal with another 'like' animal, the value may be affected by additional considerations, such as the animal's role and/or skills. The investment of time and training into a guide dog, for example, may be taken into consideration by the Court in determining the animal's 'replacement value'.

WHAT ABOUT COMPENSATION FOR 'EMOTIONAL DAMAGES'?

Valuation of an animal simply by economic considerations, however, sits uncomfortably with the reality that the relationship between many people and their pets is not based simply on economics. Pet ownership, for example, is widespread in many countries and it is common to find that a predominance of households either own, or have recently owned, a pet. Although the value of certain pets is linked to the awards that they have won or their breeding capacity, the majority of pets are kept simply as part and parcel of a family life, or even viewed by their owners as members of the family.

None the less, the depth of emotion that many people have in reference to animals (which has been referred to by a number of alternative terms including the 'emotional link', 'human–animal bond', or 'human–animal relationship') has, on occasion, resulted in people pursuing legal proceedings on the basis that 'it is the principle' (i.e., of accountability enforced by the law due to applied liability), despite the risk that they will spend more on lawyers than they are likely to recover from the Courts.

One objective measure of the 'emotional value' is the amount of money that an owner will spend on their animal, above and beyond simple calculations of replacement and/or market value. An owner of a companion animal may, for example, spend substantially more on that animal's health care and surgical repair (in the case of injury) than what it would cost to simply euthanase/kill the injured animal and replace it with another.

The disparity between the Court's consideration of 'fair market value' and the 'emotional value' of many animals to their owners has attracted criticism. In response, some Courts/jurisdictions have included consideration of emotional

172 *National animal welfare law*

consequences (e.g., on the owner) when determining the monetary sum to be paid by the defendants. If the perpetrator's conduct is deemed intentional and/or malicious, for example, it may be possible to seek punitive damages.[109] In some jurisdictions, Courts have also recognised that the unique relationship (i.e., between owners and their pets) is difficult or impossible to simply replace, and permitted the human care-taker to recover damages on the basis of 'reasonable sentimental value'.

For example, a New Zealand case addressed an instance where a neighbour 'returned' a small dog to its owner's property by throwing it through a hedge. In passing through the hedge, the dog was impaled on a broken branch, and subsequently died. The neighbour's behaviour attracted significant criticism from the Court (particularly when it was identified that the person involved was a dog breeder and a member of the local kennel club who 'should have known better'). Moreover, the dog that was killed belonged to an elderly woman whose only companion was her dog. The man was convicted and fined $1,000 with $2,000 reparation to be paid to the owner of the dog for the emotional harm caused.[110] Referencing this case shortly afterwards, another New Zealand Court ordered 'emotional reparation' to be paid by an Asian student who stomped a small dog to death after it had defecated in his room, despite allegations by the student that such behaviour was 'normal in his home country'.[111]

Each legal jurisdiction is likely to have its own sentencing rules and procedures that impact the potential success of any legal action seeking recovery of damages/ compensation concerning the death or injury of an owned animal. In the event that a defendant is found legally responsible by the Court, then the usual/common penalty imposed on the defendant is the obligation to pay a monetary sum in compensation. The starting point of reference to 'fair market value' presents a potential practical dilemma for those bringing legal proceedings on the basis that, even if the Court finds in their favour, the monetary sum that they are likely to receive is likely to be limited by reference to the cost of replacing the animal that has been injured or killed, and potentially significantly less than it would cost to engage a lawyer and pursue legal recourse. Courts now appear increasingly willing to recognise the enormous capacity of humans to form bonds with animals,[112] and the fact that non-pecuniary damages have been awarded sets a precedent that 'unlocks' traditionally accessible options to animal owners and care-givers via their legal representative.

Despite a continuing reluctance by some Courts to address the issue of compensation for emotional harm, the issue is not likely to disappear, particularly in view of the fact that animal law, as a legal discipline, continues to strengthen and evolve. The legal issue regarding emotional harm is real, and legal issues involving animals are frequently too egregious to be ignored. An increasingly animal-conscious public recognises the injustice of limiting the liability of a wrongdoer simply to the market value of the harmed, sometimes killed, animal.

109 Damages exceeding simple compensation and awarded to punish the defendant.
110 *NZ Police v Spittle* unreported, District Court (Queenstown, NZ), 3 June 2008.
111 *NZ Police v Dingshan Xiao* unreported, District Court (Christchurch, NZ), 27 August 2008.
112 *Wisconsin Supreme Court in Rabideau v City of Racine*, 627 N.W.2d 795 (Wis. 2001).

National animal welfare law 173

Criminal law recognises that animals are capable of suffering unnecessary and/or unreasonable pain and distress, and the reality is that the animal's experience is often closely associated with much more than simply human loss of property, but potential emotional suffering as well. It is predictable that the Courts and legislatures of multiple jurisdictions will continue moving toward adopting laws that make at least some provision for enhancement of damages beyond mere market value, for intentional and negligent harm to pets.

VETERINARY NEGLIGENCE

Trends acknowledging the emotional link between people and animals have enormous implications for professions and professionals associated with animals. One of the tort law subjects being addressed by animal law practitioners involves the issue of veterinary negligence.

Most veterinarians are good-hearted professionals who genuinely strive to give the best care possible to animals and owners alike. Like all other professions, there is a variety of skills and experience demonstrated amongst practitioners, and sometimes things simply go wrong. While it is reasonable to expect that veterinarians would have professional indemnity insurance for such occasions, they understandably remain in a position of prime responsibility and accountability by both the owner, the owner's legal representative and – depending on the prevailing law, facts, evidence and circumstances – the Courts.

The legal shifts in the animal law landscape are particularly relevant to veterinarians (e.g., companion animal veterinarians) who largely trade off, and derive significant pecuniary gain from the emotional value that people attach to their animals. Producers of pet products, pet foods, pet transporters and others whose activities involve animals represent additional parties who logically would stand to be affected by a shift in the law that recognises emotional harm as a potential head of claim. On consideration, the potential impact would not be limited simply to companion animals, given the reality that owners of large animals (e.g., horses, purebred herds, animals on lifestyle blocks), and animals having wider specific roles (e.g., working animals) frequently demonstrate their human care-giver's 'emotional' investment in them, and emotional value of them.

'The money' closely attached to the emotional value of animals, is demonstrated in the relevant figures. For example, in New Zealand, annual spending on companion animals is estimated to be in excess of $100 million. In the UK, pet owners spend an estimated £5 billion per year on their companion animals. In the US, pet owners spend in excess of $11 billion per year. Remembering that these figures relate to the companion-animal industry alone, it follows that the monetary sum that is attached to the wider uses of animals in companionship, agriculture, research, industry, sports and entertainment – many of which are likely to contain an element of 'emotional value' – would amount to significantly larger financial sums.

Despite the assumptions by many people that the veterinary profession would be the first to acknowledge the emotional value of animals, it has argued against the Courts including considerations for emotional harm when considering

174　*National animal welfare law*

penalties in relevant cases (e.g., veterinary negligence). Veterinary professionals have alleged that such a shift in the law would have many negative consequences, including an increase in their professional indemnity premiums.[113] Others argue that veterinarians should simply 'get insurance' and accept it is as a 'normal part of doing business'.

The issue (of awarding penalties based on emotional value) is contentious. But an increasing number of legislatures have implemented greater legal protections for animals, and questions about their value have become the topics of litigation. The legal reality remains that the precedent for award of non-economic damages exists. The door is not yet open wide, but perhaps the keyword in that description is 'yet'.

ANIMALS IN MATRIMONIAL SPLITS: 'I DON'T WANT HALF
A DOG'

It's difficult to split unique property. Animal custody cases increasingly constitute matters that may involve lawyers, and necessitate consideration to the animal's welfare.

The traditional view is that in cases of matrimonial dissolutions, there is a 50–50 starting point for splitting matrimonial chattels. This starting point depends largely on the prevalence law. In jurisdictions that function on the basis of a community property jurisdiction, all of the couple's property is split 50–50 between the husband and wife. In contrast, in jurisdictions that operate on the basis of an equitable distribution, the Court will divide the property on the basis of what it decides is 'equitable' (determinations of what is 'fair'), which may not always equate with what would be mathematically 'equal'. The Court will often consider what items lawfully constitute 'matrimonial property'. It will make an order in determining which party retains what property. This same basic procedure is used as the basis for determining which party retains a pet, on the basis that the animal is legally categorised as property.

Despite the fact that animals are legally classified as property, there is obviously a difficulty in applying a strict 50–50 split to animals. This is illustrated by one circumstance where a woman involved in matrimonial dissolutions approached her lawyer brother with instructions that he was to make sure that she got 'Rex', the family dog. Reportedly, the brother, despite being an experienced lawyer, made the mistake of commenting that animals were 'like any other property' and was subject to the traditional 50–50 split starting point. In response, his sister allegedly told him in no uncertain terms that she didn't want 'half a dog'!

The fact remains that when marriages dissolve, it is common for couples to have to decide who gets what. Some items, which frequently include the family pet, may be particularly contentious. Lawyers offering specialist legal services in

---

113　Steve Barghusen, 'Non-economic damage awards in veterinary malpractice: Using the human medical experience as a model to predict the effect of non-economic damage awards on the practice of companion animal veterinary medicine': https://law.lclark.edu/live/files/11149-171-barghusen.

National animal welfare law 175

the area of animal law, are seeing an increase in the number of pet custody battles due to the changing social attitudes regarding pets (e.g., as 'family members'), and the sheer numbers involved. For example, if 40 per cent of households have pets and 50 per cent of marriages end in divorce, then pet custody disputes are potentially an issue in about 20 per cent of households. The significance of that 20 per cent is further illustrated by considering the millions of animals that are kept as household pets. The majority (80 per cent plus) of disputes reportedly involve dogs, 5–10 per cent involve cats, and 5–10 per cent relate to 'other' species, including large numbers of ornate birds,[114] farmyard animals and horses.

Amicable dissolutions and agreed pet custody arrangements may result in the animal (e.g., the family dog) having the benefit of greater stimulation in shuttling between various locations, and interactions with wider family/friends rather than being left at home alone in the backyard. However, people involved in matrimonial dissolutions may also use animals as tools of revenge. For example, in a case where the husband went to pick up the dog from his estranged wife, he discovered that she had had the valuable breeding dog spayed, without any consultation with the husband whatsoever.

Pet custody issues reflect how societal attitudes regarding animal companions have evolved to a point where many animals are considered not just an extension of the family, to being described as 'family members' themselves. However, despite the fact that there are a significant number of people who see their pets as members of the family, this doesn't mean that the law regarding pet custody disputes is likely to change significantly in the near future. This is due to a number of factors which include, for example, practical administrative considerations surrounding the limitation of Court resources, and continuing prevailing attitudes which largely hold that while animals may warrant special consideration, they none the less remain 'different' from people.

WHAT IS WORTH CONSIDERING?

Depending upon the jurisdiction, the creativity of the Court and the individual circumstances of the people involved, a number of solutions have been implemented. Some animal lawyers make reference to what is termed 'petimony', which is an alimony-like payment for maintenance costs of the pet to the custodial owner from the non-custodial owner. Shared custody and visitation rights for the non-custodial owner have also been implemented. Such arrangements may present a problem if there is no explicit legal authority for such judgments, which is compounded where there is limited ability to police and/or enforce such orders. Where continuing problems of compliance exists, and if the Court is unable and/ or unwilling to (re-)address issues of pet custody, then the people involved may be forced to resolve the issue between themselves and/or engage lawyers to assist in creating a written contractual agreement.

---

114 Kristin Tillotson. 2012. 'When Couples Split, Who Gets the Dog?', *Wichita Eagle*, 5 April: www. kansas.com/2012/04/05/2287277/when-couples-split-who-gets-the.html#storylink=cpy.

176   *National animal welfare law*

People who are attached to their pets are often willing to pay significant sums of money to retain custody, either by paying out the spouse or engaging the assistance of lawyers. That reality raises questions about what criteria may be relevant in determining who ultimately gets custody of the family pet.

Cases illustrate that there are a wide variety of considerations that may be taken into account in the course of pet custody cases. For example, the timing of purchase of a pet can be relevant. Whether the animal was purchased by one party before or after the marriage may have a bearing. Similarly, if the animal was a gift, then the timing of that gift may also be relevant because if the gift was given after marriage, then it's usually considered matrimonial property.

While some cases demonstrate that the interests of the animals involved have been taken into account, this is usually a discretionary consideration of the Court. Decisions regarding who gets the pet must comply with relevant law, and take into account the interests of the parties involved. For example, the Court's determination about who gets the pet may be affected by whether children are attached to the matrimonial dissolution. Pet custody issues often become more contentious when there are no children involved in the matrimonial dispute, because the pets may have become 'surrogate children'. Alternatively, the children's best interests may be a consideration where children are attached to the family pet, on the grounds that the disruption and impact of a matrimonial dissolution may be reduced by ensuring that the family pet resides with the parent who has custody of the children, given that the continued presence of the family pet provides a point of consistency in the children's lives during a time of otherwise significant change.

Other relevant considerations, evidence, and interests that the Court may take into account include:

- Who spends the most time with the animal? This point may be argued in terms of what benefits not just the animal, but also the interests of the relevant person as well, including the children.
- Who is/was the primary care-giver? This involves consideration about who has provided daily care for the animal, attended to registering it, taking the animal to the veterinarian and/or paying the relevant (e.g., veterinary) bills.
- Who owns the animal? Whose name is the animal (e.g., dog) registered in? These are just some of the questions that may be relevant to considerations of ownership. While not being decisive when taken in context of all the circumstances, supporting documentation often provides valuable evidence that is potentially persuasive to the Court's decision making.
- How likely is the animal to adapt to change? This may be argued as relevant to protecting the animal's interests of avoiding unreasonable and/or unnecessary distress. Naturally, this may depend on the species and individual nature of the animal. For example, it cannot be automatically assumed that all dogs are able to adapt to any changes in their environment. However it would generally be agreed that dogs are likely to be more adaptable to change (e.g., shifting locations) than many cats.

National animal welfare law   177

- What 'benefits'/'dangers' are relevant in an animal's new environment? An unsafe yard, or the presence of other dangerous/aggressive animals, may be examples of considerations which have an obvious bearing on the well-being of the animal. However, the Court could assist the person to best fulfil their legal responsibilities concerning the animal.

Applying the principles of animal welfare law in matrimonial disputes

Discussions about pet custody inherently contain significant amounts of subjective opinion, demonstrated by the word 'should'. There are those who advocate that the interests of the animal 'should' be given as much weight as the interests of the children in any matrimonial dispute. In contrast, there are those who take the view that while the law 'should' give regard to the well-being of the animals, it is not only unlawful to regard animals as children (given that animals are legally classified as property), but is also a step too far to make such a comparison. Indeed, the Courts themselves demonstrate an unwillingness to establish animal law Courts similar to family Courts dealing with child custody disputes. Administratively, this is unsurprising given the fact that many Courts are already struggling to keep up with significant workloads and limited resources. However, civil law offers the opportunity to refer to the established interest of animals set out in criminal animal welfare law.

THE STARTING POINT OR 'THE ULTIMATE ARGUMENT'?

Criminal law has established a precedent to benchmark that there is a legal obligation to protect animals from unnecessary, or unreasonable, pain and/or distress. On assessment of persuasive arguments that have traditionally been used in civil Courts that take into account the interests of the animal (as opposed to focusing solely on the legal rights/interests of the people involved), those arguments predominantly revolve around the concept of maximising the animal's well-being, the antithesis of arrangements which results in unnecessary, or unreasonable, pain and/or distress to the animal.

While it is unlikely that any Court would knowingly make a decision that results in an animal experiencing pain, it is the animal welfare lawyer's understanding of, and references to, what constitutes 'distress', that will add veracity and credibility to arguments and/or counter-arguments proposing who should rightly/lawfully be awarded custody of the animal in question.

Referencing this established criminal law benchmark arguably adds rigour to legal arguments seeking to persuade civil Court adjudicators that the interests of the animal are a lawfully relevant consideration and not simply a discretionary consideration that hinges on the individual views and presence/absence of sympathies regarding animals of the adjudicator.

In addition to the understanding and ability of the representing lawyer, relevant law, the legal jurisdiction and the influence of the presiding Judge are all

178   *National animal welfare law*

likely to be weighty determinants to deciding who gets the family pet. None the less, mirroring strengthening concerns of the law and the public alike regarding an animal's welfare, and the well-being of the pet in matrimonial dissolutions is likely to follow a course where animals are viewed as 'unique property', rather than simply 'mere property'.

Wills and trusts: special property requires special legal consideration

If a person does not provide clear instructions as to how property is to be distributed upon their death, then the property is frequently held (e.g., in trust) while the person's estate is finalised. Domesticated animals[115] are considered a person's absolute property under the law, and obviously there are particular problems in respect of animals as animate property, given that they cannot be simply kept in a storage facility while issues of property ownership and distribution are decided.

Validity issues

The concept of ensuring legally enforceable documentation to ensure continuing care for animals after their owner's death has attracted a range of responses from humour to criticism. Additionally, outdated and/or incorrect views of estate-planning professionals which, for example, continue to view animals as if they were 'just like any other property' runs the risk that the owner's instructions will not be followed.

Legally enforceable documentation is an important prerequisite to ensuring that an owner's wishes are implemented after the owner's death. One of the first considerations is whether the owner wants to leave instructions by way of a will, or whether some other legal instrument may be more appropriate (e.g., a trust). The *will* is valid after death, and its purpose is to distribute property. Alternatively, for example, a traditional *pet trust* enlists a trustee who distributes funds and takes responsibility for ensuring that the person providing the day-to-day care for a pet follows the owner's instructions.

Pets in wills

Although looking after an animal via a will has long been held as adequate for meeting an owner's wishes and providing for the animal's needs, it also has inherent problems. If the owner chooses to address matters concerning their animals in their will, then there are a number of key legal considerations that must be properly taken into account in order to ensure that a will is practically implementable, as well as being adjudged legally valid.

---

115 Domestic animals include 'all those domestic or tame animals as by habit or training live in association with man': *Halsbury's Laws of England* (Volume 2(1)), *Animals*, 4th edn reissue (London: LexisNexis Butterworths, 2000), p. 508.

National animal welfare law 179

Given that the purpose of a will is largely to disburse property, there is a need to ensure that the will is particularly clear and contains legally binding instructions. However, it can be difficult or even impossible for a will to stipulate exactly how bequeathed property is to be treated in practical terms. Simply stipulating that a particular piece of property (albeit whether that property is a car or a cat) is to be bequeathed to an individual cannot necessarily compel the new owner to look after their new possession in a specifically detailed way.

Additionally, there are a number of important legal criteria which must be met prior to the will being considered legally valid. For example, an owner cannot 'leave property to property', so there are legal problems implementing the wishes of an owner who seeks to leave funds directly to an animal, given that the animal is, under the law, classified as property.

Validity, enforceability of the owner's instructions and delays in enactment (including consideration to whom is responsible for caring for the animal until such time as the will is enacted) are just a few of the relevant considerations which require considerable attention to detail and an understanding of animal welfare and animal law.

With these validity issues in mind, commentators have suggested various ways in which the client can provide for the animals in his or her will, for example, providing for the animals and the owner's wishes by way of outright gifts, conditional gifts, and conditional gifts in a trust. *Inter vivos* trusts have also been suggested to cover the time lapse between death and execution of an established will, with the intent of caring for the animals.

How would you make provision for one horse, two dogs, and a parrot?

The theoretical example of a person wishing to make provision for their animals including a horse, two dogs, and a parrot, demonstrates the importance of planning for each individual animal. As these are domestic animals, they are the client's absolute property.[116] If the owner does not include them in her will, the animals will be held on trust by her personal representative with the power to sell them.[117] To minimise avoidable complications with any will, it is advisable that people engage the assistance of a suitably trained professional to ensure clear compliance with legal requirements. This is particularly good advice in respect of animals, given that they are animate and frequently almost totally reliant on people for their well-being and consideration of their individual needs, personalities and preferences.

A horse is clearly a much larger animal with specific husbandry, housing and dietary needs that are significantly different to those of the dogs and the parrot. Consequently, the horse would need individualised consideration, separate to planning put in place for the dogs. Case Study 5 provides an interesting example

116 Ibid., p. 509.
117 Section 33(1) of the Administration of Estates Act 1925.

180 *National animal welfare law*

of horse neglect and whether the penalty fitted the crime. Consistent with consideration given to the individual animals, the owner and responsible/professional estate planner may consider the merits of giving attention to the relationship between animals like the two dogs. If the two demonstrate compatibility and benefit from staying together, then the owner may want them to be homed together. On the other hand, practicalities or the fact that the two dogs 'don't get along' may mean that the best option is to house each of the dogs in separate homes. Alternatively, the person to whom the dogs are bequeathed may simply not have the physical ability or space to look after two dogs. The breed would also be a relevant consideration, given that the space required to look after two Great Danes would obviously be much more then looking after two Chihuahuas. Local authority regulations, dietary and exercise needs of the animals, and relevant costs (e.g., veterinary bills, insurance) also need consideration.

Finally, not everyone is aware that certain breeds of parrots can live for eighty years.[118] A competent estate planner will recognise that there may be issues in respect of legal criteria surrounding the traditional 21-year perpetuity period as it applies to the parrot, potentially the horse which can live for sixty years[119] and the dogs, which could live for thirty.[120] Properly caring for the wishes of an owner and the needs of an animal is a legal exercise that requires careful planning, including a search for individuals who are really suited and genuinely committed – regardless of the financial incentives involved. If the owner is able to locate such people and utilises the trust method, then he may have reasonable assurance that his instructions will be followed. On some occasions though, an owner may indicate that the best option is to order their pet's or pets' destruction on the owner's death.

Case Study 5: How do you get the court penalty to fit the crime?

After identification that the gap between 'wilful' ill-treatment of an animal and standard ill-treatment of an animal was resulting in penalties that did not fit the crime, New Zealand introduced an offence of 'reckless' ill-treatment to its animal welfare legislation. New Zealand's first conviction for reckless ill-treatment involved a horse that the owner had deferred obtaining veterinary care on the basis that she had ordered, and was waiting for, medications to be sent from overseas. In the meantime, the horse deteriorated to such an extent that it was euthanased upon humane grounds when it was seen by the attending animal welfare officer. The Court provided particularly important

---

118 Encyclopaedia Britannica Online, 'Parrot': www.britannica.com/EBchecked/topic/849547/parrot.
119 Encyclopaedia Britannica Online, 'Life Span – Maximum Longevity of Animals in Captivity': www.britannica.com/EBchecked/topic/340297/life-span/63861/Perennials#toc63864.
120 Ibid.

instruction not just in terms of the definition of 'recklessness', but also the appropriate place of well-intended, but none the less criminally irresponsible actions, of owners who fail to provide for the needs of animals in their care to a standard required by law.

The defendant had stated that the horse had sustained a 'wire injury' to its rear right leg. A veterinarian had been called and although euthanasia had been discussed, treatment was commenced and the horse was described as making 'great progress'. The defendant indicated that some time later, the horse had scratched the injury and the leg had subsequently deteriorated. The defendant said that she cleaned the leg and treated the animal with penicillin. She also indicated that she looked on the Internet for treatments and alternatives, and that in the period of approximately two months that the lesion took to get to the size it did prior to euthanasia, the horse was still eating grass and happy. The defendant also indicated that the day before the animal was euthanased, she (the owner) had obtained a product from the United States that was reported to dissolve proud flesh, but she never got a chance to try it. The defendant said she had had horses on and off for most of her life, and always had the horse's best interests at heart.

Veterinary evidence regarding the animal's poor condition and related lesion stated that the time frame was a matter of months rather than days or weeks. The horse was judged as having a body condition of 0.5 (on a scale from 0 to 5), and being reluctant to move due to its lameness (which was assessed as 4 on a scale from 0 to 5). Professional assessment considered that the horse was in 'extreme pain', that the lesion was not compatible with a decent quality of life, and that any future treatment was unlikely to be warranted and unrewarding.

The Court referred to the legal definition of recklessness provided in recent Court of Appeal decisions which illustrate that 'a person will be reckless if he or she is aware of the risk and it is, in the circumstances known to him or her, unreasonable to take the risk concerned'.

Referring to, and accepting, the evidence of the experts that the horse was in a poor condition and emaciated, the Court made a point of stating that it did not accept the defendant's evidence that the horse was acting in a perfectly normal manner or eating normally up until the day prior to the horse being put down.

The Court drew attention to two key considerations:

Firstly, the defendant's actions to combat the infection were not effective in preventing the horse from suffering pain and distress. The Court considered that it was obvious to the defendant that the use of alternative remedies was having no effect, which was substantiated by the fact that the defendant attempted to obtain a cream from the United States. The Court stated that it

(continued)

182   *National animal welfare law*

(continued)

would have been obvious to the defendant that her attempts to combat the infection were not having any effect and that, as the proud flesh was growing, there was a corresponding effect on the condition of the horse which was progressively getting worse.

The second aspect to the ill-treatment was the defendant's omission to obtain proper veterinary advice. In response to argument from the defendant's legal counsel that the defendant had an honest and genuine belief that the alternative remedies would work, and that it was therefore not unreasonable in the circumstances for the defendant to refuse alternative remedies, the Court stated:

> Like many things in life distinctions as to what is reasonable or unreasonable are matters of degree. I think in this case the defendant has well and truly overstepped the boundary . . . In this case we are not even talking about an issue as to whether there was a possibility that the cream [obtained from the United States] may have destroyed the proud flesh, and the horse could [subsequently] have been nursed back to good health. The only evidence I have before me is that the wound was untreatable and the horse was going to die anyway.

In support of its finding that the Court was 'clearly satisfied that the defendant was reckless', the Court stated:

> the defendant took the risk and it was unreasonable for her to take that risk. The defendant's daily observations of the horse made it obvious that the horse was not responding to treatment and the defendant pursued both her treatment and a method to obtain proper treatment for the horse for a period of some two months.

The Court also provided clear direction on the relevance of the attachment between animals and their human owners, and owners' 'intentions' in considerations of alleged animal welfare offending:

> I think that what has occurred in this case is that the defendant had a deep attachment to the horse . . . I think that the defendant in her heart knew that she should obtain proper veterinary advice, but it was likely if not inevitable a vet would give her the advice she did not want to hear, namely, that the wound was not treatable and the horse would have to be euthanased.

> I accept that owners of animals and pets can become attached to them. That attachment can often result in making decisions that are clearly wrong and not in the best interests of the animal. Often such decisions are made with the best interests of the owners in mind rather than the

> animals . . . while I can accept that the defendant did not intentionally ill-treat the horse, she was clearly reckless in her actions'.
>
> Lisa Kirsten-McHaffie was convicted and fined.
>
> There are a number of key points and learnings from this case which include the benefit of the Court's ability to apply a penalty that fits the crime where there is an established offence of recklessness, the judicial definition of recklessness, and clarification that an owner can be guilty of reckless animal welfare offending in circumstances where the animal's interests are prioritised below an owner's intentions and/or emotional attachment.
>
> (*Citation New Zealand Police v Lisa Kirsten McHaffie*, 31 May 2011, Balclutha District Court (New Zealand), O'Driscoll J, CRI-2010-005-000479)

Destruction of animals

It is common practice for advisers to examine alternative options for providing for the animal in preference to euthanasing the animal upon the owner's death. Creating a power of appointment has been utilised to enable and identify a home for the animals. Alternatively, various organisations may undertake to care for the animals and find new homes for them.

Some owners specify that they wish their animals to be euthanased in the event of their (the owner's) death. Contemporary animal welfare law sets out that it is not unlawful to kill an animal provided it is done in an appropriate and humane manner.[121] None the less, owners should also be aware that despite traditional rules implementing the owner's wishes, provisions dictating destruction of an animal may potentially be invalidated on the grounds that they are contrary to public policy and animal welfare legislation. For example, public policy might take the view that the destruction of an animal is a waste of estate property, especially if the animal is a particular pedigree.[122] The intentional destruction of perfectly healthy animals may also be regarded unethical and immoral.[123] A number of Courts have struck down similar provisions following public outcry about their wrongfulness.[124] Although foreign jurisprudence may not necessarily be binding on a local jurisdiction, it may none the less prove persuasive, especially given the fact that animals and their welfare is a subject that has attracted significant public interest and involvement.

---

121 Section 9 of the Animal Welfare Act 2006 (England).
122 Philip Jamieson. 1987–89. 'The Family Pet: A Limitation on the Freedom of Testamentary Disposition?', *University of Tasmania Law Review*, 9: 51, 56.
123 Ibid.
124 In the American case of *Smith v Avanzino*, a statute was specially enacted by the California state legislature just to save a dog's life: No. 225698, 17 June 1980 (Super. Ct., San Francisco Country), as cited in Carlisle, 897.

184 *National animal welfare law*

There are many legal issues of providing for animals after an owner's death if it is to be done properly. The beneficiary principal, rules against perpetuities, and rules surrounding any gifts to charity are just a few of them. While full coverage of the issues involved is outside the ambit of this book, the point is that for owners wishing to make sure that their animals are properly cared for in the event of their death, then there is a need to make sure that the lawyer that they choose to assist them demonstrates not just an ability in respect of the rules pertaining to trusts, but also a competent understanding of animal welfare and relevant legal matters that goes well beyond simply treating them 'like any other property'.

Are you critically assessing national animal welfare issues?

Having covered the basics of foundational concepts that have been translated into contemporary law that governs human–human interactions concerning animals, and human–animal responsibilities, consider the following tasks and questions. In the first instance you might want to identify your immediate response, then compare it with the conclusions you reach in applying the model of critical assessment set out for you in Chapter 3:

- Discuss current debates on the property status of animals, and critically assess the proposed alternatives regarding an animal's current legal status.
- Critically assess animal welfare enforcement utilising a model which recognises voluntary assistance, assisted compliance and directed compliance as prerequisite/preferred alternatives to prosecution.
- Discuss legal standards of animal welfare as set by the law in comparison to legal standards advocated by other stakeholders including industry, and non-government organisations.
- Contrast and compare the animal welfare law of differing jurisdictions in respect of their theoretical and applied commitment to effective animal welfare outcomes.

6 International law is international 'persuasion'

This chapter extends the focus beyond national borders, and considers matters of governance (including, but not limited to, legal instruments) of global issues that are relevant to animal welfare in the international marketplace. For example, it puts national laws in the context of international organisations and obligations by identifying the key global governors impacting matters of animal welfare, identifying the issues that the government must deal with, and encouraging a critical assessment of the real drivers and mechanics of international animal law. Having identified these, the reader should then be in a position to critically assess whether or not the global governors are on track for delivering outcomes that will meet the needs of animals and humans alike in 2050 and beyond.

By the end of this chapter you should be able to:

- objectively discuss animal welfare in context of 'international law';
- identify the relationship between animal welfare and key global issues affecting each sovereign state;
- identify key governance issues of global animal welfare;
- critically assess who leads the development of international animal welfare and law; and
- discuss how animal welfare law is keeping up with contemporary global issues, debates and technologies.

Defining 'international law'

International law deals with relationships that go beyond the borders of any one country. International laws and institutions have a variety of roles which include dealing with crimes committed across or beyond borders, regulating international movement of animals, people and goods by sea or air across international land borders, and regulating contracts for the sale of goods and services (including animal products and animals) between countries. These examples are obviously just a few of the many issues that attach to the fact that the majority of countries are involved in trade of some kind.

Over centuries, law has been developed to deal with all international relationship issues through practice (known as customary international law), agreements

186   *International animal welfare law*

(known generically as treaties), general principles of law, Court decisions and contributing academic opinion.

The functions of many rules of international law are essentially the same as those of national law. They may, for example, establish constitutions of international organisations (e.g., the Charter of the United Nations), be equated to legislation (e.g., written law of United Nations Conventions), determine boundaries between nations, and/or establish bilateral or multilateral contracts involving a mutual exchange of promises and/or undertakings.

The subject matter of international law is extensive and growing, as its emphasis moves from the coexistence of states to cooperation between them, particularly as it is increasingly recognised that global opportunities are attached to global risks that affect all nations. Many areas are covered by international law and include agreements concerning international trade, finance and commerce; international communications, and the environment. Issues of animal welfare and its relevance to food supply and safety, disease control, zoonoses and other biosecurity issues, are becoming increasingly recognised.

In the beginning, Parliament was supreme . . .

'The government should do something': people frequently whip out this line as if it were the simple remedy for a whole range of societal problems, including issues related to the subject of animal welfare. But the reality is that governments don't have unlimited resources, nor can they really operate in a truly independent fashion if they are to function, thrive, or even survive – because even governments have obligations to comply with the rules of an international market. In a sense, there is no truly 'international law' that governs autonomous states. State sovereignty is a concept that sets out the idea that each state enjoys autonomy separate from every other nation state. That autonomy means that a state is not bound to comply with any international rules unless it has conceded to do so as part of its membership obligations.

State sovereignty empowers individual states, or countries, with the legal authority and autonomy to govern themselves. That autonomy implies that each state is free to decide for itself which laws it will, or will not, adopt, including rules regarding animals. Effectively, parliamentary legislative supremacy (in England and in other countries that follow the English model of law) means that the powers of Parliament are legally unconstrained. Therefore, if Parliament is persuaded of the merits of a particular course of action, then it has the inherent power and authority to translate those merits into law; it is outside the authoritative scope of the judiciary or anyone else to question the validity of Parliament's authority to act on the legislative provisions enacted by Parliament.

The doctrine of parliamentary supremacy means that in theory, Parliament has complete autonomy to decide for itself what measures it will enact in respect of animals and their protection. However, it would be farcical to assert that this autonomy, and the domestic laws which are associated with it, act in isolation of wider international obligations set out in treaties and conventions agreed to by governments as part and parcel of trading in the global marketplace.

International animal welfare law 187

State sovereignty is limited and has given way to global commercialism

While issues of state sovereignty definitely account for many of the differences that occur between legislatures, today's reality is that the independence that sovereign states theoretically have is often subsumed into larger regional[1] and global agreements that are the cost of doing business in a global marketplace. Consequently, while domestic criminal law strictly addresses issues between the state and the individual, it could also be said that national criminal law reflects wider international agreements, which are largely based on a system designed to provide a theoretically equal trading opportunity for states trading in the international marketplace. In this way, the global marketplace, complete with its opportunities and associated challenges, has a direct impact on domestic animal law.

Although nations have a long history of trading with one another, the advent of supranational organisations meant the formerly dominant and largely unchallenged authority of central government shifted to a situation where, in order to participate in the global marketplace, they assumed obligations to comply with the larger international agreements. Despite theoretical supremacy and autonomy of each legal jurisdiction to make its own laws, if the nation state is a member/signatory to a supranational organisation, treaty and/or convention, then it is theoretically bound to comply with the values and/or laws of the supranational organisation in order to operate in the global marketplace.

This shift of power has relevance to the development of animal protection. At the beginning of the twentieth century, protection of animals was secured predominantly by primary legislation of central government, which largely went unchallenged. The continued legislative development of animal protection slowed during the middle of the twentieth century as a result of a number of events, not the least of which were the First and Second World Wars which, in practical terms, meant politicians had more pressing issues to deal with. More recently, issues of animal protection have come to the forefront of the global stage as it has been recognised that they are intimately associated with the requirements of the global consumer. Food safety and supply, assurances of disease-free status, and public attention to matters of animal welfare are just a few of the relevant considerations prompting major stakeholders to pay close attention to the issue of animal protection.

'All nations are equal; it's just that some are more equal than others'

Theoretically, countries enter into treaties to comply with their international obligations on a voluntary basis. The practical reality is that in order to participate in the global marketplace, countries are induced by existing and potential trading

---

1 For example, under contemporary European legislation, sovereign states in the EU are obliged to ensure state law conforms with regional law, which states 'member States shall pay full regard to the welfare requirements of animal': Protection and Welfare of Animals, Treaty of Amsterdam, 1997.

188 *International animal welfare law*

partners to seek membership in order to provide assurances of operating on established and agreed rules of trade. Trading agreements are rarely as simple as they purportedly appear, given that they are accompanied by power imbalances and political trade-offs that go hand-in-hand with trade.

It is usually a requirement of membership that states enact supportive domestic laws that compel their citizens to comply with the conditions of a treaty's membership. The assumed responsibilities differ according to the organisation's membership. For example, as a member of the World Trade Organization (WTO), nation states have trade obligations. In contrast, as a member of the OIE,[2] there are no obligations, only recommendations for trade.

Despite the obligation of each nation to adopt the principles of an international treaty into their domestic law, each individual nation's personal animal welfare standards none the less constitutes a distinguishing feature that affects its credibility and reputation in the global marketplace. For example, New Zealand is a recognised world leader in issues of animal welfare, simply because it must be. More than half of New Zealand's GDP comes from the sale of its primary agricultural products. New Zealand's First World economy is dependent on its agricultural and marine industries and, in fact, has been described as riding on the back of animals more than any other developed country in the world. New Zealand relies on animals, and its reputation for providing the highest standards of animal management and welfare, as its primary source of trade. It logically follows that New Zealand's laws must, of necessity, continue to reflect and protect its primary source of overseas income. So the country's commitment to animal welfare is not just a matter of morality: it is also a matter of economic necessity. It is unsurprising then that New Zealand strives to lead the way with its domestic compliance and enforcement of contemporary animal welfare law.

Issues of animal welfare (and the law's governance of relevant human–human and human–animal interactions) are inseparably connected with practical realities of human economic, environmental, or societal interests. Consequently, state sovereignty and autonomy has largely been subsumed by voluntary accession to treaties and conventions of wider international obligations which include, for example, compliance with the economic drivers of the World Trade Organization.

Points of agreement, including uniform rules and agreement on minimum standards are important to the efficient and effective functioning of national trading in the global marketplace. However, an economically driven system raises questions which impact many more issues than those simply of animal protection. The questions raise issues regarding the extent to which citizens of a democratic nation should be able to determine for themselves which laws they are to be subject to, and to what extent it is appropriate to allow commercial interests to dominate national/cultural values.

---

2 The intergovernmental World Organisation for Animal Health (OIE) is responsible for improving animal health worldwide. Through international agreement, on 25 January 1924, the *Office International des Épizooties* (OIE) was established. In May 2003, the OIE became the World Organisation for Animal Health, but kept its historical acronym OIE. In 2014, the OIE had a total of 180 member states.

International animal welfare law 189

The role of commercialism and politics in law

What factors are identifiable 'needs' of an animal is primarily informed by science. The law has a role in translating that science into legal responsibilities. However, things are not that simple. Wider ethical, economic, political, health and legislative issues must also be addressed. Legislation is the result of the political process which must take into account relevant economic, environmental and societal considerations. Consequently, the subject matter and form of legislation is influenced as much by the contemporary circumstances as by principle. This means that law is persuaded, almost as much as it persuades. In this respect, law is rarely, if ever, truly neutral or objective, which in turn explains one of the reasons why the law itself is in a constant state of evolution. None the less, law demonstrates power through the interests it prioritises, the policies it accepts and advances, and the obligations/rights it either permits or penalises.

Animal welfare in context of 'international law'

There is no formal international agreement about animal welfare, although there is increasing debate as to whether animal welfare should be accepted as a trade criterion. Not all countries are members of every major supranational organisation. The countries may not meet required standards of membership, or alternatively they may have internal issues and/or be self-sufficient which means they survive without trading internationally. However, there is a difference between what it means for a country to survive or thrive, and with the objective of thriving, the majority of countries seek membership in order to more effectively trade in the global marketplace.

There are obviously a considerable number of differences between countries in respect of their attitudes to, and law regarding, animals and issues of animal protection. In the international marketplace, the reality is that rules, particularly trade-driven rules, start by referencing the similarities between nations and/or points that each nation can agree on. Furthermore, in order to facilitate the involvement of the greatest number of individuals/nations, an inclusionary approach is largely adopted which in practical terms accepts minimums consistent with the 'lowest common denominator' standards and participants (e.g., in respect of animal welfare standards and national compliance/enforcement) in order to give effect to this inclusionary principle. There are obviously inherent problems when the inclusionary approach is informed primarily by economic drivers, particularly in the face of global issues which, although having an economic component/cost, have enormous potential impacts which go well beyond simple pecuniary considerations.

Animal welfare's trinity of 'societal, economic, and environmental' global impacts

Animals are one of – but not the only – stakeholder whose interests are considered by the law. The singular interest protected by law is their protection from unnecessary and/or unreasonable suffering, pain and/or distress.

190   *International animal welfare law*

Subjective opinions may vary as to the extent this interest is adequately or appropriately defined, applies, or is limited/extended. Discussions and debates will undoubtedly continue over this, but the law remains a reference rulebook. It assumes the responsibility for the bulk of compliance and almost sole charge for enforcement of standards that are intimately associated with societal, environmental and economic 'interests'. They in turn provide a trilogy of headings that commonly assist in identifying and categorising drivers for change that influence change behaviours of people regarding animals. Of course each heading in that trilogy is related, so the categorisation is an artificial construct for the purposes of assessment convenience.

Societal impacts: seeing animals in the big picture of societal issues, perceptions and impacts

Meeting consumer needs

The subject line of 'consumer needs' potentially raises discussion about the difference between what consumers 'need', distinct from what consumers 'want', 'demand', or 'assume'. Issues such as the control of an allegedly profit-mongering industry, prevention or management of disease control, and biosecurity risks that would impact national economy and international trade are, for the most part, either topics left to governors, or addressed in the media.[3]

These statements are broad generalisations of course, and there are obviously a comparative minority of people who are very involved in matters involving animals, their well-being and issues that extend beyond occasional media interest columns. The generalisations are not based merely on subjective opinion because, due to the fact that consumer attitudes underpin consumer spending, there is a substantial amount of research investigating what consumers know (or not), care about (or not), and prioritise (or not) in respect of animals and their welfare.[4, 5, 6]

Mirroring the diversity of national opinions regarding animals, widely contrasting views exist globally of what is relevant or acceptable in terms of animal welfare. Public opinions and perceptions regarding food, agriculture, research and almost any other use of animals is influenced by multiple factors.

Surveys and polls have demonstrated that people generally have an increased awareness of issues involving animals, and that while the majority of survey respondents find certain uses (e.g., animals as a source of food) acceptable, other

---

3   D.P. Fidler. 1999. 'International Law and Global Public Health', Faculty Publications, Paper 652: www.repository.law.indiana.edu/facpub/652.

4   D. Barling. 2008. 'Governing and Governance in the Agri-food Sector and Traceability', in C. Coff et al. (eds), *Ethical Traceability and Communicating Food* (Heidelberg: Springer).

5   J. Hobbs. 2001. 'Labelling and Consumer Issues in International Trade', in H. Michelmann et al. (eds), *Globalization and Agricultural Trade Policy* (Boulder, CO, and London: Lynne Rienner Publishers). This was a key concern of US beef processors (as well as the Canadian beef industry) with proposed country-of-origin labelling for beef imports.

6   European Union, 'Animal Welfare – Surveys of Public Attitudes': http://ec.europa.eu/food/animal/welfare/survey/index_en.htm.

International animal welfare law   191

activities (e.g., the fur trade, cosmetic research and testing) are meeting with dis-approval. Mirroring the law's focus, consumers correlate acceptance, or not, of animal uses with the degree of pain, distress, or suffering of animals.

Given that food continues to be the single largest use of animals in human society, trading with consumers in order to safely provide its citizens with as many of their needs and wants as possible has consistently been the theoretical priority of responsible governments participating in the international trading market. The process inherently has trade-offs as decision makers in government, non-government organisations and industry balance competing interests in providing for the consumer's support, vote, and money.

Economic impacts: animal welfare is a 'ticket to trade in the international marketplace'

A large body of national and international law covers the movement of animals, as well as people and goods, between regions and countries. Laws involving travel/transportation of animals covers everything from people travelling with their pets through to trade in animal products and live exports of animals. In order to safeguard its biosecurity interests, nations understandably have the right to restrict entry of foreign people and products. Law governing the movement of animals, people, goods, aircraft and ships across borders is applied every day around the world by immigration, customs, agriculture, aviation and port authorities. Additionally, there are laws covering the transportation and trade of animals outside national borders.

To meet consumer needs and wants, nations need to be able to trade on the global market. Factors that provide vendors with a unique selling point that makes their product(s) more desirable have a marketing advantage that fosters ongoing trade, and ideally (from the producer's perspective) enables a premium price to be attached to the product. It is increasingly being recognised that animal welfare is a tradable commodity because of its inherent association with stakeholders' wishes and their vested interests. For example, while not all stakeholders are steak eaters, food remains the biggest single use of animals; as a result, food supply and food safety are among key wishes and interests in the food producer–consumer relationship.

Provision of 'food' is attached to a host of other requirements that consumers either demand information about, or assume that governors/government will responsibly supervise. An adequate supply of safe food and, ideally, low prices are usually the first priority, followed increasingly (but following none the less) by some sort of general assurance that the animals from whence the food came were treated humanely (or words to that effect). 'Humane' links seamlessly with rhetoric about sustainable as well, so 'humane and sustainable' (or words to that effect) increasingly appear in the content of discussions and media releases. Much of the trade is driven by reassurances to the consumer that the animals have been treated in a way which is 'humane and sustainable'.

Criticism has been directed at Western society for allegedly imposing its ethics on others largely on the basis that Western notions of animal welfare constitute the

192 *International animal welfare law*

gold standard.[7] Initiatives to impose one global region's standards on others by way of international trade agreements raises issues of 'ethical relativism'.[8] Radford has pointed out that this relativism can be viewed two ways and that the same counter-questions could equally be directed at non-Western society and a commerce-based system, which enables those nations with inferior standards of animal welfare to dictate trade criteria (and wider practices involving animals) to nations that are demonstrably far advanced in all aspects of animal welfare legislation, enforcement, and ultimately, quality of life for animals[9] and people. Again, the biggest single use of animals is as a source of food for human beings, and consequently trade in animals and animal-associated products, coupled with the need for a safe and adequate supply of food, underpins much of international trade. The impact of trade not just on the food industry but on all aspects of economic growth cannot be understated.

Global economic integration is not a new phenomenon. Early explorers and traders exchanged economically useful knowledge and technology, and the trend has been on the rise ever since. Global integration today is greater than it has ever been. Technological improvements, genetic modification, the demands of an increasingly aware global consumer, accompanied by governors seeking to meet the needs and wants of its consumers are just some factors. Decision makers now have the responsibility for balancing risks to the national economy against the economic trade opportunities such as free trade agreements. Countries and companies alike have significant economic motivation to work collaboratively to ensure that supply-chain integrity incorporates practical steps to ensure that quality, security and trade are mutually reinforcing rather than opposing.[10] The importance of trade in animals and animal products is also one of the areas where it is increasingly recognised that there is a need to transform widely held traditional perspectives on trade, including reassessing the way it is controlled and measured.

Biosecurity, biodiversity, disease control and developing technologies

The wide number of activities and interests associated with the subject of 'animal welfare' demonstrate that it is in a constant state of evolution mirroring advances in science, policy and law.

---

7 Anon. 2008. *International Animal Welfare Issues*, Europa: http://ec.europa.eu/food/animal/welfare.international/index_en.htm (19 July 2008).

8 R. Doerfler and K. Peters. 2006. 'The Relativity of Ethical Issues in Animal Agriculture Related to Different Cultures and Production Conditions', *Livestock Science*, 103: 257–62.

9 The concept of sustainable agriculture necessitates a duty of stewardship in contemporary animal welfare legislation. See I.A. Robertson. 2007. 'The Concept of Sustainable Agriculture Necessitates a Duty of Stewardship in Contemporary Animal Welfare Legislation', in W. Zollitsch et al. (eds), *Sustainable Food Production and Ethics. Proceedings of the 7th Congress of the European Society for Agricultural and Food Ethics* (Wageningen, the Netherlands: Wageningen University Press, 2007), p. 263.

10 World Economic Forum. 2012. *Global Enabling Trade Report*: http://reports.weforum.org/global-enabling-trade-report-2012/#=.

International animal welfare law   193

The international relationships and potential animal-related trading benefits are accompanied by risks. Management of the risks is addressed by a process of prevention (e.g., entry of hazardous and/or unwanted organisms into the country), eradication (e.g., if hazardous and/or unwanted organisms enter national territory despite the best efforts of risk management programmes), and/or management (e.g., if a hazardous and/or unwanted organism has entered national territory and is unable to be eradicated).

This policy approach must recognise and acknowledge via its established biosecurity systems that if animals may be a source of hazards for humans, the reverse is equally true. For example, human introduction of trans-boundary animal diseases, climate change, introduction of hazardous and/or unwanted species/organisms and reduction of biodiversity represent just a few of the hazards that humans pose to animals and thereby themselves.

In an ideal world the biosecurity systems would be adequately resourced to ensure that they are functionally efficient and effective. This nirvana is balanced by the reality that there is competition for limited resources, constantly emerging technologies and threats, underpinned by international drivers and obligations to comply with trade rules attached to supranational organisation membership (e.g., WTO obligations). See Case Study 6 for an example of biosecurity.

Case Study 6: Biosecurity, animal law, international transport and 'Bojangles'

Not every case of animal law has multi-jurisdictional impact; none the less, criminal law matters involving animals have serious potential significance to matters of national biosecurity, as illustrated by the 'Bojangles' case. Bojangles was the name given to a dog whose owners wanted to bring him from Hong Kong to New Zealand. It is common for countries to have established criteria designed to minimise biosecurity risks entering the country via imported animals. New Zealand's import standards required that dogs coming into the country be free from certain diseases including babesiosis which is caused by the parasite Babesia and is an incurable blood-borne disease that potentially results in significant deterioration and even death in dogs. Following the visit to the veterinarian and routine blood tests in Hong Kong, Bojangles tested positive for babesiosis. It was the prosecution's case that upon learning of the positive result to babesiosis, and knowing that this would consequently prohibit Bojangles from entering New Zealand, the owners collaboratively falsified the documentation to show that Bojangles had tested negative to babesiosis, then knowingly submitted the falsified documentation to the New Zealand government when Bojangles was transported from Hong Kong to New Zealand.

Upon arrival to New Zealand, a border control veterinarian conducting a routine clinical examination, located a flea on Bojangles which set in motion

(continued)

194   *International animal welfare law*

> *(continued)*
>
> a series of routine tests, including blood tests which screened for babesiosis. The blood test for babesiosis is a specialised one, and consequently only a limited number of laboratories in the world test for it. In this instance, it just happened that the laboratory that had tested the original sample that returned positive from Hong Kong were also asked, unknowingly by the New Zealand Ministry for Primary Industries, to test the new sample sent from New Zealand. In the process of conducting the tests, the laboratory identified that the dog had already been tested, and that the results were positive for babesiosis. The revelation prompted a more comprehensive investigation by the New Zealand government. Charges were ultimately laid for falsifying documentation and importing the dog to New Zealand, where it potentially constituted a risk that could put New Zealand dogs and dog owners in the same unenviable position as Bojangles and the owners, that is, dealing with an incurable, potentially fatal, clinical condition. In the course of the subsequent Court proceedings, the Court agreed with the prosecution on a 'without prejudice' basis that the appropriate starting point was imprisonment. Following conviction, the endpoint of sentencing was that the owners did not go to prison; however, they were fined – and Bojangles was returned to Hong Kong.
>
> The case demonstrates just a few of the considerable number of stakeholders and interests attached to issues of animal law which include the human–animal relationship and potential conflicts of owners' interests with national interests, issues of disease control, potential impacts on society (including other animals), and border risk management in relation to trade, transport, and import–export standards.
>
> (*Ministry for Primary Industries v Ferneyhough and Pasini*, District Court Auckland, New Zealand, October 2013)

Where there are lawful uses of animals, there are also 'unlawful' ones

The model of escalating enforcement functions on the recognition that most people will comply with rules designed to protect wider public interests from avoidable biosecurity hazards. Outside of those who voluntarily comply, or will comply once assisted, there are unfortunately those who require greater enforcement attention by proactive enforcement deterrence through a series of penalties. Experience demonstrates that despite significant communication including a visual media and border control staff to incoming passengers at airports, there are none the less those who either through ignorance or unlawful intent, seek to bring unauthorised goods across the border, prioritising their own interests above the well-being of the wider public and national interests. For example, a case where a wife whose husband owned and operated a commercial vegetable nursery

International animal welfare law   195

intentionally concealed and did not declare a number of plant seeds still covered in soil. This action was found to pose serious risks to national plant-health status and superseded his allegation that the seeds were culturally important to them on the grounds that they were given to him by his mother-in-law in China. Incidents of either ignorance or arrogance are further complicated by intentional unlawful activity seeking to sidestep the established standards and protocols for safe import (and export) of goods. There are a significant number of international treaties, agreements and international standard-or protocol-setting bodies that, in addition to taking leadership roles in developing international consensus of appropriate measures to manage specific risks, implicitly outline lawful activities which thereby define unlawful ones.

Examples of international organisations and instruments include the Sanitary and Phytosanitary Committee of the World Trade Organisation (SPS Committee), the Convention on International Trade in Endangered Species (CITES), the World Organisation for Animal Health (OIE), the Convention on Biodiversity (CBD), the Cartagena Protocol (which seeks to protect biological diversity from the potential risks posed by living modified organisms) and the Montreal Protocol (on substances that deplete the ozone layer). Competing and conflicting interests accompanied by understandably subjective opinion regarding how interests should be prioritised, provides a compelling argument for implementing standards that are objective by reference to proven science and established risk management principles. This background provides a backdrop to understand specific treaties dealing with identified species that have been recognised as being in danger of extirpation and depredation from a variety of factors. The most threatening is commonly due to one of two factors: human encroachment into the habitat (and thereby the feeding and breeding grounds of the species involved), or unsustainable commercial exploitation.

With that in mind, there are a number of key international legal instruments that the reader should know. Instruments (e.g., CITES) and issues (e.g., international whaling) are obviously not the only ones that have relevance to international law and unlawful international activities. These examples serve to illustrate the issues and complexities associated with animals, their welfare and international agreements, and seeking to deal with endangered and often migratory species.

The Convention on International Trade in Endangered Species of Wild Fauna and Flora ('CITES')

CITES is an international contract focused on the protection of plant and animal species in danger of depredation or extinction. It works by mutual agreement of its member nations, who submit to regulation and/or prohibition of international trade in the identified species. CITES differs from many other animal-related instruments in that it is a legally binding international document. Member states are obliged to enact domestic legislation that gives effect to CITES' rules.

Initiated in 1973, CITES aims to provide the best possible protection for threatened wild plant and animal species through a series of internationally agreed and

196 *International animal welfare law*

coordinated trade restrictions. The trade restrictions actively deterring and discouraging commercial exploitation are implemented with a view to facilitating the long-term survival of identified species. Prior to the initiation of CITES, international regulation of the wildlife trade did not focus on the conservation of animals and endangered species, but instead on basic economic issues such as tariffs.

Today CITES is widely supported throughout the world

Most commentators and experts agree that CITES remains the most important protection for wildlife across international borders. However, it is not without its critics, who point to the lack of enforcement and universal participation which results in a false sense of security regarding how well the interests of the international animal community are being safeguarded. Criticism has also pointed to other weaknesses in CITES, in that its regulation is limited to international trade and exploitation and does not have an effect on use, trade and exploitation of animals *within* a country, so while the actions of citizens in a particular country may severely impact and threaten the existence of many species, CITES does not apply to that conduct. Despite member countries taking on a responsibility to enact national legislation that reflects the principles of the organisational agreement, there is little actual recourse for not fully implementing the responsibilities. For example, people in the US can own tigers, lions and bears, despite the US being a signatory to CITES. However, some form of agreement and control – albeit aspirational in its purposes and fettered by its practical limitation of resources – is better than no control and/or enforcement/agreement.

The International Whaling Commission

Whales long ago captured the human imagination. Their extraordinary appearance gained them a place in literature, their size gained them a place in indigenous cultures as a source of folklore and food, and their biological similarities to humans (as mammals) have provided them with a level of interest also accorded to other visible and accessible marine mammals such as seals and sea lions, and porpoises and dolphins.

Their almost revered place in our consciousness, however, has not stopped them from almost being wiped out by commercial predators. Whales are excellent examples of the issues associated with animals in an international context, with their numbers dwindling to the point of extinction, their migratory nature through international waters, and humans' encroachment on, and pollution of their habitat – all culminate in the fact that they have attracted global support for protection.

As with every other issue involving animals, opinions are polarised, often reflecting competing and conflicting interests. For example, where national governments have got involved in the issue of protecting whales, their efforts have often been directed toward restoring the population numbers to comply with 'sustainability'. Sustainable whaling arguably accepts commercial ventures, provided there is credible scientific evidence to demonstrate that the activity is

International animal welfare law 197

indeed sustainable. In contrast, many non-government organisations advocate that adequate protection of whales requires the permanent cessation of whaling. Scientific evidence supports their own position and advocates of a complete ban frequently reference species-preservation objectives, by way of moral arguments consistent with selected definitions of sentience.

The contrasting subjective views again demonstrate the role of policy and 'international law' in obtaining sufficient objective information to assist in balancing when prioritising the interests of all stakeholders. To this end, it is important for governors to adequately understand the nuances of animal welfare. For example, how does the law regarding animals develop in different jurisdictions around the world? What are the key similarities and barriers to establishing effective and efficient agreements that deliver humane and sustainable animal welfare standards and outcomes? It becomes clear that an understanding of the foundational principles underlying the human–animal relationship is essential to identifying the answers to such questions, and their impact in relevant national and international interests. Theological, philosophical and scientific inputs continue to be evident in economic, environmental and societal policy. This trinity of broad interests must take account of fragmented sub-groups and sub-categories that include differing stakeholders, animal uses, scientific opinion, and continued exemptions to humane and sustainable animal uses based on historic, albeit frequently outdated (e.g., bullfighting), cultural and religious tenets.

In practical terms, there are a number of recognised factors which determine which species become the subjects of public favour and political/legal protection. Whales, like pandas, tigers, rhinoceroses, gorillas and elephants, have engendered public interest, in stark contrast to many other species. As with some other species, whales have benefited from the fact that a specific international organisation has been established which focuses on their conservation and preservation. However, unlike many other species, the purpose of conservation through the IWC was initially to ensure a sustainable population, so that the industry surrounding the killing of whales could continue to function. But numbers of whales continued to decline and in 1982 a moratorium banning all commercial whaling was enacted out of necessity to protect whale populations. The moratorium prohibited commercial whaling and a zero-catch quota came into force in 1986.

Although the moratorium is still in effect today, whaling still occurs across the globe – both legally and illegally. One of the major problems inherent in the IWC (and all international law) is that a member country can register an objection to a certain proposal or regulation and then not be bound by it. Norway is a member of IWC which has taken advantage of this apparent loophole and continues to allow limited whaling of minke whales.[11] Iceland is another country that has attracted significant criticism in respect of its whaling activities which it continues to conduct

---

11 'Whaling Quota Draws Fire', *Aftenposten, News from Norway*, 7 February 2008: www.aftenposten. no/english/local/article2243265.ece. See also the official Norwegian environmental policy site explaining Norway's position on whaling: www.norway.org.uk/policy/environment/whaling/ whaling.htm.

198 *International animal welfare law*

under the guise of functioning under a 'scientific permit'. After resuming 'scientific' whaling in 2003, Iceland also re-instigated commercial whaling in 2006.[12]

When discussing issues of whaling, however, there are few countries that attract as much criticism and attention as Japan, which has remained a central focus in the debate over whaling, and continues to whale under the IWC exception of 'scientific research whaling'. Lethal whale research is allowed by the IWC under article VIII of the International Convention for the Regulation of Whaling: '[A]ny contracting Government may grant to any of its nationals a special permit authorizing that national to kill, take, and treat whales for purposes of scientific research.'[13]

Both Iceland and Japan, who engage in lethal scientific research, argue that the primary goal of such research is the sustainable use of all marine resources – once slaughtered, the whales are tested for parasites, pollutants, diet and the nature of their sex hormones, as well as other tests designed to increase scientists' knowledge of whale populations. These tests are directly connected to studies of sustainable harvesting of whales.[14] Article VIII of the ICRW allows a country to do what they wish with the 'proceeds' of the research.

Mirroring continued controversy regarding policy and legal exemptions for traditional cultural practices and religious views, the IWC's allowance of whaling by indigenous peoples has also attracted criticism,[15] despite the fact that comparatively, the number of whales killed and the political dynamics associated with indigenous whale hunting is significantly lower than the impact of the activities of countries like Iceland, Norway and Japan.

As opposed to scientific research whaling, the affected groups are not powerful countries, but indigenous groups,[16] who claim to rely on whaling for their survival. Since its inception, the IWC has recognized aboriginal subsistence whaling as inherently different from commercial whaling. Therefore, the IWC has permitted some aboriginal subsistence whaling with the stated objective of 'ensur[ing] risks

---

12 However, there is some indication in the popular press that, due to a lack of market for whale meat, Iceland has ceased commercial whaling in August of 2007: 'Whaling Quota Draws Fire', *Aftenposten*.

13 ICRW article VIII, §1.

14 See 'Japan's Position on Scientific Research Whaling' pamphlet, put out by the Ministry of Foreign Affairs in Japan: www.cl.emb-japan.go.jp/doc/2008%2004%20Japan's%20Position%20(revised%20ver).pdf.

15 See Alyson Decker. 2006. 'Save the Whales – Save the Whales – Wait, Just Save the International Whaling Commission: A Fresh Look at the Controversy Surrounding Cultural Claims to Whale', *So. Calif. Interdisciplinary L.J.*, 16: 253; Richard Kirk Eishstaedt. 1998. '"Save the Whales" v. "Save the Makah": The Makah and the Struggle for Native Whaling', *Animal Law*, 4: 145; Russel C. D'Costa. 2005. 'Reparations as a Basis for the Makah's Right to Whale', *Animal Law*, 12: 71.

16 'Under current IWC regulations, aboriginal subsistence whaling is permitted for Denmark (Greenland, fin and minke whales), the Russian Federation (Siberia, gray and bowhead whales), St Vincent and The Grenadines (Bequia, humpback whales) and the US (Alaska, bowhead and gray whales). It is the responsibility of national governments to provide the Commission with evidence of the cultural and subsistence needs of their people. The Scientific Committee provides scientific advice on safe catch limits for such stocks', IWC Website, *Aboriginal Subsistence Whaling*: www.iwcoffice.org/conservation/aboriginal.htm.

International animal welfare law   199

of extinction [are] not seriously increased (highest priority) [and enabling] harvests in perpetuity appropriate to cultural and nutritional requirements'.[17]

In theory the allowance for aboriginal whaling is accompanied by significant restrictions on the methods utilised and the use of the whale after slaughter; however, the applied aspects of these criteria have none the less attracted significant attention. For example, determining which 'indigenous groups' can conduct whaling[18] has been hotly contested, particularly when, in 2002, indigenous groups in the Arctic were denied whaling privileges by Japan, after four Japanese indigenous groups were denied whaling privileges.[19] Additionally, questions were raised when an indigenous group living in the US state of Washington were allotted a yearly quota of whales – despite the fact that the same group had not whaled for over seventy years.[20] A whaling prohibition was applied to the indigenous people of Greenland after it was identified that up to a quarter of the whale meat caught ended up 'sold on supermarket shelves'.[21]

Issues regarding whaling reflect much more than simple scientific opinion about what does or does not constitute sustainable whaling. The whaling issue itself is attached to significant political undercurrents and associated complexities. This is illustrated by the fact that many IWC member countries have absolutely no association with, or history of whaling. None the less, reports indicate that a number of these countries were allegedly 'bribed' by Japan to join the IWC just to vote against the moratorium, in order to respond to 'pressure' from the United States on other non-whaling countries to join and vote for the moratorium.

Live exports – a contentious big-ticket animal practice

Literally millions of animals are transported every day across national borders. These numbers include transportation of companion animals, breeding and performance animals (e.g., racehorses), as well as agricultural animals for food. For the most part, this occurs without incident and rarely becomes the focus of media/ public attention. On the other hand, concerns have historically been raised, for example, about the number of animals that die while being transported overseas.

Some have called for a complete ban of live export of agricultural animals. Such a move has been criticised for being blind to wider human interests and realities. Critical assessment demands identification of 'the real issue'. There is little, if any,

---

17 Ibid.
18 Christopher D. Stone. 2001. 'Summing Up: Whaling and its Critics', in Robert L. Friedheim (ed.), *Toward a Sustainable Whaling Regime* (Seattle, WA and London: University of Washington Press; Canadian Circumpolar Institute (CCI) Press: Edmonton (2001)).
19 'This has nothing to do with science, and everything to do with politics' – Roland Schmitten, U.S. Delegate to the IWC, quoted in BBC News, 'Japan Blocks Indigenous Whaling', 23 May 2002: http://news.bbc.co.uk/2/low/asia-pacific/2003658.stm.
20 Russel C. D'Costa. 2005. 'Reparations as a Basis for the Makah's Right to Whale', *Animal Law*, 12: 71.
21 ABC News, 'IWC Votes Against Greenland Indigenous Whaling', Sarah Clarke, 27 June 2008: www.abc.net.au/news/stories/2008/06/27/2287381.htm.

200   *International animal welfare law*

issue with the transportation of animals provided that it is done to a standard that does not cause the animal unnecessary or unreasonable pain and/or distress – mirroring the standards which are set out in contemporary animal welfare legislation.

The real issue is not with the transportation of animals, but with the standards pertaining to humane transport of animals. The root question might therefore be identified as 'how do you implement and enforce standards which ensure that transport of animals is consistent with contemporary animal welfare legislation?' Australia is an example of a country that has established agreements with some trading partners to allow the continued monitoring of the well-being of some types of livestock, even after they have crossed into legal jurisdiction of those trading partners, and Australian exporters are held responsible for the outcomes of exported animals. Despite the fact that opinions vary on the appropriateness and/or effectiveness of the initiative, it is none the less representative of genuine responsibility for the welfare of the livestock involved along the 'farm-to-fork' continuum. It is relevant that although breaking with wider tradition of practices conducted by nations, the 'farm-to-fork' supervision in terms of a contractual arrangement is hardly ground-breaking, since this has been a long-standing practice for industries who operate across multiple jurisdictions.

Contractual arrangements where retailers demand strict compliance with specific animal husbandry procedures and standards of animal welfare by meat producers as a condition of purchase is common practice. It stands to reason that it is obviously very motivating for a producer to ensure compliance if the risk of non-compliance is the loss of a sale. Perhaps identification of the real issues attached to live exports of animals indicates that energy and attention is better spent not so much on *what* is being done (i.e., seeking to ban all exportation of live animals), but on *how* it is being done (i.e., review and enforcement regarding the standards and rules applying to transportation of live animals).

Ratings-driven media frenzies, fuelling inadequately informed public perceptions, are substantially different to credible critical assessment that fairly and accurately presents the facts, trends and options available to all stakeholders – human and animal alike. None the less, the fact remains that whether adequately or inadequately informed, the views of the purchasing consumer, costs of production, and the decisions of governors balancing and prioritising personal and public interests in a contemporary setting have a significant impact on economic outcomes.

Environmental impacts: is the environment a voiceless stakeholder?

Environment, climate control and global warming

The categories of 'economic, social and environmental' provide a useful trilogy for considering the impacts of animal welfare. Economic factors are commonly easy for people to identify as relevant to standards of animal care. Similarly, contrasts in terms of subjective opinions regarding animals, and diverse cultural and religious practices, mean that sociological aspects are easy to recognise. The environmental factors associated with issues of animal welfare may not be quite as evident as first blush, but they are just as real.

The development of the modern world has been a story of transitions of new types and uses of energy, including biomass to coal to oil through to nuclear energy sources. In each transition, the new fuel was in some way better, faster, cheaper, or generally more suited to humane demands than the fuel before it. In each transition, technical logical innovation provided new uses, and transformed energy systems and human society. Currently, there is significant focus on the next transition considering not only alternatives for clean and sustainable energy, but also the risks and impacts to the environment which animals and humans both share.

Understanding the factors that have influenced energy transitions of the past which have led to contemporary global challenges provide some insight as to the factors that may continue to drive the future. However, in balancing the increasing demands of the human consumer, there are two factors which have attracted attention and stimulated debate. The first is a deep concern about climate change and the political and policy traction associated with this issue. This is demonstrated, for example, in the existence of a wide range of mandates, incentives and regulations dealing with carbon-trading systems and aspirations for low-carbon energy uses and renewable energy resources. Information coupled with biotechnology advances are just two of the innovations predicted to provide humankind with more ability to control the planetary environment and, in effect, be a 'global game changer'.

Understanding the potential impact of animals on the environment illustrates why there is common ground between issues of animal welfare law and environmental law. This raises questions about the potential impact on the animals themselves.

The effects of climate change on animals

Humans have always utilised the environment – as well as animals – to serve their own interests, but the impact of human activities on the environment that is relied upon by people and animals alike, has been particularly marked in recent times. For example, enormous sections of temperate forest in Europe, Asia and North America have been cleared over the recent centuries in order to provide for human interests in activities such as agriculture, timber and urban development. The speed and extent of human enterprise exploiting the natural environment has been significantly driven and accelerated by the fact that there has been a six-fold expansion in the human population since 1800 and an accompanying 50-fold increase in the size of the global economy.[22] Bleak predictions are attached to the current processes associated with the planet-wide domination by human society.

The extinction rate on species of animals and wider biodiversity is reportedly up to a thousand times higher than historically 'traditional' extinction rates, and

---

22 www.skepticalscience.com/Can-animals-and-plants-adapt-to-global-warming.htm.

202 *International animal welfare law*

60 per cent of the world's ecosystems are reportedly degraded.[23] It is critical to understand that this degradation of ecosystems means that they have lost resilience and their resident populations have been irreversibly changed by human activities. The historically localised impacts of human activities have, in the modern environment, resulted in a global size to physical and biological transformations. From a global perspective, the combined effect of global warming, ocean acidification, habitat loss and fragmentation (including the development of invasive and/or hazardous organisms), and chemical pollution intensify the direct and indirect impact of climate change, making it difficult, and potentially impossible, for species to move to and from damaged areas, maintain a sustainable population size, or even survive. In effect, one threat reinforces the other and the interaction of multiple factors produces a synergised threat to species survival[24] and human interests associated with food supply and safety.

So how does law control this systematic degradation? Traditionally, law references science to provide objective and credible reference for decision making, but scientific opinions remain divided as to the actual severity of environmental and climate change impact. There are those that consider that a warmer planet will be beneficial for humans and other species.[25] In contrast, there are others already noting the impacts on traditional animal life cycles and behaviours, such as breeding and migration.

To those already involved in the science and husbandry of keeping and studying animals, it will come as no surprise that relatively stable temperatures are a key factor in the survival of many species. In addition to environmental effects of melting ice and spreading deserts, climate change has been predicted to result in disruption to, and potential extinction of, significant numbers of animal species. For example, the sex of turtles is temperature dependent (females are produced at higher temperatures); thus the potential extinction of turtles as a consequence of having an all-female population has been just one of the identified threats associated with climate change. Changes in migratory routes of birds, fish and other animals have already been noticed.

While some species are able to adapt to new conditions, other species have less flexibility. For example, subtle changes in sea temperature have marked effect on the traditional habitat of Arctic polar bears and seals, which are disappearing rapidly. However, polar bears, turtles, birds and fish are not the only animals affected by global warming. A significant number of historical mass-extinction events have been strongly linked to global climate change, but in a modern-day context, the current climate change is so rapid that many species will simply not be able to adapt in time.

---

23 Millenium Ecosystem Assessment. 2005. *Ecosystems and Human Well-being Synthesis* (Washington, DC: Island Press), p. 2: www.slideshare.net/Water_Food_Energy_Nexus/millennium-ecosystem-assessment-2005-synthesis-report.

24 www.skepticalscience.com/Can-animals-and-plants-adapt-to-global-warming.html#brook.

25 www.pbs.org/wgbh/warming/debate/singer.html%20.

Even perceptibly small changes in temperature can have dramatic impact on animals and their environment, whether they live at the polar caps or in the tropics. As is the case of many species that are already extinct or currently facing extinction, destruction of their habitat had left or is leaving these species with literally no place to go. Climate change simply exacerbates the problem. Even for species that seem able to adapt, there are concerns that the changes are happening too fast for the species to evolve new strategies for survival.

Additional climate-related animal issues include secondary impacts on animal breeding grounds and cycles. Growing water scarcity has obvious impact on the land and its resident animal population and migratory species that swim, fly and walk thousands of miles each year.

The impact of animals on the environment

It's a simple fact that there are multiple species that share one planet, one environment, and therefore, an interdependent future. Animals have historically been a part of the world's traditional environment, and others as the domestication of the species by humans that has notably resulted in secondary impacts on animals on the planet's land, sea and air.

Animals affect the environment by consuming energy/resources (i.e., food) and producing large amounts of waste and other by-products. Thus, industrial production of animals for food production raises its own environmental challenges. The human population is projected to grow by about 35 per cent between 2006 and 2050, and the number of animals raised for food worldwide is projected to double during this same time period. An increase in both human population and disposable incomes worldwide, along with changing food preferences, are stimulating a rapid increase in demand for meat, milk and eggs, while globalisation is boosting trade in both inputs and outputs. Today, an estimated 80 per cent of growth in the livestock sector comes from industrial production systems, and is reportedly one of the major causes of the world's most pressing environmental problems, including global warming, land degradation, air and water pollution, and loss of biodiversity.

Estimates that consider the entire commodity chain indicate that livestock are responsible for 18 per cent of greenhouse gas emissions, a bigger share than that contributed by transportation.[26] While the amount of greenhouse gas that agriculture and farming produces differs according to, for example, whether the livestock production system is extensive[27] or intensive,[28] livestock production is the largest source of methane production in the world from agriculturally related manure storage and enteric fermentation by ruminants. If projections regarding population growth eventuate, then livestock-related greenhouse gas emissions will potentially

---

26 FAO. 2006. 'Livestock Impacts on the Environment': www.fao.org/ag/magazine/0612sp1.htm.
27 Extensive farming is a type of agriculture that is mainly a pasture-based and land-based system.
28 Intensive systems have more concentrated operations and are often more mechanised. A feedlot is an example of an intensive system for beef cattle production.

204 *International animal welfare law*

almost double, thereby significantly increasing the amount of livestock-related greenhouse gases and posing significant risks to biological life forms.[29]

Livestock production affects water, a limited resource that is essential to biological life. Livestock production accounts for more than 8 per cent of global human water use. Water for livestock production is used for drinking, irrigation to grow crops/pasture and for different animal-related activities including, for example, cleaning. The water needed to produce feed is the major factor behind the water footprint of animal products. In addition to water usage, water contamination from animal waste presents additional environmental impacts of concern. On a local basis, the environmental impacts can be illustrated, for example, by considering the potential environmental effects of a dairy herd on the land and adjacent waterways.

People living adjacent to established commercial agricultural operations such as a piggery will be well aware of the potential air pollution (both in terms of smell and noise) that can be associated with such a sizeable agricultural commercial operation. Animal waste (manure), odour and dust are all potential air pollutants that are likely to be associated with animal-related activities including, for example, the use of medicines and pesticides.

The livestock sector is the single largest anthropogenic user of land. Feed-crop grazing occupies an estimated 26 per cent of the earth's terrestrial surface, and feed-crop production requires about a third of all arable land. Expansion of grazing land for livestock is a key factor in deforestation. Livestock account for about 20 per cent of the total terrestrial animal biomass, and the land area they now occupy was once habitat for wildlife. So animals being raised for human consumption also pose a threat to the planet's biodiversity.

Balancing conflicting interests and agendas between livestock food systems and environmental protections will predictably require greater efficiency in terms of resource use. In short, because of the finite nature of available natural resources, the predicted expansion of the livestock sector required to meet growing demand must be accomplished by initiatives which concurrently reduce environmental impacts.

Removal of price distortions at input and product level will enhance natural resource use, but may often not be sufficient. The recognised broad impact of livestock production on the environment, both negative and positive, means that environmental impacts need to be explicitly factored into the policy framework and financial compensation schemes which facilitate targeted conservation and land care objectives. For example, livestock holders who provide environmental services could be compensated, either by the immediate beneficiary (such as downstream users enjoying improved water quantity and quality), or by the general public. Additionally, incentives could be implemented for land management or land uses that restore biodiversity, and pasture management that provides for carbon sequestration. Compensation schemes could also be developed between

---

29 United Poultry Concerns. 2006. 'Environmental Impact of Animals Raised for Food Recalculated': www.upc-online.org/environment/091102animal_ag_impact_recalculated.html.

water and electricity providers and graziers who adopt grasslands management strategies that reduce sedimentation of water reservoirs.

Who is responsible for 'herding cats'[30] in the global marketplace?

Identifying the key power brokers of global animal welfare issues

The diverse uses of animals in human society, including the dramatic increases in agricultural productivity requires governors to create policy that will direct the future welfare of animals and people. If the direction is correctly chosen, then all stakeholders will benefit. If not, then the cost consequences are likely to be enormous.

Given the importance of issues associated with animal welfare that affects animals and humans alike, irrespective of country, religion, culture, or economy, who is making the decisions, and what are the criteria that they are utilising to make those decisions? Finally, and a common question for all questions of governance, who's governing the governors?

Governance of animal welfare, irrespective of whether that governance is national or international, requires an approach based on incremental change, which includes compliance with wider international relationships, obligations and undertakings. Reflecting the principle that many of society's changes nationally and internationally occur by a principle of evolution rather than revolution, the process of incremental change balances society's expectations with the constraints of the animal user. Consequently, in addition to ideally being science-based in order to provide objectivity, and incorporating laws that are ideally clear, fair and ethically principled, governors have the responsibility for ensuring that the rate of change fairly and pragmatically balances the expectations of society with the practical realities and constraints on the animal user.

In order to ensure that its initiatives are effectively and efficiently applied, governors increasingly should seek to collaborate with wider stakeholders. In jurisdictions where this ideal collaboration is being achieved in some measure, there none the less remains an important point of difference between government and wider stakeholders' roles. Although wider stakeholders (e.g., industry and retailers) demonstrate a willingness to assist in facilitating compliance with animal welfare standards (which benefits their own interests), 'enforcement' of animal welfare is still largely seen as a governors' (e.g., national government's) responsibility. This is unsurprising, given that industry, for example, remains largely reliant on membership as part and parcel of their own representative existence; approaches perceived as 'policing', that do not benefit the wider membership, are likely to attract significant criticism.

---

30 'Herding cats' is an idiomatic saying that refers to an attempt to control or organise a class of entities which are uncontrollable or chaotic. It implies a task that is extremely difficult or impossible to do, primarily due to chaotic factors: http://en.wikipedia.org/wiki/Herding_cats.

206   *International animal welfare law*

In essence, while compliance may be touted as beneficial for the wider industry, policing is fraught with the problems associated with having a conflict of interests.

There are literally hundreds of organisations, committees and forums which constitute and contribute to 'governance' of animal welfare on the international stage. Consequently, it is unlikely that any one person will be familiar with every organisation; however, there are a number of global governors that the informed animal welfare participant would be expected to be familiar with.

Defining governance and governors

Governance can be defined as the making and implementation of rules, policy and the exercise of power, within a given domain of activity. 'Global governance' refers to rule making and the exercise of power on a global scale. State sovereignty means that there is no singular 'law' that binds countries in the same way as national law binds its citizens. On the international stage, rule making and the exercise of power (frequently referred to as 'persuasion') is performed largely by those whose authority stems from parties to a general multinational agreement. This raises questions as to the identity of the global power brokers that decide the way forward, which affects the planet shared by billions of people and animals alike. Who are the governors? And how well are the governors themselves driven, observed and governed?

In terms of animal welfare, there is significant evidence demonstrating changes in the national and international landscape of animal welfare policy and law, reflecting advancement in scientific knowledge which, via modern communication technologies, has shifted public and political attitudes.

Competing voices on animal welfare

When animal welfare concepts are debated, the participants understandably reflect substantially contrasting definitions and paradigms which, in turn, result in proposals reflecting their own interests and world-views. Achieving sound animal welfare practices is obviously a key challenge for governors seeking to establish consistency and engender support in the face of controversial and contested practices involving animals. There are a number of realities linked to key players in the international arena. The first is that like many businesses, the international market functions not just on 'persuasion' of the individual participants, but also on the 'personalities' involved. In a business context, this is called 'networking', while others refer to it simply as the political 'game'.[31, 32] Different cultural norms apply and it should come as no surprise that bribery and corruption form part of international 'persuasion'. For example, it has been alleged that if you don't

---

31   E.D. Mansfield, H.V. Milner and B.P. Rosendorff. 2000. 'Free to Trade: Democracies, Autocracies, and International Trade', *American Political Science Review*, 94(2): 305–21.

32   T.S. Aidt. 1998. 'Political Internalization of Economic Externalities and Environmental Policy', *Journal of Public Economics*, 69: 1–6.

International animal welfare law 207

take sufficient funds for bribery expenses in Russia, then you simply won't trade. Japan was demonstrably purchasing the votes of various countries to facilitate its own interests in respect of whaling.[33] Such realities may sit uncomfortably with individual aspirational views regarding what 'should' be happening, but it pays to be aware of them.

The key players identified here are not an exhaustive list; however, they do represent long-standing influential organisations involved in animal welfare debates.

International governance: national voices on the international stage

National decision makers naturally contribute to international forums and decisions. The nation state and concepts on national sovereignty have historically seen themselves as almost exclusive power brokers in global governance. Nation states continue to ensure their voice and persuasion in multilateral agreements (e.g., the World Trade Organization). Additionally, nations form bilateral, regional and multilateral agreements to further their own interests in the global market.

International governing structures may vary of course. New Zealand's 'one minister, one act, one jurisdiction' theoretically simplifies governance in respect of animal welfare in that there is one appointed minister responsible for a single piece of animal welfare legislation that governs the entire country and covers multiple uses of animals. The singular governance model provides at least the opportunity for national consistency, and is in contrast to other jurisdictions (e.g., Australia, the US), where there are multiple states and territories, each with their individual governance that frequently conflict with central government. In this situation, there can be significant internal conflict, and the law relating to animals and activities concerning them (e.g., definitions of species and activities that fall under legislative protections, or not) can change dramatically as the animal and the legally recognised person in charge cross borders.

In simple terms however, each nation has an appointed representative (e.g., minister) who is supported by the relevant ministry and advisory bodies. That representative largely has the responsibility for representing the voice of each state in governing internal affairs, in a way that is consistent with the country's international obligations.

Functioning sectors on the international stage

The complexity of animal welfare debates increases as the focus moves from the national to the international stage. Internationally, there are a greater number of participant groups, with even more divergent cultural and religious opinions, proficiencies, resources, interests and agendas individually and politically. This includes varying levels of corruption.

---

33 A. Gillespie. 2001. 'Transparency in International Environmental Law: A Case Study of the International Whaling Commission', *Geo. Int'l Envtl. L. Rev.*, 14: 333.

208   *International animal welfare law*

The myriad of international groups none the less mirror the broad categories of stakeholders that occur in the national setting. Despite cultural, religious, environmental and socio-economic contrasts between countries, the welfare of animals is increasingly recognised as being important to the well-being of the wider global community. This reflects the third 'element' of animal law, which recognises a continuing relationship between the interests of people and animals.

The evolving global community has a complex interaction of self-interest and common international issues. Consequently, there is constantly a challenge associated with new players in the global governance system. None the less, there is a consistent list of long-established power brokers noted for their persistent international role, despite continuing debates about how well their historical function fits with the demands and realties of the current and future world.

International governance: the public

It is easy to assume that in a democratic system, the consumer is the ultimate power broker. This assumption, however, raises further questions regarding the identity, drivers and informers of the public 'consumer', which in turn raises questions as to whether the public is the true power broker, or simply the 'middleman' who holds the purse.

What is public opinion about animals and their welfare?

There has been substantial research[34] on public attitudes regarding animals and their welfare by both governors and industry. They have a vested interest in knowing what their supporting and purchasing public think. New communication technologies and the personal interests of individuals involved with animals show that the proportion of people interested in improving animal welfare standards has risen. Changes in people's individual attitudes and opinions are commonly the driving force behind shifts in animal-related legislation and public policy.

Legislation and public policy frequently rely on science in order to demonstrate objectivity and credibility; however, shifts in the animal welfare standards rarely eventuate as a result of scientific evidence alone. In order to be effective, the scientific evidence and legal/policy shifts need to find acceptance with at least a significant majority of public attitudes and values. Consequently, in addition to having an understanding about the historical origins of people's attitudes regarding animals, it is equally important to identify the influencers – and the drivers – of 'public opinion'.

---

34 See, for example, EU, 'Animal welfare – Surveys of public attitudes': http://ec.europa.eu/food/animal/welfare/survey/index_en.htm, European Commission. 2007; 'Attitudes of EU citizens towards Animal Welfare': http://ec.europa.eu/food/animal/welfare/survey/sp_barometer_aw_en.pdf, and the website of the Australian Animal Welfare Strategy: www.australiananimalwelfare.com.au/.

Are the public just sheep? Who, and what, influences
and informs public opinion to animal welfare?

People's moral attitudes about animals are significantly influenced not just by the foundational religious, scientific and philosophical informants, but also by other factors including the specific attributes of the animal (e.g., the species, perceived uses, and overall appeal of the animal), and the individual characteristics and experience of the person making value judgements.[35]

Contemporary research[36] has validated what an understanding of the historical basis of the human–animal relationship has consistently demonstrated: that there are two primary motivational considerations of people that impact on their attitudes and behaviours regarding animals. The first is their moral and subsequently emotional perceptions regarding an animal, which varies between degrees of empathy/similarity/identification to disassociation/fear/loathing in the eyes of the person making the value judgement regarding an animal. This is balanced by the second motivator, which is the pragmatic human/self-interest considerations frequently involving, for example, assessments of the animal on the basis of its instrumental value (either detrimental or beneficial to human interests), measured by economic and/or utility-based criteria. In short, it goes back to the very beginnings of the foundational human–animal relationship, where the emotive motivation is largely informed by how similar or different animals are perceived to be to people (consider the prevalence of arguments in gauging how similar or different animals are to people which include, for example, analogies commonly drawn between animals and children), and the human-based uses of animals (e.g., consider the emotional value attached to companion dogs and cats in comparison to agricultural animals such as dairy cows and sheep, which in turn are often valued higher than animals like opossums, rabbits, or other animals classified as 'pests').[37]

There is no doubt that the public's vote and money constitute an enormous consideration for governors (e.g., government, industry and non-government organisations) of animal welfare. But to identify the 'real' power behind public opinion, it is essential to query who and what informs public opinion.

Like most other areas where individuals hold a strong opinion despite little or no personal experience, the reality is that individuals rely primarily on being 'informed'. Being informed can come in many guises, with the media accompanied by additional initiatives, such as food labelling tailored specifically to the issue of animal welfare standards. 'Informed' may mean 'education' and 'marketing'. The public's opinion commonly relies on being informed by somebody else. There's

35 Swanson et al., 'Animal Welfare: Consumer Viewpoints': http://animalscience.ucdavis.edu/avian/swanson.pdf.
36 J.A. Serpell. 2004. 'Factors Influencing Human Attitudes to Animals and their Welfare', *Animal Welfare*, 13(Suppl.): 145–51.
37 Excerpt from Olsen, P. 1998. *Australia's Pest Animals: New Solutions to Old Problems* (Canberra: Bureau of Rural Sciences, and Sydney: Kangaroo Press): www.feral.org.au/animal-welfare/attitudes-to-animal-welfare/.

210   *International animal welfare law*

nothing unusual about this, but it highlights the reality that opinions can simply be an outcome of the most effective marketer.

Marketing experts creating campaigns on behalf of everything from politicians to industry products are well aware of this; indeed, their livelihood depends on being very good at it. Industry, government and non-government organisations all use various forms of 'education', 'promotions' and 'marketing' to advance their own ideologies, interests and agendas. This raises the question as to what portion of the public are truly critically assessing relevant animal welfare issues and are subsequently independently informed, in comparison to how many are simply voting with their (marketing-led) feet.

International governance: international organisations

People demonstrate a range of attitudes regarding governors and government. Some people appear to be constantly challenging government on the basis of everything from incompetence through to corruption and conspiracy. Other people will simply assume that governors' priorities are, for the most part, the same as their own. However, from a global perspective, policy debates about animals and their welfare in one area of the planet, particularly those that affect trade, have fuelled contentious debates about animal protection policies and related subjects (e.g., food supply and safety) in other jurisdictions.[38]

What does 'common sense' tell you is the 'currency' of political parties each vying for the power seat in national government? Obviously, answers may vary, but one of the common threads to all answers is that the governors rely on the vote of their supporters (or at least the perception of it), which in turn requires voter participation.

In this way, democratic governance is usually said to function on an inclusionary approach whereby it operates with support from the majority of authorised participants. If the party in power loses that majority support, then consequences include the possibility that it will be unseated from its place as the governing power. In a national setting, the 'members' are the country's citizens who are authorised to vote. In an international setting, the members are the countries who have indicated by their signature that they agree to abide by the rules of the new organisation as part of the membership agreement.

International governing bodies, similar to their national counterparts, function in a way that is consistent with their organisation's primary purpose(s) and relevant interests. In doing so, they naturally rely on the support of the majority of their membership, which in turn requires an inclusionary approach wherever possible.

Minimum standards as a trade-off for maximum inclusion

To facilitate maximum participation by its members, one of the frequent outcomes is that the governing body will set 'minimum standards'. This mirrors the approach generally exhibited by the law, in that the law functions on minimum standards.

---

38 C. Croney and S.T. Millman. 2007. 'The Ethical and Behavioural Basis for Farm Animal Welfare Legislation', *Journal of Animal Science*, 85(2): 556–65: doi:10.2527/jas.2006-422.

For example, a criminal offence is only considered to have been committed when an individual has breached what the law considers to be the minimum acceptable standard of conduct. Organisations, like the law, may advocate and support higher standards (e.g., 'better practice' or 'best practice'), but its rules are generally structured in a way that functions on a trade-off that balances standards that are attainable by the bulk of its membership. Standard setting becomes even more important where member consensus is required. For example, the World Trade Organization is the single largest government organisation facilitating trade in the international market, and its decisions are reportedly made by consensus, though, very rarely, a majority vote may also rule.

The World Trade Organization (WTO)

The World Trade Organization (WTO) is the largest international body dealing with rules of trade between nations. The WTO's agreements are negotiated and signed by the majority of the world's trading nations and ratified in their Parliaments. The documents set out the legal ground rules, terms and conditions of international commerce, and have a focus on enabling producers, exporters and importers to conduct business in the global marketplace.

The pervading focus of the WTO is an economic one, in that it seeks to facilitate trade between nations. Ideally, this requires rules that are transparent and predictable so that all participants to the WTO agreements are clear about the extent of their responsibilities and obligations. The WTO also serves as a forum for trade negotiations among its members, and may be called upon to settle trade disputes between member nations.

Significant controversy exists regarding the WTO, however. For example, a part of the WTO's role is to dismantle barriers to trade. Critics of the WTO have argued that since it functions as a global authority on trade and inherently has the right to review a country's domestic trade policies, then national sovereignty is compromised. This becomes a problem if a country wishes to establish regulations to protect its industry, workers, or environment which are viewed by the WTO as counter-intuitive to its central objective of facilitating free trade.

The WTO's rules largely dictate the trading policies of its member states, including trade criteria concerning animals and animal products. While the WTO and GATT (General Agreement on Tariffs and Trade) were not created specifically with animals in mind, the WTO and GATT have a major effect on member countries' abilities to protect animals within their borders or to utilise methods to aid animal protection in other countries.

Article XI of GATT prohibits bans or restrictions on imports or exports of products similar to those sold within a country, and Articles 1 and 3 states that all countries must be treated equally, and that imported products must be treated the same as 'like products of domestic origin'. This means that most countries cannot impose any trade sanctions against other countries, even if their animal welfare policies and uses of animals are offensive, cruel, or contrary to the policies of the particular country. Furthermore, the exemptions in Article XX of GATT protecting animal health, and/or relating to the conservation of exhaustible natural resources,

212   *International animal welfare law*

are not as straightforward to apply, as a number of people initially think. Article XX of the GATT refers to 'General Exceptions', and has been frequently referenced by those seeking to circumvent the WTO membership obligation which is viewed as an obstacle to the self-interests of each sovereign state, and to the progress of animal protection. However, the exceptions can only be implemented if they are based on science, and imposed only to the extent necessary. Additionally, the WTO member has the responsibility that the measures are both 'necessary' and based on scientific principles, rather than 'arbitrary or unjustified distinctions'. As a consequence, it is 'extremely difficult' for a WTO member 'to justify taking action under article 20'.[39, 40]

This raises questions as to whether the trade protection policies of the WTO and other trade-focused organisations are outdated, given that they fail to recognise standards of animal welfare as appropriate trade criteria. What if standards of animal welfare were an allowable consideration – or even a mandatory consideration – as part of multinational agreements? Radford has demonstrated that the imposition of import restrictions can be viewed two ways. The first alleges that countries attempting standards to apply import restrictions on products that have not been produced under the same animal welfare as their own are imposing their own moral view on other nation states, which may have a very different attitude towards animals. In contrast, Radford points out that it is 'equally possible to argue the same point the other way', and thus 'unconstrained trade liberalisation leads to those with low or non-existent standards imposing their view of the moral status of animals on the importing country'. Furthermore, 'the intention is not to institute a form of moral imperialism' by forcing other countries to adopt the same view as the importing country, or rather to allow the import 'to make their own moral choices, by enabling them to prohibit within their own territory, the marketing of products derived from practices which they find unacceptable'.[41]

Progress is slow, as indicated by Radford, who states that 'the underlying problem is that the WTO does not recognise the treatment of animals as a legitimate basis on which to impose restrictions'.[42] Concerns have been expressed that the WTO's rules-based trading system does not adequately address consumer interests, and as a consequence, the credibility of, and the public support for, the WTO is at risk.[43]

The realities of a global market continue to develop the norms of international trade, including what is acceptable in terms of animals and animal products. Even if animal welfare is not deemed acceptable as a trade criteria under future WTO agreements, it is possible that it will none the less increasingly feature in other instruments, including bilateral and multilateral agreements, voluntary corporate codes, and transparent product detailing that covers the animal and animal products in the producer-to-consumer journey. Ultimately, it is likely that the pressure of consumer

---

39   Radford, *Animal Welfare Law in Britain*, p. 134.

40   E.M. Thomas. 2007. 'Playing Chicken to the WTO: Defending an Animal Welfare-Based Trade Restriction under GATT's Moral Exception', 34 *B.C. Envtl. Aff. L. Rev.* 605: http://lawdigitalcommons. bc.edu/ealr/vol34/iss3/8.

41   Radford, *Animal Welfare Law in Britain*, p. 137.

42   Ibid., p. 136.

43   J. Turner and J. D'Silva (eds). 2006. *Animals, Ethics and Trade: The Challenge of Animal Sentience* (London: Earthscan), p. 251.

International animal welfare law 213

demands, coupled with demonstrated animal production gains associated with high standards of animal welfare, will in the long term compel nations to elevate standards of animal welfare in their trading criteria. See Case Study 7 below.

Case Study 7: Has the WTO seal case set a precedent for animal welfare as an acceptable trade criterion?

Issues of animal welfare have the potential to impact enormously on a range of environmental, economic and sociological matters in the global market-place. Where there are conflicts requiring resolution (e.g., trade criteria, species/environmental protection), then nations may resort to multinational organisations, including the World Trade Organization. Referencing the WTO judgments therefore provides a valuable starting point to assess the issues, judgments and outcomes relevant to animal welfare.

However, while the WTO is accustomed to dealing with issues and conflicts involving matters of trade and public morality, the WTO has historically demonstrated resistance to recognising a country's standards of animal welfare as an acceptable trade criteria. Consequently, when Canada and Norway complained to the World Trade Organization about the EU's 2009 seal trade ban, there was uncertainty about the outcomes, given that the seal ban case was a first for the WTO in that it directly required a judgment on the issue of animal welfare.

In the absence of clear provisions in trade law about what a country may or may not do regarding trade of products that have been derived from practices that are potentially deemed cruel, there is a general rule that applies. That WTO-established trade rule mandates that products which look the same and cannot be differentiated simply on the basis of the way that they are produced (e.g., potentially practices which were deemed cruel) should be permitted into the trade market.

In supporting the EU's ban, the WTO decision in respect of the seal case established a global trade precedent in respect of animal welfare and trade regulations by establishing that non-trade concerns, such as animal welfare (which formed the basis of the seal products ban), can restrict trade and still be in line with international trade law. It opens the door to the view that animal welfare is a matter of public morality, and trade bans can be implemented on the basis of animal welfare standards. If this principle was extended from seal hunting to issues of food safety and production, then there is potential for trade bans to be implemented on the basis of husbandry practices that are deemed cruel as well. Eggs from hens in battery cages, veal meat from calves housed in narrow crates, and products tested on animals where alternatives were available, are just a few examples of where the seal case trade precedent might be more broadly applied.

(DISPUTE SETTLEMENT: DISPUTE DS400: European Communities – Measures Prohibiting the Importation and Marketing of Seal Products: www.wto.org/english/tratop_e/dispu_e/cases_e/ds400_e.htm)

214   *International animal welfare law*

The World Organisation for Animal Health (OIE)

As mentioned in the previous chapter, the OIE is an intergovernmental organisation whose stated purpose is to improve animal health and welfare worldwide irrespective of the specific economic circumstance or cultural practice in member countries. It promotes itself as having a strongly scientific approach to standards of animal welfare (e.g., disease control, transport, slaughter and food safety) and is recognised as a reference organisation by multinationals including, for example, the WTO.

Since 2002, the OIE has recognised the need to set international animal welfare standards with the objective of improving not only animal health but also animal welfare, all around the world. The title of the organisation 'World Organisation for Animal Health' has resulted in a significant number of people believing that the organisation applies independent science to all uses of all animals. Although undoubtedly one of the leading organisations dealing with the related but separate issues of animal health and animal welfare, it is notable that the OIE has a mandate to focus OIE standards on matters of international trade.

With the mandate granted by its member countries, the OIE has taken a global leadership role in setting global animal welfare standards and has attained an impressive number of achievements. From an animal welfare perspective, the Terrestrial Code is particularly notable amongst those achievements. The Terrestrial Code contains general principles and specific recommendations on animal welfare. The OIE has also developed the Aquatic Animal Health Code, which contains general principles and specific recommendations on the welfare of farmed fish. The OIE standards are touted as being regularly updated to take account of latest scientific findings.

Critical assessment of the OIE's functions and role raises questions regarding its resource capabilities and independence. From an enforcement perspective, its standards are framed predominantly as recommendations and consequently it remains primarily as an adviser to those organisations with the power to implement laws which more directly bind people to behaving in a manner which complies with required – rather than simply recommended – standards.

The OIE continues to address the challenges accompanying developing political, public and science-based shifts, as it develops additional standards and recommendations. Religious slaughter, laboratory animal welfare and animal welfare standards in multilateral trade policy frameworks are examples of new and potentially contentious areas of OIE involvement in important animal welfare activities.

The WTO and the OIE are two organisations whose activities have arguably the largest impact on the welfare of the greatest number of animals and animal practices worldwide because the size of their international membership and the fact that their trade and science-based focus (i.e., WTO on trade, and the OIE on science-based standards on agribusiness practices such as transport and slaughter) is directly related to agribusiness and the biggest single global use of animals as a source of food for humans. As key global governors who actually promote themselves as leaders in the animal welfare field, the WTO and the OIE arguably have the largest responsibility to ensure that current and future initiatives correctly steer animal welfare current and future standards in a way that practically delivers what is humane and sustainable in terms of animal welfare. There are,

International animal welfare law   215

however, a number of other highly influential organisations that the student of animal welfare law should know about.

The Organisation for Economic Co-operation and Development (OECD)

The OECD's mission is to promote policies that will improve the economic and social well-being of people around the world. The OECD provides a forum in which governments can work together to share experiences and seek solutions to common problems. It facilitates the exchange of policy knowledge and experience between governments, with a view to coordinating future national and international economic policies and growing world trade. The OECD has set international standards on a wide range of global issues, which includes involvement in matters pertaining to agriculture and thereby the importance of animal welfare to wider economic and societal concerns.

The Food and Agriculture Organisation of the United Nations (FAO)

The FAO's stated purpose is to address the issue of world hunger. In the animal welfare context, the FAO is recognised as a neutral forum that serves developed and developing countries alike, providing knowledge and programmes designed to assist countries in modernising and improving areas including agriculture and fisheries, thereby facilitating improved nutrition by way of better food supply and food safety.

The European Union (EU)

The legal protection given to animals, particularly farm animals, is traditionally stronger in Europe, where countries within the European Union have banned several practices still common in other jurisdictions. In the 1990s, the EU established laws that set minimum standards for farm-animal husbandry which impacted housing for veal calves, battery-caged laying hens, pig gestation crates, and standards regarding slaughter and transport. Some European countries have gone further and adopted more stringent regulations in comparison to the minimum standards set out by the EU.

The EU arguably has some of the most advanced animal welfare legislation in the world. However, measures enforced by its members via national legislation have been criticised for incurring costs which producers find prohibitive in a competitive environment. If the same product can be imported more cheaply from a developing country (e.g., chicken from Thailand) despite having lower animal welfare standards, then domestic product may be disadvantaged, resulting in reduced profits for domestic producers.[44]

---

44   D. Wilkins. 2006. 'Outlawed in Europe: Animal Protection Progress in the European Union', in Turner and D'Silva (eds), *Animals, Ethics and Trade*, p. 224.

216 *International animal welfare law*

Bilateral and multinational agreements are key instruments of global governance[45]

Global governance is not the domain of a singular organisation. Governments, international non-government organisations and other international bodies are one part of the global governance system. Despite the fact that GATT, and its successor, the WTO, have significantly reduced trade barriers historically, major barriers to trade remain.

A feature of contemporary global governance is the evolution of regimes promoting trade, investment and competition.[46] Consequently, in addition to widespread global membership of countries to the WTO, there has also been more aggressive implementation of comparatively more flexible bilateral and multilateral trade agreements. The free trade agreements (FTAs) can have profound effects on multinational enterprises, so there is a need to consistently be alert to the substantial relationship between country context and trade strategies which, in turn, affect and are utilised by multinationals.[47]

Governments, like all other stakeholders on the international stage, understandably seek to protect trade barriers that serve and promote their own interests. With reference to debates as to who drives animal welfare in the international space, it is notable that in all the major multilateral state-to-state agreements, governments appear to have carefully ensured that any international organisation created would have limited functions and that only nation states would sit on the governing bodies of these organizations.

International governance: industry

International industry organisations

There are a literally tens of thousands of multinational corporations with many more subsidiaries in every corner of the world, each trading in products from developed and developing countries alike. Additionally, there are a significant number of global organisations representing various sectors of the animal food industry. For example, the International Dairy Federation, the International Meat Secretariat, the International Poultry Council and the International Egg Commission are examples of governing bodies which utilise science-based information gleaned from research programmes to benefit their respective sectors. Given that their industry involves animals and animal products, it follows that

---

45 Margaret Cooper. 2009. *An Introduction to Animal Law* (London: Academic Press), Chapter 9 'Foreign and International Legislation Relating to Animals'.

46 Andrew G. Brown and Robert M. Stern. 2011. 'Free Trade Agreements and Governance of the Global Trading System', IPC Working Paper Series No. 113 (International Policy Center): http://ipc.umich.edu/working-papers/pdfs/ipc-113-brown-stern-free-trade-agreements-governance-global-trading-system.pdf.

47 Sushil Vachani (ed.). 2006. *Transformations in Global Governance: Implications for Multinationals* (Cheltenham: Edward Elgar).

industry is highly motivated and influential on a global scale in matters involving animals and their welfare.

'Industry' refers not just to the food producers but also to all ancillary service providers to industries and professions involving animals. The companion animal industry, for example, involves an enormous range of services which include health care, training equipment, boarding and transport facilities, as well as a host of novelty products.

Similarly, agriculture involves ancillary service and product providers that include land care services (e.g., seed producers, fertilisers), equipment (e.g., dairy sheds, fencing, water systems, tractors and quad bikes), transportation systems, financiers and a wide association of other producers, service providers and professions associated with the 'farm-to-fork' food industry.

A common perception is that industry prefers absolute minimal standards of animal welfare in order to maximise its profit. Notwithstanding that there remain significant sectors of industry that demonstrate a purely commodity-based approach to animals, and where implemented standards of animal welfare have attracted significant criticism, there is a growing body of industry that recognises that improved animal welfare is not only profitable, but also preferable.

Industry, including producers and retailers, is increasingly conscious of the fact that improved animal welfare standards have significant benefits to people and animals alike. It is clear that certain practices in animal husbandry warrant criticism and that there is an evolving standard politically and publicly about what constitutes acceptable farm practice. Obvious examples of what was once acceptable but is no longer include veal crates, farrowing crates and certain systems of hen cages which have been banned in some jurisdictions and are in the process of being phased out in others. Despite individual attitudes of people denigrating 'all' of industry based on behaviours of selected 'sectors' of industry, industry remains not only highly motivated and influential in terms of animal welfare standards globally, but arguably industry is one of its key governors/leaders in terms of progressing practical improvements in animal welfare standards and the daily life experience of animals.

Governing organisations like the WTO wield significant influence on developed and developing countries alike, in respect of animal welfare standards – but so does industry. While trade agreements can require nations to accept non-animal-friendly imports, the same trade agreements cannot force supermarkets or restaurants to stock and/or sell the products. Industry can, however, and as a consequence, retailers have been recognised as potentially more effective than regulators in determining standards of animal welfare. Indeed, with this degree of flexibility and control, the combination of industry and retailers may be viewed as the most influential international governor, setting standards of animal welfare and the major body influencing animal welfare change.

Industry can move faster than governments, for example, it can cut off supplier's livelihoods by stopping contracts and, although bound to comply with a nation's laws, industry is not bound to the same degree as governments by international trade agreements. For example, while Europe as a whole must adhere to

218 *International animal welfare law*

the WTO and cannot bar imports on animal welfare grounds, retailers are free to do so. This mirrors statements identifying that 'the greater power in the world is not the superpower, but the supermarket.'

The visibility and name recognition of retailers has also made them sensitive targets of animal welfare campaigns promoting animal welfare reforms. For example, in 1999, in response to public persuasion, McDonald's restaurants announced the implementation of new animal welfare requirements as a condition of trade with its producers. The initiatives implemented by McDonald's included audits of slaughterhouses, increased cage space per egg-laying hen, and a ban on forced moulting. Following McDonald's' announcement, its competitors Burger King and Wendy's committed to implementing similar animal welfare improvements. Similar industry/retailer commitments to improved animal welfare standards can be recognised by other multinational/national businesses around the world including Subway, Starbucks, Coca-Cola, Heineken, IKEA and others.[48]

As retailers compete with each other over public perception, successfully negotiating welfare gains with a major retailer potentiates the possibility of a 'race to the top' of animal welfare standards by industry. The benefits to industry of greater efficiency, effectiveness and a bankable reputation for high animal welfare standards has been recognised by industry *and* a number of non-government organisations.

International governance: non-government organisations

Competing – and collaborating – NGOs

Despite the fact that the term 'non-government organisation' (NGO) does not have a strict definition and has been applied as a term to a variety of organisations with varying structures, funding, persuasions and functions, an NGO, as the name suggests, broadly refers to an organisation or body that operates independently of government.[49]

Although not all NGOs are active in global politics, there are a significant number of them that actively set out to influence public opinion engendering support for their particular purposes. There are competing interests and values between government, industry and NGOs. In broad terms, government applies an inclusionary utilitarian approach which means that enforcement is triggered primarily at a level of minimum standards. Industry's focus on profitability broadly means that despite the common perception that industry seeks the lowest possible standards of animal welfare, it would be more accurate to state that industry seeks 'profitable standards of animal welfare' which, amongst the leading producers,

---

48 Compassion in World Farming. 2012. 'Good Farm Animal Welfare Awards': www.compassionin foodbusiness.com/awards.

49 Peter Willetts. n.d. 'What is a Non-Governmental Organization?': www.gdrc.org/ngo/peter-willets.html.

International animal welfare law 219

has resulted in progressively higher standards of animal welfare that certainly exceed those expected by government/legislative counterparts.

NGOs are broadly recognised for advocating 'best-practice' standards of animal welfare. Contrasting ideologies about what constitutes 'best practice' clearly exist between NGOs but a common feature of many is a view that the animal warrants at least a stronger voice at the stakeholder table. With this in mind, NGOs' activities are as broad as the roles of animals in human society itself, and involve participation in legislative developments, policy, public education and campaigns, as well as engagement (either collaboratively or in a passive-aggressive manner) with other stakeholders, including government and industry.

Government, industry and non-government organisations share important points in common, despite their differences in world-views, responsibilities and aspirations. For example, each share a vested interest in the public's opinion and behaviour and are actively involved in development of animal husbandry practices, education and campaign programmes. Similarly, each has finite resources which must be accounted for. With the drive for greater efficiency and effectiveness in the animal welfare space, and recognition that they cannot enforce compliance on their own, a number of governments (e.g., New Zealand and Australia) have developed national strategies promoting a 'collaborative' approach between themselves and other stakeholders attached to the issue of animal welfare.

Identifying non-government organisations in animal welfare

The definition of an NGO as an organisation or body that operates independently of government assists in identifying which organisations are included in the category of NGOs. When considering which organisations are NGOs, people commonly think first about organisations which have a reputation associated with strongly animal-centric activities. The Society for the Prevention of Cruelty to Animals (SPCA) and its associates are probably one of the most well-known examples. Organisations like Save Animals From Exploitation (SAFE) and People for the Ethical Treatment of Animals (PETA) have an international profile following significant campaigns drawing attention to their own world-views and ideologies regarding animals as stakeholders in questions of animal welfare and law. World Animal Protection (formerly World Society for the Protection of Animals) Humane Society of the United States, and Compassion In World Farming are also key players.

World Animal Protection (formerly the World Society for the Protection of Animals, WSPA)

This society's remit is global animal welfare activities, particularly in respect of companion animals, commercial exploitation of wildlife, disaster management involving animals, and welfare issues related to production animals. It is widely known for its major campaigns influencing governments and other relevant

220 *International animal welfare law*

animal welfare decision makers to change or introduce policy which improves standards of animal welfare.

One of its particular initiatives is the Universal Declaration of Welfare for Animals (UDWA). It has been viewed by some people as the 'animal version' of the Universal Declaration of Human Rights, which was adopted by the United Nations in 1948. The UDWA is a grass-roots campaign, which would develop basic premises of animal welfare to be adopted by the global community. The UDWA advocates that the United Nations ratify an international agreement on the welfare of animals, which would recognise animals as sentient beings, capable of suffering and experiencing pain.

Compassion in World Farming (CIWF)

The CIWF in the UK is the leading NGO working internationally to advance the welfare of farm animals and to achieve a vibrant rural economy based on humane and environmentally sustainable farming methods. It has a strong track record in lobbying, research and education, and played a key role in achieving the UK's and the EU's phasing-out of some of the most damaging livestock production systems. The CIWF engages positively with farmers and the food industry, rewarding good practice, and has developed innovative resources on Good Agricultural Practice in Animal Welfare. The group displays a collaborative approach in its dealings with all stakeholders.

Humane Society International (HSI)

This society is the international arm of The Humane Society of the United States (HSUS), a charitable non-profit organisation which incorporates both policy and front-line programmes in countries around the world. Examples of projects which the HSI has been involved with include national and international biodiversity policy and implementation to protect habitats critical to the survival of many native species; climate change, and the protection of 'carbon sinks' such as rainforests and areas of high biodiversity value; food-labelling programmes focusing on the well-being of farm animals and unsustainable animal husbandry practices, and providing disaster relief support in developing countries to rescue stricken and abandoned animals.

It works with national and jurisdictional governments, multilateral entities, corporations, academic institutions, a range of other humane organisations and animal protectionists to identify practical, culturally sensitive and long-term solutions to common animal issues.

International Fund for Animal Welfare (IFAW)

IFAW works to improve the welfare of wild and domestic animals throughout the world by reducing commercial exploitation of animals, protecting wildlife habitats and assisting animals in distress. IFAW is active in using promotional campaigns to educate audiences about animal welfare issues worldwide. It has a large base of supporters and uses this support to influence governments and other organisations worldwide to achieve an improvement in animal welfare. IFAW seeks to motivate the public to prevent cruelty to animals and to promote animal welfare and conservation policies that influence law governing the well-being of both animals and people.

World Animal Forum (WAF)

WAF is an independent association made up of the chief executive officers of animal protection societies and other selected guests from civil society, government and business. The forum meets informally each year to exchange ideas and develop strategies to enhance and forward the animal protection movement, addressing relevant issues of education, policy and animal protection/welfare law.

Non-traditional, but none the less animal welfare-related NGOs

In addition to the traditionally known NGOs, there are other categories which also have significant influence on the international stage. They are commonly overlooked, but are obvious when their role is considered.

The World Bank Group

Financial and technical providers are as crucial to matters of animal welfare as they are to other global issues (e.g., poverty, malnutrition, disease control). The World Bank Group (WBG) aims to reduce poverty. It provides low-interest loans and grants to developing countries with a view to assisting those countries to invest in themselves by developing self-sustaining internal systems (including agriculture) and eventually becoming financially independent.

The International Finance Corporation

The International Finance Corporation (IFC) is a subgroup of the WBG that assists the private sector of developing countries with a view to enabling the recipients of funding to develop resources, expand the workplace, and achieve financial independence. In respect of animal welfare, the IFC have specific polices linking standards of animal welfare to their funding criteria.

Locally, nationally and internationally, there are literally thousands of organisations, sponsors, trusts and other groups which act independently of government, seeking to influence matters pertaining to animal welfare standards, policy and law. Not all of them can be listed here, but their influence individually and collectively establishes them as an identifiable stakeholder in matters of animal welfare and law.

International governance: the professions

There are an enormous range of professions and professionals involved directly and indirectly with animal welfare nationally and internationally, reflecting the

222 *International animal welfare law*

range of species and roles of animals in human society. There are a number of professional participants that have a role in either 'making, shaking, or applying' standards of animal welfare, and/or relevant policy and law across national and international borders.

Veterinarians, researchers and scientists

Veterinarians promote themselves, and are widely trusted by the public and the law alike, as being society's 'animal health and welfare professionals'. They are the only profession routinely and specifically identified in contemporary animal welfare legislation, as the professional who has a pivotal role in the assessment pertaining to the four words that underpin the legislatively identified and protected interests of animals: whether or not the animal has suffered 'pain' and/or 'distress' that is either 'unreasonable' and/or 'unnecessary'.

By virtue of their education and high level of credibility in the eyes of the public and the law, veterinarians are widely perceived as community care-givers with important contributions not only to animal well-being, but also in matters of public health and safety.[50, 51] Veterinarians have been identified as the only animal-oriented group, that is also a profession, and that no other animal-oriented group is invested with the same degree of trust by the public and the law alike. That trust is accompanied by expectations of knowledge and performance involving animals, their welfare and related issues of public concern.

Despite the relationship between an animal's health and its welfare, animal health has been identified as distinctly different from the subject of animal welfare. Veterinarians receive significant training in matters of animal health, but have received criticism for not understanding the relevant animal welfare law that underpins their professional activities. For example, in response to the question of what the veterinarians should do about animal welfare, the single one-word answer has been identified as 'more'.[52]

To be fair, the majority of veterinarians demonstrate a sense of responsibility and want to do 'the right thing' by their patients and their clients. But they face some significant ongoing procedural and practical hurdles which require addressing in order to help veterinarians help others. Those barriers include: a traditional lack of adequate and assessed veterinary education on animal welfare, inherent difficulties in assessing an animal's welfare, differing attitudes to

---

50 Arkow, P. 1998. 'Application of Ethics to Animal Welfare', *Applied Animal Behaviour Science*, 59: 193–200.

51 Gary Patronek. 1997. 'Issues for Veterinarians in Recognizing and Reporting Animal Neglect and Abuse', *Society and Animals*, 5(3): 267–280.

52 Catherine J. Hewson. 2003. 'Focus on Animal Welfare', *Canadian Veterinary Journal*, 44(4): 335–6: www.ncbi.nlm.nih.gov/pmc/articles/PMC372260/: 'In October 2001, the Sir James Dunn Animal Welfare Centre at the Atlantic Veterinary College, University of Prince Edward Island, Canada, hosted its inaugural annual lecture in animal welfare. Dr Mike Appleby, Vice President for Farm Animals and Sustainable Agriculture, Humane Society of the United States, spoke on the topic "What should we do about animal welfare?".'

animals within the profession, and potential conflicts of interest between the animal's well-being, the owner's wishes and the veterinarian's own professional/personal/business interests. All these have been identified as potential barriers to veterinarians demonstrating adequate fulfilment of the public trust and guardianship role of veterinarians regarding an animal's welfare.

However, there are indicators that the veterinary profession at a national, regional and international level is increasing in its understanding and participation in matters of animal welfare, and relevant policy/law. For example, decision makers in veterinary education are recognising the need for greater emphasis on animal welfare and ethics at both the undergraduate and postgraduate teaching levels.

At an international level, the activities of the veterinary profession are represented through the World Veterinary Association (WVA). The WVA is a federation of national veterinary medical associations throughout the world, and is the internationally recognised representative of global veterinary medicine. The WVA works with other organisations including the OIE, FAO and WHO, promoting initiatives including the One World-One Health concept, animal health, and programmes which demonstrate the link between animal welfare and public health.

The continued development of animal welfare standards means that the expectation of the political, public and legal minds is also shifting. The expectation of veterinarians by many stakeholders – including the veterinarians themselves – is that they will collectively, and as individuals, learn and contribute more to issues of animal welfare as part and parcel of fulfilling their professional role.

Journalists

Journalists are defined as those who present news and information to a range of audiences. The journalist fulfils many potential roles as mediator, translator, watchdog, moderator, editor, commentator and advertiser. However, many now work in a fragmented market dominated by the push for ratings and revenue. As with many professions, the list of 'shoulds' does not necessarily translate into consistent application of professional virtues such as objectivity and factual accuracy.

Major questions surround the issue of contemporary and developing journalism, relating to the impact of interpretive journalism (in the form of blogging or citizen-to-citizen communication), and arguably the disappearance of traditional forms of journalism which allegedly demonstrated greater objectivity and verifiable accuracy. These realities are particularly important in the field of animal welfare and related policy and law, in light of the fact that public opinion and perceptions continue to represent an important factor for decision makers. In turn, this is closely related to the fact that the average individual's opinion continues to be predominantly influenced by the media, complemented in part by the education materials provided by divergent stakeholders.

The credibility of journalists and media varies substantially. One of the tools that can be utilised in assessing a journalist's material is to consider not just the questions that have been asked, but also those that have not. For example, journalists have occasionally been accused of demonstrating favouritism by not asking

224 *International animal welfare law*

potentially unpopular and/or difficult questions to representatives of animal welfare institutions. Reportage of controversial animal-related issues including live exports, animal research purposes, animals for human entertainment (e.g., from zoos and rodeos to bullfighting) and breed policies (e.g., pit bulls and dangerous dog legislation) do not always represent views of many as opposed to some stakeholders.

Economists

An economist is strictly defined as a specialist in economics. Their responsibilities involve significantly more than just managing money. The role of an economist is to research, analyse and provide theories on all elements of the society and the economy in which it lives, focusing on the production, distribution and consumption of goods and services.

Globalisation has created a specific need for experts who understand the nuances of international trade including relationships between global financial markets, commodities and exchange rates. Animals and animal products are one of the commodities on the global market which, in addition to having significant relevance to trade opportunities fulfilling consumer needs, are also associated with enormous risks to public health and national economies.

Economists are frequently involved in the decision-making process involved in matters of animal welfare, determining what is affordable in terms of people, businesses, the economy and wider international obligations and relationships. Animal welfare issues involving economists include assessing consumer concerns[53] about animal welfare and consumers' willingness to pay for higher standards of animal welfare.

There are a number of readily available examples illustrating the need to have economists who demonstrate insights and proficiency regarding the subject of animal welfare, in light of its opportunities and risks to wider society, the environment and the economy. One of the most significant examples hinges on the fact that the single largest use of animals is as a source of food for humans. This use is relevant to the challenge of producing a socially acceptable agricultural product that is managed for the benefit of society, while concurrently producing an economically viable product for the producers. That in turn translates to the product's affordability for the public consumer. In some circles, the concept of ethical accounting extends the focus beyond simply financial profit, to the trilogy of 'people, planet and profit'.

Policy advisers and ethicists

A policy is defined as a plan or course of action (e.g., of a governing body such as a government, political party, or business) intended to influence and determine decisions, actions and other matters. It follows that a policy adviser's role includes

---

53 G. Harper and S. Henson. 2001. 'Consumer Concerns About Animal Welfare and the Impact on Food Choice', Final Report EU Fair CT98-3678, Centre for Food Economics.

International animal welfare law 225

functioning as a relevant expert responsible for gathering accurate information, and understanding concepts, terminologies and markets, in order to effectively communicate and advise projects and decision makers.

The prerequisite to an effective policy adviser in animal welfare is the 'accurate information' and understanding of key stakeholders, as well as the wider national and international economic, sociological and environmental factors associated with a subject. That involves much more than just 'meat for food commodity' on the one hand, or merely 'caring about how animals feel' on the other. A policy adviser's influence on government can be enormous and have a significant influence on the direction of government.

Lawyers, politicians and legislators

As has been explained in earlier chapters, the law is society's rulebook. It develops and evolves in terms of what is good practice and publicly acceptable as governors and society is informed (e.g., by science and communication technology). It is a normal and expected prerequisite to implementation that any proposal or initiative be 'lawful'.

There are a host of stakeholders and experts who influence, persuade and advise key representatives (e.g., politicians) and government decision makers on law. Lawyers have been described as the technical experts who know the law and who are licensed to represent, advise, or act for others in legal matters. The legal discipline of animal law is one of the fastest growing areas of law, reflecting increased awareness and interest of all stakeholders which include the personal and professional interests of the lawyers involved in matters regarding animals. When the discipline of animal law was in its infancy, lawyers and other involved individuals were commonly labelled as 'bunny huggers' or similarly labelled by those exhibiting their own misunderstanding and prejudice. However, stakeholders across industry, government, corporates, and other national and international organisations have recognised the enormous sociological, environmental and economic interests associated with animal welfare. And where there is money and other interests, there are usually lawyers heavily involved in drafting the rules, and giving opinion on matters of associated compliance and risk management.

Undergraduate and postgraduate training in animal law is available for lawyers in an increasing number of universities around the world. Dedicated law practices have been established by lawyers recognising that the human–animal relationship has relevance not just in criminal matters, but in a host of civil issues as well. Increasingly, more governments are recognising the value of having credible and informed in-house legal counsel dealing with animal-related matters, such as international trade risks and obligations, legal standards involving all animals whether domesticated or wild, and socially acceptable legal penalties that demonstrate that the penalty does in fact fit the crime.

While other professions frequently lobby, advise, or research on matters of animal law, it is largely the lawyers, legislators and politicians who have the responsibility for drafting and deciding on the standards and contents of society's legal rulebook concerning animals. The responsibility is significant because of the enormous consequences associated in the future by getting today's decisions 'wrong'.

226 *International animal welfare law*

Who's leading the evolution of animal welfare?

Despite their differences, the global community is highly interdependent. Globalisation in the current and foreseeable international community means that decisions by international power brokers have potentially extensive and intensive effects. In the current structure, governments and the system of multinational government-dominated bodies (e.g., the WTO, the UN) continue to be at the core of the international governance system. Despite varying degrees of flexibility and independence, multinational corporations, professions and other international stakeholders largely play a role by influencing and/or advising national governments and government-dominated international bodies. However, a shift in the balance of power means traditionally less-dominant non-state players have increasing power in the global governance system.

The traditional 'only governments decide' approach is increasingly being challenged and dismantled, as non-state players discover their own power in making many of the crucial decisions. The reality is that a large variety of organisations, including multinational corporations and NGOs, exercise authority and engage in political action across state boundaries.

Each participant – including the individuals and organisations responsible for governance – have competing and conflicting interests, drivers and agendas. The rhetoric attached to governance and management of animal welfare internationally demonstrates consistent application of fundamental principles that were established from the very beginnings of the human–animal relationship. Those principles include, for example, the dominance of humans, the categorisation of animals as property (albeit in an increasing number of jurisdictions as animate property), and recognition of the fact that healthy animals are crucial to the current and future interests of people.

The implications of animal welfare standards are significant for people and therefore all international power brokers. Globalisation means that one country which does not comply with the required standards of animal welfare and associated biosecurity may create unnecessary risks for other countries.

In order to adapt to the realities of a global marketplace, national governments may require a shift in attitudes, viewing influencers such as global media, international firms, scientific bodies and others more as peers than simply as advisers or customers. Corporate executives similarly must be accepted alongside government at the global governance table, due to their economic power in the global marketplace. Non-government organisations such as Compassion in World Farming and the World Society for the Protection of Animals have recognised the importance of influencing key economic stakeholders in order to deliver practical objectives for animal welfare interests.

Animal welfare issues are often portrayed as if they are simple matters requiring single-perspective solutions. In fact, the subject of animal welfare continues to be a multifaceted, multidisciplinary and complex policy issue. The complexity of causal relationships and patterns of influence, particularly with emerging multiple-level shifts in governance, makes simple analysis highly problematic, if

International animal welfare law 227

not impossible. Globalisation makes some degree of global-level regulation desirable in respect of many subjects including animal welfare, in order to facilitate global opportunities and minimise concurrent global risks.

Are the decision makers on track for 2050 and beyond?

Notwithstanding the progress made to date in respect of global awareness and relevant law regarding animal welfare, there is a continued need to progress the development of standards on existing and emerging areas of importance to animal welfare. For example, developments in science require continued attention to standards relating to animals used in research, testing and teaching. Additionally, the diversity of religious beliefs has required attention to methods of humane handling of animals, not just throughout their life but also in respect of their death. Similarly, the primary use of animals as a source of food for people means that providing a constant supply of safe meat to the increasing global population is a subject meriting considerable attention.

Setting standards by credible and objective systems must be properly implemented and consistently enforced if there is to be effective change. With this in mind, the national decision makers and the law must keep abreast of the linkages between animal welfare and wider national/global interests.

2050: at least 70 per cent more food needed

Reports estimate that farmers will have to produce 70 per cent more food cereals and animal proteins by 2050 to meet the needs of the world's expected 9-billion-strong population. This trend poses a considerable challenge for the agricultural sector, given the decreasing rural labour force, and the fact that most available farmland is already being farmed. Farming continues to compete with sprawling urban settlements, and there is increasing recognition of the need to change agricultural practices in order to protect and efficiently utilise limited resources of land and water.[54] There are additional expectations that agriculture will adapt and contribute to the mitigation of climate change, assist in the preservation of natural habitats, protect endangered species, and maintain a high level of biodiversity while concurrently caring for the land and producing 'more food'. Importantly, the issue is not just to produce sufficient quantities of food, but to provide sufficient quantities of *safe* and *sustainable* food and equitable access to it.

The terms 'humane' and 'sustainable' are common expressions used in the field of animal welfare. In terms of animal welfare and law, 'humane' is synonymous with concepts of 'anti-cruelty' consistent with contemporary animal welfare legislation that protects an animal from 'unnecessary and/or unreasonable pain

54 FAO. 2006. 'World Agriculture Towards 2030/2050': www.fao.org/fileadmin/user_upload/esag/docs/Interim_report_AT2050web.pdf.

228 *International animal welfare law*

and/or distress'. 'Sustainability' encompasses more than simple retention of bio-diversity and effective and efficient use of limited resources. Sustainability also advocates proactive avoidance of unsustainable production and consumption by questioning future structures and systems of livestock production. Concurrently, it should involve investing in research developing economically viable, environmentally conservative and humane animal alternatives that feed the planet.

Disease control across multinational borders

All stakeholders have a vested interest in preventing, eradicating and/or managing diseases of animals. Certain diseases are not transmissible to human beings but none the less cause devastating financial loss. For example, outbreaks of foot-and-mouth disease (FMD) continue to incur an annual global cost in excess of US$5 billion.[55]

Zoonoses (diseases transferable from animals to humans) are another category of animal-related diseases that pose a significant risk to people. 'Mad cow' disease, swine flu and bird flu are notable examples that have resulted in significant costs including loss of human life. Rabies, anthrax, tuberculosis and brucellosis are other zoonoses commonly entrenched in developing countries.

The costs are not restricted simply to producers. Consumers ultimately pay for the cost of production, and disease outbreaks commonly result in reduced availability of food products (e.g., milk, meat and other foodstuffs) and consequent increase in prices.

International trade opportunities are logically accompanied by global-sized risks. Consequently, global strategies developed by organisations such as the FAO and the OIE assist countries in developing risk management policies to prevent and/or control disease outbreaks that can affect multiple species (both domesticated and wild) and cross national borders.

In 2050, demand for meat is expected to surge by approximately 70 per cent. Demand for dairy products is anticipated to rise by 62 per cent, and estimates anticipate that egg production will also need to increase by 65 per cent to meet global consumer demand.

Strategies to address disease control must be collaboratively implemented to provide effective deliverables. Director-general of the OIE, Dr Bernard Vallat is quoted as saying 'only one country which does not comply may endanger the entire planet'.[56] A pivotal – and frequently overlooked – fact, is the estimate that 75 per cent of emerging diseases are zoonotic.[57] They are now recognised as a

---

55 OIE/FAO. 2012. 'More than 100 Nations Support New Strategy on Livestock Disease': www.oie. int/eng/A_FMD2012/Media.html.

56 'World Bank Join their Forces to Improve Animal Health Worldwide': www.oie.int/for-the-media/press-releases/detail/article/oieworld-bank-join-their-forces-to-improve-animal-health-worldwide/.

57 E.P.J. Gibbs. 2005. 'Emerging Zoonotic Epidemics in the Interconnected Global Community', *Veterinary Record*, 157: 673–9: http://onehealthinitiative.com/publications/Gibbs_Emer_Zoonotic_ %20Wooldridge.pdf.

International animal welfare law 229

major global threat to human health and sustainable development, and are a major concern for national and international agencies.[58]

Despite commonly held views that all public interest matters including, for example, issues of disease control, are the responsibility of the government, the responsibility for disease control is not limited to simply government. All stakeholders including producers, retailers, industry and non-government organisations have a vested interest in ensuring compliance with standards that minimise the risks and associated costs of inadequate disease control.

The prevalence of cross-border trade facilitates trans-boundary transference of disease and poses a regional threat that requires regional approaches and responses. Early warning of outbreaks of animal diseases and the capacity for prediction of the spread of such diseases to new areas has been identified as essential for containment and control. Past experience has demonstrated the need for rapid communication and collaboration in order to contain and eradicate diseases.[59] Since many infectious diseases are zoonotic, it is clear that information of zoonotic disease occurrence in animals is important also to public health officials. This rationale underpins the reason why agencies such as the WHO, the FAO and the OIE have developed systems to detect and respond to major animal diseases.[60]

The new context of globalisation and climate change has led to new threats that affect the global community.[61] International transportation of products and people worldwide is an important factor in the spread of viruses and bacteria. Bio- or agro-terrorism can use the flow of commodities and people to facilitate the spread of disease.

Legislation dealing with biosecurity risks, importation of hazardous substances and illegal trade are examples of wider legislation that is relevant to matters of animal welfare law. Effective law is one of the key factors identified as being important to functional partnerships between stakeholders in the public and private sector.

Are you critically assessing national animal welfare issues?

Having covered the basics of foundational concepts that have been translated into national law, and subsequently considered the principles of international law, consider the following tasks and questions. In the first instance, you might want to identify your immediate response, then compare it with the conclusions you reach in applying the model of critical assessment set out for you in Chapter 3:

---

58 Stephen Palmer 2011. 'The Global Challenge of Zoonoses Control': http://oxfordmedicine.com/oso/search:downloadsearchresultaspdf;jsessionid=3CCD2C80CEF6F918E7EADAFCB1EA1039?isQuickSearch=true&q=zoonoses&searchBtn=Search&siteToSearch=oso.
59 FAO/OIE/WHO. 2006. 'Global Early Warning and Response Systems for Major Animal Diseases, Including Zoonoses (GLEWS)': www.oie.int/fileadmin/Home/eng/About_us/docs/pdf/GLEWS_Tripartite-Finalversion010206.pdf.
60 WHO. n.d. 'Zoonoses – Outbreak Alerts': www.who.int/zoonoses/outbreaks/en/.
61 Gibbs, 'Emerging Zoonotic Epidemics in the Interconnected Global Community'.

230   *International animal welfare law*

- 'The government should do something.' Explain why governments are not truly autonomous in the global marketplace.
- 'Industry has the ability to make a quicker and more effective difference to standards of animal welfare than government.' Critically assess this statement.
- 'The most influential organisation dictating global animal welfare standards is the WTO.' Critically assess this statement.
- 'Government assurances and commitment that national standards of animal welfare are consistent with international standards simply endorse that the government is doing no more than complying with the lowest common denominator.' Critically assess this statement.

Part III

Putting the principles and law into practice

Part III provides readers with the opportunity to apply what they have learnt and test whether or not they understand, distinguish and can critically assess the concepts of animal law, animal welfare, the uses of animals in human society and society's legal criteria regarding those uses.

After finishing Part II, readers should have sufficient information and understanding of relevant animal law principles to be able to put supplementary reading in perspective, and participate in discussions about animals, welfare and law with a deeper sense of legal understanding and objectivity. These abilities will also assist the reader in critically assessing the uses of animals in society.

Part III enables readers to test what has been learnt by applying their learning to two uses of animals that attract considerable debate, namely the use of animals in research, and in agriculture. By the end of the following three chapters, readers should be able to explain what it means to 'critically assess' and, by reference to the foundational principles, explain how the law balances and prioritises the interests of competing and conflicting stakeholders and participants involved in using animals in research and agriculture.

Overall, this book identifies what has shaped – and still informs – people's diverse attitudes and in turn, the law as society's rulebook, about people's responsibilities for the treatment, protection of, and experience of, animals. Understanding the foundational principles of the relationship between people and animals assists in applying objectivity, (legal) authority and practicality to the role and uses of animals in human society, and critically assessing the interrelated future of animals and people.

7 Critically assessing the use of animals in research

Before reading this chapter assess how well you can:

- Define the term 'research' with particular reference to the four keywords that set out the interest of animals protected by the law ('unnecessary', 'unreasonable', 'pain', 'distress').
- Explain the polarised opinions of members of the public regarding the use of animals in research by reference to the foundational drivers of the human–animal relationship (outlined in Chapter 4 of this book). Identify the barriers to conciliation between contrasting stakeholders/public opinions relevant to the subject of research involving animals.
- Define the 3Rs (reduction, refinement, replacement) and relate the principles of the 3Rs to the interest of animals protected by the law.
- What are the key features of contemporary animal welfare law governing the use of animals in research? Use these principles to compare and contrast the effectiveness (or not) of the law governing research using animals in different legal jurisdictions.
- Assess arguments for and against research in context of the law's legally protected interest of animals (as set out in contemporary animal welfare law). Compare and contrast the legal assessment with a broader 'critical assessment' of the arguments for and against the use of animals in research.

'Research is painful' – and other assumptions

Historically, animal research isn't new

Records demonstrate that experiments on animals were being carried out as early as 450 BCE, when Alcmaeon revealed that animals would be blind following severance of the optic nerve. As far back as 380 BCE, Aristotle revealed anatomical differences among animals by dissecting them, and around 330 BCE, Herophilos identified a functional difference between tendons and nerves, and while around the same time, Erasistratos made a distinction between sensory and motor nerves.

234 *Assessing use of animals in research*

Despite these early records, it wasn't until the sixteenth century that experiments involving animals began to be conscientiously recorded. Respiration, heart and circulatory function, locomotion, and the study of the brain and spinal cord were all studied by scientists such as William Harvey and Leonardo da Vinci. Thus, from the earliest through to modern times, animals were frequently used in experiments, including the process of vivisection.[1]

In addition to being used to learn about the anatomical and physiological functions of living systems, animals have been used in a significant number of medical advances. The first vaccine, created in 1796 by Edward Jenner, was a result of his observing that milkmaids who had contracted and recovered from cowpox were resistant to smallpox. Jenner subsequently took fluid from the cowpox pustule of an affected milkmaid and inoculated a young boy, proving his theory that exposure to cowpox was indeed protective for smallpox. Since this discovery, smallpox has subsequently been completely eradicated as a result of an immunisation programme run by the World Health Organization – the last naturally occurring case of smallpox was recorded in 1977. This was one of many medical advances that continue to be made through to the present day, as research addresses numerous conditions including the treatment of medical conditions, such as diabetes and cancer, and the development of vaccinations, anaesthetics, surgical techniques and a wide range of pharmaceuticals.

Research, and its concurrent benefits for animals and people alike, is nothing new in the history of the human–animal relationship. What is comparatively new in context of the longevity of the relationship, is the increase in the number of animals used, the variety of experiments undertaken, and the role of the law in balancing and prioritising the polarised views of those for and against the use of animals in research.

What do we mean by the term 'animal research'?

'Animal research' is a broad term that is widely used in a way that is synonymous with other terms such as 'animal testing', 'animal experimentation', '*in vivo* testing' and 'vivisection'. Strictly speaking, there are differences between each of these terms.

'Animal research' is used in this chapter to include all of the commonly associated terms, and is broadly defined as the use of non-human animals in an experiment. In addition to activities commonly viewed as occurring in the laboratory, 'animal research' also includes any testing that involves animals (e.g., efficacy of differing treatments in separate groups of farm animals) and teaching activities (e.g., utilisation of animals in schools and universities).

In considering the use of non-human animals in an experiment, it is important to avoid making assumptions about what is meant regarding the experiment.

---

1 D. Legge and S. Brooman (eds). 1997. *Law Relating to Animals* (London and New York: Routledge-Cavendish), p. 111.

*What do you think of when you hear the term
'animal research'?*

For many people, there is an automatic assumption that the experiment which is at the centre of the research being conducted, involves pain and distress to the animals involved. Certainly there are a range of experiments which have provided visually shocking images of animals in the laboratory and that, in turn, has understandably generated significant emotion and public response.

For example, images of animals with the tops of their skulls removed, having substances applied to their eyes, or forced to repeat movements to the point of exhaustion, vomiting, and/or death, have understandably generated significant emotion in public response, despite the fact that many of the images are literally decades out of date, and that the portrayed experiments would be unauthorised and unlawful today.

SPECIES VARIATION

The fact is, experiments that use animals as the test subject vary enormously in terms of the species used, the purposes and procedures of research projects, as well as the criteria attached to each project. Mice and rats are among most common, but rabbits, guinea pigs and dogs are also frequent subjects of animal research. If the results are to be validly transferable from the research animal to humans, there needs to be a close biological and taxonomic relationship between the animal species used and humans. Furthermore, there is significant research focusing on the animals themselves, particularly in instances where there is, for example, associated benefit to wider interests (e.g., productivity and profitability). Consequently, research on a wide range of agricultural animals (e.g., dairy cows, pigs and chickens) is commonplace to increase milk or meat production. Additionally, it is clear that scientific research is also conducted on wild animals. For example, tagging and tracking is a common procedure used to study a wide range of activities involving non-domesticated species in everything from their migratory behaviour to their population size.

When considering the different species that are the subject of 'animal research', it quickly becomes clear that almost every species on the planet is the subject of some kind of 'research', and that the degree of invasiveness also varies significantly. Furthermore, people's attitudes and consequent acceptance regarding the 'necessity' of the research varies according to the level of agreement that each individual may, or may not have, regarding the purposes of the research being conducted.

PROCEDURES VARY ENORMOUSLY

Pure research investigates how organisms behave, develop and function; proponents argue that pure research may reveal significant benefits warranting further applied research (i.e., research that has a specific practical aim). Embryogenesis,

236 *Assessing use of animals in research*

developmental biology, gene research, toxicology, drug testing and the study of diseases and medical conditions/disorders, xenotransplantation and behavioural studies are all examples of research that may involve animals. However, the degree to which animals may be involved in the research may vary significantly – from pure observation through to experiments which involve varying degrees of internal and/or external modifications and potentially pain and/or distress to an animal.

The point in terms of critical assessment of animal research is that in the first instance, it is important to be clear about the nature of the experiment itself, which is consistent with the first part of the two-part test (i.e., whether reasonable or necessary) in respect of an animal's welfare and the law. Some experiments do indeed cause pain and distress to an animal – others simply do not. However, debates continue regarding the ethical basis for conducting research on animals at all.

What makes animal research acceptable or not?

Polarised opinions on research reflect the same basis for contrasting opinion regarding any use of animals. On one hand, animals are 'different' from human beings, and there is a prevailing attitude that human domination gives people the right to use animals for the benefit of the human race. Despite this difference in status, animals are seen as sufficiently similar to humans biologically to validate research and testing on animals, frequently as a prerequisite to identifying potential risks and benefits that may apply to people.

On the other hand, abolitionists advocate that animals are sufficiently 'similar' to humans that they should be viewed and protected as individual experiences of life, rather than the subjects of research. Objections to animal research were also raised on the basis that the benefit to humans didn't justify the harm to animals, and that because of the differences between animals and humans, the results obtained in animal research could not reliably be applied to humans. The continuing debate, of course, is where to draw the line between these two polarised views.

Those in favour of continuing animal research

Proponents of continuing to use animals in experimentation almost universally point to the important contribution animal research has made to medical and surgical advancements which have benefited both humans and animals. Those in favour of experimentation are quick to point out that animal research has played a vital role in virtually every major modern advance in medicine for both animals and humans, and contributed to an extended life expectancy of people in excess of twenty years.

In addition to pointing to a lengthy list of medical and surgical benefits derived from the use of animals in research, it has been argued that animal research should continue in order to search for solutions to yet unsolved medical problems including, for example, cancer, genetic disorders, neurological and cardiovascular conditions, and immunodeficiency syndromes. There is also a need to subject cosmetics and beauty products to animal testing, before they can be safely sold for use by humans.

The claim is that it is simply not possible to eliminate animal research completely and still produce new or improved treatments for disease, which the general public has identified as a priority. Issues of drug safety are also referred to by those advocating continued use of animals in research. It is claimed that banning animal experimentation would severely restrict development of new drugs, or require researchers to use human beings for safety tests. It has been pointed out that animal experiments cannot guarantee that drugs are safe and effective in human beings, but the experiments assist in deciding whether a particular drug is sufficiently developed to be tested on people. The experiments utilising animals theoretically identify whether certain drugs are either ineffective or too dangerous to use on human test subjects. Effectively, if the drug meets test criteria in animals, then it may be tested on a small group of people prior to being rolled out for larger clinical trials.

In the view of those who support the use of continued animal research, the benefits of animal research can be demonstrated by considering the repercussions of discontinuing the practice. It is claimed that millions of people and a similar number of animals would suffer or die unnecessarily if animal research work were to cease.

On a cost–benefit analysis, proponents argue that there is a case for continuing animal experiments if the benefits to humanity mean that it is morally acceptable – even 'necessary' and/or 'reasonable' – to harm a comparatively few animals. In contrast, the anti-vivisection lobby alleges that the number of animals involved is so high that the benefits derived by human beings do not provide moral justification to continue animal research.

BIOPREJUDICE

Selected species have been singled out as the beneficiaries of specific protection. 'Bioprejudice' is a word inferring that certain species of animals have benefited from greater protections as a result of their greater human appeal. Large, iconic and endangered animals such as pandas, elephants and whales are notable examples where it is accepted that the public are much more likely to associate positively with, than alternative species such as insects, or other 'creepy-crawly' species.

The great apes (identified as the orang-utan, gorilla, chimpanzee and bonobo) are some of the more notable species to benefit from targeted conservation efforts and legal protections and there is little surprise at identifying why the great apes engender particular feelings of sympathy and empathy among humans.

Reference to specific considerations for decision makers contemplating the use of great apes in research has been set out in certain jurisdictions. For example, New Zealand legislation specifically states that any research, testing, or teaching conducted on non-human hominids must be 'in the best interests of the non-human hominid', or 'in the interests of the species to which the non-human hominid belongs and that the benefits to be derived from the use of the non-human hominid in the research, testing, or teaching are not outweighed by the likely harm to the non-human hominid'.[2]

---

2 Sections 80(1)(c) and 85(5)(a) Animal Welfare Act 1999 (New Zealand).

238   *Assessing use of animals in research*

The legislation highlights an important point to be considered by those critically assessing issues of animal welfare and law. In addition to considering the paper benefits of any legislation and/or policy, it is equally important to be alive to what practical benefits are actually delivered and/or derived.

Furthermore, the often-overlooked occurrence of bioprejudice resulting in certain species being singled out for special attention by the public and the law, further demonstrates that questions regarding acceptability of the use of animals in research is likely to be a multifactorial consideration. The line between acceptable and unacceptable varies considerably. A multitude of factors come into play: personal, societal and ultimately political – and, consequently, legal – attitudes regarding animals and the balance of public risks and benefits. For example, society and the law have obviously indicated that despite the variance in opinion regarding the ongoing use of animals in research, it continues to be a legally acceptable practice. None the less, legal criteria regarding research utilising great apes has distinctions from those applying to the use of other animals in research (e.g., mice, rabbits, chickens). Furthermore, individuals who support the use of 'government-supervised' research may accept that animals such as cats and dogs will be used for research purposes – provided it is not *their* cat or dog.

The responsibility for setting standards of research, and facilitating compliance and enforcement with the standards, largely falls to the government. The government, via the law, has the responsibility for balancing the varied opinions that exist in the public while at the same time promoting the interests of the public. In fulfilling this naturally tenuous responsibility, the government has the task of drawing the line that enables scientific research to continue in a lawful and ethical manner, while at the same time addressing accusations that scientists operate behind a perceived veil of secrecy.

Viewing research through the eyes of the activist, in comparison to the scientist

Research through the eyes of the scientist

Transparency and accountability are laudable aspirational ideas, which none the less face significant barriers when research scientists are forced to contend with personal and unlawful attacks on their person, families and personal property. The nature and degree of extremist actions against research scientists have resulted in certain governments (i.e., the US and the UK) to develop criminal law which categorised animal extremist actions alongside acts of terrorism (in the US) and serious organised crime (in the UK).

Research through the lens of the activist

Some people have alleged that there is a 'veil of secrecy' pertaining to the use of animals in research. They claim that the closed doors of science laboratories are further complicated by perceived inadequacies of the law requiring accountability and openness from those conducting animal experiments. It has been claimed that research continues in the absence of a genuinely independent review of compliance with the principles of the 3Rs (reduction, refinement, replacement) and relevant research guidelines, and that ethics committees can be selectively made up of sympathetic researchers.

Costs and benefits for animals as a research stakeholder group

While animals are frequently portrayed as the victims of animal research, a balanced perspective also recognises that animals as a stakeholder group potentially benefit from the practice of animal research. Human well-being is closely related to animal health, and the animal health industry is an enormous national and international business. A significant number of medicines – including vaccines, anthelmintics, surgical techniques and additional treatments, devices and procedures – have been developed specifically with animals in mind.

The similarity between certain animals and humans means that animals have frequently been used as a model for testing developing treatments and surgical techniques to be used in humans. This process of development means that there is frequently substantial research data and information available in respect of particular animal species well in advance of treatments and/or other medical advances being available to people. Antibiotics, insulin for diabetes, whooping cough vaccines, heart–lung surgery, kidney transplants, polio vaccines, drugs to treat asthma and surgical anaesthetics are all medications and procedures that benefit human beings which have been previously tested and developed utilising animals, and can now also be used in veterinary practice for the benefit of the animals.

Additionally, there are a significant number of features within the animal kingdom that have potential benefits to people. For example, Australia's 'gastric brooding frog' incubates its young inside its stomach, and the young literally emerge from the mother's mouth after they have developed beyond the tadpole stage. Scientists have been intrigued by the frog's ability to 'turn off' the digestive processors of the stomach during the incubation period. This may have significant relevance to people who, for example, suffer from gastric ulcers. The benefits for the animal in this instance are that efforts are made to maintain the existence of the species itself.

An often-overlooked benefit of animal research then, is the greater understanding that science gains of animals and nature. That understanding has resulted in an informed effort to conserve habitats and species. While humankind remains as one of the key influences on the planet, the greater understanding of animals, habitats and human impacts which results from animal research provides the potential to consider how to minimise further negative human effects.

Society's legal rulebook: what makes animal research 'lawful'?

There may come a day when research involving animals is deemed unnecessary – however, at present, the fact remains that animals continue to be used in the breadth

240 *Assessing use of animals in research*

and complexity of scientific research products. The risks, advantages and diverse public opinion regarding the continued use of animals for research purposes necessitates a system of governance and practical control/enforcement regarding the use of animals in research projects. The need for such governance raises questions about what constitutes an *ideal* system of governance and enforcement, which benefits and protects all stakeholders and their interests, including the legal interest of animals.

Animals are one of the stakeholders – not the only stakeholder

In circumstances where animal protection/legislation is enacted, then it is usual to identify that the law sets out considerable regulation consistent with its purpose of protecting animals from unnecessary and unreasonable pain or distress of animals, including those that are used in research. Legislation that governs the use of animals in research usually includes an objective to balance the aims of research considered to be essential and necessary against the possible harm to the animals.

Applying the four key words defining animal welfare to the subject of animal research

The law's demonstrated definition of animal protection/welfare centres on the four key words – 'pain', 'distress', 'unnecessary' and 'unreasonable' – and can be summarised as the prevention of an animal's unnecessary and/or unreasonable pain or distress of an animal. This is the sole and continued interest of the animal and its experience that is protected by law.

This is the same principle applied to the use of animals in research. Firstly, the law draws some clear lines between animals and human beings. As demonstrated by the law's definition of an 'animal', it recognises a distinct difference between humans and all other species. Furthermore, in jurisdictions where the principles of anti-cruelty law are recognised, there is recognition that any pain or distress caused to an animal in the process of conducting research should be demonstrably necessary and/or reasonable.

The fact is, not all research necessarily implies that the animal has experienced pain and/or distress. In the event that it is determined that the animal has actually experienced pain or distress, then the law determines whether the pain or distress experienced was either unnecessary or unreasonable.

'Unreasonable' can be considered as making a determination regarding the degree of pain or distress experienced by the animal. 'Unnecessary' includes determinations as to the purpose and alternative available options of the act/omission which has allegedly caused the animal pain and/or distress. This two-part legal test is broadly the same in research as it is in regards to other uses of animals. Even if there is agreement that pain or distress is experienced by the animal, then potentially contrasting and conflicting views exist as to whether or not the animal's pain and/or distress is 'necessary'.

Assessing use of animals in research   241

The law largely has a responsibility to reflect societal attitudes and requirements in determining how the animal's species, environment and circumstances (e.g., its situation/role), and its legally protected interest is appropriately balanced and prioritised in context of all the facts, law and circumstances.

The reality is that if 'research' is given its broadest definition, spanning documented and planned procedures (e.g., laboratory procedures involving drug tests) through to approaches that might be described as 'let's try it and see what happens' (e.g., crossing different breeds for the purposes of production or visual aesthetics), then almost every role of animals in human society involves some kind of animal research.

Of course, in the majority of cases, it's the more formalised research, testing and teaching procedures that come under the scrutiny of legislative regulators, who have the responsibility of ensuring there is compliance with established standards, protocols and procedures.

The 4Rs

BUT FIRST: THE 3RS

There is wide acceptance that the decision-making mechanism regarding legislative determinations of what is either necessary or reasonable in terms of an animal's pain and/or distress, should take into account wider ethical principles including, for example, the tenets of the 3Rs (reduction, refinement, replacement) and overall 'responsibility' for legal and ethical research.

Reduction, as the term indicates, advocates reducing the number of animals used in experiments. This may be achieved, for example, by improving experimental techniques and data analysis techniques, and sharing information with other researchers.

Refinement demands that the experiment, in particular the way in which the animals are handled, should be conducted in such a way as to reduce their suffering and ensure the most comfortable and humane conditions possible for the animals during the course of the experiment. This might be achieved, for example, by utilising less invasive techniques, providing better medical care, and by providing adequate living conditions for the animals during the course of the experiment.

Replacement advocates replacing experiments on animals with alternative techniques wherever possible. This includes, for example, experimenting on cell cultures instead of animals, utilising computer models wherever possible, conducting research and studies on human volunteers, and making efficient use of epidemiological studies.

THE 4TH R: RESPONSIBILITY

Despite common reference to the three Rs, there is a relevant fourth issue that warrants adding an additional R to the tradition 3R formula. The fourth R broadly refers

242 *Assessing use of animals in research*

to the concept advocating that all research should include a level of 'responsibility'. The word 'responsibility' underpins all of animal law, in that the law dictates that people are responsible for treating animals in a way that complies with legal standards. In reference to the use of animals in research, the responsibility principle promotes the concept that research not only complies with the law's utilitarian minimal standards in respect of 'reducing, refining and replacing', but reaches further by responsibly applying the highest standards of professionalism to the animals each research programme utilises and is responsible for.

What makes animal research legally acceptable?

The practice of animal research largely hinges on what the law considers 'necessary'

Broadly speaking, the dominant ethical view is that the use of animals in research is acceptable in order to achieve scientific, public safety and medical goals, provided that animal suffering is minimised, and that the human benefits gained could not be obtained by utilising alternative methods.

Considerations of what is necessary often incorporate an in-depth decision-making process in jurisdictions where legal criteria are set out. Traditionally, the decision-making process involves a cost–benefit analysis that goes beyond simply considering weighing up the financial outlay necessary for establishing the research project, to incorporate considerations which assess the cost to the animal against the proposed purpose of the project.

The degree and nature of the protection accorded to an animal depends very much on the situation and circumstances. Regulatory relativism hinges heavily on the degree of human responsibility regarding the animal's experience of unnecessary and/or unreasonable pain and/or distress. It would be a misconception to conclude, however, that all research – or prohibitions of it – are consistently based on common sense, rational needs and/or a formulaic approach to decision making. There are a number of well-established guidelines – but research, like any other endeavour, can be subject to the whims and realities of everything from resource restrictions through to political point scoring. Familiarity with the theory, however, is a must for competent students of animal welfare law.

The ideal model of animal research governance looks like this . . .

In terms of the principles of animal welfare law, the question is raised as to how best to regulate and control animal experimentation. Given that a total ban on animal experimentation appears to be an unrealistic expectation at present, then essential aspects of regulating and controlling animal research would include five factors:[3]

---

3 Ibid., p. 167.

Assessing use of animals in research   243

- a legislative framework which outlines functions and procedures in respect of the animals involved;
- an effective range of sanctions which includes formal prosecution of offenders and removal of licences/funding;
- a national review and data collection body which has the ability to recommend or directly implement changes;
- the establishment of ethics committees representing a wide range of interests which have the power to prevent an experiment from going ahead; and
- representation and influence from different interest groups to facilitate public confidence.

Elements of these five factors can be identified in regulatory mechanisms from various countries. Leading animal welfare legislation either incorporates or refers to state legislation which is monitored by external agencies and/or government enforcement. There are critics and supporters of all systems that have been established. Ethics committees which are made up of a variety of interest groups continues to be a widely supported initiative, though attention to the number, constitution and education of its constituents has been highlighted as warranting attention to avoid 'loading' the committee in a way which results in committee bias (e.g., in favour of research projects) and simply window-dressing transparency and compliance. Ensuring that there is a wide representation and influence of various stakeholders is not always an easy task, however. Some groups have indicated an unwillingness to have any involvement with ethics committees on the grounds that participation may imply a degree of acceptance of animal experimentation. Additionally, while having a 'lay person' (i.e., member of the public) is an increasingly common feature of many committees, careful consideration would obviously need to be given to the education, potential conflicts of interest and personal opinions of the layperson to ensure that the chosen person provides a balanced and informed perspective rather than a predetermined bias.

The UK is frequently referenced as the legal jurisdiction exhibiting one of the most highly regulated systems of animal research. It has a dedicated piece of legislation (Animals (Scientific Procedures) Act 1986 – ASPA), governing the use of animals in experiments and testing. Under ASPA, three licences are required prior to authorisation for testing to be conducted on animals. The three-tiered system involves a personal licence for each person carrying out a procedure on animals, a project licence for the programme of work, and an establishment licence for the laboratory or site where the work/research is to be carried out.

In addition to the required personal, institutional and project licences, the UK is the only country to require an explicit cost–benefit assessment of every application to conduct animal research. The legislation is further supported by a system which incorporates a local Ethical Review Process and an established inspectorate. All research establishments are subject to frequent (usually unannounced) inspections, and are reportedly visited an average of approximately four times per

244 *Assessing use of animals in research*

year.[4] UK inspectors deal exclusively with persons, places and projects involved with animal research, and have a reputation for their considerable experience in laboratory animal science. In contrast, inspectors in the US and France are frequently general practitioners in veterinary medicine who have wider responsibilities for animals in zoos, circuses and commercial farms, and may have little hands-on experience with laboratory animal science.[5]

New Zealand does not have a stand-alone piece of legislation dealing with animal research, but incorporates legal standards pertaining to the use of animals in research in its Animal Welfare Act. It relies heavily on ethical committees and, in contrast to its UK counterparts, does not have a stand-alone inspectorate dealing exclusively with animal research facilities.

Other jurisdictions engage a variety of agencies, inspectorates and ethical committees as a package of enforcement to support relevant animal research legislation. The US, for example, references primarily animal welfare legislation which is enforced by the Animal and Plant Health Inspection Services (APHIS) of the United States Department of Agriculture (USDA). However, a 2002 amendment meant that rats, mice and birds fell outside the legislative protection. In addition to the USDA, other agencies (government and non-government) are involved in enforcement and accreditation assessments of research facilities. The comparatively complex and mixed system of regulation and accreditation has resulted in questions regarding the reliability that the public can put on reported procedures, numbers (e.g., of animals used) and assurances provided by research institutions.

From a legal perspective, prosecutions in respect of research are notably few and far between. There may be several reasons for this, one of which is recognition that prosecution is arguably a significantly slower and less effective sanction than the alternative, which is to withdraw the relevant licence or certificate allowing the institution/premises to continue conducting research. The withdrawal of the relevant licence naturally has a much more immediate impact on those who fail to comply with required standards. Consequently, the potential forward role of the licence would be expected to constitute a significant motivation for facilities and the scientists involved to ensure consistent compliance with research requirements.

The relatively few number of prosecutions associated with research institutions might also indicate that there is a high level of compliance by the scientific fraternity, or alternatively, it might raise questions about the effectiveness of the inspectorate. In jurisdictions with established law governing animal research and an adequately resourced inspectorate, then, in terms of issues pertaining to animal welfare, the question is how many of the breaches actually identified by the inspectorate are primarily technical (e.g., a lapse of the licence or certificate) in comparison to those which directly result in unnecessary suffering of an animal.

---

4 UK Parliament. 2002. 'Select Committee on Animals in Scientific Procedures Report': www. publications.parliament.uk/pa/ld200102/ldselect/ldanimal/150/15004.htm.

5 Ibid.

Assessing use of animals in research   245

Legal assessment focuses on the relevant credible facts, applicable law, and 'all' the circumstances, and ultimately considers whether an act or omission (in this case, an act or omission involving an animal in research) causes an animal unnecessary and/or unreasonable pain and/or distress to the point that it is 'unlawful'. Case Study 8 provides some examples of where animal researchers have been taken to court, resulting in prosecutions.

Case Study 8: If your income stream depends on compliance, why would you stray outside your research licence?

The use of animals in research continues to be a hotly debated topic, exhibiting starkly contrasting perspectives, so it is unsurprising that in many jurisdictions those debates are taken to Court. The use of primates in research, the appropriateness and purposes of research (e.g., for cosmetic purposes), the alleged alternatives to using animals as research subjects, and questions about the application of research results from animals to humans – each represent examples of 'big picture' debates involving the use of animals for research and teaching. In addition to those ongoing debates, there are also strict enforcement criteria that none the less apply to researchers undertaking projects that do not ordinarily receive wider media coverage.

The 3Rs, for example, underpin a routinely very strict system of assessment addressing the use of animals in research. This strictness of application and supervision in respect of the people, place and procedures is naturally necessary in view of the fact that some of the procedures permitted inside the laboratory would potentially constitute criminal offending outside the laboratory. It follows that variation from the strict guidelines attracts potentially serious consequences for the researcher and for the authorised institution. Opinions vary as to how accountable researchers actually are, but that background puts the offending of one researcher in context, when it was identified by an inspector in Victoria (Australia) that the researcher had not complied with the terms of the issued research licence.

After a Scientific Procedures Premises Licence was issued, the Monash Medical Centre Animals Ethics Committee subsequently approved an application by the researcher, Elizabeth Williams, to use animals, namely mice, for scientific purposes in research and teaching.

Williams's project was designed to examine how advanced prostate cancer develops. There was a specifically identified experimental endpoint defined by the size of the tumour or the duration of the experiment (whichever occurred earlier). There was also a defined humane endpoint which

(continued)

246 *Assessing use of animals in research*

> *(continued)*
>
> stipulated that if, during the course of the experiment, an animal demonstrated evidence of ill health, then the mouse would be humanely euthanased.
>
> As a condition of application approval, the procedures expressly specified in the application become conditions of the project which are to be strictly complied with, and no variation or departure from those conditions is permitted without the express written authority of the appointed Animals Ethics Committee. As part of the conditions of this project, and only when either the experimental or humane endpoints were reached, tumours and mouse organs could be surgically removed and collected for histological and molecular analysis. The surgical removal of tumours and organs, however, could only occur after the animal had been euthanased. To do otherwise would be a breach of the conditions of the project and in turn a breach of the scientific procedures premises licence. As Williams was the chief investigator of the project, she had personal responsibility for all matters relating to the welfare of animals used for scientific purposes.
>
> It was identified that Williams surgically removed tumours from 30 individual mice under anaesthesia rather than post-euthanasia. Consequently, the surgery was in direct breach of the project conditions and of the scientific procedures premises licence. Following the identification of non-compliance, the relevant Animals Ethics Committee withdrew all approved applications under Williams's name and all remaining animals were transferred to another scientific procedures premises. Williams was formally interviewed and criminal charges were subsequently laid for failing to comply with research requirements.
>
> Williams pleaded guilty and was sentenced, without conviction, to an adjourned undertaking for twelve months, with a special condition that she pay a contribution of $800 to the Court Fund.
>
> In sentencing, the Court is obliged to take the potential impact on the defendant into consideration, and while personal opinions may vary regarding the level of penalty, the case is significant since, among other lessons, it demonstrates the willingness of the regulatory body to prosecute breaches of research licences, and illustrates the potential significant consequences for the researcher for non-compliance.
>
> (*Department of Environment and Primary Industries v Elizabeth Williams*, Moorabbin Magistrates' Court Melbourne (Australia), 14 January 2014)

Keep the facts in context

The commonly accepted practice of reporting alleged numbers and species of animals used in research provides a useful illustration of the importance of being fully informed as part of critically assessing projects and practices associated with animal research.

Assessing use of animals in research   247

While global figures for animal testing are difficult to ascertain, it has been estimated that 50–100 million animals are utilised in animal research around the world on an annual basis.[6] Critical assessment of any report requires an understanding of which animals have been included – and excluded – in the quoted numbers.

For example, dependent upon the jurisdictional legislation, traditional laboratory animals such as rats and mice, which form a high percentage of animals used widely in laboratory research, may or may not be included in the legal definition of an 'animal', and therefore may or may not be included in the national figures indicating the number of animals used in research. The same consideration applies to other species such as frogs, fish, rabbits, other rodents and even poultry.

Similarly, figures may or may not include animals bred for research then killed as surplus to requirements, or animals used for breeding purposes. Almost certainly, the figures will not include invertebrate animals such as shrimp or fruit flies.

Is the law keeping up with research developments?

The technologies associated with animal research continue to evolve, which raises questions about what happens when technology moves faster than the law's apparent ability to keep up. There are certainly a significant number of stakeholders and stakeholder interests involved in these 'future developments'. In addition to the animals, the financial interests of investors, the livelihoods of researchers, and the well-being of each person benefiting, to one degree or another, are at stake. Each of these interests are considerations that must be prioritised and balanced by lawmakers.

The subject of animal research demonstrates the third element of animal law: that the interests of humans and animals are invariably connected. Critical assessment takes a broader perspective which includes, but is not restricted to, questions of lawfulness.

When critically assessing the subject of animal research, it is important to remember that the 'critical' component of critical assessment relates to a depth and breadth of thinking that goes well beyond simply criticising. With this in mind it is helpful to review the 'critical thinking check list' of Chapter 3, which demonstrates key concepts that are common to both legal and wider critical assessment of the use of animals in research. Key words/phrases include, for example, balance and prioritisation (e.g., of contrasting interests, perspectives and representation of all stakeholders), relevance, credibility and veracity (e.g., of facts in terms of their method of collection and presentation), measurability, practicality and implications/consequences.

It's one thing to argue that the use of animals in research is justified for purposes of medical advancement, but what about using animals for purposes which have been classed as human vanities (e.g., cosmetics, fashion industry furs), or pure human pleasures (e.g., party drugs). A detailed discussion of the ethics of such practices is beyond the scope of this chapter, but suffice to say that public opinion has led to the development and marketing of a range of cosmetic products labelled as 'not tested on animals'.

---

6 Nuffield Council on Bioethics. n.d. 'What Animals are used in Research?': http://nuffieldbioethics. org/report/animal-research-2/animals-research/.

248 *Assessing use of animals in research*

Are you critically assessing the use of animals in research?

Conflicting opinions exist regarding the continued use of animals in research. Try to critically assess statements and/or articles and/or publications from the websites and media. For example:

- Certain references have been made alleging that research scientists operate behind a 'veil of secrecy' – critically assess this, and other, allegations/claims/perspectives.
- Critically assess the following statement: 'Whether diseases affect us directly or someone we love, we want to know that researchers across the world are working towards a cure. Unfortunately, there are people who want to stop medical progress and are using a variety of tactics to publicise their message from mild to extreme and life-threatening. But research is unlikely to be stopped, and humanity will continue to look for ways to improve the quality of our lives. I, like every reasonable person, am all for the ethical treatment of animals, but also recognise that in order to treat human suffering and advance medical science, animal testing is a necessity.'[7]
- Critically assess the following statement: 'Although modern alternative test methods exist, huge multiproduct manufacturers, including Unilever, Clorox, Church & Dwight, Johnson & Johnson and others, continue to poison and harm animals in tests that aren't even required by law. Rats, mice, guinea pigs, rabbits and other animals are forced to swallow or inhale massive quantities of a test substance or endure the pain of having caustic chemicals applied to their sensitive eyes and skin – even though the results of animal tests are often unreliable or not applicable to humans. Even if a product has blinded an animal, it can still be marketed to you.'[8]

7 Kristina Cook. 2006 (4 April). 'Stand up for Science: Why Animal Research is Important AND Needed': www.pro-test.org.uk/2006/04/why-animal-research-is-important-and.html.
8 PETA. n.d. 'Animal Testing 101': www.peta.org/issues/animals-used-for-experimentation/animal-testing-101.aspx.

8 Critically assessing the use of animals in agriculture

Before reading this chapter, consider these issues:

- The biggest single use of animals is for food. What are the political, economic and practical considerations for decision makers in delivering safe and sustainable food?
- What defines agriculture? What principles do agriculture and aquaculture have in common, and what is different in terms of the animal's welfare and legal protections?
- What meaning do you personally attribute to the term 'factory farming'? How does your definition fit with the principles of animal welfare law? Explain any apparent lawful 'gaps' in terms of current legal justification.
- Is the legal definition of an animal wide enough to protect the species that are farmed?
- List ten issues other than the welfare of the animal, that are associated with 'agriculture'. For example, you might include land care, antibiotic resistance, international trade criteria, biodiversity and genetic modification. Food safety, food supply, sustainability concepts and disease control including zoonoses might also come to mind. Economic cost of meat production, environmental impacts (e.g., water and air pollution, deforestation and global warming) and the growing human population are also relevant. What other issues can you identify that the law is – or should – be monitoring and controlling?

Thinking practically about the objectives of agriculture

Defining 'agriculture'

In the broadest sense, agriculture is defined as the science, art, or occupation concerned with cultivating land, raising crops, and feeding, breeding and raising livestock. Essentially it's about producing food for human consumption (as well as fibres, such as wool or fur) and therefore is not restricted to simply the interests of the animals.

In the context of animal welfare and law, the term 'agriculture' therefore means the raising of animals for food and fibre. It's a simple definition that obviously

250 *Assessing use of animals in agriculture*

has significantly wider implications for all animals and people involved. Those implications vary from one legal jurisdiction to another. For example, the legal definition of an animal may vary enormously. One of the criticisms by animal welfare groups in the United States is that animals used in agriculture are specifically excluded from legal protections that would apply to the same animal used in a non-agricultural context. Balancing the voice of animal welfare groups are powerful lobby groups with vested interests in farming, which seek to maintain the exclusion of animals from potentially problematic animal protection laws.

Animal welfare law involves continual assessment of the well-being of the animal which must take into account not just the condition of the animal but also the reasons for the animal's condition. This requires careful and often expert assessment of an enormous range of factors that are external as well as internal to the animal including, for example, the land (e.g., shelter, nutrition), the human care-giver (e.g., abilities, resources), and the internal health of the animal (e.g., parasitism, metabolic conditions).

Aquaculture is a specific type of farming in that it involves the farming (e.g., breeding, rearing and harvesting) of aquatic organisms such as finfish, shellfish and even plants in all types of water environments including ponds, rivers, lakes and oceans. Aquaculture is increasingly recognised as an effective way to meet the dietary demands of a growing human population. As a result, aquaculture is one of the fastest growing forms of food production in the world. Some people view aquaculture as separate to more traditional, land-based farming agriculture, while other people view it simply as a subset of agriculture distinguished only by the fact that it is water based rather than land based. It is noteworthy that aquaculture demonstrates the same enormous economic, environmental and societal interests as does land animals and the same principle of interdependency between people, fish and the environment – as well as the consequences of getting it wrong. For example, harbour pollution in larger cities impacts the environment of fish and potentially the entire local food chain, given that there are frequently detrimental impacts on the sea plant life which is a source of food for the fish. Welfare issues such as overcrowding and disease control in intensive aquaculture are becoming increasingly apparent.

Historically, farming was self-rewarding or self-punishing . . .

Animals have always had a place in the development of humankind. Theories vary as to how and why this actually occurred but it is widely accepted that as the practical lives of early humans became less nomadic and more organised and settled into a routine that was less mobile and involved more possessions, then it simply became easier to produce food rather than gather it. Animals were integral to the food production, either as work animals assisting in producing the food (e.g., horses and cattle for transportation and working farming machinery such as ploughs, and operation of irrigation systems), or kept and grown for their use as food (e.g., meat, milk) and products (e.g., wool) that they provided.

Consequently, the livelihoods of families and villages became highly dependent upon their animals. It is little wonder that the practical value of animals meant that they were identified as a key feature of people's lives as a means of food production, a sign of wealth, and sacrifice objects in religious ceremonies which involved the death of an animal. The well-being of the animal was very closely associated with the well-being of the people who depended on it. This trait can still be recognised today, particularly in certain poorer communities such as nomadic pastoralists, which depend highly on their animals. Some criticism has been made of places that do not have established animal protection law, assuming that the husbandry systems are inferior. Such views commonly demonstrate a lack of understanding of practical realities pertaining to the resources available to poorer communities. Despite the absence of documented law and welfare codes dealing with care of an animal (e.g., shelter, disease control) and potentially differing attitudes regarding sentience, it is often clear that communities do the best they can with what resources are available to them. The law of nature prevails and dictates that in circumstances where the community so heavily relies on its animals, the people do well only if the animals do well. Inadequate and improper care of an animal, as it was in early agricultural systems, was self-punishing in that an ailing animal did not produce or perform well. The death of an animal naturally meant the complete loss of investment in the animal, its production and its work performance.

Allowing for differences due to contrasting cultural/societal/political, economic and environmental drivers, the fact is that the real welfare problem for animals in terms of agriculture have occurred relatively recently in human history.

What is meant by 'factory farming'?

This is a simple term that evokes different images for different people. For some, it embodies the epitome of cost-efficient production of animal protein and products. For others, it illustrates a reprehensible example of animal suffering, and associated criticism that factory farming is non-sustainable and unethical. Factory farming is synonymous with another term used to describe intensive production of animal protein, namely a 'Concentrated Animal Feeding Operation' (CAFO). The criteria identifying a CAFO may vary but essentially a CAFO involves 'a production process that concentrates large numbers of animals in relatively small and confined places, and substitutes structures and equipment (for feeding, temperature controls, and manure management) for land and labor.'[1]

Mirroring other animal welfare-related issues and uses, factory farming, or CAFO, demonstrates the diverse opinions and competing interests involving environmental concerns (e.g., animal waste/manure production affecting land, water

---

1 J.M. MacDonald and W.D. McBride. 2009. 'The Transformation of U.S. Livestock Agriculture: Scale, Efficiency, and Risks', Economics Information Bulletin No. 43, US Department of Agriculture: www.ers.usda.gov/publications/eib-economic-information-bulletin/eib43.aspx.

252 *Assessing use of animals in agriculture*

and air quality), economic concerns (e.g., market demands, costs/efficiencies of production), and sociological concerns (e.g., human health risks, animal health and welfare issues). The reality is that livestock production (e.g., poultry, cattle, pigs) by means of intensive animal production operations is reportedly increasing, and likely to increase even further given the predicted 70 per cent increase in demand for animal protein by the year 2050.

Governors, via the law, have the usual challenges in balancing and prioritising competing interests. Predictably, opinion is divided not just on the need for intensive production systems, but also on how well the governors are doing.

From an animal welfare legal perspective, the question is whether or not these operations are 'lawful'. The fact that they exist should, in the first instance, demonstrate that such operations are currently legally permitted. Indeed, where there have been proposals to establish super (dairy) farms, alternatively known as 'mega-dairies', the successful counters to their establishment have primarily been based on environmental impacts, rather than evidence establishing that the animals' welfare would be legally substandard.

To understand this outcome from an animal welfare legal perspective, it is important to remember that the standards of animal welfare law refer to what is unnecessary, or unreasonable, pain and distress – qualified by the species, environment and circumstances of the animal. Thinking about factory farming objectively through the legal lens therefore requires consideration of the *definition* of factory farming, and specifically the species and systems being considered. This then enables assessment of how the specific system of factory farming being considered complies, or not, with legal obligations associated with applicable animal welfare law. The law functions by firstly establishing benchmark criteria regarding standards of human responsibility regarding the care and treatment of animals (i.e., prevent unnecessary and unreasonable pain and/or distress of animals), then qualifies that responsibility in terms of the circumstances of the animal, particularly its use and associated dependency on its human care-giver.

Defining factory farming

The term 'factory farming' involves raising livestock in intensive conditions involving cost-efficient use of space with high stocking density, and a focus on efficiencies of feed-conversion rate, with the broad objective of achieving the highest output at the lowest cost, and incorporating contemporary systems involving science, technology and monitoring systems controlling the animal's environment (e.g., light, temperature), inputs (e.g., food science, pesticides) and the animal itself (e.g., biotechnology).

Balancing morals, perceptions and progress with lawfulness

For the law, mirroring progress in science and communication systems which now inform the paying public and political voters, the catchphrase in respect of animals and animal products is the concept for food production that is 'humane and sustainable'. Humane refers to the animal's experience and concepts of welfare. Humane is distinct from sustainable which refers to retaining the presence and biological integrity of the animal, the environment and other resources for future human use.

Despite broad agreement that animals warrant protection from unnecessary and unreasonable pain and distress, there is no universal agreement about what is 'necessary' in terms of agricultural practices, or the degree to which various animals fall under the ambit of legal protections. Nor are there any guidelines to how legal obligations and corresponding responsibility should be effectively implemented and efficiently enforced, given the variety of species, drivers and circumstances involving animals in agriculture.

Like it or not, intensive farming systems are widespread globally and provide almost 40 per cent of the world's meat production. As intensive farming methods have been adopted, there has been concurrent increased automation, an increase in the development of larger farms and corporate ownership structures, and a continued exponential growth of the global population of people who are the end users of agricultural products.

Advocates of factory farming claim that it provides a means of meeting existing and future demands for meat by the expanding global population, which concurrently has benefits for the animal due to improvements in animal housing, nutrition and disease control. Critiques of factory farming claim it results in unacceptable levels of cruelty (i.e., pain and distress to the animals farmed in intensive systems) and commonly point to the unsustainability of farming practice by reference to concepts such as environmental impacts, resource efficiency and the comparative (larger) cost of protein production by meat production and consumption over alternatives such as grains.

The fact is, on a global basis the majority of people like to eat meat. So despite the logic of production costs or alleged health benefits, most people will eat meat when they can. This is evident in poorer communities that largely exist on rice and other grain substitutes, who will none the less eat meat as one of the first lifestyle changes that occurs when their socio-economic status changes. Predictions to 2050 and beyond reinforce this human behaviour, when it is assumed that the global population of an estimated 9 billion people will require an additional 50 per cent of meat in their diet,[2] largely as a result of the changing socio-economic status and growth of populations in existing Third World and developing economies. The law then has a responsibility to balance and prioritise the interests of all stakeholders, where animals and humans are each one, but not the only, stakeholder.

Animal-based agriculture has the task and primary responsibility for meeting the predicted increase for dietary meat. The fact that factory farming is practised should give a clear indication that in the first instance, the practice is lawful and only becomes unlawful where practised in a way that fails to comply with existing law.

---

2 In comparison to 2013 figures and global population.

254 *Assessing use of animals in agriculture*

Do animals feel pain and distress in intensive farming systems? The resounding answer must be yes, there are some practices that undoubtedly cause an animal pain and distress. But it must be clear that the objective is not to alleviate all pain and distress, but to alleviate unnecessary and/or unreasonable (i.e., unjustifiable) pain and/or distress. So it's a two-part test. The law that governs almost all human societal interactions, which includes humans' responsibilities regarding animals, first questions whether or not a practice causes an animal pain or distress. If so, then is the practice necessary and/or reasonable in consideration of all the wider responsibilities, risks and diverse interests?

For some, the changes in law and animal husbandry are frustratingly slow. None the less, the procedural aspects of a democratic society, the economic realities for the people and livelihoods involved, and the law's obligation to refer to proven science rather than simply the opinion of potentially vocal minorities (i.e., risking the 'tyranny of the minority'), all take time. But there is discernible change.

Delivering sufficient, safe and humanely produced food

Putting animal welfare law in the 'paddock-to-plate' process

First of all, animal welfare law applies to live animals. Contemporary animal welfare law makes it clear that it is not unlawful to kill an animal provided that the method of killing does not cause the animal unreasonable or unnecessary pain or distress. Furthermore, while dead animals may provide an indicator of animal welfare offending (e.g., starvation of livestock), the simple fact is that you cannot cause pain and distress to a dead animal. So in terms of animal welfare law and most farmed animals, it applies from the moment the animal is born to when it is lawfully and humanely killed.

The law applies standards based on minimums, and does not legally compel producers to implement standards of best practice. Animal welfare is therefore just a part of the farm-to-fork process of meat production, and law related to food safety.

General Objectives of Food Safety Law

Consumers not only want an adequate food supply – they also want assurances of food safety. This requirement for safe and sufficient food naturally involves multiple stakeholders along the food supply chain. To maintain consumer confidence, it is obviously important to establish mechanisms that maintain the integrity of the food production process and compliance from all participants along all steps of the food supply chain. Effective and enforced law, engagement of stakeholders, and overall transparency are naturally essential to assuring the consumer that they will have sufficient safe food that responsibly takes account of wider environmental, societal and economic considerations, including the health and welfare of animals.

Managing the risk

Primary and secondary food safety legislation aims to ensure that food for sale is safe and suitable for human consumption, and prevents misleading conduct in relation to the sale of food. The existence of law as part of an overall mechanism including compliance and enforcement resourcing, established policy, stakeholder involvement, and communication programmes doesn't mean of course, that there is 'no risk' to the public from potential food associated health hazards. However, the procedures try to provide a level of monitored and managed acceptable levels of risk, using science, technology and communication.

There are more than simply national interests at stake. International trade and agreements also set standards for participating countries to demonstrate compliance. While few aspects of food safety can guarantee complete safety, the legal provisions are put in place to prevent, manage and/or mitigate risks posed by the food business to the community. As a general principle, the more risk that exists, then the more food safety regulation is applied. Licensing of premises, the product, labelling and traceability of food – often right back to the farm of origin – are initiatives widely put in place in jurisdictions with existing law and reliable enforcement systems.

Like other governance decisions, assessments consider the risks in the context of a range of wider information including, for example, the practical aspects of controlling a risk, the steps along the food chain where incursions will yield the most cost-effective outcomes, and wider results including socio-economic effects and the environmental impact.

Defining sustainable food production

The ordinary meaning of sustainable means something that is able to be maintained, and to conserve (e.g., natural resources) as well as meet future demands and objectives. In terms of sustainable resources, for example, there is a need to ensure that people use resources in a way that does not exceed the ability of natural processes to replace or restore them.

As with most systems of governance, the key consideration revolves around a sense of human responsibility to balance and prioritise current consumption and development in a way that retains sufficient quantity and quality of resources to meet current demands and future requirements. The way objectives and definitions are commonly framed and presented reflects a predominantly human-centric approach, as demonstrated by the oft-quoted definition of sustainability of the United Nations which says 'sustainable development is development that meets the needs of the present without compromising the ability of future generations to meet their own needs.'[3]

---

3 World Commission on Environment and Development (the Brundtland Commission). 1987. *Our Common Future* (Oxford: Oxford University Press).

256 *Assessing use of animals in agriculture*

For example, environmental sustainability broadly focuses on maintaining and protecting the quantity and quality of land, water and air. Recognising that these resources are borderless, environmental law of most jurisdictions sets out both national and international obligations regarding these resources that affect the global commons. Debates arise about how well each jurisdiction is doing in complying with its often politically motivated paper undertakings, but a jurisdiction's law, usually reflecting obligations under wider international treaties and obligations, demonstrates at the very least a recognition that environmental resources should be properly managed.

Environmental, economic and social considerations constitute the three pillars of sustainability, and the issue of sustainability has attracted attention to all aspects of human existence and activity. Specialist subject areas include, for example, specialties addressing sustainability of energy, tourism, transportation, living conditions and lifestyle, building and architecture, and trade.

Specialty interests and expertise exist in respect of animals, given that animals and issues concerning their welfare are impacted by, and have impact upon, almost all aspects of the environmental, economic and social matrix. For example, the impacts of consumerism on matters involving animals and conservation are broadly recognised in debates involving conservation of biodiversity, and habitat protection. In terms of agriculture, and the primary planetary use of animals as a source of food for people, issues of sustainability sit alongside questions, systems and laws pertaining to the animal's welfare.

Animal welfare in the sustainable food chain

A sustainable food system is broadly recognised as more than simply providing sufficient food to people. It involves providing safe and healthy food to people in a way that meets current food needs and concurrently minimises negative impacts to the wider environment (e.g., physical elements of land, air, and water, including raw resources of plant and animal material), so that future species – both human and non-human – have proper and sufficient food. A sustainable food system therefore incorporates considerations of production and distribution systems/ infrastructure in a way that makes food nutritious, accessible and affordable to all people and animals.

The multifactorial nature of animals and their welfare as part of the food chain is reflected in the variety of stakeholders and diverse interests. Balancing the predicted demand for more meat to meet the demands of more people with greater disposable income, there is a move promoting healthy, sustainable eating as a major component of overall dietary consumerism. Amongst the range of initiatives is a school of thought, which includes the WHO's published Global Strategy on Diet, Physical Activity and Health,[4] which recommends a diet that is comparatively low in meat, by reference to current Western consumption figures. The

---

4 www.who.int/dietphysicalactivity/strategy/eb11344/strategy_english_web.pdf.

Assessing use of animals in agriculture 257

ancillary benefits focusing on greater cost efficiency of protein production (e.g., of plants as opposed to animals), and arguments advocating that the current animal agricultural systems are unsustainable must none the less accommodate the stark reality that, generally, people like to eat meat.

Whether the meat is sourced from land-based agricultural systems, or seafood that is either fished or farmed, the public's idea of 'humane' is reflected in the concepts of animal welfare law which dictates that animals must be raised and/ or caught and killed in a way that avoids causing the animal's unnecessary and/or unreasonable pain or distress.

The 'sustainability' element of the 'humane and sustainable' oft-quoted phrase, seeks to maintain and increase meat production in a way that meets current and future dietary demands of people and animals, in a way that facilitates growth without unnecessarily or unreasonably degrading or destroying the ecosystems from which the meat was acquired.

The politics of animal welfare and food production

Trade, politics, and technologies and patterns of demand, including differing dietary preferences and consequent health patterns, impact considerations regarding animals' welfare and their role as food, as well as the livelihoods of all those involved in the food chain, which takes meat from the paddock to the plate.

Even a cursory glance at how animal welfare has evolved over the last two hundred years, and its impact as an issue on current global trade, demonstrates that as science and technical/communication systems evolve and subsequently influenced consumers' views and buying behaviours, then agricultural producers and retailers have similarly evolved. For example, the legal changes regarding (non-)acceptability of battery hen cages, veal crates and pig stalls clearly demonstrates the shifts in public opinion and subsequently the law. Producers seeking to cash in on a consumer who will willingly pay more for products that have been derived from free-range pigs and poultry have, in turn, faced legal challenge regarding the definition of 'free range'. See Case Study 9.

Case Study 9: Mislabelling: profiteering from free-range misrepresentation

Good animal welfare is big business, as demonstrated, for example, by retailers and supermarket giants like Coles, Tesco, McDonald's, Burger King, Nestle, Marks and Spencer and Woolworths, implementing policy that impacts not only the quality of the animal product, but also the animals' welfare as part of the production process. Reflecting the increased interest in matters of animal welfare by the public, there has been considerable pressure demanding transparency and accountability from industry, regarding the animals' experience in delivering the end product.

(continued)

258 *Assessing use of animals in agriculture*

(continued)

Retailers have demanded a higher price for products derived from animals that have allegedly received above-average care, and debates about what defines 'free-range' chickens, and eggs derived from 'free-range' birds, have extended to the Courts.

In 2014, the Australian Federal Court fined egg producer Pirovic Enterprises Pty Ltd $300,000 for misleading consumers that their eggs were free range, where Pirovic's idea of free range was not consistent with the legal definition. The decision has significant potential relevance to ongoing debates seeking to establish a legal definition of 'free range', given that the decision utilises a definition that birds must be able to move around freely on an open range on an ordinary day. An 'ordinary day' is considered to be every day other than a day when on the open ranges weather conditions endangered the safety or health of the laying hens, or if predators were present or the laying hens were being medicated.

(*Australian Competition and Consumer Commission v Pirovic Enterprises Pty Ltd* (No 2) [2014] FCA 1028)

'Mega-farms' are another emerging issue associated with animals, which is increasingly finding its adversaries taking their arguments to the courtroom. Intensive animal farming is known by different names, which include 'industrial livestock production', 'concentrated animal feeding operations' (CAFOs), 'confined animal feeding operations' (CFOs), and/or 'intensive livestock operations' (ILOs). In the public sector, these animal production systems are widely referred to as 'factory farms'. The terms all refer to a form of intensive farming that refers to the keeping of livestock in conditions where there are higher stocking densities than is usually the case with other forms of animal agriculture. Mega-farms are widely viewed as taking traditional factory farming to a significantly higher level of stocking density. For decision makers, producers, retailers and the public alike, there's a key issue in trying to improve the conditions for animals raised in industrial farming units while concurrently meeting humanity's insatiable demand for an increasing supply of safe, low-cost meat.

Outside the Courts, there are numerous examples of additional initiatives seeking to reassure the consumer, and distinguish one animal product from another on the basis of standards of animal welfare. Farm assurance and certification schemes abound, and in the UK, the RSPCA's Red Tractor food label is just one of many labelling programmes that have been developed.

From animal welfare concerns in both traditional and organic agriculture, and transportation of the animals to slaughterhouses, through to retailers dictating standards of animal welfare as a prerequisite criteria to stocking and selling products either for general consumption or specific needs (e.g., halal meat), the shifts

Assessing use of animals in agriculture 259

mean that it would be fair to say that all parties in the entire 'farm-to-fork' process have been impacted by the consumers' heightened awareness regarding the well-being/welfare of animals.

The diversity of national social, environmental and economic abilities and objectives is reflected in equally diverse, competing and conflicting systems of governance despite participation in common global forums. This raises questions about how the dynamic of conflicting interest and common goals in the global food production network will change in the future.

Looking at the future of animal production for food

Towards and beyond 2050

The human population is predicted to reach approximately 9 billion people by 2050. In order to meet the food demands of the projected 2050 global population, the UN Food and Agricultural Organisation estimated that agricultural output will need to be increased by 70 per cent.[5] This presents a natural challenge for governors and producers alike in establishing sustainable food systems utilising the same – or even less – limited resources in terms of available agricultural land.

On one hand, there are those that contend that increased meat production from the animal sector of the agri-food industry is not sustainable and would incur unacceptably low standards of animal welfare. It is claimed that the food demands of the 2050 global population would best be met by reducing livestock production; proponents of this argument point to individuals and cultures who consume minimal amounts of animal protein food, who none the less lead healthy lives. Proponents of reducing animal production and human protein intake also point out that livestock themselves consume energy derived from plants/crops that might otherwise be consumed by people, and that the available land utilised to produce plant materials for livestock is predicted to decrease in terms of quantity and quality.[6]

There are a number of counter-arguments to this proposed grain and plant-focused solution. Firstly, pigs, poultry and cultivated fish in established intensive agri-systems and aquaculture systems are, for the most part, excluded from the list of species which require considerable amounts of arable land. Additionally, animals kept in traditional pasture-grazing systems consume food that would not traditionally be used by humans. These efficiencies of production, which involve farm species that take up less room and consume foods that humans wouldn't eat, point to the possibility that such species and systems may become more important in meeting global food demands in the future.

---

5 FAO. n.d. 'How to Feed the World in 2050': www.fao.org/fileadmin/templates/wsfs/docs/expert_paper/How_to_Feed_the_World_in_2050.pdf.

6 Philip Lymbery, with Isabel Oakeshott. 2014. *Farmageddon: The True Cost of Cheap Meat* (London: Bloomsbury).

260 *Assessing use of animals in agriculture*

It has been anticipated that the predicted increased demand for animal protein by the year 2050 will come primarily from developing countries as they become more affluent. In reality, vegan or vegetarian diets are unlikely to be widely accepted as a solution to objectives seeking to provide the global population with sufficient amounts of safe food. Moreover, it is also unlikely that global-sized food security strategies will be achieved by government-driven changes in eating behaviour, or by individuals' well-intended dietary changes as they abstain from ingesting animal-derived products. Campaigns promoting the reduction of meat intake on health grounds have been largely unsuccessful, as evidenced by the widespread prevalence of obesity in some developed (and even developing) countries. Even if health campaigns resulted in a degree of reduction in meat eating, it is unlikely that the reduced meat intake in developed countries would be greater than the predicted growth of meat consumption in emerging economies countries like India and China, where there is increasing demand for quantity and quality of meat.

Scientific advancements may meet some of this demand. The production of artificial meat in cell culture (known as *in vitro* meat) may be produced on a scale that makes it economically viable for sale to, and purchase by, the future public. But questions remain as to whether *in vitro* meat will realistically replace the continued production of meat from live animals, given that the cost of *in vitro* meat is likely to be prohibitive at least in the medium term, and the fact that livestock will remain an integral part of wider cultures and future society.

The predicted increased demand for animal-derived protein, in association with other human interests attached to agriculture (e.g., international trade, disease control and zoonoses, livelihoods and economic interests of producers, retailers and the public alike) poses particular challenges for political and legal governors who have the responsibility of balancing and prioritising the public's demands for animal products from livestock production systems, while at the same time fulfilling wide obligations (e.g., climate change and reduction of environmental footprints).

With these multiple obligations and responsibilities, governors increasingly recognise the role of animal welfare in providing healthier animals that make better use of feed and thereby reduce waste products and environmental impacts. Additionally, the law's benchmark of what constitutes 'good practice and scientific knowledge' is also changing, as governors recognise the need for shifts beyond traditional entrenched animal husbandry methods to incorporate biotechnological solutions which solve problems associated with providing the public with sufficient quantities of safe food.

From an animal welfare perspective, genetic improvement is closely associated with animal production objectives which incorporate concepts of efficiency (e.g., food conversion rate) which maximises both the quantity and quality of the final product. While current factory farming methods continue to incorporate these objectives, it is increasingly recognised that concepts of sustainability and standards of animal welfare have a direct impact on farming efficiency, productivity and quality.

While selective breeding programmes have resulted in welfare problems for the animals, a balanced perspective also recognises that when breeding programmes incorporate appropriate standards and objectives, there are a significant number of positive outcomes for all stakeholders involved, including the animal. Considerable advances have been incorporated into animal husbandry systems, resulting in better welfare for the animal – examples include selection of breeding animals that have enhanced disease resistance, polled cattle (cattle without horns), and reduction of wool and folds of skin on sheep, which reduces the incidence of fly strike. Temperament is also recognised as a heritable trait and has been used to breed lines of animals that demonstrate, for example, reduced aggression.

Some people take the view that human manipulation of animal behaviours and appearance is unethical. As with so many questions associated with issues of animal welfare, and the law that governs standards pertaining to an animal's welfare, the word 'responsibility' is central to critically assessing whether practices are acceptable in terms of the law's animal welfare criteria. These are whether the practice causes pain or distress to an animal to the extent that the pain or distress is deemed unnecessary and/or unreasonable. Humans have a long history of selectively breeding from animals that suit the various purposes and uses to which the animal is put. Aggression, for example, may be a desired trait in a security dog, but in farmed domesticated animals such as horses, cattle, pigs and deer, overt aggression in a large animal poses significant potential danger to the human care-giver.

The concept of human responsibility is central to the obligations attached by the law to human–animal interactions. Commonly relying on science and scientific advancements, the law demonstrates a preference for facts that show an authoritative basis which incorporates rational and quantifiable measurements of welfare, to balance frequently anthropomorphic and emotive measures.

More science, more efficiency, more compliance...

Global governance and law continue to rely on greater
efficiencies of animal husbandry and scientific advancement

Animal-based agriculture has been very successful at supplying the public, particularly of developed countries, with enormous quantities of comparatively inexpensive, high-quality meat. Producers have been able to compete in an increasingly international market primarily by increasing efficiency of production and distribution systems, while concurrently utilising improved genetic-selection technologies in selecting breeding animals and animal feeds.

Reliance on progressive science is viewed as a panacea by some people, and a cause of great alarm to others. Concerns have been raised regarding how the advancements may impact not only the animal's welfare, but potentially the health of humans, as animal products and additives progress along the food chain to people as the end consumer. Responsibility for the adequate supply of safe food ultimately falls to the governor.

262 *Assessing use of animals in agriculture*

Unfortunately, the governor's responsibility is easier stated than fulfilled. Significant political, social and economical barriers continue to defer to acceptance and development of more sophisticated animal genetics and biotechnology as solutions to problems of meeting the predicted increase in global demand for animal protein. Personal opinion, reflected in segments of public opinion, are understandably cautious about the risks attached to new technologies. Economic constraints are visibly evident in agriculture, where governments widely reduce expenditure/investment in the agricultural sector and defer enforcement and development responsibilities to industry and other non-government organisations under the guise of 'improved cost efficiencies' and 'collaboration (with industry)'.

The reality is that the subject of animal welfare is a multifactorial issue with enormous impact on wider society and national economies. Animal welfare is obviously not the only issue that governments must address in their governing role, but given the central role of food supply and safety to the issue of 'public good' from both a national and international perspective, agriculture is a responsibility that governments simply cannot abdicate to wider stakeholders, including industry and pharmaceutical companies.

The fact remains that despite political, social, religious, professional, economical and cultural views that advocate understandable caution regarding the risks attached to new technologies, the desires and demands of the public often result in the eventual adoption of new technologies. This is evident in most aspects of society by a simple assessment of historical change and progress in matters of transportation, communication – and agriculture. Similarly, adoption of biotechnologies and genetic-selection programmes which ultimately affect economies and the public, require substantive investment of expertise and money by competent governments appropriately serving the public good by fulfilling their role in objectively assessing and minimising the enormous risks.

A final word on agricultural fallacies, realities and misconceptions 'on the farm'

The aspirations of animal welfare in agriculture are commonly quite different to its realities. Similarly, there are common misconceptions regarding the theoretical model of ensuring compliance with standards of animal welfare on the farm.

The role of science in legal decisions involving issues of animal welfare and agriculture

Despite the reliance of governors and enforcement on science and scientific experts, the scientists themselves have questioned whether the law relies too much on science and scientists. Science doesn't provide all the answers – it provides some of the answers and explanations in, for example, the form of the Courts. Additionally, although certain aspects of science are widely accepted as definitive (e.g., the law of gravity), the reality is that science and scientists frequently disagree. This is demonstrated, for example, with animal welfare offending that

Assessing use of animals in agriculture 263

comes before the Courts. It frequently involves lawyers that each have their chosen '(scientific) expert witness'.

It has been repeatedly stated that the practical significance of animal welfare as a multifactorial issue is that even in cases where there may be scientific agreement rather than competing scientific views or equivocal scientific findings, decision makers are often obliged to take account of considerations in addition to, rather than restricted to, purely scientific information.

Economics is not a justification for all agricultural practices

Despite widely held beliefs that farmers would ensure high standards of animal welfare because their livelihood depends on the animal's health and production, the fact that farmers are prosecuted for animal welfare criminal offending clearly indicates that some farmers do not meet the standards of animal welfare that are set out in animal welfare law. That is, *some* farmers – not *all* farmers. Like most professions, most farmers/producers quietly get on with the business of farming. So, for example, a media report about a poultry farmer who was prosecuted does not mean that all poultry farmers are failing to look after the animals in their care.

In short, surveys of farmers have demonstrated that while profitability is understandably a consideration for any person in business – including farmers – the people who are farming commonly demonstrate significant concern regarding the well-being of animals in their care. If animals are put under the heading of 'planet', then the concerns for the well-being of animals is consistent with a new accounting which moves from considerations of just profit, to a trilogy of auditing and assessment protocols referred to as 'people, planet and profit'.

Good practice and scientific knowledge

Agriculture is an evolving subject and animal husbandry practices concurrently change with that evolution. Legal benchmarks and assessments recognise this process of evolution in legislative wording that facilitates incorporation of contemporary standards.

To put animal welfare law in context, remember that the whole subject of animal-based agriculture, and animals produced for the sole purpose of human consumption, requires an appreciation that animal agriculture is a multifactorial public policy issue and it requires much more than a singularly purist view (e.g. social, economic, religious). It helps to remember that the law focuses on minimum standards and like many laws, enforcement is necessary in respect of the few in order to protect the wider interests of the many.

The majority of people involved in farming never come to the attention of enforcement personnel because how they look after the animals in their care usually exceeds the minimum standards set out by the law. Similarly, while the livelihoods and economic interests of many people and businesses along the food production chain are governed by the law, the interaction between humans

264 *Assessing use of animals in agriculture*

and animals does not always warrant the involvement of enforcement to either educate, assist, direct and/or prosecute.

In terms of animal welfare law as it governs activities on the farm, when matters of alleged animal welfare offending are brought to the Court, adjudicators must give due attention to the relevant law (e.g., animal protection law, the species covered by the law), admissible facts and evidence (e.g., standards of good practice and scientific knowledge in respect of the particular species, the farming calendar, prevailing weather conditions, usual practice in respect of farming activities) as consideration to all other relevant circumstances.

Like most areas addressed by animal welfare law, the well-being of animals depends primarily on the abilities, skill and responsibility of the human care-giver. Proper care of animals in agriculture, that complies with and/or exceeds the standards set out by animal welfare law, requires skills and ability that manage and plan for all aspects of the animals' environment as part of caring for the animals, which are totally reliant upon their human care-giver for their food, water, shelter, health care and ability to behave in a way that is normal for their species. Some people do exceptionally well at farming, and others require assistance to one degree or another. At the other end of the spectrum, there are certain people that simply do not have the skills or aptitude for running a farm that contains living creatures, which the law recognises are capable of experiencing pain and/or distress.

While personal opinions may vary, the focus of the law is not on the number of animals that are raised for human consumption, or the pros and cons of horizontal versus vertical integration of animal production corporates, or even subjective views alleging that life on the farm for the animals is institutionalised animal suffering. While anthropomorphic and emotional opinions are respected, as is the fact that people vary on their opinion of what is normal or justifiable, the central constant of contemporary animal welfare law is its focus on the unnecessary or unreasonable pain or distress of an animal considered in context of its species, environment and wider circumstances.

Animal welfare is part of the bigger objective of delivering safe and sustainable food – not the other way around.

Are you critically assessing the use of animals in agriculture?

The use of animals in agriculture is one of the most discussed and disputed subjects involving animals. This is unsurprising because the predominant use of animals is for human food, and because of the impact of food quantity and quality on human health, lifestyle and wider economic interests. Animals as food is another illustration of the third element of animal law, which states that the interests of humans and animals are invariably connected.

In assessing the use of animals as human food, it is important to remember that critical assessment means more than simply criticising, and that critical assessment considers – but is not restricted to – questions of lawfulness. It's one thing to argue that the use of animals in research is justified for purposes of medical

Assessing use of animals in agriculture   265

advancement, but what about using animals for purposes which have been classed as human vanities (e.g., cosmetics, fashion industry furs) or pure human pleasures (e.g., party drugs)? Critically assess the status of the law (by country and/ or region) regarding the use of animals in research that falls outside mainstream advocated purposes.

The degree and nature of legal protection attached to an animal depends significantly on the circumstances in which it is located, and demonstrates that the law's substantive consideration of the purpose/use of the animal and its correlating dependency on the human care-giver, rather than simply its species. Conflicting opinions exist regarding the continued use of animals in research. Critically assess statements and/or articles and/or publications from websites and media. Also, critically assess the following statements:

- What's the real problem with live exports of production animals? Animals are transported every day to and from medical facilities and across national borders, so what is the root problem with transport of live animals for slaughter?
- In 1995, author Bernie Rollin wrote a book called *The Frankenstein Syndrome*,[7] stating 'genetic engineering of animals cannot be stopped – it is too simple and relatively inexpensive to accomplish'. Critically assess the lawful standards of animal welfare, factory farming and genetic engineering in context of this statement.
- How can one country dictate to another country about the conditions of slaughter of exported animals?
- Is the WTO doing 'enough' in respect of animal welfare?
- Are governors on track to provide sufficient safe food that is humanely and sustainably produced?
- If 'people, planet and profit' are the accounting benchmarks, then what are the alternatives (if any) to factory farming?

---

7 Bernard E. Rollin. 1995. *The Frankenstein Syndrome: Ethical and Social Issues in the Genetic Engineering of Animals* (Cambridge: Cambridge University Press).

9 The continuing journey of animal welfare and law

The shakers, makers and users of animal welfare law

Issues like food safety and supply, international trade, disease control and zoonoses are just a few of the issues impacting national and international social, environmental and economic interests. Consequently, government, industry, non-government organisations and the public have increasingly recognised the importance of this multifactorial subject called 'animal welfare'. From both a moral and commodity-based perspective, law regarding animals and their welfare has also developed in a process of incremental change.

With the increased attention to matters around welfare, defining and assessing the term has become the subject of a significant amount of work. Scientific perspectives benchmark the coping abilities of the animal by reference to the animal's immunological, physiological and behavioural responses.

From a policy perspective, the OIE has set out a definition of animal welfare that incorporates and extends the science-based approach. The World Animal Health Organisation describes animal welfare as a complex, multifaceted public policy issue with important ethical, economic and political dimensions. The definition of animal welfare as identifiable in contemporary animal welfare legislation is of the protection of animals from unnecessary and/or unreasonable pain and/or distress.

Arguably, this has always been the singular statement setting out the law's definition of animal welfare, or synonyms of animal protection and concepts of anti-cruelty and humane treatment of animals. Indeed, study of the historical development of animal protection law demonstrates that in truth, it is only human/legal considerations of what is unnecessary or unreasonable that has changed, and that human perceptions have largely developed in response to greater scientific knowledge and technical advances, which have enabled the public to learn and understand more about animals and their experience.

Despite these definitions and significant progress, however, there is no singularly accepted definition of animal welfare and thus it remains potentially sidelined, misunderstood, or subsumed into self-serving interests. For example, concerns have been raised that recognition of animal welfare as an international trade policy issue may be used for 'trade protectionism' in a way that inappropriately denigrates from the central purpose of our welfare legislation, which is to protect the animal.

In order to maintain the integrity of purpose set out in animal protection law and balance it with other competing and potentially conflicting human interests, it has been suggested that animal welfare policy and standards should be complemented by robust ethical analysis and draw on credible scientific consensus while taking an incremental approach to animal welfare change management.

Governance of change management still demonstrates a widespread misunderstanding of two of the three features of animal law itself, namely the animal's experience (e.g., pain, distress, the ability to suffer, with arguments toward legal recognition of sentience), and the inseparable connection between people and animals.

The fundamental principles demonstrate that human attitudes regarding animals have been polarised from the very earliest of times. Entrenched individual attitudes of governors and other professionals result in a predilection for debates to simply spiral into advocacy positions. What is needed is a genuinely knowledgeable and objective approach which enables identification of the important issues – a prerequisite to rectifying current and foreseeable problems. In short, misinformation and misunderstanding create barriers preventing leaders to be politically and publicly credible in the area of animal welfare. It is oxymoronic to claim national 'leadership' in animal welfare law, when national standards are based on minimum standards which are the 'lowest' common denominator for international agreement.

The concept of leadership itself is distinctly different from simple management. Management has been described as doing things right. In comparison, leadership is doing the right thing at the right time. Chapter 4 illustrates the dramatic contribution of historical leaders to the subject of animal welfare law which, in turn, has had an enormous impact on the world today. Current law regarding human–human and human–animal interactions has developed incrementally over a long period of time. Similarly, our understanding of animals and the wider social, environmental and economic consequences of animal welfare standards has also developed over an extended period of time. Indeed, people are prone to take these significant historical contributions regarding animal care and human responsibility almost for granted.

Who are the shakers, the makers and the users?

The 'shakers' of animal welfare law include all those who advocate for change and subjective opinion in one form or another. Non-government organisations are probably the most common example of a 'shaker' that comes to mind. The 'makers' refers to those involved in drafting and enacting legislation which sets the standards of animal welfare that the public are to comply with, and the penalties for non-compliance. The 'users' refer to all those whose lives and livelihoods are directly – or indirectly – affected by the standards of animal welfare prescribed by the law. One of the key elements of animal welfare law is that it is law relating to a live animal, which takes account of the inseparable connection between people and animals.

268   *Animal welfare law: the continuing journey*

Applying a broad interpretation to this element means that all people and all animals are arguably 'users'.

The literature generally references organisations and groups, listing them as government, non-government organisations, producers, industry, retailers and consumers. Alternatively, broad groups of interests may be referenced including, for example, the environment, society, the economy and the animals.

There are a number of professions which clearly have a role in affecting and deciding the rules that govern the public's responsibilities regarding animals. Veterinarians and lawyers are commonly the first two professions identified. Recognition that animal welfare is a multifactorial public policy issue leads to the inclusion of policy advisers and ethicists as key professions included in the highly influential 'makers' group. When the impacts of animal welfare decisions are described as having wide 'societal, environmental and economic' outcomes, it becomes clear that environmentalists, sociologists and economists also joined the group of 'shakers and makers'. Additionally, recognition of the fact that the public is increasingly better informed and highly influential to political decisions, raises questions about who is informing the public. In addition to various stakeholders and stakeholder promotions/education programmes that deal with matters pertaining to animal welfare (e.g., government, non-government organisations, industry and retail chains) it is usually identified that the media (e.g., journalists) are also highly influential in that the degree of accuracy, balance and objectivity provided by a frequently ratings driven profession has significant potential to influence public opinion, and thereby political action or inaction.

How good are the key professionals?

Consideration of which professions have key animal welfare roles and responsibilities provides the possibility of assessing how well-informed current and future leaders are in respect of animal welfare matters. For example, assessing the existence and/or quality of undergraduate and postgraduate tertiary education programmes on the subject of animal welfare provides some indication of how confident the public can be in professionals who subsequently take on the government's responsibilities.

In understanding key issues that need to be addressed, the reader is in a better position to critically assess animal welfare literature, policy, decisions and law. Combining these insights with recognition of the drivers that affect each stakeholder also provides the ability to distinguish lip-service from genuine leadership in matters of animal welfare.

There are challenges associated with each of these key professions. The public relies on politicians, legislatures and their advisers to 'get it right'. Animal welfare is one of a number of key considerations that is highly relevant to expanding human populations, urbanisation and income growth. These developments demand knowledgeable and informed leadership in order to adequately meet public demands in a way which minimises avoidable risk of potentially devastating consequences that happens when governors 'get it wrong'.

Animal welfare law: the continuing journey 269

The veterinary profession is widely recognised and trusted for its role as society's 'animal health and welfare experts'. Contemporary animal welfare law commonly identifies 'the veterinarian' as the singularly identified expert who is entrusted with the responsibility for making critical animal welfare decisions (e.g., euthanasia of an animal). While veterinarians undoubtedly have significant training in matters of animal health, assessment of undergraduate and postgraduate education programmes raises questions about how familiar veterinarians are with welfare concepts and the legal criteria that apply to almost all their professional activities and the animals that are under the veterinarian's supervision and care. When asked to provide a definition of animal welfare, veterinarians commonly refer to scientific benchmarks, make reference to the Five Freedoms (see Chapter 4), or reiterate undergraduate training and media reference to 'happy' animals and commonly unclear concepts regarding 'anti-cruelty' and 'humane'.

Contemporary animal welfare law certainly relies on science for objective information and explanation, sets standards that reflect the principles of the Five Freedoms, but does not make any mention of 'happy' animals as objective criteria for the Courts. In the minority of cases, reference is made to the legal obligation to minimise an animal's suffering, pain, or distress.

Veterinarians are not the only key professional in the process of learning the foundational principles and benchmarks of animal welfare law. Despite being identified as one of the key professionals responsible for drafting, advising, enforcing and litigating matters of animal welfare, a substantial number of the legal profession remain blissfully unaware of developments in animal welfare law. To be fair, animal welfare law is an emerging legal discipline. While issues involving human–animal and human–human interactions involving animals are scattered throughout traditional legal pillars of contract, criminal, tort and public law, the discipline itself is widely misunderstood and therefore attracts a variety of responses that range from interest and curiosity right through to bias and criticism. In this regard, animal law has similarities to the beginnings of environmental law which, in its beginning, was also widely misunderstood. Today, of course, environmental law is a recognised legal specialty that has a direct impact on all people and organisations whether they are aware of it or not, simply by virtue of the fact that environmental law governs uses and impacts of any activity involving air, land and/or water. As lawyers learn that animal law involves much more than simply dog bites and animal rights, and actually has enormous impacts on wider societal, environmental and economic interests, then it is predicted that just like environmental law specialists, organisations will also recognise the need and benefit of having animal law specialists at their decision table.

The scientific community faces challenges and criticism for being the professional body heavily relied upon by the law, given that consensus is difficult to achieve. The reality of a divided community has raised questions about the scientific community's ability to be a credible reference to the law makers. Similarly, in recognition of the fact that the continuation of many scientific projects relies on demonstrated compliance with the law and funding resources, concerns regarding conflicts of interest are commonly considered in determining whether a particular

270 *Animal welfare law: the continuing journey*

scientist or scientific group can be relied upon to act as an empirical expert or is simply a political and/or funding puppet. Indeed, eminent scientists have themselves raised the question as to whether the law relies 'too much' on preferred interpretations of science in order to promote its own agenda while conveying a persona of objectivity to the public.

Economists face a continual litany of rhetoric alleging that decisions pertaining to animal welfare are almost exclusively based on profitability. Undoubtedly, cost efficiencies factor into any decision-making process and it demonstrates business naivety to suggest that any organisation – government, NGO, or industry – has a bottomless pocket of money. None the less, while certain bodies continue to focus simply on the cost of animal welfare initiatives, there are economists actively applying a broader cost–benefit assessment, which gives consideration to the interaction between profit, people and the planet.

It is said that individual opinion is important because it creates public opinion, which in turn influences political opinion. This raises questions about how well the voting consumer is truly 'accurately informed'.

Those involved in the media have a pivotal role in informing the public. Aspirations to protect the freedom of the press are laudable, where such freedoms are provided; however, the responsible utilisation of that freedom requires that the profession and its members consistently provide information that is accurate, balanced and objective. This may present challenges for less-skilled or dedicated journalists who may consider it a necessary and/or acceptable trade-off in order to highlight or ignore certain animal welfare issues on the grounds that they are more/less emotive and attractive in a ratings-driven industry.

Identification of the fundamental principles of animal welfare and law provides the ability to governors and professionals alike to exhibit genuine leadership. Importantly, there are a number of identifiable animal welfare trends where leadership has been shown, and where continuing leadership – in doing the right thing at the right time – is required.

Future trends to watch for in animal welfare

Standards acknowledging the positive aspects of an animal's experience

The World Animal Health Organisation has advocated that the totality of animal welfare as a subject includes proper treatment of the animals and the animals' experiences. Contemporary discussions on animal sentience and how that might be incorporated into law demonstrated that the jurisdictions with leading animal welfare law are significantly further along the development path than the early beginnings of animal protection, which faced challenges, for example, even recognising animals as anything more than a simple commodity, or the legal acknowledgement and protection of an animal from experiencing pain or distress.

A significant amount of study and literature exists on the subject of pain and how to avoid it in both animals and humans, because humans are highly motivated to avoid their own pain. The human life-experience model broadly demonstrates that the next step after avoiding unnecessary pain is the pursuit of pleasure.

Existing law effectively draws the line on the basis of minimal standards that are based on preventing an animal from experiencing 'unnecessary or unreasonable' pain. While legal standards of animal care progress from minimal standards, to standards of best practice, the focus is still on avoidance of pain rather than pursuit of pleasure. The principles of the Five Freedoms, for example, have been incorporated into standards set out in animal welfare law with a view to preventing an animal from suffering avoidable pain. Of course, the challenge for science has been how to put objective empirical measurements to the subjective experience of pain, where the response to the same stimulus can vary enormously between individuals. None the less, a significant amount of research and literature exists on the subject of pain, and how to avoid it. This driver has, in practical terms, meant that a significant amount of knowledge exists in respect of the animal's experience of pain as well.

Moving toward 'animal-friendly' standards, rather than just away from unnecessary pain benchmarks?

Interestingly, eminent scientists utilising emerging technologies of neuroscience have already turned attention to the subject of identifying how to measure an animal's experience of pleasure, rather than simply restricting studies to avoidance of pain. This revised and refreshed approach to empirically measuring the positive, rather than just the negative, life experiences of animals has the potential to further shift perceptions of what the law considers 'good practice and scientific knowledge'. While such a concept may appear fanciful to some people, history none the less demonstrates that people of the past also scoffed at the suggestion that animals actually experience pain, and ridiculed the idea that legal protections should be established to prevent animals from experiencing unnecessary pain. Indeed, once the eighteenth-century philosopher Jeremy Bentham had turned the debate from whether or not animals had souls to whether or not they could suffer pain, it was only humankind's knowledge of animals' ability to experience pain, as validated by improved science, that has in turn shifted the benchmarks of what the public consider acceptable regarding animal husbandry practices, which have eventually been translated into revised human legal responsibilities.

A review of the development of animal welfare law contains additional lessons for people, professions and organisations involved with matters pertaining to animal protection. In short, it is a process that most people would consider very slow by a process of incremental 'evolution not revolution' change.

The development of animal law from its early beginnings is already over two hundred years old. Even canons of animal welfare law are literally several decades old. For example, consider the evolution of what is known as the Five Freedoms. In 1964, *Animal Machines*, written by British author Ruth Harrison, described intensive livestock and poultry farming practices, and became widely viewed as a seminal text and exposé of factory farming. In response to the ensuing public

272 *Animal welfare law: the continuing journey*

outcry, the British government appointed a committee to examine the welfare of farm animals. In 1965, the committee, chaired by Professor Roger Brambell presented the 85-page 'Report of the Technical Committee to Enquire into the Welfare of Animals Kept under Intensive Livestock Husbandry Systems',[1] which became known as the 'Brambell Report'. The report made reference to 'freedoms' that should be given to animals. In 1979, those freedoms were codified into the format in which they are known today. The principles of the 'Five Freedoms' (freedom from thirst, hunger and malnutrition; freedom from discomfort; freedom from pain, injury and disease; freedom to express normal behaviour, and freedom from fear and distress) continues to form the basis of standards ('positive duties of care') and relevant offences in contemporary Westminster animal welfare law. The entire animal law development spectrum demonstrates that dramatic overnight change in almost any use of animals is unlikely to happen. Animal welfare is a process of continual involvement informed by science, influenced by the public, and reliant upon a range of political and economic resources and initiatives. In this regard, the development of animal welfare and law may be viewed as a journey rather than a destination.

Debates regarding animal sentience are likely to increase and concepts referencing the totality of the animal's life experience will be incorporated into strong, complete and practical animal welfare legislation.

Recognition of animal welfare as a distinct academic discipline

Mirroring the growing realisation that animal welfare has direct relevance to people's finances, health and lifestyle, there has been a significant increase in the provision of education regarding animal welfare and law. While undergraduate and postgraduate courses in animal welfare and law were originally considered by traditional tertiary education providers as somewhat 'fringey', there is now an increased number of institutions incorporating courses on animal welfare and law into their syllabus.

Animal welfare professorial Chairs have been established in universities in jurisdictions including Canada, the US, the UK, several European countries, New Zealand and Australia.

In recognition of societal expectations of veterinarians regarding animal welfare rather than simply animal health, leading veterinary schools are proactively implementing measures to ensure that graduates are adequately informed, not just on matters of animal welfare, but also on associated legal obligations which the veterinarian may be involved in as a professional expert or, in certain circumstances, potentially a party to criminal offending and/or civil liability.

---

1 Great Britain – Scottish Office, Francis William Rogers Brambell. 1965. *Report of the Technical Committee to Enquire Into the Welfare of Animals Kept Under Intensive Livestock Husbandry Systems* (London: H.M. Stationery Office).

While veterinary schools are doing this, there is a veritable burgeoning of law schools providing education on animal welfare law, meaning that in certain jurisdictions, undergraduate and graduating lawyers know more about animal welfare legal obligations than undergraduate and graduate veterinarians.

Not only are professionals being better educated on matters pertaining to animal welfare and associated legal responsibilities, academia also demonstrates a trend to recognition of specialist animal welfare qualifications encompassing disciplines, for example, of science, ethics and law.

Trends indicate that the animal's experience will not only be increasingly recognised by the law, but that the subject of animal welfare will spread as a subject available in the curriculum of wider university studies offering education in law, ethics, veterinary science and ethology. Developments in the curriculum of formal education providers can be expected to be complemented by wider community education and reference material including, for example, official, complete and public databases on animal welfare-related procedures and compliance.

Increased priority to animal welfare matters by organisations

Reflecting the opportunities and risks associated with animal welfare-related activities, there are a significant number of major international bodies that are heavily involved and invested in matters of animal welfare.

The subject of animal welfare has been a long-established matter for organisations like the OIE and the WTO. Animal welfare-related matters (e.g., disease status) pervade a variety of import and export standards which are vital for market access to trading bodies such as the European Union. There have been important developments in the creation of animal welfare conventions which deal, for example, with issues of farm animals, transportation, animal welfare at slaughter and the welfare of companion animals. As an international trade policy issue with considerable relevance to societal, environmental and economic issues involving disease control and public health, animal welfare-related issues and law continue to be a major topic requiring careful governance to maintain an organisation's credibility and engender continued support from organisational members.

Non-government organisations such as World Animal Protection (formerly the World Society for the Protection of Animals (WSPA), Compassion in World Farming (CIWF) and the global organisation Society for the Protection of Animals (SPCA) provide just a few examples of well-resourced and highly influential groups conducting effective targeted lobbying activities to the government and public consumer. A number of industry producers and retailers have also implemented initiatives in recognition of the fact that animal welfare-related public interests, such as humane treatment of animals and food safety as well as food quality, has a direct effect on profits.

Despite economic constraints, a number of governments also have standards recognising the importance and value of maintaining nationally consistent

274   *Animal welfare law: the continuing journey*

policies to enhance existing animal welfare arrangements which, in turn, assists in maintaining a credible international reputation and international trade.

To facilitate continued improvement and development, it is essential for all stakeholders to have a measure of ownership and 'buy in'. There are obviously political and strategic advantages in ensuring that all stakeholders collaborate wherever possible to increase effectiveness and efficiency in meeting both domestic and international requirements.

That said, it is clearly inappropriate to utilise just the rhetoric of 'collaboration' as a simple cost-reduction exercise that advocates responsibility and puts all individuals (including people and animals) at unnecessary and unacceptable risk. The need for governance and monitoring cannot be understated to avoid such programmes simply becoming, for example, a thinly disguised revenue exercise that confuses market standards and participating stakeholders.

With the advent of the Internet, news of serious animal welfare offending can be broadcast to the international community in a matter of minutes. Consequently, if a case involving serious animal welfare offending is not seen to be adequately addressed by government enforcement and compliance agencies, then existing and future trading opportunities may be lost as a result of producers and retailers who do not want to take the risk that continued association – real or even perceived – risks tarnishing their own reputation in the public eye as an organisation that can be relied upon to maintain high standards of animal welfare. Such occurrences appear to validate the comments of the former chair of the UK's Farm Animal Welfare Council (FAWC), Colin Spedding, who proposed that the marketplace would emerge as the new regulator.

It is then perhaps unsurprising to note the trend in organisations responding to public demands by revising their own real, perceived and promoted self-compliance with higher standards of animal welfare. *Trends indicate that animal welfare will increasingly be recognised and consequently feature more prominently in the policy documents, agreements and laws of persuasive and influential government and non-government organisations.*

The end of the beginning

In considering the journey of animal welfare and law, the question has been asked whether the current state of contemporary animal welfare law represents the ultimate codification of human responsibilities involving animals. Alternatively, it might be argued that the last two hundred years of legal development in the animal welfare space was simply 'the beginning', and that with the assistance of improved science and communication systems enabling people to better know about and understand the life experience of animals, then exponentially faster and improved systems of care and protection can be implemented. The views demonstrate contrasting perspectives as to whether contemporary animal welfare law represents 'the end of the beginning' or 'the beginning of the end'.

Irrespective of the reader's individual view, it is indisputable that the development of animal welfare and law is an ongoing journey of expectation for animals and people, facilitated by emerging technologies and global demands. The law's definition of animal welfare, encapsulated in the synonymous terms of 'anti-cruelty', 'animal protection' and 'humane treatment', has remained the same since its inception in eighteenth-century England. If scientific technological advances identifying the empirically measurable neurological pleasure centres of animals ultimately result in future generations engaging in animal husbandry systems which benchmark not only the avoidance of pain but the promotion of pleasure for animals, then arguably that too is simply an extension of the predominant consensus. It might be codified in law, that animals should not suffer unreasonable or unnecessary pain or distress.

Such aspirations may seem far-fetched to a number of people today; however, one can only wonder at what eighteenth-century animal protection advocates Sir William Putney, William Wilberforce, Richard Martin, Lord Erskine and Jeremy Bentham might think at seeing today's official recognition of animal welfare, public concern regarding animal care, and the law's codification of human responsibilities regarding animals. Undoubtedly, they would also marvel at the technologies available today, which further enable the development of animal welfare and law, both nationally and internationally. With that retrospective view to refer to, it is at least reasonable to conclude that today's population will similarly have a limited idea of the technologies and society that will exist in two hundred years' time.

Despite these significant and encouraging developments, there is also a harsh reality that none the less balances progress made in respect of animal welfare. That reality centres on the very fact that people are at the heart of all decisions affecting animals, their welfare and related concerns.

It is evident that with advances in science and easier access to global communication systems, there is a raised awareness in many countries about the range of animal welfare issues. While a certain amount of that awareness undoubtedly comes from people being interested in animals and the way they are treated, it is likely that the awareness is primarily a result of external pressures which force people to confront realities of the constant interaction between human well-being and animal welfare. Food supply, food safety, antibiotic resistance, disease control, the direct and indirect effects of animal uses and practices on communities and people's livelihoods stand as just a few of the more obvious examples where people are personally affected. Additionally, grass-roots campaigns utilising modern technologies to document ongoing cruel practices in farming, research and production systems are also enormously important in raising public awareness.

Unfortunately, awareness does not always translate into people's propensity to act. Despite the fact that people know more about the wonderful complexity and depth of animals' lives than they ever did before, and despite the fact that issues of animal welfare are increasingly included on organisational agendas, awareness regarding matters of animal welfare has attracted criticism for being simply lip-service and window-dressing in the face of the continued and increasing exploitation of animals in many countries.

276 *Animal welfare law: the continuing journey*

Putting aside contrasting moral views regarding the animal's experience just for a moment, basic assessment of the extent and degree of animal exploitation, the loss of biodiversity, the secondary impacts of animal exploitation to the environment, and the mass extinction of plants and animals largely attributable to human causes, makes it difficult to argue that education and awareness alone is enough to counteract the losses attributable to human exploitation.

In this regard, the law may not be a panacea, nor may it succeed in stemming the tide of destructive change associated with exploitation of resources that is unfettered and/or compliance with the law that is rendered weak or impotent due to inefficiencies and/or administrative corruption. None the less, it remains a check in doing what it can to ward off the realisation of Hardin's 'tragedy of the commons',[2] by preventing, mitigating and managing overt exploitation and non-compliance.

In comparison to more entrenched legal disciplines, the subject of animal law is still in its infancy. On its journey of development, perhaps animal welfare and law has reached the end of its beginning now that the public, politicians, legislators and wider governing bodies recognise that the subject of animal welfare goes well beyond the altruistic moral views of a minority, and constitutes what has been described as a complex international public policy issue with important scientific, ethical, cultural, religious and trade policy implications. With increased recognition of the considerable interests and investments attached to the multifactorial issue of animal welfare, it is expected that the law will continue to develop and codify human responsibilities regarding human–human and human–animal interactions that involve an animal, recognise its ability to experience pain – and pleasure, and the inseparable connection between human well-being and animal welfare.

Eventually, common threats and interests may result in consensus on global animal welfare standards. The notion of approaching animal welfare change management on a truly global, rather than a national basis, represents a paradigm shift from traditional interactions between independent national players jostling for primacy on the international stage. The concept of unified global animal welfare standards and protection is an objective that has so many political, social, cultural and economic hurdles that it could appear unrealistic and unattainable. Yet the evidence would suggest that in spite of these apparent obstacles, there are people, organisations and states who, although sharing a variety of motivations, are actively involved in trying to achieve it.

---

2 Garrett Hardin. 1968. 'The Tragedy of the Commons', *Science*, 162(3850): 1243–8: doi: 10.1126/science.162.3859.1243.

Suggested key further reading

Animal Welfare Act 2006. 2007. (commencement No. 1) (England) *Order 2007: Statutory Instruments 499* (C.20) (London: HMSO).

Appleby, M.A., Mench, J.A., Olsson, I.A.S. and Hughes, B.O. 2011. *Animal Welfare*, 2nd edn (Wallingford: CABI Publishing).

Ascione, F.R. (ed.). 2010. *The International Handbook of Animal Abuse and Cruelty: Theory, Research, and Application* (West Lafayette, IN: Purdue University Press).

Bayvel, A.C.D., Rahman, S.A. and Gavinelli, A. (eds). 2005. 'Animal Welfare: Global Issues, Trends and Challenges', *Scientific and Technical Review* 24(2), special issue, published by OIE (World Organisation for Animal Health).

Beauchamp, T.L. and Frey, R.G. (eds). 2014. *The Oxford Handbook of Animal Ethics* (Oxford: Oxford Handbooks in Philosophy, Oxford University Press).

Beirne, P. 2009. *Confronting Animal Abuse: Law, Criminology, and Human–Animal Relationships* (Rowman and Littlefield).

Cooper, M. 1987. *An Introduction to Animal Law* (London: Academic Press).

Eisenstein, Y. 2013. *Careers in Animal Law: Welfare, Protection, and Advocacy* (New York: American Bar Association).

Favre, D.S. 2011. *Animal Law: Welfare Interests and Rights*, 2nd edn (New York: Aspen Publishers/Wolters Kluwer).

Feinberg, J. 1974. 'The Rights of Animals and Unborn Generations', in W. Blackstone (ed.), *Philosophy and Environmental Crisis* (Athens, GA: University of Georgia Press).

Francione, G.L. 1995. *Animals, Property and the Law* (Philadelphia, PA: Temple University Press).

Fraser, D. 2008. *Understanding Animal Welfare: The Science in its Cultural Context* (Chichester and New York: UFAW Animal Welfare Series, Wiley-Blackwell).

Grandin, T. 2007. *Improving Animal Welfare: A Practical Approach* (Wallingford, UK: CABI Publishing).

—— (ed.). 2014. *Livestock Handling and Transport*, 4th edn (Wallingford, UK: CABI Publishing).

Gregory, N.G. 2007. *Animal Welfare and Meat Production* (Wallingford, UK: CABI Publishing).

Halsbury's Laws of England. 2000 (Volume 2(1)), *Animals*, 4th edn reissue (London: LexisNexis Butterworths).

Harrison, R. 1965 (2013 edn). *Animal Machines* (Wallingford, UK: CABI Publishing).

Hauser, M.D., Cushman, F. and Kamen, M. (eds). 2005. *People, Property, or Pets?* (New Directions in the Human–Animal Bond) (West Lafayette, IN: Purdue University Press).

278 *Suggested further reading*

Hubrecht, R. 2014. *The Welfare of Animals Used in Research: Practice and Ethics* (UFAW Animal Welfare Series, Universities Federation for Animal Welfare) (London: Wiley-Blackwell).

Ibrahim, D. 2006. 'The Anti-cruelty statute: A study in animal welfare', *Journal of Animal Law and Ethics*, 1: 175–89.

Legge, D. and Brooman, S. (eds). 1997. *Law Relating To Animals* (London and New York: Routledge-Cavendish).

Linzey, A. (ed.). 2009. *The Link Between Animal Abuse and Human Violence* (Eastbourne, UK: Sussex Academic Press).

Lymbery, P., with Oakeshott, E. 2014. *Farmageddon: The True Cost of Cheap Meat* (London: Bloomsbury Publishing).

Maehler, A.H. and Trohler, U. 1987. 'Animal Experimentation from Antiquity to the End of the Eighteenth Century: Attitudes and Arguments', in N. Rupke (ed.), *Vivisection in Historical Perspective* (London: Routledge).

Mellor, D.J. and Bayvel, A.J.C. (eds). 2014. 'Animal Welfare: Focusing on the Future', *Scientific and Technical Review*, 33(1), open access journal special issue, published by OIE (World Organisation for Animal Health).

——, Patterson-Kane, E. and Stafford, K.J. 2009. *The Sciences of Animal Welfare* (UFAW Animal Welfare series) (Chichester and New York: Wiley-Blackwell).

Miller, L. and Zawistowski, S. 2012. *Shelter Medicine for Veterinarians and Staff*, 2nd edn (Chichester and New York: Wiley-Blackwell).

Moberg, G.P. and Mench, J.A. (eds). 2000. *The Biology of Animal Stress: Basic Principles and Implications for Animal Welfare* (Wallingford, UK: CAB International).

OIE. 2014. *Terrestrial Animal Health Code* (Paris: OIE, World Organisation for Animal Health).

O'Sullivan, S. 2011. *Animals, Equality and Democracy* (The Palgrave Macmillan Animal Ethics Series) (Basingstoke: Palgrave Macmillan).

Radford, M. 2001. *Animal Welfare Law in Britain* (Oxford: Oxford University Press).

Regan T. 2004. *The Case for Animal Rights* (Berkeley: University of California Press).

—— and Singer, P. (eds). 1989. *Animal Rights: An Human Obligations*, 2nd edn (Pearson).

Ryder, R.D. 2000. *Animal Revolution: Changing Attitudes Towards Speciesism* (Oxford: Berg).

Singer, P. 1995. *Animal Liberation* (London: Pimlico).

Schaffner, J.E. 2010. *An Introduction to Animals and the Law* (The Palgrave Macmillan Animal Ethics Series) (Basingstoke: Palgrave Macmillan).

Sunstein, C.R. and Nussbaum, M.C. (eds). 2006. *Animal Rights: Current Debates and New Directions* (Oxford: Oxford University Press).

Taylor, A. 2009. *Animals and Ethics* (Peterborough, Ontario: Broadview Press).

Turner, J. and D'Silva, J. (eds) 2006. *Animals, Ethics and Trade: The Challenge of Animal Sentience* (London: Earthscan).

Wagman, B.A., Waisman, S.S. and Frasch, P.D. 2009. *Animal Law: Cases and Materials*, 4th edn (Durham, NC: Carolina Academic Press).

Waldau, P. and Patton, K. 2009. *A Communion of Subjects: Animals in Religion, Science and Ethics* (New York: Columbia University Press).

——. 2011. *Animal Rights: What Everyone Needs to Know* (Oxford: Oxford University Press).

Webster, J. (ed.) 2011. *Management and Welfare of Farm Animals: The UFAW Farm Handbook*, 5th edn (UFAW Animal Welfare Series) (Chichester and New York: Wiley-Blackwell).

Suggested further reading   279

Wise, S.M. 2001. *Rattling the Cage: Towards Legal Rights for Animals* (London: Profile Books).

Wolfensohn, S. and Lloyd, M. 2013. *Handbook of Laboratory Animal Management and Welfare*, 4th edn (Chichester and New York: Wiley-Blackwell).

Yeates, J. 2013. *Animal Welfare in Veterinary Practice* (UFAW Animal Welfare Series) (Chichester and New York: Wiley-Blackwell).

Zollitsch, W., Winckler, C., Waiblinger, S. and Haslberger, A. (eds). 2007. *Sustainable Food Production and Ethics. Proceedings of the 7th Congress of the European Society for Agricultural and Food Ethics* (Wageningen, the Netherlands: Wageningen University Press).

Index

abetting 160
absolute liability 111
academia 272–3
accountability *see* responsibility
activism 238–9
Acts of Parliament *see* Parliament
actus reus (guilty act) 110–11, 113–14
acute pain 97
adjudicators 101–2
agriculture 217, 249–65; definition
    249–50; economics 263–4; fallacies
    262–4; future perspectives 259–62;
    history 250–1; humanely produced
    food 254–9; misconceptions 262–4;
    practical perspectives 249–54; USDA
    244
aiding 160
Animal Liberation (Singer) 58, 73
Animal Machines (Harrison) 73
Animal and Plant Health Inspection
    Services (APHIS) 244
Animal Protection Act 1911 4
Animal Welfare Act 51, 77, 84, 100, 140,
    142, 157–8
anthropomorphism 64
anti-cruelty concepts 82–3, 151
APHIS *see* Animal and Plant Health
    Inspection Services
Appeals Court 144–5
Aquinas, St Thomas 48
'a shield, but not a sword' codes 154
astronomy 49
A Theory of Justice (Rawls) 57
attitudes regarding animals 41–3
'attitude test' 144–5
Australia 71–2, 98, 162

Australian Code of Practice for the Care
    and Use of Animals 98
authoritative perspectives 11, 34–5
awareness 29, 72–4, 152–3, 165

Babesia parasite 193–4
balanced perspectives 11, 28–9
Banner Committee 92
battery-hen cages 122
Bentham, J. 21, 57, 60–1, 74
Bernadone, G. Francesco di 46
best practice 115–19
'beyond reasonable doubt' 113–15
Bible 48
bilateral agreements 216
'bioprejudice' 237–8
biosecurity 192–4
bird flu 1–2, 65
birds 1–2, 65, 179–80
Blackstone, W. 88
border control 228–9
bovine spongiform encephalopathy (BSE)
    1–2
'Boycott Australian Wool' campaign 71–2
British Empire 79, 81–3
British law 15–16
broad net of liability 117–19, 158
brokers 205–6
Brooman, S. 26
BSE *see* bovine spongiform encephalopathy
bullbaiting 72
bundle of rights 23–4, 87–8, 91

CAFOs *see* Concentrated Animal Feeding
    Operations
calculating of damages 170–1

Index 281

care-givers 78, 106, 109, 158, *see also* duty of care
case law 15
cattle 80–1, 102, 104, 120
CCO *see* Community Corrections Order
certification 153–4
CFOs *see* confined animal feeding operations
Christian teachings 48, 49
chronic pain 97
CITES *see* Convention on International Trade in Endangered Species of Wild Fauna and Flora
civil law 15, 88–9, 165–84
CIWF *see* Compassion in World Farming
climate change/control 200–3
Code of Practice for the Care and Use of Animals 98
Codes of Welfare/Practice 115
commercialism 187, 189
common law 15, 121–4
'common sense' 64
Community Corrections Order (CCO) 130–1
Compassion in World Farming (CIWF) 71–2, 220, 226, 273
compensation 167–77
competing/collaborating NGOs 218–19
compliance 124–31, 245–6
Concentrated Animal Feeding Operations (CAFOs) 251–2, 258
confined animal feeding operations (CFOs) 258
confinement systems 102, 104, 122, 168, 258
consumer needs 190–1
consumption of food 29–30, 46, 191, 227–8, *see also* agriculture
contemporary animal welfare law: halal slaughter 51–3; historical roots 43–7; inherent value 59; utilitarianism 60
Convention on International Trade in Endangered Species (CITES) of Wild Fauna and Flora 195–6
counselling 160
Court of Appeal 144–5
Creutzfeldt Jakob disease (CJD) 1–2
criminal law: civil practice 165–6; compliance and enforcement 124–31;

distinguishing of standards 117–19; interest of animals 114–15; nature and degree 160–1; proof 113–14; property perspectives 88–9; religion 44–5
cruelty 82–3, 93, 114, 151, *see also* Society for the Prevention of Cruelty to Animals
Cruelty to Animals Act 82
crying 97
cultural perspectives: national law 77; religion 44, 49–50
'currently lawful' 103–4

dairy cows 120
'damages' 167–77
Darwin, C. 62–4
death *see* fatalities
decision-making processes 145, 168, 227–9, 262–3
definitions 14–18; agriculture 249–50; animal law 16–17; of animals 156–60; animals/legal lens 18–19; 'beyond reasonable doubt' 113; distress 98; early protection 83–7; ethics 54; factory farming 251–4; governance/ governors 206–7; 'humane' treatment 92–3; international law 185–6; law 14–16; 'necessary' 100–1; pain 96–7; precautionary principle 156–60; research 234–6; sustainable food production 255–6; treatment of animals 17–18; unnecessary 99–100; unreasonable 99–100; uses of animals 17–18; welfare/legal lens 19–20
DEFRA *see* Department for Environment, Food & Rural Affairs
delegated legislation 15
Denmark 52–3
Department of Agriculture (USDA) 244
Department for Environment, Food & Rural Affairs (DEFRA) 65
derivative liability 159–60
Descartes, R. 46, 55–6
destruction of animals 183–4
deterrence 129
developing technologies 192–4
'development continuum' 84–5
difference between animals and humans 47–8

282   *Index*

dignity 58–9, 79–80, 153, 165
direct interest in animals 2–3
disease control 1–2, 65, 192–4, 228–9
disqualification 125–6, 160
distress: agriculture 254; animal
   law definitions 17; definition 98;
   international governance 222; national
   law 77–8, 93–8, 104–5, 115, 167;
   principles 23; research 240; welfare
   definitions 20
dogs 179–80
dolphins 42–3, 123
domestic animals 83–4
domesticated animals 18
donkeys 45
'drawing the line' 22–3, 66
duty of care 83, 114–15

Economic Co-operation and Development
   (OECD) 215
economic impacts 1–2, 189, 191–2, 263–4
economists 224
education 209–10
Edwardian Empire 82–3
effectiveness of animal welfare law 106–7
emotions 23, 32–8, 96, 171–3
empathy and anthropomorphism 64
Endangered Species (CITES) of Wild
   Fauna and Flora 195–6
enforcement, national law 124–33, 135–40
English Supreme Court 130–1
entertainments industry 9
environmental impacts 1–2, 189–200
equality 187–8
Erskine, T. 72, 80, 81, 90–1
Ethical Treatment of Animals (PETA)
   71–2, 219
ethicists 53–4, 77, 224–5
European Union (EU) 1–2, 152–3, 215
Evans, E.P. 45
'everything is permitted...' 89–90
evidence 144, 157, *see also* proof
evolution, theory of 63–4
exclusionary rules of evidence 141–2
'exemptions', national law 122–3
exports 199–200

fabrics industry 9
factory farming 102, 251–4

factual perspectives 62–3, 140–1, *see also*
   proof
fair market value 170–2
FAO *see* Food and Agriculture
   Organisation of the United Nations
Farm Animal Welfare Council 92
farming *see* agriculture
fatalities 104–5
Favre, D. 107
fearful emotions 23
Feinberg, J. 28, 109
feral animals 18, 84
Five Freedoms concepts 73
flu virus 1–2, 65
FMD *see* foot-and-mouth disease
Food and Agriculture Organisation (FAO)
   of the United Nations 215, 228, 229
food chains, sustainable agriculture 256–7
food production and consumption 29–30,
   191, 227–8, *see also* agriculture
foot-and-mouth disease (FMD) 1–2, 228
forfeiture 125, 160
foundational principles of animal welfare
   law 20–31, 39–184; international law
   185–230; national law 76–184; religion
   41–75
fox hunting 123
Francesco di Bernadone, G. 46
Francione, G. 28, 107
'free-range misrepresentation' 257–8
free trade agreements (FTAs) 216
fundamental principles of animal welfare
   law 20–31

GATT *see* General Agreement on Tariffs
   and Trade
Geldart, W. 167
General Agreement on Tariffs and Trade
   (GATT) 211–12
Germany 80
global animal welfare 5, 205–16
global commercialism 187
global governance: agriculture 261–2;
   animal law definition 16; context 30–1
global impacts of international law
   189–200
global warming 200–1
God 47–8
'good egg award' 71–2

'good practice and scientific knowledge'
155–6, 263–4
governance/governors: agriculture 261–2;
global animal welfare 5; international
law 206–11, 218–27; research 242–7
government: national law 147–8;
righteousness 70–2; state involvement
69–70
'greater good' concepts 60–2, 73
Greek culture 44
groaning 97
guardianship debates 108–9
guilty act *see actus reus*
guilty mind *see mens rea*

halal 50–3, 123
Hamilton-Johnson, K. 130–1
happy emotions 23
Harrison, R. 73
hen cages 102, 104, 122
history: agriculture 250–1; contemporary
law 5, 43–7; national law 76–8; research
233–4
horses 80–1, 179–80
HSI *see* Humane Society International
HSUS *see* Humane Society of the United
States
human–animal relationships: factual
perspectives 62–3; pain 95; sheep
mentality 209–10; starting point 5
Humane Slaughter Act 51–3
Humane Society International (HSI) 220
Humane Society of the United States
(HSUS) 220
humane and sustainable concepts 92–3;
agriculture 252–9; international law
227–8; whaling 196–7
hunting 123, 168
husbandry *see* agriculture

ideal standards 148–9
IFAW *see* International Fund for Animal
Welfare
IFC *see* International Finance Corporation
ill-treatment concepts 80–3, 112, 160–1
Ill-Treatment of Horses and Cattle Bill
80–1
ILOs *see* intensive livestock operations
imprisonment *see* criminal offences

inadequate enforcement 136
inanimate property 88
incremental change 85–7
indirect interest in animals 2–3
industry 147–8, 216–18
influenza 1–2, 65
inherent value 58–9
injury 97
'innocent until proven guilty' 119
intensive livestock operations (ILOs) 258
interest of animals 25–8, 78, 114–15,
152–3
International Finance Corporation (IFC)
221
International Fund for Animal Welfare
(IFAW) 220–1
international law: context 189; decision-
making processes 227–9; definitions
185–6; environmental impacts 200–5;
global impacts 189–200; governance/
governors 206–11, 218–27; herding cats
205–16; industry 216–18; Parliament
186–9; professions 221–5
International Whaling Commission (IWC)
196–9
'irrationality' of animals 44
IWC *see* International Whaling
Commission

Japan 123
Jewish communities 52–3
journalists 223–4
judges/the judiciary 15

Kant, I. 56–7
Key Performance Indicators (KPI) 150
key power brokers 205–6
key professionals 268–70
Koran (Qur'an) 47–8
kosher meat 50
KPI *see* Key Performance Indicators

Lawrence, J. 69, 90–1
lawyers 101–2, 225
leadership 148–65, 226–7
learned tendency to evaluate things 41–2
legislators 225
liability 110, 111, 117–20, 158–60
licensing 153–4

284 *Index*

Lisbon Treaty 66, 152
live exports 199–200
livestock operations (ILOs) 258
Locke, J. 56

McDonald's restaurants 218
mad cow disease 1–2
Magistrates' Court 130–1
'makers' of animal welfare 266–70
marine mammals 42–3
marketing 209–10
Martin, R. 72, 80–1, 90–1, 161
matrimonial splits 174–5
maximum inclusion 210–11
meat consumption 30, 46
'medieval mind' 45
Memorandums of Understanding (MOUs)
   138
mens rea (guilty mind) 110–12, 113–14,
   121
minimum practice/standards 115–19,
   210–11
'ministers of justice' 143
mislabelling and misrepresentation 257–8
Moberg, G.P. 98
Moore, J.H. 64
morals: conflict with science and law 67;
   culpability 44; factory farming 252–4;
   national law 103–4; rights/obligations
   67–8; treatment of animals 53–4
MOUs *see* Memorandums of
   Understanding
multinational agreements 216
multinational border control 228–9
Muslims 47–8, 50–3

national law 76–184; best practice
   115–19; categorisation of animals
   107–8; civil practice 165–84; common-
   law defences 121–4; creative use
   of property status 109–10; criminal
   law 113–15, 117–19, 124–31,
   160–1, 165–6; distress 77, 78, 93–8,
   104–5, 115, 167; early protection
   83–7; enforcement 124–33, 135–40;
   guardianship debates 108–9; hallmarks
   149–65; historical viewpoints 76–8;
   investigations 142–3; leading animal
   protection/welfare law 79–83; liability

117–20, 158–60; minimum practice
   115–19; 'negative' duties 90–3;
   offences 110–15, 117–19, 160–1; pain
   77–8, 93–8, 104–5, 115, 167; penalties
   124–31, 160–1; practical perspectives
   107–8; principled prosecutions 143–6;
   proof 113–14, 119–20, 140–2; property
   perspectives 77, 87–93, 105–10, 177–8;
   single interest of animals 78, 114–15;
   SPCA 138–40; standard practice
   115–19; standards drivers 146–9;
   unnecessary 78, 95, 97, 99–100, 104–7,
   167; unreasonable 78, 95, 97, 99–100,
   104–7, 167; VADE models 133–5
natural law 68–70
'necessary': definition 100–1; minimum
   standards 117; research 242;
   stakeholders 102–3; subjectivity 101–2
'negative' duties 90–3, 115, 151
negligence 173–4
nervous systems 96
Netherlands 80
New Zealand: animal definitions 157–8;
   biosecurity 193–4; common-law
   defences 122; court penalties 180–3;
   emotional damages 172; halal slaughter
   53; ideal standards 148; international
   governance 207; national law 77;
   'precautionary principles' 67; religion
   51; treaties on equality 188; veterinary
   negligence 173; 'victims' of crime 125
non-government organisations (NGOs)
   196–7, 218–27, 273

objective thinking 34–5
obligations, morality 67–8
occupiers liability 170
OECD *see* Organisation for Economic Co-
   operation and Development
offences, national law 110–15, 117–19,
   160–1
Offray de La Mettrie, J. 46
OIE *see* World Organisation for Animal
   Health
onus of proof 119–20
Organisation for Animal Health (OIE) 19,
   214–15, 228–9, 273
Organisation for Economic Co-operation
   and Development (OECD) 215

organisations and welfare 19, 188, 196–7, 211–15, 218–29, 273–4
outdated legislation 4
ownership 158, *see also* property concepts

'paddock-to-plate' processes 254–9
pain: agriculture 254; animal law definitions 17; definitions 96–7; international governance 222; national law 77–8, 93–8, 104–5, 115, 167; principles 23; research 233–8, 240; welfare definitions 20
parasites 193–4
Parliament 15, 54–5, 150, 186–9
parrots 179–80
Pease, J. 81, 90–1
penalties, national law 124–31, 160–1, 180–3
People for the Ethical Treatment of Animals (PETA) 71–2, 219
perceptions: factory farming 252–4, *see also* public opinion
permits, whaling 197–8
persons in charge *see* care-givers
persuasion *see* international law
PETA *see* People for the Ethical Treatment of Animals
pets: custody 174–7; wills 178–9
philosophy 46, 54–5; factual perspectives 62–3; key philosophers 55–8; national law 77; treatment of animals 53–4
pigs 45, 102, 104
Plant Health Inspection Services (APHIS) 244
policy advisers 77, 224–5
politics/politicians 72–5, 189, 225, 257
positive duties of care 83, 114–15
positivist law 68
Posner, R. 22, 24
power brokers 205–6
practical perspectives 11, 34–5; agriculture 249–54; inherent value 59; national law 107–8; property classifications 24
'precautionary principles' 66–7, 156–60
prejudice 237–8
pressure of prosecution 146
primary law 150–3, 154, 155, 166
principled prosecutions 143–6
principles of animal welfare law 20–31

prison *see* criminal law
private law 2–3, 15
pro-dignity initiatives *see* dignity
production of food 29–30, 191, 227–8, *see also* agriculture
professionals 221–5, 268–70
proof, national law 113–14, 119–20, 140–2
property perspectives: classification of animals 23–4; national law 77, 87–93, 105–10, 177–8; state involvement 69
prosecutions 143–6, 160
Protection of Animals Act 82–3, *see also* Royal Society for the Protection of Animals
protection terminology 25–8
public opinion: attitudes regarding animals 41–3; awareness 29, 72–4, 152–3, 165; international governance 208–10; philosophy 58; utilitarianism 60–2, *see also* national law
purpose of animals *see* use of animals
Putney, W. 72, 80

qualifiers 114–15, 122
'quietness' 97
Qur'an 47–8

Radford, M. 27–8, 60, 64, 74, 107
Rawls, J. 57
Reagan, T. 21
'reasonable excuses' 120
'reasonable steps' 120
reckless concepts 112, 161
reduction 241
refinement 241
Regan, T. 59
registration 153–4
rehabilitation 129
religion 41–75; attitudes regarding animals 41–3; first law 47–75; historical roots of contemporary debates 43–7; national law 77
replacement 241
research: acceptability 236–8, 242; activism 238–9; 'bioprejudice' 237–8; critical evaluation 233–48; definition 234–6; governance 242–7; history 233–4; keeping updated 247; legality 239–47; pain 233–8; profession 222–3; scientists 238

286 *Index*

'responsibility' 105–6; national law 114–15, 137–8, 158; research 241–2, *see also* liability
retribution 129
rights: inherent value 58–9; morality 67–8; property perspectives 23–4, 87–93; terminology 25–8
risk management in agriculture 255
rites of passage 42–3
Royal Society for the Protection of Animals (RSPCA) 65, 85, 130–1, 138, 139
'rule of law' 32–3

sad emotions 23
SAFE *see* Save Animals From Exploitation
safety: agriculture 254; biosecurity 192–4
St Francis of Assisi 46
St Thomas Aquinas 48
Sandøe, P. 66
Save Animals From Exploitation (SAFE) 219
science: agriculture 261–3; conflict with morals and law 67; definitions of welfare 20; human–animal relationships 62–3; knowledge 155–6, 263–4; precautionary principle 157; and religion 50–1; whaling permits 197–8
scientists 222–3, 238
secondary legislation 150, 153–6
self-interest 148
sensory receptors 96
sentencing 128–31
sentience 29, 72–4, 152–3, 165
service animals 123
seventeenth-century animals 46–7
'shakers' of animal welfare 266–70
sheep mentality 209–10
sheep and wool industry 71–2
Singer, P. 21, 58, 73
slaughter methods 50–3, 123
social impacts 1–2
societal impacts 1–2, 189–91, *see also* public opinion
Society for the Prevention of Cruelty to Animals (SPCA) 138–40, 219, 273
sociological perspectives 49–50
South Korea 80
sovereignty 186–7

sow stalls 102, 104
Spain 122–3
SPCA *see* Society for the Prevention of Cruelty to Animals
'specialist property law' 87–9
speciesism 21–3, 60
species variation in research 235
stakeholders 102–3, 239, 240–2; environmental impacts 200–5; established strategies 162; hallmarks of protection law 152–3; ideal standards 148–9
standard practice, national law 115–19
state involvement, 1840s 81–3
state involvement 69–70; enforcement 136–8; 'negative' duties 90–3; sovereignty 186–7
Statute Law 15, 150–3, 154, 155, 166
stimuli 96
'stocking rates' 120
stray animals 84
stress 98
strict liability 111, 119–20, 158
subjectivity, 'necessary' 101–2
subsidiary/subordinate/delegated legislation 15
suffering: national law 93–8; principles 23, *see also* distress; pain
'survival of the fittest' 63–4
sustainability *see* humane and sustainable concepts
swine flu 1–2
Swiss Animal Protection Act 79–80
systems that deliver 162–5

tame animals 18, 83–4
Tariffs and Trade (GATT) 211–12
technologies 192–4
theology *see* religion
Theophrastus 46
The Origin of Species (Darwin) 63–4
theory of evolution 63–4
Thomas Aquinas (Saint) 48
'total agreement' 30–1
totality of offending 118
training devices 168
transport 168, 193–4
treaties on equality 187–8
treatment of animals 17–18

Treaty of Lisbon 66, 152
trusts 178–9

UDWA *see* Universal Declaration of Welfare for Animals
unique property 177–8
United Kingdom (UK): common-law defences 123; Parliament 15, 54–5, 150, 186–9; philosophy 54–5; 'precautionary principles' 67; RSPCA 65, 85, 130–1, 138, 139; sentencing 128, 130–1; veterinary negligence 173; Westminster Law 15–16, 79–80, 84–5, 88–90, 128, *see also* Parliament
United Nations (UN) 215
United States Department of Agriculture (USDA) 244
United States (US): halal slaughter 52; HSUS 220; precautionary principle 156; primary legislation 151; research 244
Universal Declaration of Welfare for Animals (UDWA) 220
unlawful uses of animals 194–5
unnecessary: definitions 99–102; national law 78, 95, 97, 99–100, 104–7, 167; research 240; subjectivity 101–2; welfare definitions 20, *see also* 'necessary'
unpaid enforcement 139–40
unpleasant/undesired experiences 93, 96, *see also* distress; pain
unprincipled prosecution 145
unreasonable: definitions 99–100; national law 78, 95, 97, 99–100, 104–7, 167; research 240; welfare definitions 20
USDA *see* United States Department of Agriculture
users of animal welfare 266–70
uses of animals 17–18; common-law defences 123–4; religion 47–75; seventeenth-century animals 46–7; unlawful 194–5
'usual practice' 120
utilitarianism 59, 60–2

validity issues of wills and trusts 178
Vallat, B. 228–9
valuation of damages 170–1
veal crates 102, 104
vegetarianism 30, 46
'ventilation shut down' 65
veterinarians 155, 171, 173–4, 222–3
'vicarious' liability 110
'victims' of crime 124–5
Victorian Empire 80, 82–3, 90–1
Voluntary Assisted Directed Enforced (VADE) models 133–5

WAF *see* World Animal Forum
Welfare for Animals (UDWA) 220
welfare paradigm 28–9
welfare terminology 25–8
Westminster Law 15–16; development continuum 84–5; leading animal protection/welfare law 79–80; property perspectives 88, 89–90; sentencing 128
whales 42–3, 196–9
whimpering 97
Wilberforce, W. 80
wild animals 18, 84, 157–8
wills and trusts 178–9
witnesses of fact 140–1
wool industry 71–2
words as evidence 140–1
working animals 123
World Animal Forum (WAF) 221
World Animal Protection 219–20
World Bank Group (WBG) 221
World Organisation for Animal Health (OIE) 19, 214–15, 228–9, 273
World Society for the Protection of Animals (WSPA) 219–20, 226, 273
World Trade Organization (WTO) 188, 211–13, 273
World Veterinary Association (WVA) 223

'younger cousin' perspectives 11–13

zoonoses 228

eBooks
from Taylor & Francis

Helping you to choose the right eBooks for your Library

Add to your library's digital collection today with Taylor & Francis eBooks. We have over 50,000 eBooks in the Humanities, Social Sciences, Behavioural Sciences, Built Environment and Law, from leading imprints, including Routledge, Focal Press and Psychology Press.

Choose from a range of subject packages or create your own!

Benefits for you
- Free MARC records
- COUNTER-compliant usage statistics
- Flexible purchase and pricing options
- All titles DRM-free.

Benefits for your user
- Off-site, anytime access via Athens or referring URL
- Print or copy pages or chapters
- Full content search
- Bookmark, highlight and annotate text
- Access to thousands of pages of quality research at the click of a button.

Free Trials Available
We offer free trials to qualifying academic, corporate and government customers.

eCollections

Choose from over 30 subject eCollections, including:

Archaeology	Language Learning
Architecture	Law
Asian Studies	Literature
Business & Management	Media & Communication
Classical Studies	Middle East Studies
Construction	Music
Creative & Media Arts	Philosophy
Criminology & Criminal Justice	Planning
Economics	Politics
Education	Psychology & Mental Health
Energy	Religion
Engineering	Security
English Language & Linguistics	Social Work
Environment & Sustainability	Sociology
Geography	Sport
Health Studies	Theatre & Performance
History	Tourism, Hospitality & Events

For more information, pricing enquiries or to order a free trial, please contact your local sales team:
www.tandfebooks.com/page/sales

www.tandfebooks.com